IBM—small and
medium systems

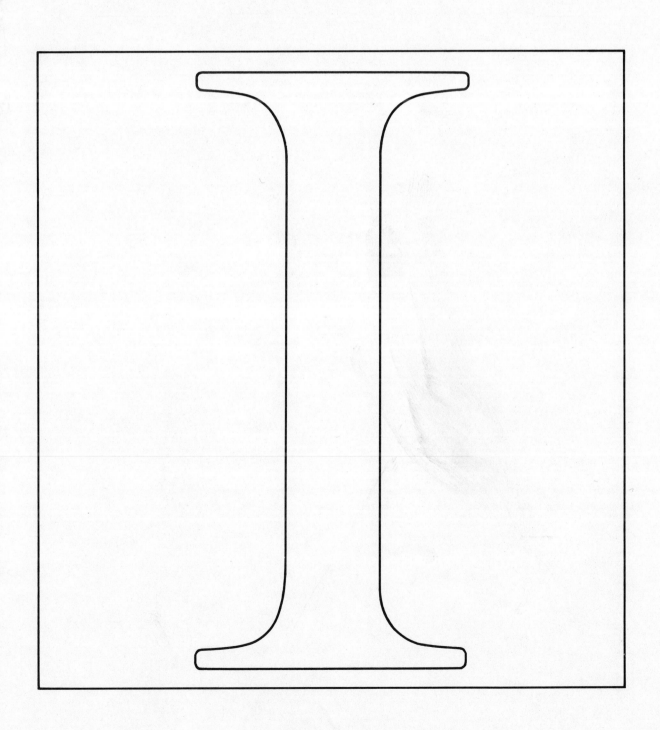

# IBM – small and medium systems

State of the Art Report 14:1

Pergamon Infotech Limited    A member of the Pergamon Group    Oxford    New York    Toronto    Sydney    Beijing    Frankfurt

Published by
Pergamon Infotech Limited
Berkshire House  Queen Street
Maidenhead Berkshire
England SL6 1NF.

Telephone: 0628 39101
International + 44 628 39101
Telex: 847319
(Answerback INFO G)

Printed by
A Wheaton & Company Limited
Exeter Devonshire
England.

UDC     681.3
Dewey   658.505
ISBN    0 08 034 0903

# Contents

## Analysis

## Bibliography

## Index

# Foreword

The year 1985 was not a good one for International Business Machines (IBM) — its profits were stagnant for the first time in many years — but many others fared much worse. In a year full of losses, redundancies and failures amongst high technology companies, for IBM merely to maintain its existing profit levels has been something of an achievement. For IBM the year was also one of new product announcements, of which the token-passing local area network was perhaps the most important, even if the least unexpected. As we enter the later 1980s, the relevance of these announcements will become more clear and we will be able to see whether the current stagnation is but the forerunner of a massive increase in sales and profits.

## The dominance of IBM

The progress of computing and data processing has been led by two types of influence — on the one hand advances in technology and methods, from a wide variety of sources, on the other hand the *de facto* standards set by a few major suppliers, among whom IBM has traditionally been the most important.

IBM's dominance has not spread to every part of the computer marketplace — for instance it quickly abandoned the 'supercomputer' area to suppliers such as CDC and later Cray — but it achieved and held a dominating position in the mainframe computer market which for the first 20 years was virtually all there was to the industry. The complexities of IBM mainframe systems and their software continue to provide almost unlimited scope for comment and speculation. In this State of the Art Report however, we are concerned with the other part of the computer spectrum — the small- and medium-size systems whose importance in value terms is now overtaking the mainframes and among which the most dynamic changes are occurring.

## Small and medium systems

IBM's share of the small and medium systems market, once negligible, has now become very significant. Indeed, at the bottom of the 'serious' business market the IBM PC has not merely captured the largest share, it has effectively redefined the market in the same way that the System/360 did for mainframes years ago. In the medium systems area, the current picture is a plethora of products and architectures left over from a previous era. Some of these will no doubt wither away as IBM faces the need to rationalise its architecture and its offerings.

## Small business computers

Two products in particular stand out in the medium systems area: the System/36 and the System/38. Presented by IBM as part of the line of 'small business computers' which sprang from the System/3, these two models have far less in common beneath the surface than the similarity of the numbers might imply:

the System/36 is the real descendant of the System/32 and System/34, but the System/38 is a horse of a different colour.

The System/36 appears to have an assured place in the IBM scheme. It has been widely recognised as the natural middle element in a hierarchy of computing to match the structure of a large business organisation — the mainframe at the corporate level, System/36 as the departmental machine, and the PC for the individual — all interworking and exchanging files via SNA. For office automation in particular, there is now a more or less consistent range of packages, such as DisplayWrite and Personal Services, available on the System/36 as well as the PC and mainframe. This commonality of software supports the view of the System/36 as a strategic machine at departmental level. However, it may be significant that the System/36 was not initially integrated into the new local networking system: does this mean that IBM has something else in mind after all?

Of IBM's medium systems, none has provoked more interest than the System/38. Initially planned as a possible new mainframe architecture, it was targeted, for marketing reasons, at the top of the 'small business computers'. Today it is something of an anomaly as a machine with plenty of power and capability, but no growth path to speak of. Although no longer new, its architecture is in many ways still far in advance of the competition. The time seems ripe to re-examine it, to see how its innovative aspects have stood the test of time, and how it fares as a vehicle for use in a commercial environment.


## The IBM PC

Both the System/36 and System/38 are very specific IBM machines. Their architecture, operating systems, and application packages are all very different to anything available outside the IBM fold. By contrast, the PC end of the market is, in all its major features, a product of developments outside IBM. However, if the overall shape of the PC was market-led, at the detailed level it is the IBM PC which is setting the standards and that is what the rest of the industry is striving to be compatible with.

The history of the IBM PC — its enormous success in dominating its market and in leading the growth in this area — is well known, but the future is not so clear. With sales no longer growing at the same rate, and with prices and hence profit margins severely cut back, it is not the glamour market it once was. Clearly however, the PC range is a strategic one. We can expect that IBM will exploit it to the full, bringing in new up-market models, while still perhaps keeping open the option of entering the home and educational markets. Moreover, the PC is taking on a new role as a multi-function office workstation, linking to a variety of IBM systems, and is seen increasingly by IBM as the personal link in a corporate network rather than a stand-alone machine.

At the time of writing, the original PC and PC Portable are at the end of their life and the PC/XT (with or without hard disk) is a mature product, exploited to the limit of its capabilities, and with third-party products available to extend them. By contrast the PC/AT is beginning to sell widely, but with little of the distinctive software that will take advantage of its advanced features. A 'PC 2', perhaps filling the gap between the XT and the AT, is confidently expected. In the longer term, the growth of processor technology means that IBM could advance the PC into the 32-bit arena without losing compatibility with its present range.

One of the success factors of the IBM PC has been its openness — the ability to add software products and hardware extensions and the relative ease with which third-party suppliers have been able to produce 'compatibles'. This competition has not proved to IBM's detriment: arguably the existence of compatible machines helps to legitimise the PC standards and thereby swell the PC's market.

The standards set at the launch of the PC — the disk formats, the expansion cards, the keyboard layout, the screen size, the MS-DOS/PC-DOS operating system — have all proved durable and merely evolved under IBM guidance. However, the evolution, particularly in software terms, has reached a breaking point. There is a clear demand for more sophisticated personal computing, with windowing, concurrency, and multitasking, but as yet IBM has set no clear guidelines, and far more solutions are being offered than the market has room for. One solution to the PC problem could be UNIX — effectively the industry standard multi-user operating system. IBM's key product here is XENIX for the IBM PC/AT, which may yet succeed in establishing a market for small multi-user systems in the very small company or department.

## Networking

Networking is a key aspect of any IBM installation today and its complexities are still baffling for the uninitiated. The situation is becoming slightly less clouded with the continued growth of Systems Network Architecture (SNA) and the move at last toward standardisation in local area networks. IBM's SNA has been described as an IBM solution to an IBM problem — that of linking together a variety of machines with originally quite different interfacing standards. It will become still more important in the future but will also need to coexist with other standards, particularly the international standard for Open Systems Interconnection (OSI). Fortunately the gap between SNA and OSI can be bridged. A limitation of SNA has long been its emphasis on control from the centre, but peer-to-peer communication is at last being supported and will be essential in the future for office automation and links from company to company.

Local area networks are the other part of the networking picture. They have been developing for some years in the non-IBM area, but IBM's response has been confusing, with a long-term commitment to the token-passing ring and a number of stop-gap products using other architectures. IBM's announcement in 1985 of a token passing product has clarified the longer-term prospect, although other standards can be expected to coexist with it. Again we see IBM taking an 'open architecture' approach, following international standards and making the hardware (at chip level) available to the industry. We can expect that this openness will be to IBM's advantage.

## Some themes

A number of themes run through the papers making up this Report and are summarised in the Analysis.

### IBM itself

The company's strengths and its weaknesses, its inheritance from the past in terms of products and architectures, and its promise for the future. The marketing aspects, as always with IBM, are the key to its success, but its research and development strengths should never be underestimated.

### Hardware and technology

The various product ranges are examined and their future prospects assessed, with special reference to the PC and System/38. Will the medium systems be thinned down to a much reduced number of ranges which IBM will support for a long time to come? Or will they be caught in a pincer movement as the mainframe and PC meet in the middle?

### Operating systems

On the medium range machines the IBM operating systems are unchallenged, but how long will it be before Pick or UNIX is readily available? In contrast, industry-standard operating systems are the norm on the PC. Digital Research and Microsoft are battling it out, but UNIX and Pick are waiting in the wings.

### Networks and applications

The smaller range machines are increasingly used for non-traditional applications, such as office automation. A key factor will be the ability to link them with each other and to mainframes. Having dominated data processing in the past, IBM's aim must be to dominate office automation in the future, as the long-heralded electronic office finally takes shape.

### The future: where will IBM go next?

The history and present position of IBM give the best guide to its future, but there are some new elements in the picture. As IBM moves away from its traditional market areas, which it has dominated for so long, into the new age of convergence between computing and communications, competition with AT&T will become more important. IBM's newly acquired interests in Rolm and MCI have given it a toe-hold in AT&T's own sphere of influence — will AT&T be provoked into retaliation? IBM clearly has the superior marketing skills and a comparable research base, but the contest between the two will be interesting to watch. In the computer business itself, a number of technological changes are almost ready for widespread application — intelligent knowledge-based systems, parallel processing, voice recognition, flat panel displays. It is the Japanese competition that seems most threatening here.

Such is the strength of IBM that it is easy to assume that it will always dominate the market, but the information processing industry of the future will be far more diverse and complex than the computer industry of the past, and more difficult for any one company to encompass. Even IBM has made mistakes, and we should not readily assume that its future dominance is assured in the uncharted waters that lie ahead.

*Ross Burgess: Editor*

# Publisher's note

This Report is divided into three parts:

1  Invited Papers.
2  Analysis.
3  Bibliography.

The Invited Papers in this State of the Art Report examine various aspects of IBM small and medium systems. If a paper cites references they are given at the end of the Invited Papers section, numbered in the range 1-99 but prefixed with the first three letters of the Invited Paper author's name.

The Analysis has the following functions:

1  Assesses the major advances in IBM small and medium systems.
2  Provides a balanced analysis of the state of the art in IBM small and medium systems.

The Analysis is constructed by the editor of the Report to provide a balanced and comprehensive view of the latest developments in IBM small and medium systems. The editor's personal analysis of the subject is supplemented by quotations from the Invited Papers, written by leading authorities on the subject.

The following editorial conventions are used throughout the Analysis:

1  Material in Times Roman (this typeface) is written by the editor.

2  Material in Times Italic (*this typeface*) is contributed by the person or publication whose name precedes it. The contributor's name is set in Times Italic. Numbers in parentheses in the ranges 001-099 or 100-199 following the name refer to the original source as specified in the Analysis references or the Bibliography, respectively, which both follow the Analysis. References within the text are numbered in the same way. A contributor's name without a reference refers to an Invited Paper published in this Report.

3  The quotations in the Analysis are arranged at the discretion of the editor to bring out key issues. Three or four dots within a single quotation indicate that a portion of the original text has been removed by the editor to improve clarity.

The Bibliography is a specially selected compilation of the most important published material on the subject of IBM small and medium systems. Each key item in the literature is reviewed and annotated to assist in selecting the required information.

# Invited Papers

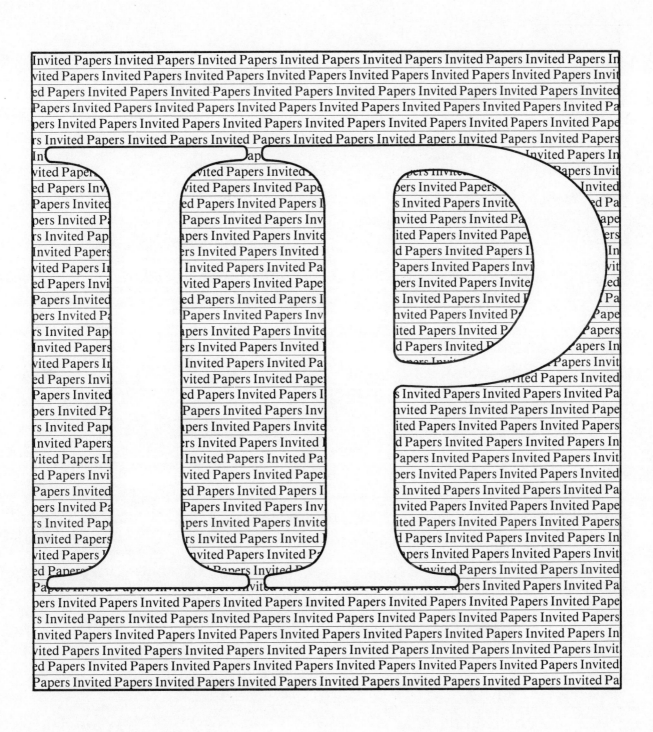

# 1: Concurrent™ DOS operating systems

P Bailey

Digital Research
Newbury
Berkshire
UK

**Digital Research's Concurrent DOS is unique among operating systems for the IBM PC range, and for IBM compatibles and other personal computers in providing true multitasking and multi-user capability incorporating user-controlled windows for viewing concurrently executing tasks; Local Area Network (LAN) software providing a multitasking file-server capability which eliminates the need for dedicated fileservers; background modem-based communications with other computers; intuitive icon-based Graphics Environment Manager (GEM) user interface, available also for IBM-DOS and MS-DOS; and compatibility with IBM-DOS and MS-DOS at version 2.1 level, and with CP/M, for the widest possible choice of applications software. This paper reviews the current state of the Concurrent DOS/GEM system and its future.**

*P Bailey*
Paul Bailey is Vice-President of European operations for the US-based company, Digital Research. He holds an honours degree in Electrical Engineering from the University of Bristol (UK) and has worked for the UK Ministry of Defence in a research and development capacity, and subsequently as European marketing manager for the Computer Graphics Division of Tektronix. In August 1982 he took up his present post, managing the establishment and development of four Digital Research operating companies in the UK, France and West Germany, marking Digital Research's strong emphasis on European markets.

## The IBM PC and the user

Since the introduction of the popular 16-bit IBM PC in 1981, the working habits of many hundreds of thousands of users have been radically changed. Their experience has proved that personal computing amplifies personal creativity and productivity in almost every walk of life. However, the experienced user can become frustrated by the limitations imposed by an environment in which only one task can effectively be carried out at any one time. Added to this, the arbitrary command syntaxes of the PC operating environment and of applications programs have to be learnt. In short, many users are dissatisfied with the PC's primitive 'user interface'.

'User interface' is an industry catch-phrase which refers to the way in which the user controls a computer system or program. Regrettably it is still true that it is the *user* who must make the major effort to interface to the kind of personal computing software available today, not the other way round. In common with many of the popular application programs, the original 'gang of three' 16-bit PC operating systems, IBM-DOS, MS-DOS and CP/M-86 are serious offenders in this respect.

Frustration with these broadly similar user interfaces then, has two main causes: *obstinate singlemindedness* and *immemorable user dialogue*. The Concurrent DOS solution to singlemindedness — the inability to perform more than one task at a time — is discussed immediately below, while the Graphics Environment Manager (GEM) user interface, the Digital Research answer to the often obscure and frustrating nature of user dialogue in operating systems and applications software, is described further on in this paper under the heading 'The GEM user interface'.

## Obstinate singlemindedness

Operating systems control programs in PC memory. The operating system is responsible for servicing program requests for keyboard input, screen output, file access, communications, and other numerous housekeeping tasks, in the right order and at the appropriate times. However, most PC operating systems can run only one application program at a given time. As we explain below, this *single-tasking* restriction can severely limit user satisfaction and productivity.

## The user problem

Few of us work like computers, so the sensible arrangement is to make computers work more like us. It is a fact that most people who do not work on a fixed production line interrupt their current work to perform other tasks which become necessary from time to time. This is because we have a human tendency to identify our workload by major objectives, not enquiring too deeply about details unless and until they have to be faced. Until recently, personal computers could not fully support this human creative pattern. Micros were either running the program you needed or they were not: to break out of a word processing package or a spreadsheet to enter a financial model or a graphics presentation program, the user had to save current files, swap diskettes, and load the new program and any necessary files. This is extremely trying, especially when pressure is high.

## Concurrency and multitasking — a natural way to use a computer

In 1982, Digital Research introduced Concurrent CP/M for personal computers. Concurrent CP/M lets a single personal computer run several CP/M programs at the same time in areas of reserved user memory. This means that a number of the user's most valuable applications can be up and running throughout the working day, supporting the normally interrupted pattern of the user's work.

Next, in April 1984, Digital Research launched Concurrent DOS, an operating system that runs not only CP/M programs but also programs written for IBM-DOS and MS-DOS, allowing the user a wide selection of available PC applications.

Under Concurrent DOS, one program, known as the *foreground task* is always available for user input while others are running as *background tasks*. Any program running in background may be brought into the foreground and *vice versa* with a single keystroke. This is possible through the Concurrent DOS provision of a number of *virtual consoles*. Virtual consoles are areas of memory, separate from the physical screen memory, which contain screen output and buffer data for each task-specific area of reserved memory. Because output from tasks is directed to their respective virtual consoles, it is possible to fully or partially window (or completely suppress) their outputs to the physical screen as required. Task windowing is discussed below.

Under Concurrent DOS a manager may temporarily leave a word processing package, in which he or she is composing a letter, to do some calculations in a spreadsheet; here a useful feature of Concurrent DOS enables data to be 'piped' from the spreadsheet to the document on the word processor. The updated letter is completed and sent as electronic mail by a communications application and while this process is going on as a background task, the manager can use the word processor to write another letter. This is *multitasking*: it saves time and indirect cost, and generates a good deal of user satisfaction. As configured for the IBM PC version, up to four user-controlled tasks may be run, depending on total user memory availability.

'Concurrent', as an adjective and as a trademark, was chosen carefully to indicate how programs run under Digital Research's CP/M-derived 16-bit microcomputer operating systems. The adjectives 'parallel' or 'simultaneous' for example, are not applicable because the current IBM PC range of hardware cannot deal with more than one 'task' at any time, but Concurrent DOS makes the hardware switch its attention between several applications in memory, gainfully using the 'dead' time in which programs wait for input from user or from peripherals to sequentially service all current program requests. Competition for service between programs is decided by Concurrent DOS on the basis of the nature of the fundamental system or machine processes currently requested by the individual programs. Some of these processes are interruptable by others of higher priority, while some have absolute priority and may not be interrupted. However, such processes operate in micro- and milliseconds and are normally of very brief duration compared with stretches of 'dead' time. The user can therefore interact with one of a number of concurrently-running tasks at his or her customary pace.

## Task windowing in Concurrent DOS

Windows are topical, but they entered the popular business micro market in early 1984 as an advanced aid to multitasking under Concurrent DOS. Windows are a logical enhancement enabling the user to stay visually in touch with a number of programs on one physical screen. Before task windows were available the Concurrent user had to switch out of the foreground task to discover the state of a background program. Now, up to four windows in Concurrent DOS can be individually positioned, sized and overlapped at will by the user to take up all or part of the physical screen (excepting the prompt line at the bottom of the screen). In addition, each window can be operated in two modes: in *buffered mode* the window is frozen until it is selected as the foreground window, when all updates are played out in sequence before control is handed over to the user; in *dynamic mode* the window is altered on updating. Dynamic mode is especially useful for monitoring the current progress of potentially long-winded programs such as complex predictive models, or communications tasks in which the window is logged onto a remote mainframe, or a videotex or electronic mail service.

6

These windowing operations are based on the virtual consoles operated for each task by Concurrent DOS. Because virtual consoles are copied to the physical screen in whole or in part, the user can also control the foreground and background colours of task windows, a further aid to task monitoring.

## Multiple users and multitasking

The availability of Concurrent DOS to maintain several programs in memory also allows a number of users to work simultaneously with a suitable machine. Given enough user memory, they may each perform multiple tasks at low-cost serial terminals connected to the PC's processor unit. Concurrent's *multi-user capability* therefore has direct cost advantages. However, due to the memory overhead imposed by each user, multiple user multitasking is practical mainly on hard-disk machines with the full 640 Kbytes of user memory, such as the PC/XT or PC/AT.

PC multi-user operating systems alternative to Concurrent DOS include Microsoft's UNIX variant, XENIX, and perhaps versions of other systems such as BOS. None of these, however, has Concurrent's advantage of support for IBM-DOS, MS-DOS *and* CP/M-86 applications, which gives multiple users of Concurrent DOS the widest possible choice of applications software.

In addition to multitasking and multi-user capability, Concurrent DOS features and utilities provide further enhancements of the user interface concerned with file handling, networking and communications, as well as other important extensions of system capability. These are discussed directly below.

Most work performed on personal computers involves disk file handling: creation, updating, saving, deleting and copying. Business users each generate a large number of disk files which must be managed safely and efficiently and must be easily identifiable. Under Concurrent DOS, both IBM/MS-DOS 2.1 and CP/M systems of file organisation are supported on both DOS and CP/M formatted disks.

A useful filing feature of DOS 2.1 is *hierarchical filing*. This enables subdirectories of files to be contained within a single file name which appears on the disk (or 'root') directory. In turn, subdirectories can contain other subdirectories. Subdirectories tidy the disk directory by suppressing the names of the files they contain; by specifying the subdirectory, a group of related files and/or applications can be conveniently isolated for use. CP/M filing under Concurrent DOS features *password protection* to prevent unauthorised reading, writing or deleting of files. Concurrent DOS also provides for locking of files and individual records within files.

## Networking — the multitasking fileserver

Networks distribute expensive resources such as corporate data held on personal computers or on remote minis and mainframes, as well as the capabilities of costly peripherals such as hard disks, and sophisticated printers and plotters. The distribution of messages and data is accelerated by networking desktop computers together in local area networks (LANs). This is especially useful in corporate environments.

To support the trend to networking, Concurrent DOS has been equipped with DR Net, an optional networking extension. While LANs based on other operating systems often require expensive dedicated supervisory hardware known as 'fileservers' to accept and correctly route messages across the network, DR Net fulfils this function as a background task under Concurrent DOS: each networked Concurrent DOS machine has its own soft fileserver, limiting the direct cost of the LAN to low-cost physical cabling and interfaces.

DR Net is organised on the basis of the International Standards Organisation's OSI model for networking software and is hardware independent. It may be interfaced to many major network protocols, such as those of Arcnet, Ethernet, and Omninet, and may also serve as a gateway between LANs, and also between a LAN and other communications services.

Integration of DR Net with Concurrent DOS provides a networking operating system in which remote resources and even remote tasks on other computers in the net can be accessed with simple commands. The network is transparent to the user under DR Net: only the small set of DR Net commands reminds the user of the existence of the net. DR Net is accessible from any user task running in either single or multiple user configurations.

## Communications

DR Talk is a Concurrent DOS utility which links all models of the IBM PC with remote computers or database services, over public or private telephone networks using an asynchronous communications port and a modem with suitable functionality. DR Talk-based applications can easily be configured to send and receive data at rates required by all major videotex and electronic mail services, database providers and bulletin boards. A DR Talk-based application can operate in background, for example while receiving the results of a long database search, or when a task is operating as an auto-answer bulletin board, to provide information to remote callers.

## Print spooler

Concurrent's print spooler is a standard background task which uses no virtual console. It stores files for printing in chronological order and offers them to the printer when it is free. The print spooler thus eliminates the need for a task to be connected to a printer for output of hard copy. The user can continue with a full complement of applications while hard copy is being generated.

## Support for maths coprocessors

The Intel 8087 and 80287 maths coprocessors are specially developed for rapid handling of arithmetical computations. Pixel-based graphics operations, which involve a high level of such calculations, are also much faster when supported by these coprocessors. Concurrent DOS supports the 8087 for 8086 machines like the PC and PC/XT, and the 80287 for 80286 machines such as the PC/AT.

## RAM disk

Portions of main memory may be configured as a fast RAM disk under Concurrent DOS. This is useful for holding frequently used utilities or files. The RAM disk may be loaded with files or applications by starting the system with a suitable batch file. Speed is the main advantage, but wear and tear on disks and disk drives is also reduced.

## Exploiting the full power of the AT

The PC/AT's Intel 80286 CPU has a memory address space of 16 Mbytes, which is all addressable in 'protected' mode by Concurrent DOS-286, an 80286-specific version of Concurrent DOS. In the 80286's IBM-DOS mode the PC/AT is restricted to a total of 640 Kbytes memory like the PC or PC/XT, and in this mode acts simply as a faster version of the earlier PC machines. Concurrent DOS-286 is designed to release the full capabilities of the PC/AT.

## Future support for memory expansion

Concurrent DOS for 8086 machines will soon be extended to support memory expansion boards capable of providing up to 8 Mbytes of additional random access memory (RAM) for the PC, PC/XT, PC/AT and compatibles. Full support will be provided for the advanced AST specification for such boards. Ever larger amounts of memory in excess of the 8086's 1 Mbyte address space and the 640 Kbytes limit imposed by IBM-DOS are becoming necessary for multitasking of big applications, and even for some sophisticated single applications such as large spreadsheets and modelling packages.

## Concurrent DOS support for software development

It is a strength of Concurrent DOS that it is easily modifiable by the computer manufacturer. All hardware-dependent code in Concurrent DOS is located in one module, the Extended Basic Input/Output System or XIOS.

The advantages conferred on the software developer by this modularity are strategic: easy implementation across a wide range of hardware broadens the Concurrent DOS machine base and provides a larger target for software developers' new products. Because Concurrent DOS is available for many machines based on the Intel and other manufacturers' 16- and 32-bit CPUs, it also offers an expansionary pathway for software development. A package supported by Concurrent DOS on one machine can readily be modified to move it onto another Concurrent DOS machine, even one based on a different CPU.

## Concurrent DOS and TopView

TopView is IBM's single user, multitasking environment (with windows) for the IBM PC range and requires the presence of IBM-DOS. It is fair to point out to the potential user that TopView does not run CP/M-86 applications, and does not currently permit communications tasks to run in the background. In addition, TopView and IBM-DOS together occupy over 180 Kbytes of user memory, up to 40 Kbytes more than Concurrent, depending on the implementation. TopView is a proprietary product and is not readily available to manufacturers of IBM compatibles and non-compatibles.

## Immemorable commands

Having dealt with multitasking and the other major features of Concurrent DOS, we shall now turn to Digital Research's second radical enhancement to the PC user interface. This is concerned with improving the quality of user dialogue. Few users enjoy employing the lengthy commands or key sequences which must be entered to perform basic tasks under the IBM-DOS, MS-DOS or CP/M operating systems. The following command in CP/M, entered at the A> prompt, PIP B:= *.* copies all non-system files on disk A to disk B. Of course, it would be perfectly possible for an operating system to use a command line like COPY A TO B which bears a closer relationship to English, but textual commands slow down the majority who use computers only to boost personal productivity. Worst still for the industry, the cryptic nature of system commands and the lack of information on options available in command-driven user interfaces, presents a significant barrier for a major potential market of new customers who may well be individuals and organisations with little or no practical experience of personal computing. Something much simpler and more intuitive is called for.

## Making the user interface more friendly

DOS and CP/M-86 systems all owe a structural debt to CP/M-80, which was introduced by Digital Research in 1975 for Intel 8080 and Zilog Z80-based 8-bit microcomputers. Resulting directly from the technical climate of that period, these systems' command-driven user interfaces have changed little.

A first level of true user friendliness is found in the Concurrent DOS customisable menu system, which enables users to replace difficult to remember command lines with single keystrokes chosen from a number of options. Having set up their own menus, users can largely forget the complexities of the system's underlying command structure, although, of course, in order to exploit this feature to the full, they must first gain some working understanding of this command structure.

A second and more fundamental level of user-friendliness is the icon-based visual interface, represented in the IBM-DOS, MS-DOS and Concurrent DOS environments by Digital Research's GEM products. GEM replaces command complexity with mouse or pointer-driven cursor movements among a small set of icons — familiar desktop objects ('graphic metaphors' for analogous system and application resources), plus a number of short 'dropdown' menus.

Because graphic metaphors can condense large amounts of information onto the screen, they can be used to provide an effective map of the system and to indicate the options available to the user whatever the system's condition. By contrast, a solely command-driven interface provides only a system prompt and an expectant blank screen, and the user must correctly recall and use the correct command syntax. Moreover, the command user always has the option of miskeying complex sequences, a problem which is almost entirely eliminated in the iconic interface. Menu-only interfaces are helpful, but they cannot show as many options, nor can they represent system resource interrelationships, with the same degree of clarity as does the iconic interface.

## The GEM user interface

The basic ergonomic research underpinning the iconic user interface was carried out in the early 1970s by Xerox at its Palo Alto Research Centre. The Xerox work determined that most computer users found visual interaction with screen objects more satisfying than the use of commands or menus. The Xerox iconic interface was implemented in the Smalltalk environment on the Xerox Star machine. It is satisfying to note that Xerox is one of the most recent companies to adopt the GEM user interface.

A further contribution to the spread of the iconic user interface to popular personal computing has been the recent advent of low-cost, high-performance, pixel-mapped screen graphics, which enable the fast drawing of icons and object-oriented screens.

The GEM user interface is available as a graphics extension for IBM-DOS, MS-DOS and for Concurrent DOS. It consists essentially of a library of standardised graphics routines devoted to icons, windows and other graphics objects, together with the GEM Virtual Device Interface, a computational module which converts the idealised coordinates used by the graphics routines into device-dependent coordinates suitable for use by graphics screens, plotters and printers and other output and input devices. GEM also contains 'device driver' routines which modify GEM's graphics output for direct use by these peripherals. A further GEM module provides concurrent operation for up to six specialised 'desktop' programs referred to as 'desk accessories'. Typical desk accessories include a calculator, a clock, a print spooler and a communications utility.

GEM applications call the standard graphics routines in the GEM operating system extension to provide the characteristic GEM iconic environment. Therefore, all GEM applications operate in the same familiar way. The GEM user interface represents a much-needed user interface standard which is independent of machine and operating system, and which can be applied across a varied range of applications.

As a collection of virtual graphics routines, GEM is an invariant, with the hardware interface provided by the operating system. So programming techniques for GEM applications are also independent of hardware and operating system. This means that GEM applications can be readily transferred by software developers between machines and across operating systems.

## GEM Desktop

The GEM applications base was started by Digital Research with GEM Desktop, a program which replaces DOS commands with icons and mouse control. The basic components of a GEM Desktop screen are as follows:

1  An arrow cursor controlled by moving the mouse on the physical desktop.

2  A menu bar at the top of the screen containing basic options.

3  Dropdown menus which descend from the menu bar when the user moves the cursor to menu bar options.

4  Icons representing disk drives, as well as icons identifying files, subdirectories, application programs and utilities.

5  Up to six desk accessories, depending on the implementation, including a clock, calculator and/or print spooler, screen snapshot (a small camera), and others.

6  Windows containing disk directories or subdirectories which can be scrolled vertically by clicking the mouse on various portions of the window borders.

Using the mouse, or other pointer device or (slow!) keyboard cursor control, the user can intuitively perform most file operations and can run application programs without using operating system commands, although these are available as an option within GEM Desktop.

To use any system resource represented by an icon, the user points to it with the mouse, and clicks the button. This action is called 'clicking on' the icon. For example, a disk directory can be called by clicking on a disk drive icon. The icon turns from light to dark or changes colour depending on the implementation of GEM Desktop, and a new disk directory appears in a window on the screen. Within a disk directory window, icons represent files (documents with a turned over corner); application programs (flat documents with a dark band at the top) or subdirectories (tabbed document folders). The individual icons are further distinguished by design patterns depending on the file or program type. Again, the user clicks on the appropriate icon to run an application program, or to access a file or subdirectory. To copy a file from one disk to another, the user clicks on the appropriate icon, and drags it to the destination disk drive or folder icon, when copying takes place. By clicking on a number of files before dragging the cursor to disk

10

drive or folder, groups of files may be copied. Clicking on a document folder opens a subdirectory in a new window.

## Error handling

Notification of errors in DOS and CP/M systems is as cryptic as their commands. GEM error handling, presents full information in a user dialogue box which indicates how to proceed. Instead of CP/M-86 or Concurrent's:

BDOS ERR ON A: Bad Sector

which appears whenever the system finds that there is no disk in drive B when it expected to find one, or that the disk in drive B is improperly formatted, the drive latch is open or the power to the drive is off, GEM Desktop outputs a user dialogue box containing a hand upraised in warning, with the following helpful text:

Disk drive A is not ready. Be sure the drive is on-line or check that the diskette is the right type and is inserted correctly before retrying

plus two smaller boxes labelled Cancel and Retry, which can be clicked on by user action. This kind of helpful error handling is used in all GEM applications.

## Other GEM applications

GEM Desktop is included with all GEM applications and it will be the first GEM application that most users meet. The visual effect of selecting any other GEM application from GEM Desktop is minor — the iconic environment is retained, albeit with different accessories and icons representing different resources, such as: fill textures in the unstructured drawing package (GEM Paint) or text typefaces in the word processing package (GEM Write). However, on selecting a DOS or CP/M application which does not call GEM graphics routines, GEM Desktop disappears, turning over the whole screen to the foreign application. GEM Desktop will reappear when this application has been shut down.

At the current state of the art, Concurrent DOS permits one GEM application to run per system in a full-sized task window, because GEM routines address the whole screen. Developments are in hand to permit full multitasking of both GEM-based and non-GEM applications under Concurrent DOS.

To date, a number of significant OEMs in the IBM PC compatible and non-compatible markets have taken GEM on board, including Philips, Olivetti and Apricot. In addition, GEM-based software is available as retail products for IBM and COMPAQ personal computers. A fast growing number of independent software developers are also producing GEM applications. By early 1986, it is expected that over 50 GEM applications will have been launched as retail packages for the IBM PC or COMPAQ ranges. These currently include the following:

1  GEM Paint: an unstructured interactive artwork program.

2  GEM Write: a full function word processor with graphics capability.

3  GEM Draw: a structured drawing package.

4  GEM Graph: a multiple format graphing package accepting major spreadsheet files.

5  GEM Wordchart: produces impressive presentation quality text foils.

6  GEM Presentation Master: uses GEM Draw, GEM Graph and GEM Wordchart to prepare high-resolution business quality slides and prints.

7  Open Access: GEM version of Software Products International's popular integrated package which includes word processing, database, spreadsheet and communications functions.

8  Business: integrated sales and invoicing package by ABC Software.

9 Vicom: a modem-based communications package by AM Technology offering TTY/ASCII, VT100, VT52, videotex, V21/V23, and other communications standards.

Success of GEM software in the retail market is already apparent. Satisfying volumes of US and European retail sales have been based on a low-cost package, GEM Collection, containing GEM Desktop, GEM Paint and GEM Write. GEM Draw has already appeared on distributor Softsel's US 'hit list', a chart of top-selling software packages.

## The future of Concurrent DOS and GEM

Concurrent DOS and GEM will continue to develop according to a strategic development plan with the following objectives:

1 Maintenance of compatibility of Concurrent DOS operating systems with the existing IBM PC business software base.

2 Maintenance of compatibility with IBM and other manufacturers' impending hardware and software developments based on the Intel family of microprocessors.

3 Provision of highly productive multitasking environments supporting multiple users and networking.

4 Application of the best available user interface technology based on research into user interaction needs.

## Appendix

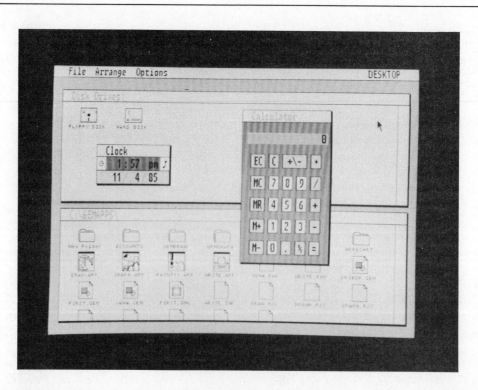

*Figure 1: GEM Desktop screen replaces DOS commands. All resources are accessed with pointer and mouse, including those represented in menus which drop down from the options in the menu bar at the top of the screen when the pointer passes over them. Up to six desk accessories, such as clock and calculator, are available depending on the implementation.*

*Figure 2: GEM Paint lets both novice and expert manipulate and improve the developing work on the screen. Icons (left) and palette (right) give the pointer the power to draw lines, shapes and solids of various colours, patterns and textures; and the ability to size, erase or modify the results. Text in various fonts can be inserted.*

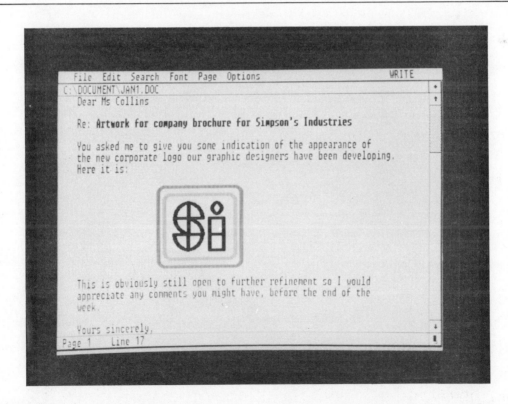

*Figure 3: GEM Write is a professional but easy to use word processor with advanced features controlled by the pointer. It can incorporate into the text images originated as graphics files in other GEM applications such as GEM Paint and GEM Draw.*

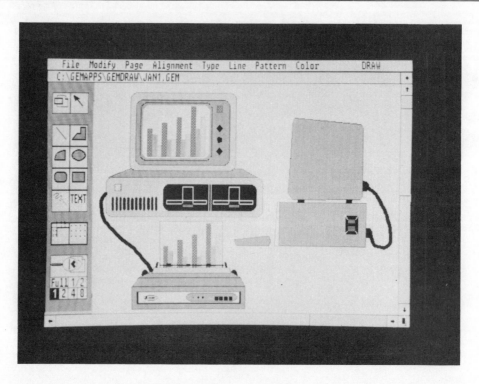

*Figure 4: GEM Draw is a popular business presentation drawing package with superb design features, such as the ability to hide or expose overlapped features, to rotate and copy images, to zoom in or out, and to automatically pack images into a given framework. Text is treated as graphics images.*

# 2: IBM office automation and networking

## C Brett

BIS Applied Systems Ltd
London
UK

**This paper provides a practical definition of office automation and examines the component parts, among which communications plays a vital role. IBM offers numerous products which fit, but do not complete, the OA model. Where do these gaps exist and how will they be filled?**

*C Brett*
Charles Brett is concerned
with the development of 'on
the desk' office automation
services for BIS and its clients.
As a user of equipment from
many different manufacturers
(but particularly IBM), he is familiar with the
problems of automating the non-technical office.
His recent projects have involved software integration, mass correspondence (image) storage
and decision support.

## Introduction

Office automation is an all embracing term. Too often, today's approach to office automation (OA) is generalised and unclear. Indeed, many observers are very puzzled as to what exactly OA does embrace. With IBM products, the situation is no different and it might be said that the position here is even more puzzling because of the vast repertoire of offerings available from IBM. At BIS Applied Systems, we have a working definition of OA which is shown in Figure 1.

The most significant factor in the figure is the user interface to all the services. If it is not friendly, approachable and 'on the desk' OA cannot work, for it is a truism, though often ignored, that OA is only productive when it is as simple and as effective to use as current office practices.

The presentation of these elements through a single consistent interface is simple to appreciate. Less obvious, perhaps, is the requirement for a 'seamless' interface between the individual elements in the OA mix. A system has little value if a user cannot readily transfer information from one element to another.

For example, data should be readily extractable from a data processing (DP) system, modelled in a decision support system and incorporated in text prior to distribution and final filing — a fairly common sequence of events. If users have to copy data from a screen onto paper, then re-enter it into a spreadsheet, the process is cumbersome, inefficient and prone to error. OA involves the integration of as many of these elements as are required by a user, combined with a single interface and seamless interactions between the components of the system.

Currently, IBM and other OA suppliers group applications together, but that means different methods are used in different application areas, both within and across the above elements. This is neither elegant or easy to use. Preferably, all OA applications should have a single consistent user interface. Keyboards and commands — including fundamentals such as create, delete, move and copy — should be identical in word processing (WP), spreadsheet, graphics and every other application within the system. By making the system easy to learn, users are encouraged to explore the system to the full: narrow use of facilities is discouraged, because the obstacles to acquiring new skills have been minimised.

Essentially, therefore, OA is a grouping together through electronic or automated means of all the activities performed in a conventional office. Given such a broad definition, the next problem is to assess exactly which facilities need to be supported in terms of interworking and communication across both users and systems. Indeed, it is generally correct to suggest that the provision of acceptable communications for the office is one of the major challenges in OA. At BIS, we have identified the following key factors:
- Ability to meet office (application) requirements
- Physical characteristics
- Cost.

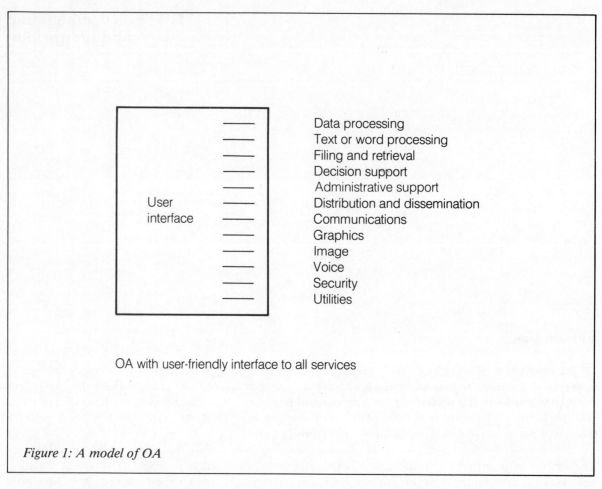

OA with user-friendly interface to all services

*Figure 1: A model of OA*

Such requirements of the working office tend to be ignored in favour of the more easily definable technical facilities. Yet these requirements must be fulfilled if ease of use to non-technical staff is to be attained. In summary, characteristics which are invariably in existence in today's manual (human) offices and are, therefore, required in automated office systems, may be defined as follows:

1 Reliability: systems may fail only if alternatives exist which meet the need to 'keep functioning'.

2 Simplicity: all staff — whether junior or senior, technical or non-technical — must be able to comprehend and use 'systems' without distraction, discomfort or difficulty.

3 Flexibility: the office is a real-time, event-driven 'system' with people responding to a wide range of events, many of which are unpredictable.

4 Accessibility: information must be readily to hand and obtainable.

5 Expandability: requirements change and both expansion and contraction must be achievable. In practice, offices expand — and it is one of the objectives of OA to increase throughput without a proportionate increase in cost.

6 Effectiveness: the office must accomplish its objectives.

These factors must be applied to communications just as much as to the actual OA applications themselves, if such facilities are to be viable for the office. It is necessary that communications provide the integration and adaptability to carry the information which forms the basis of office practices. Therefore, the key communications — and thus networking — characteristics required for the office are those currently present. These are summarised, in order of importance, as follows:

1 The choice must fit human capabilities, motivations and skill. It is important to match communications characteristics to meet immediate OA needs and to cater for conceivable new demands, but cognisance should be given to emerging technologies.

2  The selected networking must assist in addressing the issues of increasing individual and corporate effectiveness. It should permit the dynamic sharing of resources but it should not retard OA usage development by generating premature capability problems. It should be designed for long life: the installation costs of replacing an obsolescent network are substantial but clinging to an outdated network risks losing the benefits of new OA opportunities.

3  The choice must be technologically correct. It is important to analyse the nature of the workstations that will use the network services and to determine the bandwidth demands. It is important to study the types of office traffic generated by workstations and the services they access in terms of the nature and the time duration of a connection.

## How do IBM's products fit the OA model?

Given the breadth of the definition in Figure 1, a substantial problem arises when examining what IBM can provide because of the multiplicity of products. Using Figure 1 as the base, the shape that emerges can be seen in Figure 2.

The variety is vast, even dazzling. The choice is, superficially, bewildering — and some argue that even IBM is puzzled. Yet this list is by no means exhaustive: certain applications, for example VS/Script and QBE/OBE, have no immediately precise role in the conventional office. While the list may appear Gargantuan, in practice there are significant omissions and the way these products or systems link together is enough to cause those thinking of turning to IBM, for OA, considerable concern.

It is in communications and cross-element interfacing that IBM is most vulnerable. Distributed Office Support System (DISOSS) for example, requires an ICS environment and, therefore, cannot run under VM. Professional Office System (PROFS) only runs under VM. There is a formal commitment by IBM that PROFS and DISOSS will 'communicate' but it appears that one will need both VM and CICS under DOS or MVS — which is an expensive way to provide OA. This incompatibility is important because

| | |
|---|---|
| Filing | DISOSS, TMS (S/36), PROFS, X Services |
| Text/WP | OMS (S/36), DisplayWrite(r), 5520, DOSF, ETs (electronic typewriters) |
| Distribution | DOSF, DISOSS, PROFS, X Services |
| Administrative support | PROFS, OMS, 5520, 8100 |
| Decision support | PROFS, PC |
| DP | All varieties from PC via S/3X to 308X |
| Communications | SNA, DIA, DCA, etc |
| Image | Scanmaster, 6670, IVF/GDDM, PC graphics |
| Voice | ADS, 1750, 3750 |
| Utilities | Many forms |

*Figure 2: IBM products fitted to the OA model*

DISOSS is the key OA product, according to IBM, and it is here the fundamentals of the Document Content and Document Interchange Architectures (DCA and DIA) are embraced. On the other hand, however limited it may be in text applications, PROFS is the main professional office tool on VM 3270-type systems.

Examining the products on a wider basis, certain other key omissions become apparent. IBM is fond of discussing 'peer-to-peer' SNA communications, particularly for the old 'GSD' products (S/34, S/36, S/38 and 5520).

What is peer-to-peer communication? It is certainly not full networking in IBM's current offering. An S/36 cannot interact with another S/36 (or S/38) as though it is a remote screen onto the second system. It can only initiate pseudo-interactions which are, in fact, file access and transfers. This is only effective if the name of the sought after file is known. In the office the user will be searching for informal, or 'soft', information, the filing structure of which will inevitably be oblique. In this respect, IBM's current 'peer-to-peer' is quite unsatisfactory for practical OA.

Of course, multiple 370 systems can be linked together for peer-to-peer communications via SNA. This indicates the direction that IBM wishes to follow; DISOSS and mainframes at the centre with GSD-type products as nodes.

However, OA is as much about the location of information and its exploitation as it is about systems. The weakness in the current IBM networking lies not so much in 43XX/308X communications but in 43XX/308X to GSD communications and GSD to GSD communications.

It is not yet feasible to have a central system controlling the network which allows users to access, either directly or via the centre, non-370 IBM systems. Given the popularity of GSD systems in Europe, this is absurd. GSD users will not be interested in buying a 43XX mainframe for OA alone.

For voice it is apparent from the relationship with Rolm, that IBM perceives its own Private Automatic Branch Exchange (PABX) voice systems to be in decline. The 1750/3750 analogue exchanges are outdated. The ADS voice messaging system, based on the seemingly eternal Series/1, is a first and expensive step towards reducing the 70 per cent failure rate on telephone calls. More can be expected, although the ability to connect to non-IBM PABXs in Europe remains in question — as much because of IBM marketing policy as technical difficulty. The fact that Rolm has its own voice messaging system only further complicates the issue.

For highly centralised systems, such as in insurance companies, the 8100 remains the OA choice. The dependence of 8100s running Distributed Office Support Facility (DOSF) upon DISOSS is quite clear.

The functionally similar 5520, a stand-alone, shared-logic word processor with excellent administrative handling, is still remote from all systems, including other 5520s. IBM's mainframe products are equally estranged.

In the image area the 6670 (laser printer/copier) has not been a success — despite the attractiveness of both its office and general-purpose printing. Scanmaster, with the recent announcement of 3270 viewing of image documents via IVF/GDDM under MVS, is unique. It is a blend of facsimile, photocopier, scanner (onto DASD devices) and near letter-quality printer. At £8000 its price/performance is remarkable — if you have a host DISOSS environment.

Finally, the ubiquitous PC and its older (and some would say better) relative, Displaywriter, continue to sell beyond IBM's ability to satisfy demands. Displaywriter, though venerable, still has possibly the most powerful WP software of all and the announcement of DisplayWrite/2 for the PC suggests that IBM's direction is to provide this facility on PCs rather than stand-alone, dedicated WP. Provision of DisplayWrite/36 and a Statement of Direction for Displaywrite/370 confirm the view that IBM is intent on producing a single DCA standard WP document across all main OA systems. Conversely, those systems without Displaywrite may be about to disappear: the chances are that the 8100 and 5520 have reached their final development.

This discussion of IBM OA products is, necessarily, incomplete, but it does indicate that even for the products so far announced, things are not as clear cut as might be expected. It highlights the difficulty of providing OA with seamless interfaces, full communication abilities and accessible data storage. There may be just too many options over too many products to allow full integration.

## Networking and connecting IBM's OA

The necessity to have networking that is operable by non-technical users has been argued earlier in this paper. The provision can take many forms, some of which are no more than broad 'advice', such as the wiring recommendations for cabling links within a building or site. However, there are a few key uses which need to be discussed. These are: SNA, Local Area Networks (LANs), DIA/DCA and PABXs.

### SNA

The importance of SNA in the office is absolute — it provides the physical and logical backbone for communication — but it is not the preserve of the user. If the user is aware of SNA itself, then the user friendliness is not available.

It suffices, therefore, to suggest that, while SNA is a major building block for IBM for its host-based systems, it is not yet sufficiently flexible to handle either genuine non-370, peer-to-peer links or LANs. This is significant, particularly in the context of small groups of users, departmental systems and organisations which are not 370 host-oriented.

Users who wish to capitalise on existing IBM DP equipment are currently frustrated in any attempt to obtain full SNA networking — unless they are prepared to incur the penalty of installing a 43XX (or larger) processor. It has been suggested that IBM may be preparing a '4301' (a 43XX under the desk). BIS finds this an attractive idea: it could provide both storage capacity and a host controller for networking. On the other hand, BIS is not of the opinion that IBM's commercial policy would allow the healthy 43XX market to be threatened by a significantly less expensive processor. Furthermore, even if the '4301' could fit under a desk, the main storage by itself would take up far more room, at least until the practical advent of the optical disk which IBM is apparently so keen to disavow.

The more attractive option, from a marketing view, might be to use existing machines (as discussed below) with SNA facilities enhanced through greater implementation of SNA LU6.2 rules. If this provides S/3X communications services (including interactive facilities), then OA and SNA would coalesce. From that base, IBM could swiftly move to lock out all those vendors who are so earnestly attempting to surround IBM DP with non-IBM OA.

### LANs

IBM's history with LANs has not been noted for its success. There are several significant intentions — each with troublesome implications because of the lack of sufficient information. The key products are:
- PC Cluster
- PC Network
- Token-passing LAN.

Of these, the PC Cluster is the least important. It is a convenient low-cost method of pulling together a number of PCs but without special qualities. The PC Network has far greater implications. As a broadband network it has the potential for many more activities (see Figure 3).

Whereas neither microLANs nor baseband utilities can conveniently (if at all) integrate voice or real-time image onto the network, broadband systems are able to do so. Broadband enables many services to share the same cable simultaneously. For example in hotels, video films and television can be distributed to bedrooms at the same time as supporting room reservation, mini-bar monitoring and billing. In hospitals, broadband systems are used for video-camera monitoring of patients as well as providing access to hospital and patient records to support security surveillance in parallel with process control management, warehouse management, time and attendance recording and even a voice broadcast tannoy system.

PC Network has a capacity of only 2 Mbit/sec. This is not sufficiently fast for many of the above applications. For example, where DP is involved, capacity is rarely an issue. There is plenty of time for activities such as bulk text input (20 typists working at 100 words per minute is less than 20 000 bit/sec of

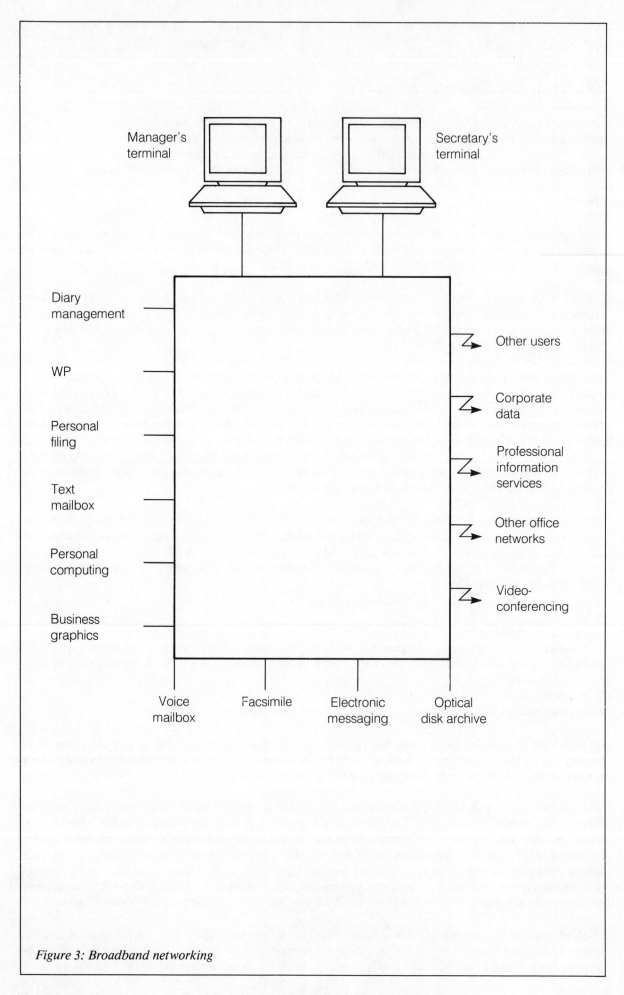

*Figure 3: Broadband networking*

maximum throughput). If blocked, rather than character, input is exploited, much less than one per cent of the throughput is used, although many users scanning through multiple page documents will utilise much higher percentages. Similarly, images of 400 Kbit/sec per A4 page compressed will require large proportions of capacity if retrieval speed is to be acceptably fast.

However, PC Network has the capability to support traffic between PCs and SNA nodes, such as mini or mainframe computers. Such a utility can provide the basis for closer integration of OA and DP within an organisation.

Because PC Network can theoretically accept voice, connection to PABXs becomes feasible — along with multifunction, telephone-inclusive traffic. Typically, a voice channel requires 64 Kbit/sec: the 2 Mbit/sec would quickly be absorbed in any large configuration.

Hence the need for a high-speed LAN — the so called token-passing LAN which has been in development and rumoured as being imminent for the past three years. Two theories are most common to explain this delay. One, the least credible in many ways, is that the chip agreement with Texas Instruments has not been fruitful. The other theory is that full integration of the token-passing LAN and SNA has proved far more complex than IBM envisaged. This seems quite reasonable. SNA is hierarchical in nature: a LAN is the opposite. Providing a convenient entry and access mechanism in both directions (LAN to conventional SNA network and *vice versa*) is conceptually a difficult problem. The practice must be far worse.

The importance of the LAN to IBM was demonstrated by the May 1984 'Cabling System' announcement. IBM does not wish other vendors to capitalise on its current weakness. Cabling the office for OA is expensive and is not an exercise to be repeated lightly. The concept of the 'data expressway' to enable differing IBM hardware to interface with those resources — including voice connection — is critical in achieving the penetration of the OA market that IBM wishes.

## DIA and DCA

IBM's greatest strength in OA is its size. Such size not only allows it to produce divergent systems but also means it has the extensive research and development necessary to recombine such systems into a single approach. Such expenditure is apparent in DIA and DCA — and it is around these architectures, and IBM's ability to support them, that the future will unfold.

DIA/DCA can realistically be regarded as an IBM solution to an IBM problem. While this is a valid viewpoint, it completely underestimates the quality and thoroughness of the thinking which underpins these architectures. This is manifest in the implicit inclusion of not only text and image — Scanmaster images are stored under DIA/DCA within DISOSS — but also the potential for voice.

Simultaneously, IBM is said to be examining the inclusion of a single ROM with all Western character sets in every output device, be it printer, screen or whatever. This would provide the base for accommodating different nationalities in the office — without a recurrence of the problems that have arisen with non-European keyboards and software, for example.

DIA and DCA represent a structure upon which, or within which, OA can be built. The architectures surpass any of the research performed by other vendors. That is confirmed by the army of vendors who are adopting DIA/DCA (or at least some elements of the architectures). These include Wang, Digital Equipment and Data General. The scale of IBM's research can be assessed with one example. On average a word processor uses about 30 or 40 control characters: DIA/DCA have over 256 defined.

These architectures are undoubtedly important both to IBM and to third parties. Because IBM does not recognise other vendors (it does not provide CO3, VT100 emulation etc), any user on an IBM host cannot communicate with non-IBM OA vendors' systems. However, because many of the vendors can perform 3274 emulation they can communicate to IBM hosts. With DIA/DCA transforms, these vendors can envisage such a picture as shown in Figure 4.

The only DIA/DCA transforms in this instance are final-form documents which are effectively print image documents being passed into the IBM host environment for IBM users and/or DISOSS. If this were to occur, IBM would be vulnerable extremely quickly.

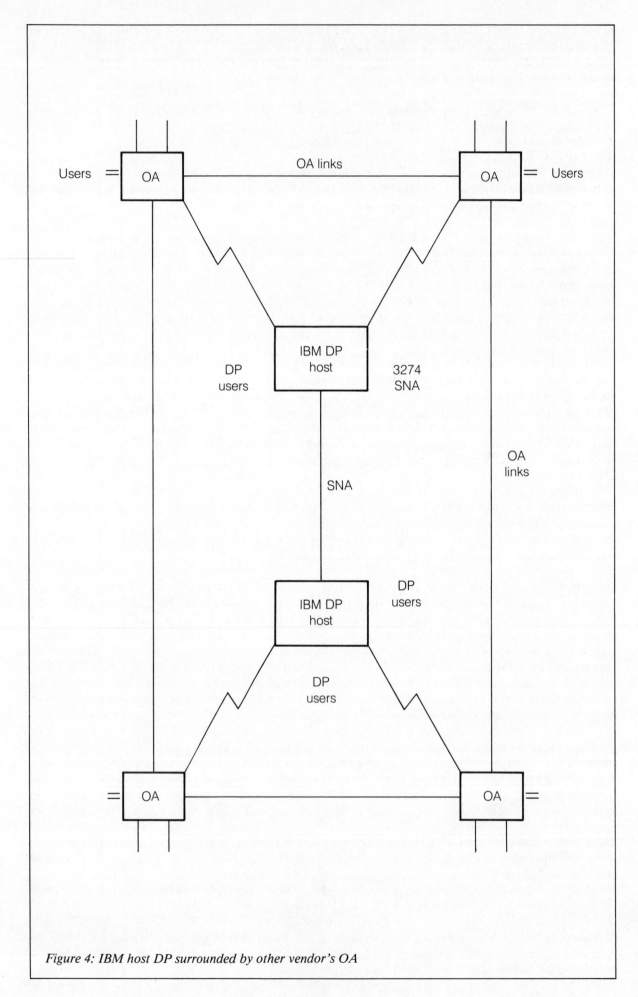

*Figure 4: IBM host DP surrounded by other vendor's OA*

24

However, the inherent requirement for SNA, as the carrier for DIA and DCA, may continue to frustrate the non-IBM OA vendors — just as it has so well in the past. Vendor emulation of 3274 SNA will be inadequate for DCA at its best.

## PABXs

The notion of the PABX as an all-purpose network switch for information is not new. Unfortunately it is not available: fully digital PABXs will come but are not yet ready. Additionally, the cost of attaching a workstation to a digital PABX is prohibitive. At around £500 per workstation and a further £500 per PABX to host line, the cost of providing a screen can be doubled. IBM's position is no different from that of other suppliers except that its 3750 and 1750 PABXs are analogue and, now, obsolete. IBM also has no experience of selling PABXs in the US.

The acquisition of Rolm gives IBM the opportunity to address this weakness. The Rolm CBX II is a powerful, almost fully digital PABX. Until the uncertainties clear after the acquisition, the long-term strategy will be difficult to discern. The probability is that IBM's action and manufacturing expertise will lower current costs of attachment via the PABX. However it seems reasonable, given IBM's other products, that it will be hosts or controllers rather than individual screens that will be attached via PABXs.

## IBM's omissions and future directions in OA

In the US over 60 per cent of sales are mainframe-oriented; such a market cannot be ignored. Until late 1984, the DIA/DCA structure did not provide effective text processing on IBM mainframes. It accommodated non-revisable form documents (from whatever allowable source) for display and no more than single character alteration. This is quite inadequate for the average professional who needs to amend documents before approving or despatching them.

How IBM proposed to address the inadequacy was unclear. The conventional mainframe user could not have had full OA because no WP was available. A multitude of 3270 users were excluded from the most common practice of the office — acceptable text handling — and documents need amendment or revision, not just the very minor corrections which the final form allows.

This weakness arose because it was deemed wasteful to use mainframe power for WP. However, not providing WP for 3270 users begged the question of information provision if mainframe users cannot effectively handle text. One way has been to adopt the distributed intelligent terminal approach, similar to the Z80 in every Wang WP workstation, but using the PC as the base, as in a 3270 PC.

There are clear indications that IBM is rapidly rationalising its screen offerings. Not only have the conventional monstrous 3270s been replaced by lower cost 317Xs but the PC's role as a terminal is beginning to assume major importance. Indeed, it has been suggested that there is a movement towards a standard screen box for which one specifies the type of local processor board that is required. This could include a 317X board, a PC board or a 529X board. In 1984 a Displaywriter board would have been included but the advent of DisplayWrite on the PC indicated that a PC board will be quite sufficient. Each board could operate alone or in parallel, using the communications network and main processor only when needed. This would be one way of introducing full text to the future 3270-type population and, by the by, encourage faster sales of 317X screens at a higher margin through the PC manufacturing base.

Another way forward was provided in November 1984, with a Statement of Direction to provide DisplayWrite on all IBM mainframe operating systems. This was very significant. All 3270 users would, at least, have access to full WP facilities within PROFS and DISOSS — at the revisable form document level. No doubt the consequent increase in CPU resource usage encouraged users to acquire more mainframe systems — and IBM would not be unhappy.

A further, radically different, alternative exists. This takes account of two significant factors: the general perception of IBM's mainframes as batch processors and the unpredictability of OA loading. DP systems are finely judged as to the throughput and workload but OA needs cannot be so finely judged. The office is an event-driven, interrupt-bound combination of processes covering every activity in an office environment. Rather than implement OA on mainframes, IBM could choose to leave message switching, store and forward and central filing to DISOSS. (This is all file transfer (batch) work and suitable for 370 architecture.) Interactive OA could be implemented via subordinate processors supporting several or many professionals. While these processors would not be closely coupled to the mainframe, their communications to both hosts and, possibly, themselves would be comprehensive and cover most of the OA activities in Figure 1 (except voice). Indeed the position would be little different from Figure 4 — except that all systems would be IBM's.

The structure can be extended further. If these subordinate processors become over-tasked by OA, further redistribution of processing could be undertaken by PC type products communicating with OA processors. The net effect of such a host/subordinate/PC approach is to concentrate processing where it is needed, as in WP, and where it makes best use of IBM systems. This may seem unlikely, given that a general-purpose machine with appropriate software is required, yet IBM's current systems, such as 8100, 5520 and S/36, all approach these requirements in different degrees.

The 8100 seems to be on uncertain ground because of the dependence of DOSF on DISOSS and the host. It is not known either for its user friendliness or extensive DP, never mind other aspects of OA. If the 8100 continues, it will be because of its suitability in congrous organisations, for example, where central control is all important. For decentralised companies, the 8100 is inapplicable.

The 5520 has a similar deficiency — a total lack of DP. It also lacks a reasonable screen (the 5253 is not a common screen) and does not provide anything which is not duplicated in the 529X line or elsewhere within IBM. Indeed, the 5520, despite the IBM label of a 'strategic' box looks as if its life is over — at the whim of IBM and to the inconvenience of current users. Indeed, the November 1984 announcement of a new software release may have been the last significant announcement about this administrative, but not professional, support system.

By deduction, this leaves the S/36 as the most interesting of all. It has the office management and text management software. 1984 saw the announcement of S/36 Personal Services, with links to PCs and upwards to 370 Personal Services. There are extensive communications facilities, including X.25 and 3274 emulation. Both PCs and Displaywriters can, to a greater or lesser degree, interact with it. Although many of these facilities are available with either the 5520 or 8100, the S/36 scores in three areas: the breadth of software available, the existence of graphics and its extremely low cost. Indeed, as a low-cost option for either DP or OA — or both — it has great attributes, once the software is improved and full (interactive) S/36 to S/3X and 43XX to S/36 communications are implemented. Yet the S/36 may not be the answer. Rumours abound of a 4301, the 43XX 'on a board' for the office (possibly as an office controller).

S/38 also offers possibilities. As a purpose-built database machine it looks attractive for supporting comprehensive office structures. Additionally, there are suggestions that a 'DISOSS/S/38' may become available. Using the power of the new Model 20 and Model 40 machines, a lower cost OA host with important ease of use and lower running costs than 43XX/308Xs would be attractive as a general-purpose OA controller. That this may become the case is further indicated by the implementation of 317X/327X screens onto S/38 via 3274 controllers.

Other areas where IBM has weaknesses are in genuine peer-to-peer communications, LANs and voice, all of which have been commented upon earlier.


## Summary

IBM's push towards dominating the OA market has begun. Key issues either have been addressed (image with GDDM and Scanmaster) or will be (WP on mainframes using DisplayWrite).

OA is about communications and integrated software. The advent of Personal Services on PC, S/36 and 43XX/308X is indicative of an increasing functionality which is common. The 3270 PC, with its multiple windowing, allows users to 'simulate their desks', where many sources of information are available simultaneously.

1984 was the year in which IBM failed with its major LAN, acquired genuine telecommunications expertise and for the first time showed the general direction of its OA products. The future will prove whether or not the multilevel approach is possible.

Users can now choose from several options (once, of course, all are available) and match IBM's OA to their commercial needs, as follows:

1  The secretary has the new IBM typewriters, which can be attached to the PC.

2  The professional has the PC which can be attached to:
   - The secretary's typewriter as a printer
   - S/36
   - PC Network attachment
   - Hosts.

3  The department might have a DP/OA S/36 with:
   - Expansion by attaching PCs
   - Increased OA via PCs as word processors
   - Node connection to corporate resources (be they current SNA hosts, as with 43XX/308X, or possibly an S/38)
   - The potential for LAN connection.

4  The corporate resource is on mainframes with all the above levels reaching down to the individual in the office, especially when full peer-to-peer communication is available.

No other supplier can match IBM's range of products over the OA model in Figure 1 and no other supplier has the problem of matching and integrating so many variations. To achieve this comprehensive coverage, including full peer-to-peer and LAN, SNA is needed. Once, or if, this is provided, non-IBM vendors of OA equipment should beware.

# 3: The power and influence of IBM in the European marketplace

**P H Dorn**

Dorn Computer Consultants
New York
US

**Apparently unstoppable by either competitors or government, IBM moves on towards total domination of the information technology industry. In Europe, as elsewhere, it has sought to appear almost native within its host countries while truly retaining power and policy in Armonk. How has IBM gained such dominance and can it ever be restrained? The major Japanese corporations, united under MITI, seem secure but what of the European companies?**

*P H Dorn*
Philip Dorn has been involved
in information processing for
over 26 years and for the
past 13 years has operated his
own consulting organisation.
His areas of specialisation in-
clude operating systems, office automation, telecommunications and the legal implications of
computer-related activities. He is a member of
ACM, IEEE and the BCS, and is a contributing
editor to 'Datamation'.

# The power and influence of IBM in the European marketplace

## Introduction

IBM dominates the information technology business. In any measurable terms — revenues, profit, market share — IBM is far ahead of all its alleged competitors. More striking, however, than any purely objective measure, is IBM's near total domination of the psychology of the industry — its customers at all levels and the computer-using community.

To reach this position, IBM has adopted a series of positions, sometimes understandable but often inexplicable to even the best informed outsiders. A brief glance over IBM's history reveals many unanswered and highly arguable questions, for example, IBM's apparent disinterest in the mini-computer business.

However, as much as it may be interesting to debate and discuss the past, it is the present and near-term future which must be of greatest concern to all involved in the industry. History may suggest lessons of considerable importance and ought not to be discarded lightly, but there are important issues on which IBM has a very limited span. Today's IBM is by no means bound to the past. Those who predict actions based upon historical precedent may fall into the same traps as have many competitors of the recent past.

While IBM continues to stress its strength in US markets, the European markets increasingly offer attractive opportunities. But there is no such thing as '*the* European market', rather there is a set of sometimes separable but often collectably treatable opportunities. Perhaps no other US-based corporation understands the difficulties and potential profits of the European scene as IBM does.

A brief paper can neither detail all the changes, nor suggest all the reasons behind IBM's actions. Therefore, this paper will assert, without much in the way of explanation, and describe, without indicating 'why'.

## IBM: yesterday and today

IBM has been well described in a variety of books and business publications. The IBM Corporation spent 60 years until 1979 building a worldwide reputation as the high-quality, high-priced seller of solutions to business problems. Product profitability was maintained at all costs. Pricing was based on costs. Technology was all home-grown, slightly behind the state of the art.

To external appearances, the old IBM was so low key as to nearly disappear from sight, except for quarterly financial results. The press was treated as the enemy, to be put down if there had to be a discussion and quizzed endlessly on 'Why do you want to know that?' if by some accident an authoritative IBM executive was reached. To its competitors, IBM was a large, slow moving, highly predictable organisation which could be counted upon for incremental improvements to a well-defined timetable. To its customers, IBM was polished, careful, willing to discuss principles but never giving much information and, most of all, a supplier of manpower when there was a true crisis.

On a worldwide basis, IBM operated on some fundamental principles long ago defined and codified by Thomas J Watson, Snr. The rules were simple: wherever IBM exists, it must be a good corporate citizen of the host country; pay all taxes; not engage in currency speculation; employ citizens of the country in which business is being done; adapt to local custom. However, while there was some local flexibility, on many points IBM was identical the world over: no deals on price; no volume discounts; no partnership arrangements, IBM dealt directly with its customers. Most of all, there were no 'under the table' dealings: IBM was above suspicion, even in parts of the world where cash payments are a normal way of life.

Governments worldwide came to know IBM as the bountiful US-based company on whose local board of directors sat some of its nation's leading citizens. It was hard for a government to get annoyed with IBM when princes of the realm were directors, along with leading industrialists. What was seldom realised was how limited a set of powers were enjoyed by such an IBM company. In truth, 99.9 per cent of all major decisions, and almost as high a percentage of minor matters, were dealt with in Armonk. A beautiful fiction existed.

The IBM of the past no longer exists. It is hard to pinpoint exactly when the change occurred but it is likely that it started in 1979 when the then chief executive officer, Frank Cary, decided that IBM was going to win the long running US Government anti-trust litigation. The decision may have been guesswork, it may have come after serious analysis or it may have been from a computer projection, but it was correct and led to a set of decisions and major changes within IBM. These included:

1 Immediate entry into the soon to explode microcomputer business.

2 Announcement of a steady stream of new products without worrying about legal implications or the impact of the announcements on competitors.

3 A restructuring of IBM, permitting the development of a group of smaller, more fast moving organisations, equipped to deal with emerging technologies.

4 A change in philosophy to emphasise buying necessary components, rather than building everything in-house.

5 Use of IBM's vast cash reserves to acquire companies in businesses in which it wanted to participate.

6 Accepting the changes in IBM marketing required by the rising cost of a sales call and reduced product price: leading to dealerships, distributors and joint venture arrangements.

7 Continued heavy investment in new plant and facilities to create the most modern, highly automated production facilities in the industry.

8 Shortening of product cycles, which greatly reduced the second-user marketability and life-cycle of IBM systems.

9 Movement away from short-term rentals to long-term leases and outright sales, generating immediate cash at the expense of a revenue base.

10 Creation of the IBM Credit Corporation to provide leasing capabilities and to recapture some of the revenue base 'lost' in the sale philosophy.

11 Increased emphasis on having customers do more system installation, testing and first-level diagnosis, even on comparatively complex systems.

12 Entry into the retail business.

13 Vastly increased advertising budgets, utilising expensive nationwide television, as well as traditional media.

14 Development of a 'consultant industry' network to aid and support consultants rather than treating them as 'non-persons'.

15 A new press policy which, while still short on information and facts (especially pre-announcement), nevertheless opened channels for discussion and permitted appropriate events and entertainment.

16 Development of a series of 'statements of intent', suggesting to customers the directions in which IBM was proceeding without announcing specific products.

This list, which is by no means complete, when taken collectively describes a company which has little relationship to the IBM of as recently as 10 years ago. This is, to all intents and purposes, a new company, the common points of which appear as follows:

1 The IBM logo, the colour 'blue' and a conservative dress code.

2 Emphasis on keeping total control of key accounts — the top 200-250 national and international accounts which buy the largest percentage of the equipment.

3 Emphasis on market share, revenues and profitability.

4 Exceptionally skilled internal use of cash for investment purposes.

5 Promotion from within with ample rewards for those who are able to withstand the pressures and rise to the top.

6 Quiet concern for manufacturing technology.

7 Continued IBM philosophy of being a good corporate citizen of its hosts.

Within the overall guiding points, today's IBM must be dealt with as a different company from its predecessor. Those who anticipate an IBM action based on years of precedent have missed the point. IBM today can be predicted only on an extremely short history.

## The world scene

The information technology industry of today is an international industry. It is obvious that there is no special knowledge base inherent in any country or group of countries which can be restricted to within national boundaries. Attempts to restrict the flow of technology are futile, whether based on national policies, use of tariff or non-tariff barriers, thinly disguised hints of national security or any of the various other possible approaches. There are few commodities in the world which move as freely as those dealing with information technology. Consider for example the following:

1 Semiconductor memory circuits designed in Texas, manufactured in El Salvador, installed in computers designed in Denmark, sold to users in Taiwan.

2 Software originally developed in South Africa, marketed in the US by an American company and sold to users worldwide through a series of distributors.

3 Terminals designed in California, built in Singapore, added to computers originally designed in Japan, which are sold by American sales forces to users in South America.

4 Modems built in Florida by a British-owned and managed corporation and distributed worldwide.

5 Software developed in New Jersey, on a computer system being designed in Sweden, to be built in the Benelux countries and sold by nationals of various countries.

These are just a few examples to illustrate the scale of movement. The technology moves around the world freely, legally or illegally, and appears whenever and wherever a need arises. It can be stopped no more easily than the tides.

While there are many reasons why the technology floats so freely (not least is the size of the potential profit involved), it must be noted immediately that there is an overriding technical factor involved. IBM has set the standards, the interfaces, the connections, into which all others can easily plug their products and services. It is not an official worldwide standard approved by ISO but a *de facto* standard accepted by the worldwide user community.

The computer industry in its formative stages existed in many countries. History will record the earliest significant developments in Germany and the UK. The German efforts disappeared in the post-war era, while the UK lead, stemming from World War II codebreaking efforts, was allowed to dissipate as the UK turned towards research and ignored commercialism.

By the mid-1950s, the world centre of computer system development was the US and there it remained, virtually unchallenged, until 10 years ago. The first significant non-US efforts began to emerge from Japan in the middle of the last decade, especially in memory chips, but these were not a real threat until recently. Today, however, the power of the leading Japanese companies — Fujitsu, Hitachi, NEC, Sord, Sanyo, Sony, Epson, Toshiba, Canon and others — is well recognised.

Japan is a serious competitor in a wide variety of information technology products, from supercomputers to microcomputers, peripherals to copiers. What the Japanese seem to lack is software capabilities — but they do not lack for manufacturing technology, high-volume production capabilities, a dedicated workforce and immensely strong national barriers to competition in their lush home markets. This is, in part, a tariff question but, more to the point, it is a cultural matter. Major Japanese buyers will purchase home manufactured goods at any opportunity and without special urging. It is inherent in the national culture. No matter how much talk there is of free trade and access to their markets, Japanese buyers are unlikely to respond.

Europe is in a vastly different position from Japan. The essential area of development is a viable semiconductor industry, which Japan has and Europe does not. European-owned companies supply less than five per cent of the world's chip suppliers, which is probably less than 25 per cent of European needs, and almost all of this comes from only two companies, Siemens and Philips. Europe is an importing, dependent market.

Lacking truly protected home markets, European computer vendors have not done well. Even in those markets which were protected (for example, UK governmental buys), the European companies have struggled. Protection can allow a company to develop financial strengths but it also allows a company to neglect user needs and become vulnerable to tougher, profit-driven competitors. A clear view of European manufacturers is not very uplifting. The winners seem to be those companies which did not receive much protection and have had to scramble to survive, for example Norsk Data, Dansk Data Elektroniks, Racal, Nokia and Nixdorf. The other side of the ledger includes the famous names of European-based computing whose collective trading losses probably exceed the gross national products of most European countries: ICL, Siemens, Philips, Bull, Olivetti and Ericsson.

Of course, there are constant changes. Today's ICL is no longer the financial weakling of the past 10 years, it now has strong backing. Olivetti, for years a struggling office equipment company with almost no serious electronics, has turned itself around. Ericsson, a major force in worldwide telecommunications, is starting to come to terms with the computer industry elements it has inherited.

All in all, though, annual surveys of European industry reveal the domination of European markets by US and Japanese firms, both at the system and component levels.

Unconfirmed reports suggest that IBM has focused on one target — what it calls 'Japan Inc' — as the major competitor for the next five to 10 years. The combination of Hitachi-Fujitsu, with support from Toshiba, Canon and others, is a large company. It becomes especially large when backed by the protective wing of the Japanese government, MITI, which provides cash and sets a series of unified goals and directions. Only NEC, perpetually non-conformist and non-IBM in its architectural approach, appears to be taking a different direction. The traditional Honeywell-NEC relationship has now reversed: NEC is designing for large-scale systems, Honeywell has become the sales agent — a remarkable reversal in 20 years.

IBM does not appear to take most European competitors too seriously from a technology or marketing view. It does, however, recognise the inherent governmental power of corporations owned by host country political authorities (such as Bull in France) or those with whom there is a long-standing close relationship (the Bundespost and Siemens, British Telecom with Plessey, STC and GEC). It is perhaps against these relationships that IBM works its hardest, striving to inculcate itself into national cultural institutions, claiming in advertising that it is a 'British/French/German/etc' company and bringing leading citizens into the fold.

Worldwide, IBM's objectives remain consistent. While local tactical moves may differ, the end result is usually the same. The industry as a whole has largely freed itself from national boundaries, IBM would do the same on the marketing side. Competitively, while every manufacturer is of some importance, IBM seems to watch the Japanese very carefully, while amiably tolerating the Europeans.

Business practices differ from country to country and IBM seems willing to adapt when necessary. In Japan, it has set up a joint venture with one of the major Japanese office products dealer organisations to handle low-end and entry-level products.

Today's IBM seems willing to carry out joint ventures in countries where foreign ownership is not permitted, although it must be noted it will not do a deal if the outsiders obtain control of the venture. Even in Mexico, with rigid rules against non-Mexican ownership, IBM was able to circumvent the regulations through political astuteness. Countries in which IBM has had serious ownership problems in the past include India, Nigeria and Indonesia. While none of these are major markets, IBM does not like being excluded and has been able to work out arrangements for all except India.

In 1985 the worldwide information technology industry slowed down somewhat after the explosive growth of 1982 and 1983. The slow-down began in mid-1984 and continues. In the new climate, which is doubtless another short-term cycle, a number of once-feared competitors are sure to fall by the wayside. It is too early to predict failures precisely, much will depend on short-range buying patterns among major corporate customers. However, it is not speculative to assert that there are a fair number of companies with international reputations in less than good condition. These include both long-term players and start-ups, hardware and software companies, and organisations from micro, mini and main-frame markets.

## Users: the last competitors

Habitually, the computer using community is thought of as dedicated and loyal to IBM, willing to accept the dictates from Armonk and not likely to cause trouble. There are several explanations for this alleged behaviour, not the least of which is the 'comfort index'. IBM is extremely good at making senior management and top data processing (DP) executives familiar and comfortable with the IBM company, the IBM approach to computing and the way IBM deals with management. Making a pro-IBM decision is very easy. Making an anti-IBM decision makes people uncomfortable. It is not untrue to say, as many veteran DP personnel often do, 'You never get fired for going with IBM'.

Conversely, every senior DP practitioner has personal stories of what happened to a DP manager who elected to take a different route. These range from an occasional success to a great many instances of being downgraded from executive status. Tradition holds, if a manager goes against IBM and it does not work, the manager is no more. This might once have been an idle fantasy; today it is a self-perpetuating truth.

In IBM sales schools, going back to the 1920s, the magic term is 'account control'. To achieve this exalted status, the senior IBM marketing representative on a major account stays 'glued' to the responsible executive, ensures there will be no surprises, fights for machine positioning, takes the executive on carefully selected visits to IBM locations, personally delivers all major announcements within seconds of the release time and exercises full and complete discretionary management powers over junior IBM staff on the account, especially supervising their information collection efforts. Having account control translates itself into big orders for new equipment (almost automatically on announcement day), removes worries over the competition 'sneaking in the back door' and, if a competitor happens to slip in a disk drive or terminal, guaranteeing there is always the IBM equivalent on the system.

Having 'account control' in the 1979 to 1981 period meant putting off the installation of Personal Computers (PCs) until August 1981, invention of the Information Centre as a way to substitute on-line, terminal-based computing for a PC and keeping Apple on the outside looking in. To Apple's eternal regret, the tactic worked well. Today, Apple is a negligible factor on the corporate scene.

There is little doubt though that typical senior executives are well aware of what is happening. IBM control is by no means absolute. Why then do senior corporate executives accept the IBM manipulation? There are a number of possibilities worth examination. They are, as follows:

1 It is simply easier to buy IBM than to analyse a dozen or more choices, not merely in equipment but also in methodology and approach (this has been called 'option overload').

2 Equipment decisions today are of considerably less importance than in the past; the potential savings of a Plug Compatible Manufacturer (PCM) buy are relatively minor (in comparison to the total corporate DP budget).

3 Decisions with regard to add-on software or hardware are 95 per cent predetermined because of historical factors — an installation does not have many options to change to another supplier in an era of database systems or the IBM hardware interface.

4 The comfort and ease factor.

5 IBM offers more options, more functional capability and more direct-line upgrades than the competitors, with firm statements of intent as to future direction.

6 Upon real analysis, many of the so-called choices prove to be of the 'you cannot get there from here' category.

In spite of this it is undoubtedly true that many senior corporate DP executives are thoroughly disturbed over the lack of choice. One observer, Hesh Wiener, publisher of 'Computer and communications buyer', said in January 1985: 'Actually, we think the users are more unhappy than anyone. They buy IBM, but they want alternatives. They like to have more choices; they sense that in choice there is control. It is their money paying the piper and they want to call the tune, which seems reasonable enough.'

Yet 'choice' still implies 'within the IBM framework'. A vendor must work inside the interface, hardware or software already defined by IBM — outside, it is very bleak.

The computer-using community wants choice. There is no other explanation for why so many installations stayed with Amdahl and NAS when both companies were late in delivering IBM equivalent systems. At the PC level, the same remarks can be made about Victor Technology, Eagle, Corona and Columbia. Of this PC clone group, only COMPAQ emerged as a really viable alternative. In software, one reads at length about UNIX, even with its known flaws, against VM. Yet on any objective measurement, UNIX's penetration into classic IBM markets is so minor as to be indetectable. This should be clearly marked as the author's opinion. It cannot be documented or proven in any scientific way. Yet there is a discernible sense that the computer-using community — the important major users — want some sort of choice to continue to exist.

There are increasing, easily readable signs of discomfort among major users, even those with long histories of 100 per cent IBM positions. Discomfort cannot be measured or quantified. Will it be translated into any sort of definitive action? Will a user-manager buy a mainframe from Sperry, CDC or ICL just because it is different — a choice? I think not. Rather, the management will elect to stay with products within the interface, such as NAS-Hitachi or Amdahl-Fujitsu machines.

The one group which has the power and strength to deal with IBM is the major computer-using community. There is no recent evidence of important changes in IBM policies occurring as a result of user actions. Inhibited in the US by the conspiracy statutes, the user groups are strong on technical matters but essentially impotent on business factors. On occasions, the Computer Users' Association has provided 'yeoman-like' services to its membership but it, too, operates under constraints. In the final analysis, account control seems to have won over the uncomfortable lack of choice in the information technology industry. Senior management, non-DP in outlook, sees nothing wrong with today's situation, so long as the DP budget stays under control.

## Europe and European manufacturers

Analysts spend inordinate amounts of time arguing about the future for Europe and European manufacturers. Stepping back and re-examining the question alters the perspective. Who are European manufacturers? Does this mean companies which build, companies which sell, or companies which are European owned? The result of any inquiry depends on the base from which the analysis begins. The 1983 version of the 'Datamation' European Top 25 (published on August 1 1984) has two charts, one listing the top 25 European-owned companies and another listing the top 25 sellers in Europe. Of the top 25 sellers, number one is, of course, IBM, and half of the remaining 24 are US-owned companies or US dependencies. What is even more startling is the dollar gap. IBM Europe is listed at $10.758 billion; the nearest competitors, Bull, Siemens and Olivetti, are about the $1.3 billion mark.

What might be more interesting would be to consider profitability, which is a critical item for the non-governmental firms. Regrettably, the accounting for such companies as Philips, Ericsson, Siemens and Olivetti is so complex as to make analysis of DP revenues and profits virtually impossible.

The difficult question, 'Can a European-based manufacturer of information technology survive?', is avoided by these numerical exercises. Is the real question not another level deeper? Can any vendor, regardless of location, survive the current beating IBM is giving everybody?

Looking at the world, Europe represents approximately 20 to 25 per cent of the total information processing sector. The US is about 48 to 50 per cent and Japan is about 20 per cent. The remaining elements are scattered. If one looks clearly at any individual country in Europe, there is a reasonable market, not a big one in comparison with the entire US, but, nevertheless, one sufficiently large to permit a company to make a living. To really prosper, though, a company must successfully penetrate neighbouring markets. Finally, to be a world factor, a company must expand outside Europe. Of all European-based companies, perhaps only a handful have recognised these basic facts and figures, and acted upon them. The majority seem content to hide behind localised barriers.

Those who have proven capable in world markets come in two varieties. The first group is the international telecommunications companies who have long known they must sell to the entire world if they are to prosper. This group, led by Siemens, Ericsson, Thomson-CSF, Philips, Racal, Ferranti and GEC, has proven many times that a European-based company can compete successfully. The second, computer-based, group is smaller and includes Nixdorf, Norsk Data, Dansk Data Elektroniks and one or two other smaller players.

One of the more curious points is the broadly-based telecommunications success of such companies as Philips, Ericsson and Siemens, matched by the near total DP failures within the same companies.

Other European-based companies have not been successful in the general sense. They have survived, somehow, but have never become serious players in world markets. These include Bull, ICL and Kienzle. Even where they have done well, the impact is highly localised.

One of the more interesting European submarkets has always been French service companies. Consider the differences between SG2, CISI and CGS, which are all the same general size and shape: SG2 and CISI are prosperous but almost unknown outside France; CGS (Cap-Gemini-Sogeti), which is aggressively expanding all over Europe and the US by growth and acquisition, is moving ahead much more rapidly. Thus, is there a real future for a one-nation company?

The fundamental question to be determined is the viability of a European-based company. It is obvious the question has been answered many times by companies based in many different countries. There is nothing inherently positive or negative about being European-owned, provided the company is willing to aggressively chase business worldwide, make the commitment to expand abroad, invest the cash and understand the markets.

The success of Japanese companies, who must export to survive, has been noted. In spite of far more difficult cultural and language barriers, the 'Hitachi-Fujitsu-NEC-Canon-Toshiba' invasion proceeds. These companies have long been willing to pay the price to enter new markets, whether by direct sales, through partnerships or joint ventures, or by direct government-to-government deals. The

Japanese have taken the position they must to sell to the entire world and, having taken the position, will back it up with investments.

If, indeed, there is nothing fundamental to prevent European-based companies from attacking worldwide markets, why are the success stories so infrequent? Consider the following as part, or all, of the potential answer; European-based companies are:

1 Unwilling to invest hard cash in ventures without a well-defined and obvious short-term payback.

2 Short-sighted and lack a serious long-term strategic sense; they are too concerned with conservation of resources.

3 Managed by employees rather than entrepreneurs; there is little interest in a high-risk/high-growth opportunity because there is no personal reward structure.

4 Sheltered, over-protected and simply cannot compete without assistance from their governments.

5 Largely government supported, do not believe they have to keep pace with the technology and tend to rely on tariff barriers to keep out advanced producers from other nations.

6 So concerned with being different from IBM that they have followed ill-defined technical paths and trapped themselves in positions of no interest to major users.

At one time or another, each and all of these explanations have been suggested. Where the truth actually lies is extremely difficult to determine but it is likely that all these factors contain a grain of truth. In looking at the success of such non-governmental ventures as Norsk Data and Nixdorf, it is worth noting that there is a single entrepreneur at the helm in both cases: they do not enjoy the blessing of their government and they have both attacked international markets joyfully.

## Alternatives for 1990

A number of possible scenarios for the remainder of this decade in the information technology industry have been generated. These deal not with technological progress, which is assumed, or with any questions as to the development of markets, because there is no reason to suspect the demand for computational power will slacken, rather, there are several possible industry structural changes to consider across the next few years. These are discussed below.

### Do nothing

This scenario assumes nothing will change from the January 1 1985 base, except for normal growth. Today's trends toward more million instr/sec per user and emphasis on on-line, transaction processing systems will grow. No government action will occur to inhibit IBM's growth. World economies will progress in a growth/recession cycle, as the West moves to an information base and the Far East takes control of 'smoke-stack' industry.

From this pattern, in 1990 IBM can be expected to reach the $110 billion level. Most of today's smaller competitors will have disappeared. Survivors might include Hewlett-Packard, Wang, perhaps Apple, and Sperry (based largely on military business). IBM's market power in this scenario is so strong as to virtually prevent new entries. However, the user community will not be entirely unhappy as it will have a firm *de facto* interface standard with which to deal. By 1990, IBM will have moved in on most independent software companies, although the applications specialists will survive, especially in financial areas. In Europe, small struggling remnants will remain to support governmental purchases. Constant clashes between IBM and the major European telecommunications suppliers will occur at the interface but, by and large, the present 'telecom' people will be relegated to voice systems, with IBM dominating the mixed voice/data switch business.

### Revival of the giants

This scenario postulates that IBM will continue to wield power for a few more years, crushing smaller competitors outright (for example, Apple and Digital) or by 'deadly embrace' (for example, Amdahl and

Microsoft). However, new competitors will arise later in the decade, as AT&T prepares to enter new markets, Eastman Kodak makes a final, firm determination to enter the business and ITT picks up pieces shed by Xerox, Philips, Ericsson, CDC and others.

This scenario is curiously silent on the possibilities of a European-based aggregation of companies becoming a serious competitor. The general feeling is that there is too much political in-fighting for such a scenario to occur in Europe, too many deep cultural differences, as well as direct product line clashes. A merger of efforts between Siemens, Philips and Bull has already been tried. Add to this set, Thomson-CSF, Ericsson and ICL, and a large company would result. However, all are strong in telecommunications and comparatively weak in basic computational skills, marketing and strategic planning.

A major player in the 'giant' scenario is the Japanese. While an irrevocable merger between Hitachi and Fujitsu is unlikely, it is equally likely there will be close cooperation under MITI's watchful eye. The scenario suggests the presence of a Japanese giant may alter the expected results. Working within the IBM software standard, the Japanese can deliver more price/performance than any other giant. Therefore, the end result suggests a Japanese market share increase to 25 per cent of the mainframe business worldwide. In Europe, the Japanese can be expected to assume at least 40 per cent of the business, perhaps 20 per cent in the US. (Note that the current US sales agencies, Amdahl, NAS and Honeywell, are likely to be assimilated later in this decade.)

## Government intervention

This scenario projects that governments, worldwide, will grow uneasy about the size and market power of IBM and revive anti-trust proceedings. In the US, this is in the form of private anti-trust suits as there is no serious possibility of anything legal until the present administration passes from the scene in 1989. In Europe, this takes the form of EEC actions. In Japan, no legal action is required as the Japanese simply raise the cultural barriers.

This scenario has no serious impact until 1990 because of the time required to generate and define the cases, suggest the alternatives and bring the actions against which IBM will fight with all its legal brainpower (which is not inconsiderable). Even a major action started in 1986 would be unlikely to be heard in a court of law before the end of this decade. It is generally felt that there is no possible serious relief for beleaguered competitors in this decade from legal actions. Even the oddly structured EEC 'Undertaking' took four years to negotiate and does little except codify what already exists.

As IBM grows, the chances for long-term legal action rise. There is an ever broadening stream of notes, papers and articles suggesting IBM is too big and needs to be restrained. Most of this is still a semi-underground movement and little widespread, cogent reasoning has appeared in reputable media supporting a 'break up IBM' movement. Two major negatives to such an action are:

1 The politics of the present Washington administration.

2 The unhappy experience of US corporations and individuals with the judicially mandated break-up of AT&T.

1985 to 1990 may seem like a long timeframe but in the normal course of American litigation (the last IBM anti-trust case ran from 1969 to 1981 with no decision) it is a very short run.

## Unilateral European action

Several attempts have been made to model the possible outcome of unilateral actions by one or more European governments to simply take over IBM's holdings in a particular country. While such actions would seem extremely unlikely under present governments in the UK, Germany or Denmark, such nations as France, Italy and Sweden have different social philosophies.

It takes little projection to visualise IBM's reaction to such an effort. Instantly, massive public campaigns would be launched with a pro-IBM theme. Secondly, IBM would quietly but forcefully begin to suggest why cutting a country off from the world (or the world according to IBM) can only lead to second rate national status. Thirdly, the full force of the US government, with its long-standing IBM relationships, would come into play. While one cannot visualise military actions in the scenario, one can easily postulate a

US counter-move of freezing financial assets, taking over properties owned by overseas investors and governments, and massive legal actions on a scale not seen before.

The French Government in office has taken over several French-owned private financial and manufacturing institutions. A previous French government took over properties owned by ITT and Ericsson. However, the size and impact of these takeovers was small compared to the assets of IBM France and it does not seem likely that it will be taken over.

While the possibilities of this scenario are slim, they cannot be disregarded completely, especially if a government becomes politically disadvantaged and needs to impress its electorate. A politician under pressure often suggests some strange things, merely to divert attention. Threats to nationalise an American-owned company are very attractive for a significant percentage of the electorate in a number of European nations. On balance, such actions are unlikely in the near future. By 1990, however, the percentages might change.

## The 'all-fronts' attack

This scenario is based on the notion of increasing uneasiness about IBM's continued growth, with no special triggering point but a general reaction occurring in many countries simultaneously. The scenario suggests multiple private lawsuits (some with merit but others based on little more than a bad decision by the litigating company), some governmental control actions in selected European countries, increased pressure from 'Japan Inc' and a major competitive effort from one of the 'sleeping giants'.

Even IBM does not have unlimited resources. While it can fight on several fronts, there is a limit. Given IBM's propensity for defending aggressively rather than giving in on even the most minor issues, it is not difficult to come up with a sequence of events which would stretch its resources. Perhaps half a dozen lawsuits from reasonably large competitors (say Apple, Wang, Hewlett-Packard, Digital Equipment and Amdahl) timed to coincide with actions in (for example) the UK and Germany to establish the national companies as preferential suppliers, together with a major Japanese effort in Europe and the continuing battle to fight off AT&T in key US markets, would see IBM stretched to its limit.

This approach is reminiscent of Sir Winston Churchill's proposals for how best to attack Germany during World War II: he proposed to ring the Continent, cut off all transport of goods, attack by air, aim minor offensives at as many points as could be supported, make no commitment to any one attack so large as to sap the strength of the attackers and generally wait and see which avenue (Western France, the Balkans, Italy or the Low Countries) should prove most successful. This is an interesting approach but one which was set aside for the 'one punch' effort in Normandy. In larger terms, the 'all-fronts' theory has greater potential than direct attack but, to be brought off successfully, it would seem to require a certain amount of possibly illegal conspiracy round the world. It is not easy to visualise the Japanese Government cooperating with private litigants in the US.

Perhaps enough publicity and articles can set the tone and alter the environment so that these things simply happen with no pre-arrangement.

Of all the scenarios postulated, the strongest possibilities exist here. All that has to happen is that a few corporate officers in various organisations become angry enough to act. Selective European controls are always imminent. In almost every country there are bureaucrats working on a variety of schemes to control IBM at the expense of their national (and nationalised) company.

## Scenario evaluation: a conclusion

Does IBM need to be restrained? If it is thought that nothing needs to be done aside from ensuring it obeys all laws and statutory requirements of each host country, read no further. If it is felt something needs to be done, regardless of whether the feeling is based on objective fact or subjective uneasiness, which scenario seems most likely? It would appear there is little likelihood of significant actions stemming from governments in Europe or the US. The other giant companies are far from being real threats. Therefore, any genuine hope for restraining action must come from the 'all-fronts' effort. If Chairman Mao was correct, 'the journey of 1000 miles starts with a single step', then necessarily each small action must be part of a total, albeit uncoordinated, attack. Given IBM's strengths, aggressiveness, deep influence in the end-user community and technology, no single company, user or competitor, can hope for a clear-cut victory. Rather, the entire scenario must come into play before results can be achieved.

In the final analysis, government restraining actions have always proved inept. IBM either circumvents the rules, changes the rules to suit itself or just fights off the hostile government. In general this occurs because few governments have the technical depth to deal with IBM. They do not understand the game being played (for example, the EEC in the 1980s or the US Department of Justice in the 1970s).

It is difficult to peer into the future. At the moment, there is little upon which to build an action case. General uneasiness needs to be translated into specific complaints. It is not enough to wish Gavilan, Coleco, Osborne or Otrona had survived. Rather, there must be some precise examples of what IBM did which was illegal, unethical or immoral and, more important, provable in a court of law, before the forces which generate action coalesce into a single attacking aggregate.

# 4: Microsoft operating systems

**P R Harrison**

Research Machines Ltd
Oxford
UK

**Until 1981, most microcomputers used the Z80 CPU and offered Digital Research's CP/M operating system. Now the picture has changed completely. Most micros are based on Intel processors and Microsoft has become the dominant operating systems supplier with MS-DOS. Microsoft's recently announced agreement to continue joint operating systems development with IBM seems to assure Microsoft's continued dominance, with Digital Research reduced to producing MS-DOS applications and operating systems which more or less emulate MS-DOS. This paper outlines how Microsoft achieved dominance of the market and examines its current range of systems products.**

*P R Harrison*

Peter Harrison entered the computer industry 10 years ago as a member of the Numerical Control Group at the Aircraft Research Association. After two years he joined Real Time Control where he gained his first experience of microcomputer operating systems. After working at Digital Electronics on medical applications of micros, he joined Research Machines where he is currently Systems Software Manager. Over the last two years he has been responsible for all systems software for the RM Nimbus, one of the fastest microcomputers based on an Intel processor. During this period he kept in close contact with developments at Microsoft and Digital Research and gained considerable experience with both companies' products before the decision was taken to adopt Microsoft operating systems as standard for the Nimbus. He has been responsible for the implementation of MS-DOS, MS-Net and MS-Windows on Nimbus.

## History

MS-DOS started life with a small company called Seattle Computer Products, which produced a single board S100-bus microcomputer based on one of Intel's 8086 microprocessors, and decided to write its own operating system for it. The system Seattle Computer Products produced was known as 86-DOS and was clearly based on CP/M, offering almost identical interfaces at both user and program levels.

At about the same time IBM decided to enter the microcomputer market and set up its entry systems division. Lacking experience in this field, IBM chose as a partner Microsoft, which had been involved with micros since 1974 and was known mainly as the producer of the standard BASIC interpreter.

The entry-level machine IBM intended to produce was really very ordinary, being cassette-based with just 16 Kbyte RAM and Microsoft BASIC in ROM — a specification which was clearly based on the Apple. However, among the possible peripherals were disk drives which required an operating system. At that time Microsoft had only just produced XENIX, which was clearly unsuitable for IBM's machine, and in any case Microsoft had a very good relationship with Digital Research (DRI). So when IBM asked Microsoft what it should do for an operating system, Microsoft sent IBM to DRI. There are many rumours about what happened next, but it is clear that Digital Research was unable to make a deal with IBM. Instead, IBM returned to Microsoft and asked it to supply an operating system. Having no in-house expertise, Microsoft promptly bought 86-DOS from Seattle Computer Products and a few months later, in August 1981, 86-DOS had been transformed into PC-DOS 1.0 and the IBM PC was launched.

The machine IBM launched was not the one the industry had anticipated, and the initial reaction of many other manufacturers was one of relief. Apple even went so far as to publicly welcome IBM. With hindsight it is easy to see that IBM's competitors failed to appreciate the importance of the extra speed and larger address space offered by the 8088, or indeed the importance of the similarity between PC-DOS and CP/M. Such features, however, were not lost on the software houses.

Three standards were available to software houses at that time:

1 The Apple, with its 6502 processor and proprietary operating system.

2 CP/M coupled with the Z80 processor, a strictly limited standard due to the lack of any standards for disk formats and the need to tailor most software for each machine.

3 Microsoft BASIC, which was available on most machines regardless of the processor and operating system used, but was not the ideal language for most real applications.

All these suffered from lack of memory. Certainly some machines had more than 64 Kbytes, but there was no standard way to access the extra memory, making it useless to anyone wanting to write software for a range of machines. The only way to write larger, more powerful software was to overlay part of the code on disk, a technique used by WordStar and dBASEII. The problem with overlaying was that it tended to be slow, effectively limiting the power of programs which could be written for these standards. When the IBM PC was released, this limit had already been reached.

The similarity of PC-DOS to CP/M allowed software houses to move their 8-bit products onto the IBM PC very quickly. The additional speed and memory could handle new, more powerful software and soon the software available on the IBM enabled it to out perform its rivals. In order to stay competitive, the other manufacturers had to emulate this and MS-DOS, the generic form of PC-DOS, allowed them to do just that.

## MS-DOS 2

As an operating system, MS-DOS 1 had a number of advantages over CP/M. It provided the user with more detailed information about the files on his disk, gave him command line editing facilities and a batch facility considerably more powerful than that provided by SUBMIT. It removed the need to type ^C every time a new disk was inserted and allowed the use of imperfect disks where CP/M insists that disks must have no bad sectors. MS-DOS allowed the programmer to choose the record size of his files rather than being stuck with an arbitrary number chosen by the operating system.

On the other hand, MS-DOS 1 did not provide any equivalent to CP/M's user numbers for organising the files on a disk. While the largest disk available was a 320 Kbyte floppy, this omission was not serious, but IBM had plans to produce an enhanced version of the PC with a 10 Mbyte Winchester. Such a disk could handle over 4000 files, making it totally unmanageable unless some means was provided to organise it.

Microsoft's solution was MS-DOS 2, released in February 1983. Building on the base of MS-DOS 1, Microsoft added a number of significant new features, many of them borrowed from XENIX, making MS-DOS into a far more powerful operating system. The major additions were:
- Hierarchical directories
- I/O redirection, pipes and filters
- Device-independent I/O
- Loadable device drivers
- Print spooling
- New standards.

### Hierarchical directories

Hierarchical directories were Microsoft's solution to the problems of organising large numbers of files. Instead of all the files on a disk appearing in one large directory, MS-DOS 2 disks have a comparatively small root directory (the only directory on a newly formatted disk), but files in this directory can be designated as subdirectories containing information about further files, some of which may themselves be subdirectories.

There was nothing particularly new about this type of directory structure, but such powerful methods of organising disks had previously been restricted to users of larger, more expensive systems. This was the first industry standard stand-alone microcomputer operating system to offer such a feature.

Unfortunately the added power of hierarchical directories brought with it an increased vulnerability to failure. A single bad sector on an MS-DOS 2 disk can result in the loss of a large number of files. Microsoft does supply some utilities which attempt to rectify this, but they still leave the user a lot of work to recover his disk. Thankfully disk technology is now sufficiently reliable that this is not a serious problem.

### I/O redirection, pipes and filters

It is often convenient to set up a file with the keyboard input for a program and leave the program to run, sending its output to disk file or hard copy device for later examination. I/O redirection allows the user to do this by instructing the operating system to take a program's keyboard input from one file or device and send its screen output to another file or device.

Pipes are a very closely related facility, allowing the screen output from one program to be used as the keyboard input for another. This feature is especially useful when associated with utilities known as filters which modify screen output in some way, for instance sorting.

## Device-independent I/O

MS-DOS 2 included a range of new calls for the programmer, covering functions such as memory and directory management. The most significant of these was a complete new set of file handling calls using UNIX-style handles rather than CP/M-style FCBs (a handle is a number used to refer to an open file). These call work identically for both disk files and devices. When a program specifies the name of the file it wants to open, MS-DOS first looks to see if a device of that name exists. If it does, the handle that is returned will refer to the device rather than a disk file. If a program wants to know whether it is talking to a device or a file it can find out, but it can carry out I/O operations successfully without knowing anything about the nature of the object it is talking to.

This can occasionally result in the system behaving in unexpected ways. Half an hour spent trying to decide why CON.ASM could not be assembled is an example — a problem which was solved by realising that the assembler was trying to input the source from the keyboard. However, such problems are few and far between, making this feature a very useful tool for the programmer.

## Loadable device drivers

The microcomputer market changes fast and it is very difficult for a manufacturer to anticipate all the add-on devices he will supply for a new machine as well as the devices other companies may offer if the machine is successful. Ideally, all these devices should be supported by the operating system. In practice, the first release of the operating system will only support those devices the manufacturer has anticipated. Under MS-DOS 1, the only way to support new devices was to make a new release of the operating system. With MS-DOS 2 the problem can be solved by shipping a device driver with the new add-ons. MS-DOS will load the new device driver at boot time and will then be able to talk to the device just as if it were supported in the manufacturer's original BIOS.

## Print spooling

Printers are typically much slower than other parts of the system and printing a file can take quite a long time during which the computer cannot be used for anything else. Print spooling on MS-DOS 2 solves this problem by allowing printing of files concurrently with other operations.

This feature is quite simple to implement on a multitasking operating system, but is quite tricky on a non re-entrant single-tasking system. It only works at all on MS-DOS because the operating system and the print spooler were written by the same person. Essentially what happens is that MS-DOS passes control to the print spooler whenever it is called by a program. The spooler outputs some data to the printer, then returns control to MS-DOS. Since most programs call MS-DOS many times a second, the performance of this system is perfectly acceptable.

## New standards

CP/M was the standard on 8-bit microcomputers but was unfortunately deficient because machines generally could not read each other's disks and every machine had different screen handling. As a major software house Microsoft was acutely aware of the difficulties caused by these deficiencies, so it set out to ensure that MS-DOS users did not suffer the same problems. With MS-DOS 2 Microsoft introduced a standard for disk layout designed to ensure that reading sector zero from a disk would give all the information needed to access the rest of the disk correctly. At the same time, Microsoft introduced a standard for screen handling via escape sequences based on the ANSI/ISO standard.

Standards have to be followed to be useful. Unfortunately some manufacturers, such as Apricot, have chosen to ignore these standards, though enough have followed Microsoft's lead to ensure a much higher portability of disks and software than was available with 8-bit CP/M.

## MS-DOS 3.1

MS-DOS 2 was a major advance in single-user single-tasking micro operating systems. It rapidly became the industry standard and was supported by a huge range of software. Digital Research managed to hold its own in Europe, but Microsoft enjoyed an enormous success in the American market. As a result of this, the major software houses increasingly produced software for MS-DOS only, thus increasing its dominance.

Meanwhile, in Seattle, Microsoft was working hard on a new version of MS-DOS to provide support for networks. That version materialised in May of 1985 as MS-DOS 3.1. From the user's viewpoint, MS-DOS 3.1 is not very different from MS-DOS 2. It offers a handful of new utilities allowing interesting features, such as making a disk appear to be a subdirectory of another disk, or making a subdirectory of a disk appear to be a disk! It also allows over 16 000 files on a disk and makes it easier for the user to run programs which are not in the current directory. Apart from a few minor details, these are all the changes the user sees. All his existing MS-DOS software will run on MS-DOS 3.1 without change.

From the programmer's point of view, MS-DOS 3.1, as a stand-alone operating system, offers all the functions of MS-DOS 2 plus a few useful new ones. The changes do little more than slightly reduce the difficulty of writing good, sophisticated software.

As a stand-alone operating system, MS-DOS 3.1 has few advantages over MS-DOS 2. Used as a network operating system, it really comes into its own.

## Microsoft Networks

MS-DOS 3.1 alone is not a complete network operating system. It requires Microsoft Networks (MS-Net) to provide it with the full network capability. MS-Net, illustrated in Figure 1, is the industry standard network operating system. It is used by PC-Net, the IBM network, and it provides the same program interface. The main features of MS-Net are:
- Hardware independence
- Transparency to software
- Sharing of disks and printers
- Print spooling for multiple printers
- File and record locking
- Access control/passwords.

### Hardware independence

As with MS-DOS, MS-Net will run on any system based on an 8086-family processor. Microsoft's code constructs the packets of data to be sent on the network and decides where they should be sent. Code supplied by the manufacturer transports the packet reliably to its destination. In essence, this is the same technique used by MS-DOS — a logical, invariant section running on all machines and a manufacturer-supplied section to drive the underlying hardware.

### Transparency to software

It is absolutely vital that a network is completely transparent to existing software, otherwise many packages will not work or will need modifying. This is an area where many older network products failed. MS-Net achieves this goal. Remote resources on the network behave identically to local resources as far as the program is concerned. New programs written to make use of the features of the network can find out what is going on if they want to, but existing programs work just as they always did.

### Sharing of disks and printers

Sharing of resources has to be a feature of any true network. Without these facilities it is merely an electronic mail system. MS-Net provides these facilities by means of a dedicated server (or servers). The network manager decides which of the server's directories and printers are to be available on the network and the names by which these resources are to be known — a very useful feature which allows the manager to reorganise the server completely without the network users having to know anything about it. The user

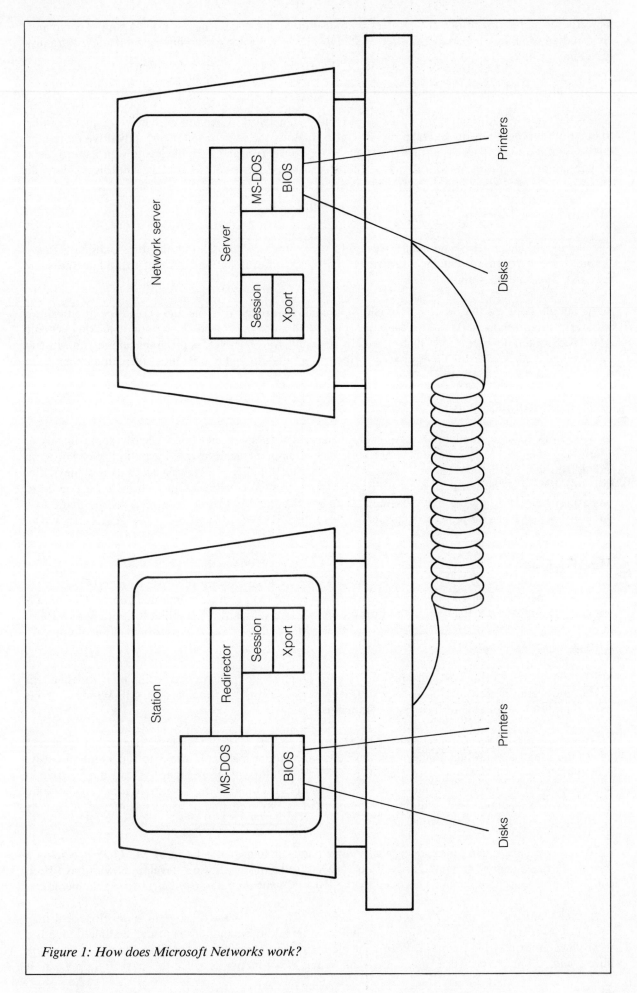

*Figure 1: How does Microsoft Networks work?*

maps these remote directories and printers onto disk drive and printer names using a simple command. He can then use these resources as if they existed locally — he just seems to have gained a few extra disk drives and printers.

## Printer spooling for multiple printers

This is the type of feature most people expect to find on a network. Each server manages a queue of files to be printed, potentially on several printers. Unfortunately, the server cannot currently drive more than one printer at a time. There is a single print queue on each server and each file has to wait its turn, even though the printer it is destined for may be idle. In practice this is rarely a problem, but this is clearly an area where we can expect improvements in future releases.

## File and record locking

File and record locking are essential for true multi-user software. Without these features, attempts to use the network to provide a database server will fail when several stations attempt to update the same record in the same file simultaneously.

Some people believed that Microsoft would be unable to provide true file and record locking facilities without a multitasking server. Microsoft has proved them wrong by implementing a locking scheme which is considerably better than that offered by its main rival, DR-Net. A program running on MS-Net has detailed control over the types of access other programs can make to its files, and can lock any area of a file, down to a single byte.

## Access control/passwords

In a network a large number of users can gain access to a single machine. Clearly some means of controlling that access is required. Some networks attempt to achieve this by putting passwords on individual files. Research Machines' experience as a major supplier of networks leads us to believe that this does not meet the needs of most users. Microsoft's system of allowing passwords to be related to directories, and allowing the network manager to restrict the types of access which can be made to a directory, seems to be far more appropriate.


## MS-Windows

One area in need of standardisation is not covered by any of the products mentioned above. That area is graphics. Digital Research attempted to introduce GSX as a standard for graphics for both 8- and 16-bit micros, but failed for lack of GSX applications. MS-Windows represents Microsoft's attempt to introduce such a standard.

MS-Windows offers a standard software interface for graphics input and output, completely independent of the underlying hardware. As such, it should increase software portability, but MS-Windows is far more than just a graphics interface for programmers.

MS-Windows offers the user a friendly, graphic interface to the system with extensive use of icons and allows the use of a mouse or similar input device. It allows multiple applications to run simultaneously, each with its own window on the screen. It is not a full multitasking operating system, but its pseudo multitasking meets the needs of most users. MS-Windows also allows multiple invocations of the same application to share code, reducing the amount of memory required, and provides facilities to allow easy information exchange between programs.

MS-Windows has a much more advanced memory manager than that offered by MS-DOS providing a form of virtual memory system. This will be very useful to those software developers who have been complaining about the limitations imposed by the IBM PC's maximum of 640 Kbyte of usable memory.

A further feature of MS-Windows is dynamic linking. Currently when a program is developed, it may consist of several modules plus a number of routines from a library, and these must all be linked together to produce an executable program. With dynamic linking, it is possible to link the modules without the library and still produce an executable program. When MS-Windows is asked to run such a program, it will load in the library as well as the program and complete the linkage process. Using this feature, several applications can share a library even if the remainder of the code cannot be shared, thus reducing the amount of memory required.

In some quarters much has been made of the fact that MS-DOS does not provide any emulation of the IBM ROM BIOS, so that a significant number of PC-DOS programs will not run on MS-DOS machines other than IBM clones. MS-Windows tackles this problem by emulating the ROM BIOS interfaces.

MS-Windows will run all existing MS-DOS applications. If the application talks directly to the hardware, MS-Windows will retreat, let the program run and then restore the Windows environment. Most programs will run in Windows and new applications written for MS-Windows will be able to make use of its full range of services. It is even possible to produce software which uses the services of MS-Windows and can run even if MS-Windows is not present!

MS-Windows is a powerful application environment and is clearly in direct competition with Digital Research's GEM. IBM could again determine which system becomes dominant.


## XENIX

The various operating environments described so far make up the MS-DOS family. This family is the dominant operating environment for single-user stand-alone microcomputers. There is, however, a growing market for multi-user microcomputers, UNIX being a popular choice of operating system. With XENIX taking over 80 per cent of the microcomputer UNIX market, Microsoft dominates here too.

XENIX was Microsoft's first venture into the operating system market. It consists of UNIX adapted to run on microcomputers and enhanced to provide a more commercially usable and user-friendly operating system. Like all versions of UNIX it is large, needing a 512 Kbyte system with a 10 Mbyte hard disk to be sensibly usable, but the arrival of IBM's PC/AT and similar machines have made it viable. The adoption of XENIX as an option for so many 80286-based machines augurs well for the future of this operating system.

When MS-DOS 1 was released, there was no compatibility between it and XENIX. Clearly it was in Microsoft's interests to bring the two environments closer together, and a number of steps have already been taken in this direction. MS-DOS 2 adopted many of the features of XENIX, including the directory structure and file system, although not always in a totally compatible manner. Utilities have been added to XENIX to allow it to access MS-DOS disks, and a range of cross-development software has been produced. It should soon be possible for MS-DOS and XENIX machines to run on the same network sharing a common server, and Microsoft has hinted that a XENIX version of Windows may be on the way.

All of these things help to increase the level of compatibility between the systems, but they do not achieve the ultimate goal of running the same binary on both XENIX and MS-DOS. This could, perhaps, be the major benefit of the dynamic linking feature of MS-Windows, for it will now be possible to write a program in, say, C and distribute it without linking it to the C library. When the program is run, the dynamic linking mechanism would link it to the appropriate C library for the operating system. If Microsoft's intention is to achieve compatibility in this way, the realisation of this benefit will depend on language developers and software producers, so we may still have to wait some time before the average user can buy a single copy of a software package to run on both operating systems.


## Conclusions

Microsoft dominates the microcomputer operating systems market, MS-DOS is the industry standard stand-alone operating system and MS-Net is the industry standard network operating system. At the time of writing it is not clear which product will dominate the applications environment market, but MS-Windows is clearly a major contender.

Currently there is no industry standard for stand-alone multitasking operating systems. Concurrent DOS is the only major product in this area, but it needs to be accepted by users, manufacturers and software houses before it can become the standard. We can expect Microsoft to produce a multitasking version of MS-DOS in the near future and judging from its history, Microsoft will have learnt from the mistakes of others and will probably produce a superior product. Certainly Microsoft is aware that its competitors will find it almost impossible to step in and set a different standard as long as it continues along the path of complete compatibility. We can expect Microsoft's dominance of the operating systems market to continue for the foreseeable future.

_____

# 5: TopView and the future

**M Healey**

University College
Cardiff
UK

TopView is the major IBM announcement, possibly the most significant yet in the microcomputer market. It effectively declares IBM's intention to get out of the standard world of MS-DOS and to move into IBM created and owned system software. This paper examines the applications and features of TopView and suggests that a new version may be available soon, allowing IBM to exert even greater control over the software industry.

*M Healey*
Professor Martin Healey is a consultant in the use of mini and microcomputers in factory control systems, data process- ing and office automation with particular emphasis on inte- gration with mainframe systems. His research specialisations include data communications, local area networks and workstations. He has presented more than 200 seminars on minis and micros and has authored eight text books and numerous articles. Professor Healey holds a BSc and PhD, and is a member of the Institute of Electronic Engineers and a fellow of the British Computer Society. In 1985 he became a non-executive Director of Network Designs Limited.

## Background

Despite its success, the IBM PC is a very low-specified product. In many areas it is below the desired minimum level and only IBM's superb marketing machine could have moved such a product; without IBM's name it would have been unsaleable. The key problems are as follows:

1  Low performance. A low clock rate, 8-bit bus machine with wait states.

2  Unergonomic keyboard. The layout is different from a typewriter keyboard, with no 'lock' indicators and no 'shift-lock' mechanism.

3  A very low-resolution display. When characters are displayed on the colour screen they are nearly unreadable and surely below any health standard recommendations.

4  PC-DOS.

Unlike the first three items, which were unforgivable, totally avoidable and prove that IBM is not above providing users with substandard products, PC-DOS was not an immediate problem. It satisfied the requirements of the first phase of PCs; that it still exists in 1985, however, *is* a key problem and one that information and management centres will regret in a few years' time.

PC-DOS is a rewrite of Digital Research's (DR) old 8-bit CP/M operating system with detail enhancements and support for specific IBM PC hardware features. Some of this support is so poorly implemented that most applications programs have been written to bypass the operating system and to write direct to hardware, a common feature of computing in the 1960s! In effect PC-DOS is a resident suite of subroutines, accessed by making software interrupts, which map the physical PC into a logical set of units. It contains none of the features of a real operating system, eg memory management, processor scheduling, multitask support with intertask communication and synchronisation mechanisms.

In the early days of the PC the simplicity of PC-DOS provided just the vehicle for quick rewrites of old 8-bit CP/M applications, with no further frills. The extended addressing of the 8088 allowed for bigger programs than the old 8-bit system and this fact alone has given scope to programmers to produce the current generation of superior micro applications, particularly Lotus 1-2-3.

PC-DOS is available in three major releases, Version 1.X, Version 2.X and Version 3.X. Version 2 introduced the concept of 'tree-structured' directories and 'handle' file I/O. Version 3.0 introduced support for the larger disks of the AT and a mechanism for 'locking' byte strings, inside files. Version 3.1 extends Version 3.0 to include a trap for BDOS calls and to 'redirect' them into a network operating system such as MS-NET or PC Network Program.

## The need for improvement

By failing to improve the whole concept of PC-DOS with Version 3.X, IBM has created a millstone for the computer industry. It is now time to move on to a full operating system, of which DR's Concurrent DOS is a definitive example. Such a system must provide true multitasking support with a task scheduler and memory management; it must also provide a message-passing intertask communication mechanism, implemented in Concurrent DOS for example by queues. Why should this be so?

If the user needs to run only one program in an exclusively stand-alone mode PC-DOS is adequate. If he or she is used to a mainframe terminal and has not experienced the user friendliness of a multitasking OS then there will be few complaints. There are, however, major aspects of corporate usage that need re-thinking, most of which revolve around the need to communicate with other resources. Some examples are as follows:

1 User-friendly interfaces. The smalltalk concept pioneered by Xerox is now commonly available courtesy of Apple with Macintosh and, even more impressively, with Atari ST 520. To use the display as a graphic 'object-oriented' user interface requires a system-level display manager to control the windows and the programs using them. The contrast between the disastrous concept of embedding windowing and multiple applications into an application program, eg Symphony, and an extension to the OS, eg TopView and Graphics Environment Manager (GEM), will be explained later.

2 Multi-user capability. The PC and PC/XT do not have this capability, but the AT does, and is capable of presenting enough processing power to support one or two added users via VDUs.

3 Micro-to-micro communication. With PC-DOS each user has to run the appropriate software at the same time. If the communications program could be ready to acknowledge an incoming call at all times while the user performs another task, then the 'communicating word processor' concept would be a reality.

4 Micro-to-mainframe communication. It is easy with PC-DOS or 3270 PC-DOS to emulate a mainframe terminal; it would be better if the emulator(s) and other local tasks were concurrent. However, we are now in the age of distributed processing such as the LU6.2 capability of SNA. Using LU6.2 an application on one processor can directly coordinate and execute with an application on another processor. The user only conceives one program, despite the use of two CPUs. The 'program' comprises two separate tasks on two machines joined by LU6.2. Typical examples would be a database server on the mainframe, accessed by an application program in a PC. But PC-DOS does not support multitasking! Thus only System/36, the 8100 etc support LU6.2; the PC user remains a terminal. Thus all the diabolical inventions (all commercial failures) based on the IRMA concept are serious problem areas. File transfer based on extracting/inserting data in 3270 screen-oriented data sets is inadequate.

5 Local area networks (LANs). There are two basic methods of creating a multi-user departmental computer as follows:
   - A central minicomputer with VDUs, eg System/36, DEC's 'All-in-one', DG's 'CEO'
   - Joining PCs together by means of a high-speed LAN so that they can share the services of database, file, communications, printer etc.

The PC/AT is a good workstation and an adequate server. Specialised servers would soon follow. The latter method is so obviously superior that IBM has had to stop it in order to protect the more profitable System/36 sales. However, LANs could not be ignored for fear of creating opportunities for competitors, so IBM produced a 'half-baked' solution in PC Network. This ensures inferiority in many respects to the System/36, but superficially offers an IBM LAN. The IBM LAN has problems of hardware but these are not the main problems; users can opt for superior hardware, eg Ethernet, G-NET etc and still use IBM PCs. The problem is that LANs, like PC/Mainframe, should be multitasking, a task in a workstation being linked to a task in a server. DOS 3.1 traps BDOS calls and can therefore map an access to a file across the network to a fileserver. Multi-user applications, however, need to share a data server (ISAM or DBMS); PC-DOS does not provide the intertask call to link an application to the DBMS so there is nothing to trap! Thus applications which share files, eg program development, electronic mail and word processing work, but applications which share data, eg data processing do not (see Figure 1).

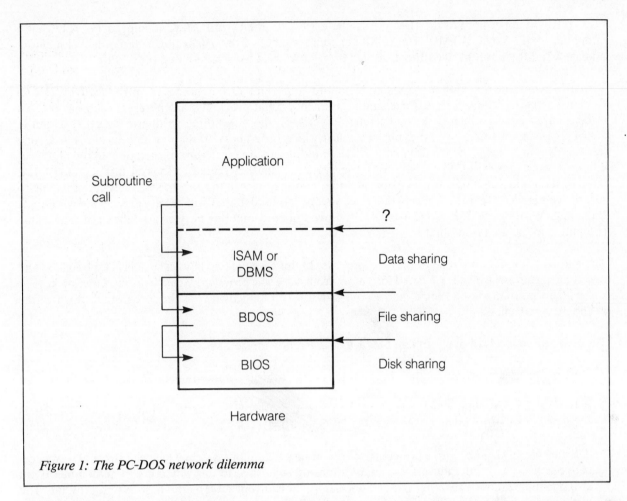

*Figure 1: The PC-DOS network dilemma*

In summary, IBM's continuing endorsement of PC-DOS is a controlling mechanism to slow down the real development of PCs as alternatives to more lucrative products. A multitasking OS opens up too many prospects too soon.

However, even IBM cannot stop progress. Thus innovative software houses have accepted the limitations of PC-DOS and have tried to work round them by building non-existent features into the application program itself. Thus each different application 'suite' has its own executive which will clash with any other such 'suite'; there is no longer a defined system-level interface. Thus there is going to be an ever-growing list of examples (complaints?) of incompatibility and the MIS centres will have to take care of these problems.

Two areas of the PC-DOS saga however do not suit IBM. First, users have seen the Macintosh and are demanding similar user-friendly interfaces from the PC, and secondly, the modular integration at the application program level, eg Symphony, has strengthened the software houses at IBM's expense. Thus in order to retain the inferiority of PC-DOS *and* to control the user interface (and indirectly the software houses) IBM has introduced TopView.

## Virtual screens and windows

The traditional 'one program, one display' approach, the only one practical with a terminal-based system, is well suited to data processing but not to office, decision support and communications systems. By simply providing processing power at the user end of a communications cable a much more useful information display can be achieved. IBM's approach was very limited, eg stand-alone (Displaywriter), graphics displays or multiple logical terminals in one display (3290). Given that the visual display is within the address space of the processor, far more flexible user-friendly techniques are possible.

Two basic techniques of screen management are common nowadays: virtual screens and windows. Both require far more memory than terminals or simple personal computer systems: 256 Kbytes is a minimum;

the 640 Kbyte upper limit of the IBM PC can be easily absorbed (with 256 Kbit chips, a 16-bit PC has a minimum of 512 Kbyte RAM!). The 16 Mbyte address space of the 68000 and, better still, the memory managed 16 Mbytes of the 286 processor, will prove attractive for screen-based processing.

Virtual screens, in the author's opinion the more important technique, were introduced by DR in Concurrent DOS. The OS runs, for example, four individual programs for one user; each has its own screen output one of which is the real screen (keyboard), the other three writing to a virtual screen in RAM. By using function keys, the user can select which program is on the real screen and is accepting keyboard input. Thus, as on a normal office desk, multiple activities can run concurrently; in the middle of editing a word processing file, a secretary can switch to another screen to look at an incoming telex, interrogate a diary or start a transmission of a file, and then return to the edit session without having to reload. This is such a 'natural' concept that once anyone has used it, they will be very dissatisfied with single threading. With this feature Concurrent DOS moved microcomputing very clearly ahead of mainframe computing in the area of usability.

The natural extension to virtual displays is windows. In this case the one physical display is subdivided and one area, a window, which is allocated for output from a specific program. Again by using function keys or some other 'pointing device' (eg a mouse) one window can be activated as the foreground to which the keyboard is 'attached'.

There are three levels of management of windows currently in use:

1  Only the program currently in the foreground is active: this is common on kluges to PC-DOS.

2  A time-slicing scheduler which gives CPU and screen resources to each task running. Such schedulers run as a control program on top of, say, PC-DOS, eg IBM's TopView. Lisa and Macintosh are similar.

3  A true multitasking OS with a pre-emptive (real-time) scheduling system which can share all resources between tasks with full intertask communications mechanisms. In this way not only screen-based but also communications programs can be concurrent. Concurrent DOS is the best example by far. The elementary scheduling mechanisms of UNIX have also been used to good advantage and, while nothing like as powerful as Concurrent, some good examples have been developed as long as communications processing is off-loaded to an intelligent controller.

The first method is frustrating and the second merely a stepping stone to the third. IBM will supersede TopView and PC-DOS V3 with its own multitasking OS, TopView *and* DOS compatible; Concurrent can today be used as a specification for IBM's OS until IBM deems to make a proper announcement.

## Object-oriented processing

### Smalltalk

Given the display concepts of virtual screens and windows, object-oriented processing can be carried further into processing commands and data via the display. The concept of object-oriented processing is amusingly referred to as WYSIWYG (wizziwig) — What You See Is What You Get. The origins stem from the Xerox research programme which defined the operating environment Smalltalk. The Smalltalk concept first appeared in a product in the Xerox Star workstation and, more recently, in the Apple Lisa and Macintosh. Now IBM with TopView, Microsoft with MS-Windows and DR with GEM are providing 'Smalltalk' concepts on top of conventional operating systems. Of these, Digital has taken a step forward, providing virtual screens and object-oriented processing in a far more flexible combination than, say, Macintosh. It must be noted, however, that Macintosh includes a number of integrated application programs as well; IBM and DR are aiming at encouraging microcomputer software suppliers such as Ashton-Tate, Lotus, Micropro, etc to provide the applications, broadening the base over their own products. Application-level integration such as demonstrated in Symphony, Framework and VisiOn are dubious.

What then is object-oriented processing? Basically, commands and data I/O are performed by reference to physical screen locations. Commands can be issued via the use of 'pop-up' menus. On entering command level, a window is presented containing an appropriate set of icons, pictorially defining the process

58

required. The cursor is then moved until it lies over the appropriate icon, the corresponding procedure then being initiated by pressing a specific key. To improve the user interface Xerox introduced the trackball and later Apple introduced the mouse. These devices allow the cursor on a graphics display to be moved more quickly and easily, the function key or keys being provided by push buttons on the 'pointing device' itself. Technically the computer software uses the cursor X-Y coordinates to identify the particular icon selected and, via look-up tables, causes a jump to the appropriate processing program. Alphanumeric displays can be used but graphic displays allow greater flexibility and better icons.

The second level of operation involves using the screen for data I/O. Again, the cursor and mouse buttons are used to mark a section of the screen in one window and to 'pick it up' and move it into another window. Thus data is output from the program serving one window and input to the program serving the second window; not only is the display updated but so is the corresponding dataset.

## TopView

TopView is the major IBM announcement, possibly the most significant yet in the microcomputer market. It effectively declares IBM's intention to get out of the standard world of MS-DOS and to move into IBM created and owned system software.

TopView is an executive which uses DOS 3.X as an I/O handler. It provides a simple timesharing executive (IBM calls it multitasking, but to date it is only time slicing) and memory manager (which allows multiple applications to share memory), a screen and keyboard. One program is selected as master, having use of the keyboard by the use of menus. The system provides a user interface by 'pop-up' menus as demonstrated in the Apple Macintosh, so that, say, a word processing program could run in one window, a spreadsheet in another, etc. However, applications must be 'well behaved' and make all I/O calls via the executive so that they can be controlled by TopView. Thus, programs that write direct to memory, such as Lotus 1-2-3, cannot run under TopView. A further feature of TopView is support for 'cut and paste' operations, moving data from one program to another via the screen. If applications program suppliers do not rewrite their products to run under TopView, IBM's dominance is such that somebody will provide an equivalent product which does.

The key factor now is that TopView, not PC-DOS, controls applications programs. A next release of 'TopView' (possibly in the first quarter of 1986) will be a native mode 286 operating system with TopView and PC-DOS compatibility but with the true multitasking capability needed for taking the LAN products from the interesting but limited PC Network into true SNA software. At that point IBM will have 'gone it alone'. Only the application providers will be welcome from the outside world. MS-DOS, products like VisiOn, Framework MS-Windows, Desq, are all eliminated. Integrated suites like Symphony and Open Access are dubious since, correctly, the user can choose his own set of modules from the software catalogue to run under TopView — the use of multiple modules in an application program, rather than an operating system, as in Symphony, is wrong anyway.

Thus with TopView, IBM is creating an enormous gap between itself and the other personal computer suppliers, including the clones. An IBM PC/AT clone is going to be strangled by software, not hardware, pricing.

The rest of the personal computer world must look for an alternative, possibly UNIX, possibly multitasking MS-DOS, but almost certainly Concurrent DOS. With Concurrent, DR has a field-tested product which can be made compatible with IBM on IBM, but more particularly, on foreign hardware.

Being menu-driven and using icons, TopView must have a 'pointing device', eg a mouse or bit pad. It will run on DOS 2.X on a PC or PC/XT, but will run much better on the higher powered AT. TopView works only in alphanumeric mode, so it will be enhanced to full graphics mode when the real OS is introduced. It must be noted that DR's GEM and MS-Windows already offer graphics equivalents of TopView and IBM may incorporate them in its new OS, rather than write its own.

## TopView versus the competition

Object-oriented processing requires a far more extensive executive than PC-DOS *viz*:
- It must manage the display, mapping logical display locations into appropriate parts of the physical display as defined by the windows

- It must manage the loading of multiple programs into memory
- It must provide allocation of CPU resources to the active window: ideally it should be multitasking to allow programs in background to continue to execute
- It must provide executive calls to manage the data interchange between windows, eg cut and paste.

The general requirements are shown in Figure 2.

Ideally there is only one way to produce such a system and that is to build the task scheduling, memory management etc into the operating system. This is possible with Concurrent DOS or UNIX (and MS-DOS 4.0 when it appears), the display manager then being a device interface (eg GEM or UNIX), does not have the real multitasking capability, making it nearly impossible to run a communications task for instance, nor will it run PC-DOS programs.

However, retention of PC-DOS presents a major problem, so that the executive is added as a module on top of the basic BDOS. Once a program is in BDOS it will not come out until the task is complete so true multitasking is impossible. Two mechanisms have been introduced. The first is to embed the executive in the application program, excluding other application modules. Symphony is the prime example, Framework another, although the latter tries to present 'hooks' for including other programs. They should not be used in any circumstances. The second method involves loading an executive on top of PC-DOS; the extended executive plus PC-DOS then provides a *very* badly designed multitasking operating system with poor facilities. The leading example of this concept is of course TopView. MS-Windows is a more advanced product, providing graphics support. DR's GEM is designed to sit on top of Concurrent DOS, the correct architecture; mounted on top of PC-DOS GEM only provides single tasking. Sadly DR is bowing to pressure and is sampling a version of GEM with multitasking on top of PC-DOS.

IBM must release a new enhanced version of TopView. The current version has limitations (no graphics) and performance problems. It is obviously far better suited to the reasonable performance of the AT than the problematic PC or XT. True multitasking is not possible, the executive providing time slicing to allow 'background' programs to execute. Communications programs for instance will be difficult to mount.

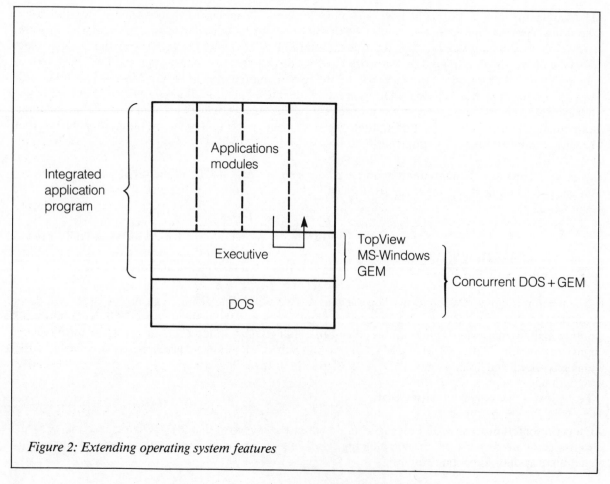

*Figure 2: Extending operating system features*

## The 286 processor and bank switching

The 286 processor used in the PC/AT offers greatly extended possibilities. It will run in either its own protected 286 mode with addressing extended to 16 Mbytes, or in 8086 emulation mode. Thus a true 286 operating system such as UNIX or Concurrent-286 could run new 286 software *and* an old PC-DOS program as a task. Unfortunately there is a major problem with the 286 in that the time overhead to trap absolute operations, eg reprogramming a segment register of the 8086 program, is unacceptably high. Thus a step backwards has been taken by introducing 'bank-switched' memory and running the 286-based AT as a fast, unprotected, XT. Bank switching was re-introduced by Lotus/Intel and is a relative failure. AST is producing a more flexible switching mechanism which DR is using for a bank-switched version of Concurrent-86 (Version 5.0).

Now IBM has the same problem. An IBM 286 protected-mode operating system is a likely development. This would integrate TopView properly and, being IBM owned, would separate IBM from the clones. However, even IBM must provide PC-DOS compatibility so it must retain the 8086-mode for the AT. PC-DOS 3.X provides a basis and TopView 2 (or whatever it will be called) will provide the graphics mode executive. What IBM will do for bank-switched memory support is as yet unclear, but it will be provided by TopView 2.

For true multitasking 286 applications IBM will use Concurrent-286, but a native IBM system must follow.

## The effect of TopView on applications

To run under TopView (or GEM or MS-Windows) an application program *must* make executive calls to access the display. 'Badly behaved' programs such as Lotus 1-2-3, which write direct to hardware, cannot be 'managed' by the display manager and will not run in the windows environment. Further, to take advantage of 'cut and paste' for instance, applications programs must include system calls to implement the integrated features. Thus a program written for TopView is *not* a PC-DOS program, although well-behaved PC-DOS programs can run under TopView with no integration.

The major effect of TopView is to force software houses back into writing program modules rather than monolithic integrated systems. In this way IBM fragments the PC software houses and regains control. A major advantage accrues to the end user in that software houses will at last write to a common interface standard and the user can choose the module he or she likes best, building an integrated system from a 'Chinese menu' of modules.

Unquestionably, TopView's current performance limitations are a serious impediment, but with the total commitment of IBM behind it, it will undoubtedly become a market leader, albeit only with the next (graphics, expanded memory support) release. TopView 2 plus PC-DOS will be, effectively, a proprietary IBM operating system. DR and Microsoft must provide GEM and MS-Windows upgrades to make them TopView 2 compatible as soon as the specification is known.

Integrated applications on PC-DOS will live on for some while because of the performance limitations on the PC and XT, but they will eventually be replaced in the next, AT, generation.

## The effect of 'clone' manufacturers

IBM has now successfully separated itself from the clones, albeit not as far as it would like. Special products such as the 3270-PC, loosely based on PC-DOS, provide features proprietary to IBM far beyond a 'PC plus IRMA' system. TopView plus PC-DOS provides an IBM operating system again only loosely based on MS-DOS. The LAN software, PC Network Program, is IBM's own which must be made to work with TopView 2. The AT hardware is virtually impossible to clone in detail, making full IBM compatibility with both hardware and software (being IBM proprietary) impossible.

Thus while PC and XT clones flourish (who would be foolish enough to buy an IBM PC when faster clones are less than half the price?) IBM must open the gap with 286-based products. The clones must look to *software* compatibility and the applications programs must try and make their offerings portable. The clones are now more important to Lotus than IBM!

## Summary

With TopView IBM has inserted a wedge between itself and the other micro vendors. Assuming a new and superior version of TopView to be just around the corner, IBM can now exert more control over the software industry. By staying with PC-DOS IBM has introduced multitasking via TopView, creating a very poor, modern micro operating system. This appears to be deliberate policy since the real operating systems with the desired architecture are available now. The PC-DOS policy ensures that communications and LANs remain inferior products and thus are not really competitive with System/36 in the departmental computing role. IBM is guilty of deliberately retarding microcomputer distributed processing progress to suit its own ends; this is to the major disadvantage of the corporate user. Because of IBM's dominance, the 'real' system is available only in separated parts and IBM is relying on no user or computer vendor being big enough to piece all the parts together and to eliminate the archaic System/36 concept.

The multiplicity of application program-based kluges to bolster PC-DOS must clash with each other causing extreme aggravation among users with a resulting backlash to the DP departments. Only by choice of a proper operating system could a healthy applications industry grow avoiding IBM-inflicted wounds.

# 6: IBM Personal Computers and the manager

**J R Hemsley, S M Green, M Popham**

Brameur Ltd
Aldershot
Hampshire
UK

**The importance of managers as users of personal computers will increase in the future. This will heighten the need for improvements, particularly to the 'manager/machine' interface. An analysis of managerial use of computers supported by interviews with a sample of managers indicates that resistance to their use is reducing. This paper reviews IBM's domination of the personal computer market in terms of its historical development and the comparative position of the XT and AT with leading competitors. Selected current issues and future developments are discussed including the AT and its successor, the 80386 machines and the potential impact of IBM's token network system, which is viewed as likely to have a similar impact on the general local area network scene to that which the IBM PC had on personal computers — IBM domination.**

*J R Hemsley*
Most of Dr Hemsley's career has been in management consultancy, mainly with Booz Allen & Hamilton, the US consultancy firm for whom he worked in West Germany, South America and Japan. He is a director of John Bell Technical Systems Ltd, a real-time software house based in Fleet, Hampshire. His responsibilities have ranged from sales and operations to finance. His main interest now is Brameur Ltd, specialising in management research, consultancy and education in information technology, a particular focus being on strategic competitive analysis. He was educated at Oxford and has a PhD in Mathematics from Imperial College.

*S M Green*
Sandra Green was educated in Horsell and at Woking Sixth Form College. She has a BTEC in Computer Studies from Farnborough College of Technology and a Certificate in Computing from the National Computing Centre. She began work as a computer systems analyst for Brameur Ltd in Aldershot and has played a considerable part in writing and researching a Managers' and Buyers' Guide to Computerised Personnel Packages.

*M Popham*
Mark Popham has been working in information technology for two and a half years. Prior to this he attended The City University, London, where he studied Actuarial Science for three years and was awarded a BSc in 1983. Initially he worked for a small software house as a microcomputer programmer where he became interested in the wider implications of computers. He joined Brameur Ltd in August 1984 and has since worked on several research projects, in particular a large study into personnel systems in conjunction with the IPM.

## Introduction

The history of the IBM PC demonstrates that even the largest companies can break the mould formed by past success to create a different product for a different market and sell it in a different way. IBM achieved PC market leadership within a couple of years, much to the surprise of most of the rest of the information technology industry. The history of the follow-on products to the PC shows that one spectacular success is not necessarily followed by others — even by IBM. The failure of the PCjr, the 'Peanut', and the relatively poor results obtained by the Portable PC together with the limited success, so far, of the AT have given cause for concern. However, the announcement of IBM's new networking systems indicates that IBM may do for networking what the PC did for microcomputing. This paper reviews the history and explores the future of IBM in personal computing with particular attention to its impact on management. We sketch the historical progress of the IBM PC range and discuss their strengths and weaknesses compared to competitors. The software side is then reviewed, before turning to the managerial use of the personal computer, firstly from a conceptual viewpoint and then by reporting on a series of interviews with managerial users of personal computers. The paper concludes with selected key current issues and expected future developments including the situation of the AT, networking, and multi-user systems. In addition to these topics, which every significant user of IBM PCs must consider, we also look at two issues which could have a major impact on the way computers are used in the future — especially by managers. These two issues are expert systems and natural language processing — the former in vogue and the latter pre-vogue in 1985.

In such a fast-moving dynamic field as personal computers it would be pretentious to assume that the future is easy to project. However, decisions must be made based on current projections, despite their flaws and limitations. Perhaps the only point one can be really sure of is that in the future there will be much more use by management themselves of personal computers. The impact that this will have on IBM and compatible manufacturers should be interesting.

## The history of the IBM PC — its strengths and weaknesses

### History

The success of the IBM PC is well known. Its origins lay in a burst of entrepreneurial energy, remarkable for a large corporation. IBM's Entry Systems Division (ESD), consisting of a small number of staff, was set up under Philip Estridge (who tragically died in an air crash in 1985) outside the normal corporate framework. In less than four months the group produced the PC and then quickly launched it despite substantial scepticism in the marketplace. A range of related products then followed including more powerful and portable versions. Figure 1 shows the key features of the PC products launched in the UK. In addition the PCjr was developed for the domestic market, but the 'Peanut' as it was termed did not meet market expectations and was not introduced into the UK market. The timetable of launches in the UK was as follows:

| | |
|---|---|
| IBM PC | 18.1.83 |
| IBM PC/XT | 8.3.83 |
| IBM PC Portable | 24.7.84 |
| IBM PC/AT | 11.9.84 |

The IBM PC's production and marketing strategy was based on major changes from IBM policies. Particularly the following:
- Low-cost easily available parts were brought in from third-party suppliers
- Distribution was through dealers instead of IBM's own sales force.

The launch of each member of the PC family has been quickly followed by the launching of 'compatibles' from many other manufacturers such as Zenith, Olivetti and ITT. These machines are nearly always lower priced and more powerful than the IBM 'model type' they are supposed to be compatible with, but in general only make a limited impact on IBM sales. However in the case of COMPAQ, they succeeded in beating IBM to launch a 'transportable' personal computer of a quality and price that IBM has since been unable to match.

## IBM strengths and weaknesses

The decision to buy an IBM PC or a competitor's is dependent upon the particular situation of the prospective client. However, a general evaluation of IBM's PC range can be a valuable exercise. A number of consultancies and research organisations offer assistance in this. One recent interesting analysis is from a leading German systems house and consultancy company, ADV/ORGA of Wilhelmshaven *(HEM1)*. They evaluated 10 leading personal computers. The ADV/ORGA conclusion was a clear victory for the IBM AT E with a particularly strong showing in performance flexibility and the various screen options as shown in Figure 2.

The only criteria for which the IBM AT E did not take first place were as follows:
- Design and ergonomics
- Keyboard
- Peripherals.

However, in all of these the AT E was placed in third position. The XT was judged to be in the fourth position following the home contender, Siemens, and by a very small margin, the HP 15011. The XT benefited from several of the general IBM strengths including documentation and training, but was viewed as comparatively weak (eighth position) in design and ergonomics. Another three areas of poor showing at seventh position were:

1 System: technical features and configuration.
2 CPU/ROM/RAM: technical features and configuration.
3 CPU/RAM: specific performance.

It is striking however that in each of these three areas the IBM AT E was placed in first position indicating that IBM design engineers have made a good effort to eliminate weaknesses when moving from the XT to the AT.

However, despite such an objective technical view of the quality of the AT it does not appear to have sold as well as anticipated due in part to the likely arrival of its successor as discussed under 'Key current issues and future developments' below, its lack of market success as a multi-user machine, and the absence of sufficiently powerful software to really differentiate it from the PC and XT for replacement purchases.

Not all IBM's products in the personal computer area have been successful though the Portable PC and the PCjr proved particularly disappointing.

### The Portable PC
The Portable PC faced a superior competitive product from COMPAQ which led to significant price

| Selected features | PC | XT | Portable | AT E | AT |
|---|---|---|---|---|---|
| Processor | Intel 8088 | Intel 8088 | Intel 8088 | Intel 80286 | Intel 80286 |
| ROM | 40 Kbytes | 40 Kbytes | 40 Kbytes | 64 Kbytes | 64 Kbytes |
| RAM | 64-640 Kbytes | 128-640 Kbytes | 256-512 Kbytes | 512 Kbytes – 4 Mbytes | 256 Kbytes |
| Expansion slots | 5 | 8 | 5 | 8 | 7 |
| Operating systems | DOS 1.1 | DOS 2.0 | DOS 2.1 | DOS 3.0 | 3/3.1/XENIX |

*Figure 1: The IBM PC in the UK*

| Maximum points | Evaluation criteria groups / Selected IBM compatible PCs | IBM AT E | Siemens PC-D | HP 15011 | IBM XT | Tandy 2000 | Sirius 1 | COMPAQ DESKPRO | NCR PC4i | Ericsson PC | ITT XTRA |
|---|---|---|---|---|---|---|---|---|---|---|---|
| 24 | 1 Manufacturer's reputation | 1 = | 7 | 3 = | 1 = | 8 | 9 | 10 | 3 = | 6 | 3 = |
| 47 | 2 Systems and service environment | 1 | 2 | 3 | 5 | 6 | 4 | 9 | 8 | 7 | 10 |
| 54 | 3 Documentation, training, introduction | 1 | 9 | 4 | 2 | 3 | 6 | 7 | 5 | 10 | 8 |
| 62 | 4 Design and ergonomics | 3 | 1 | 2 | 8 | 9 | 6 = | 6 = | 5 | 4 | 10 |
| 39 | 5 System: technical data configuration | 1 | 2 | 3 | 7 | 6 | 5 | 4 | 8 | 9 | 10 |
| 39 | 6 Technical data configuration CPU/ROM/RAM | 1 | 2 = | 5 | 7 | 2 = | 6 | 4 | 8 = | 8 = | 8 = |
| 47 | 7 Screen: technical data configuration | 1 = | 5 | 3 | 1 = | 6 | 4 | 9 | 7 | 8 | 10 |
| 47 | 8 Keyboard: technical data configuration | 3 | 2 | 1 | 5 | 9 | 10 | 6 | 4 | 7 | 8 |
| 39 | 9 Disk memory: technical data configuration | 1 | 4 = | 8 | 4 = | 6 = | 3 | 2 | 6 = | 9 | 10 |
| 31 | 10 Peripherals: technical data configuration | 3 = | 2 | 9 | 3 = | 10 | 1 | 3 = | 3 = | 3 = | 3 = |
| 47 | 11 Enhancement capability & flexibility | 1 = | 4 | 3 | 1 = | 5 | 6 | 7 = | 7 = | 7 = | 7 = |
| 62 | 12 Specific performance CPU/RAM | 1 | 2 = | 5 | 7 = | 2 = | 6 | 4 | 7 = | 7 = | 7 = |
| 62 | 13 Specific performance disk memory | 1 | 3 | 10 | 4 = | 7 | 4 = | 2 | 6 | 8 | 9 |
|  | 0 Total points | 436.8 | 395 | 391.5 | 388 | 377.3 | 374 | 357.3 | 356.2 | 333.6 | 314.1 |
|  | Overall ranking | 1 | 2 | 3 | 4 | 5 | 6 | 7 | 8 | 9 | 10 |

Source: ADV/ORGA Report (1985)

Figure 2: Comparison of AT and XT with a selection of compatibles

reductions in mid-1985. Until then the Portable PC cost virtually the same as the standard one and therefore it was perceived as expensive.

Another reason for the relative failure of the portable model was its advertising image, as an aid to the travelling executive, because it now appears that a major contribution to sales of the portable will come from firms that require mobile machines *within* their office.

## *The PCjr*
The PCjr or 'Peanut' was a failure in the US and was not even introduced into the UK. The basic home computer market is highly competitive and price sensitive so that highly priced products — even with the IBM name — cannot overcome domestic budget limitations.

Despite these errors and faults, there is no doubt that IBM has succeeded in establishing market dominance in the personal computer field due primarily to the IBM PC itself, the engine of this dominance. Even at its launch, many regarded it as technologically old but its market success is now undisputed thanks largely to IBM's powerful overall position in the corporate computing world and its superlative marketing capability which, although not infallible, is certainly difficult to beat.

## Applications and operating systems

### Applications

The use made of a microcomputer depends almost entirely on software. Therefore the first microcomputers were of limited use, not only because they were low-powered and immobile, but also because there was a distinct lack of professional software. It is well known that software development always lags behind hardware development, so when IBM announced its PC, people were not surprised to find its uses initially limited by software. However, this situation quickly changed as software houses realised the market potential afforded by the IBM PC's market success. In 1986 there will be over 1000 separate PC applications packages ranging from psychology to animal feeding. As IBM claimed in a 1985 advertising campaign a new software package for the IBM PC was being produced every day.

The most obvious areas for software application are word processing, finance, and database management. By 1983 the PC could produce effective spreadsheets for financial planning, keep company accounts, be used as a fairly effective word processor and maintain with easy access many types of database. These are still the four main areas as shown by the table of top selling software packages in Figure 3.

By October 1985 the sales breakdown of these top selling areas and the 'integrated' packages was reported by a leading computer magazine as follows:
- Word processing              40 per cent
- Spreadsheets                 20 per cent
- Database management systems   20 per cent
- Accounting                    10 per cent
- Integrated                     10 per cent.

## *Word processing*
The biggest success in 1985 in this area is still the WordStar package from MicroPro, with Microsoft's Multimate gaining great popularity. Though sales of Microsoft packages no longer top those of the Lotus software package, word processing is still the most important application area. Word processor software packages range from as little as £25 to over £600 in price and encompass a broad range of facilities. The simplest form is that of a line editor, the most complex a text processor. Since the introduction of software to save, edit and print text the basic requirements have remained the same. This means that new software packages have distinguished themselves by 'improved' user interfaces. These improvements involve special keycaps or keyboard maps and screen handling, eg text to be underlined appears underlined on the screen, with many users now demanding 'WYSIWYG', a new 'buzzword' meaning 'What You See Is What You Get'.

## *Financial packages — accounting and spreadsheets*
These packages fall into two distinct areas, that of accounting, eg the keeping of ledgers, and that of forecasting, eg spreadsheets.

| Rank | Name | Supplier | Word processing | DBMS | Spreadsheet | Accounts | Integrated | Price |
|---|---|---|---|---|---|---|---|---|
| 1 | Pegasus | Pegasus Software | | | | 1 | | £350 |
| 2 | Lotus 1-2-3 | Lotus Development | | | 1 | | | £430 |
| 3 | dBASEIII | Ashton-Tate | | 1 | | | | £550 |
| 4 | WordStar 2000 | Compsoft | 1 | | | | | £440 |
| 5 | Multimate | Multisoft | 2 | | | | | £450 |
| 6 | Delta | MicroPro | | 2 | | | | £495 |
| 7 | Multisoft | Microsoft | | | | 2 | | £390 |
| 8 | WordStar | Ashton-Tate | 3 | | | | | £295 |
| 9 | Multiplan | Lotus Development | | | 2 | | | £190 |
| 10 | dBASEII | Ashton-Tate | | 3 | | | | £395 |
| 11 | Symphony | Lotus Development | | | | | 1 | £595 |
| 12 | DisplayWrite 2 | IBM | 4 | | | | | £275 |

*Source: PC Business World, October 1985*

*Figure 3: Leading computer software package sales in the UK*

Improvements in the area of accounting software have mainly come about through an increase in the complexity of the reporting that is possible. The inclusion of payroll and pension packages, as well as a large number of personnel routines, has made computerised accounts very attractive to financial management.

Spreadsheets, such as VisiCalc and SuperCalc, were an instant success in the personal computer market. The ability to produce many 'What if?' enquiries quickly and without laborious manual recalculation, has been invaluable to management. However the only qualitative addition that could be made to these packages has been slow in coming. The ability to produce pie charts and graphs seems a natural extension to such programs and although the software to provide these facilities was slow to arrive, many packages now have colour graphics capability.

By the end of 1984 software which could only be used to manipulate numbers in boxes had fallen out of favour and been replaced by more powerful software, the most widely used of which is Lotus 1-2-3. These packages maintain the traditional grid format of spreadsheets, but also include the facility to program several manipulations through the use of macros. The most significant advantage of the programmability is that the spreadsheet can be used as a database of about 2000 records. Recent improvements have more than quadrupled this providing that the operating system has the ability to handle RAM greater than 640 Kbytes.

## Databases

At first there were no database management packages available for personal computers. Each application had to be specially developed in a standard applications language, which was slow and expensive unless the user was an experienced programmer. There was a clear market for generalised database management systems enabling semi-expert users to create useful databases. The huge sales of packages such as dBASEII, dBASEIII, Delta and KnowledgeMan indicate the extent of such a market. The real advantage of a DBMS is the speed with which a particular application can be generated and maintained.

Two problems which inhibit the use of database management packages are as follows:

1  The need for some degree of computer literacy.
2  The slow responses in comparison to application software.

Developments in graphics and user interface design (see under 'Key current issues and future developments') will alleviate the first of these problems and increases in hardware specification will eradicate the latter.

## Integrated packages

The term integrated package has been used to describe any program which will accomplish more than any single application, eg Symphony, currently the top selling integrated package. An early example of the integrated package was Silicon Office which provides a combined word processor and database management system. In order to have a 'true integrated package' the user must be given, in one package, a user-friendly interface to the operating system, a 'WYSIWYG' word processor, a spreadsheet, a database management system and perhaps as an option, an accounting system. Though all these facilities can be easily acquired as separate packages the true integrated package will allow information to be transferred between 'modules' easily. Another approach to providing this information exchange has been provided by IBM in the form of its TopView package which will allow the user to run a number of packages concurrently and exchange information between applications.

## Operating systems

When the IBM PC was first introduced in this country the recommended operating system was a version of Microsoft's disk operating system called PC-DOS. This operating system provided several useful 'external commands' (separate programs) which gave it a substantial edge over the then predominant Control Program/Microcomputer (CP/M).

As hardware improved and disk storage capacity increased, the need to organise data storage became more urgent. Hard disk storage of over 10 Mbytes became readily available. To cope with this new demand Microsoft brought out a new version of MS-DOS called MS-DOS 2. IBM PCs are able to run versions of MS-DOS 2 called PC-DOS 2. The main difference between this operating system and others available at the time of MS-DOS 2's launch was the ability to divide the data stored on a hard disk using directories rather than by partitioning into different logical devices. This gives greater flexibility of data file size and enables a disk to be effectively reconfigured without removing files.

The next generation of operating systems which provide for multi-user access has been developed because of rapid increases in the power of hardware. At this point however there is a divergence between the mainstream development of MS-DOS 1,2,3 and the entrance of UNIX-based operating systems such as UNIX System V and XENIX into the market.

Advertising and 'informed users' are behind the UNIX-based systems. Nevertheless their sales have not matched expectations and no clear leader between MS-DOS and UNIX has yet emerged in the personal computer marketplace.

## The personal computer as a management aid

### Conceptual views

With regard to computers, managers are generally held to be unwilling horses dragged to drink water they do not particularly enjoy — especially after tasting it! Many views as to the reasons for management resistance to using computers have been expressed including the following:
- General fear of the unknown
- Fear of looking foolish by inadequate performance especially in the learning stages
- Inability to spell or write properly
- Loss of status by being seen to carry out 'secretarial' duties
- Insufficient time to learn
- Complexity of use
- Inappropriateness of the microcomputer to 'real' managerial work.

Although the first four of these reasons are not ones that should be readily accepted as they can be overcome, others are valid for many managers to a certain extent. The time needed to learn, and stay proficient in, the use of personal computers will be reduced as they become increasingly user friendly. The Macintosh was a major step in the direction of increased user friendliness and there is a rapidly increasing awareness of the importance of man/machine interface design. A basic problem still arises from the nature of managerial work which is not, in general, an idealised calm work scene where planning leads to organisation which gives rise to the type of leadership which results in total control. If it were, one could readily appreciate the need for the manager to spend days solidly working at plans with the support of his trusty personal computer followed, after a period of 'organisation' and 'leading', by further use of the personal computer to control the results. Unfortunately, however, the reality of managerial life according to a practical research school of management is more likely to be characterised by:
- Decision-making and planning in open-ended situations of a highly varied nature
- Handling of exceptions, interruptions and emergencies in fragmented units of time *(HEM2)*.

If these circumstances held for all managers all the time, the degree of management use of even user-friendly personal computers would be very low. However, an increasing number of managers are becoming 'computer literate' so that they are using computers for non-managerial tasks, such as writing memos and letters, as well as managerial tasks using tools such as spreadsheets for planning.

As the present computer-literate student generation moves into the business world and up the management ladder it is safe to expect substantial management use of computers due also to increasing ease of use, as discussed further below (see 'Key current issues and future developments'). It is already no longer an oddity to see a terminal on a manager's desk that is actually used for upwards of an hour a day.

Figure 4 provides an overview in diagrammatic form of the positive and negative forces acting on the management use of computers.

### Management user views

As part of the preparation of this paper we interviewed a selected sample of managers who, despite the negative forces described above, actually use micros in their day to day work. These managers were with eight firms with a large number of personal computers and either had their own on their desks or made

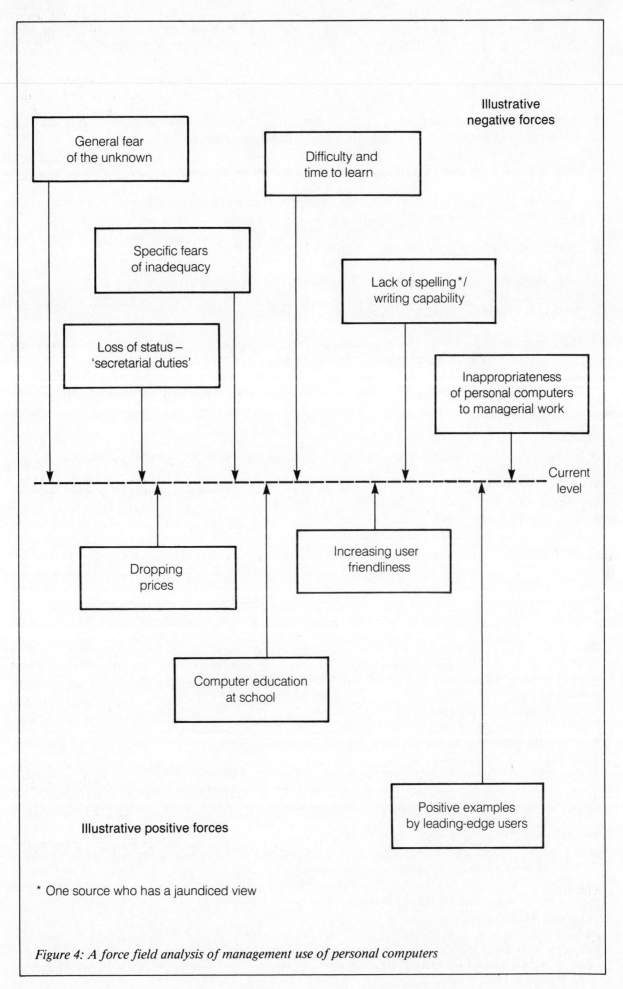

extensive personal use of one. They were asked to discuss their current usage of the machines, what opinions they held of hardware and software and their suggestions for future developments by IBM.

## Current usage and users

The survey showed substantial variety in personal computer usage patterns:

1 There was no consistent use made of them. In some of the firms surveyed all senior managers had their own at work, while in others there was no usage by senior managers.

2 Those managers with one had had, on average, over a year's experience with it.

3 On average 50 per cent of management made some personal use of them at work, and this use was as high as 15 hours of active computing in a week.

4 Approximately half of those who used them at work also used them at home.

The uses made of their personal computers by managers were as follows:

1 Spreadsheets were the primary application for all managers interviewed.

2 The next highest use was for report generation. This involves use of a database applications program (usually written by a DP professional) to produce reports from financial data in a database.

3 The third significant use was for communications with central computers (minis or mainframes) to obtain data.

## Opinions

In this section managers discussed their opinions of hardware and software, documentation and support.

There was a great divergence of opinion on hardware. Here is a selection of comments which illustrate the differing management views. First the positive:
- 'Good workman-like tool'
- 'Excellent design: I like the large screen'
- 'Very reliable'.

and the negative:
- 'Ugly and mediocre — the Ford Cortina of personal computers'
- 'Slow and expensive'
- 'Too large to keep on my desk'.

By far the greatest proportion of managers used Lotus 1-2-3, a minority used Symphony, dBASEII and Delta. No other packages were used to a significant degree. The opinions held of software were virtually all complimentary:
- 'Well designed.... Good use of keyboard' (Lotus)
- 'Lotus' macros make it easy to use'
- 'It gets the job done without too many frills' (Lotus)
- 'Very good documentation'.

Some user managers commented on the necessity of using a Lotus system disk when starting the system for the first time, although this is no longer necessary since the release of version II in October 1985.

The divergence of opinion shown on IBM PC hardware reflects the varying amount of experience with other machines. There is no doubt that an assessment of the IBM PC in terms of price and speed would not give complimentary results. It appears that buying decisions are made with only minimum operational requirements being set. The main criteria are the reputation of the supplier and the availability of services and software, as shown earlier in the German study.

## Future

Managers were asked to supply their view of what IBM's next development in the PC area should be and what their own plans for personal computing were. Again answers were coloured by the degree of experience with other systems. Half of those interviewed immediately mentioned networking. This indicates a great deal of interest in the idea of exchanging information directly between personal computers and working with other managers on a common database or spreadsheet. The recent announcement of IBM's own token passing ring network should stimulate a large demand from corporate PC users. Very few managers talked of widening the scope of the software they use or of buying a portable. Several mentioned the high price of the Portable PC and the fact that the COMPAQ portable was a better buy.

These interviews, although a small sample, support and give insight into the general conclusions developed elsewhere in this paper.

## Key current issues and future developments

A number of key current issues have been identified for discussion:
- The AT and its likely successor
- IBM's Local Area Network (LAN)
- Multi-user systems
- Natural languages
- Expert systems
- User friendliness and management use.

### The AT and its likely successor

Following an initial period during which demand outstripped supply, the AT has been slow to sell. According to dealer reports insufficient effort has been made by software developers to exploit the machine's expanded memory potential or multi-user features under Microsoft's XENIX. A Dataquest analyst termed the AT as follows: 'It's just a big fat PC'. The installed AT base as of autumn 1985 was only 175 000 versus some 4 000 000 PCs and XTs, according to an Intel source. Software developers are more likely to direct their efforts at the latter major installed base unless there are good prospects of strong 80286-based markets. Although it is rumoured IBM will launch another 80286-based machine in 1986 in order to encourage software development and sales, it is now questionable whether these 80286 machines will make a major impact on the market. The crucial issue is the size of the market window for the 80286 chip from Intel. Its successor, the 80386 introduced in October 1985, is much more powerful and is expected to be the processor on which IBM will build its next PC generation. The first such machine should be available in 1987; it will feature a new version of DOS and will be aimed at the multi-user, multitasking market.

### IBM's local area networks

The most important initiative of IBM in 1985 is likely to be its token passing ring network. This long awaited announcement means still further waiting for its European users since availability is not planned for Europe until autumn 1986. During this period, however, there will be ample time for users to prepare, including the cabling with which IBM itself is reported to have had difficulties. Highlights of the token network as announced at its launch are as follows:

1 The number of users can be up to 260, based on a star configuration with eight users per star, each star being connected to the ring by a multistation access unit.

2 The recommended cable length is initially set at only 60 metres, although with special signal enhancement equipment at the prototype stage in late 1985 this could be extended up to 600 metres.

3 There are two types of cable, both telephone-type copper twisted pair cable, which can support voice and data transmission simultaneously. Type 1, shielded, supports up to 260 users. Type 2, using unshielded voice-grade cable, supports up to 72 users but would not be as cheap for UK users who cannot 'loop' off telephone cables and would have to rewire, whereas US users could link into existing telephone wiring.

4 Data transmission will be 4 Kbit/sec.

Over 40 other companies were provided with the samples from Texas Instruments, manufacturers of the chipset to implement the token ring, including IBM's major competitors. This should ensure a large number of compatible, competing and complementary products leading to *the domination of the LAN market by IBM in the same way that its introduction of the IBM PC led to its domination of the personal computer business.*

## Multi-user systems

Multi-user systems are becoming more prominent in the market. IDC Europe, the market research company, estimates that packaged software for small system users (2-15 terminals) shows very strong growth at 30 per cent per annum. Many software companies are bringing out multi-user versions of their programs. A multi-user system consists of a central computer which shares its attention between several users with their own screens and keyboards. All users will be sharing the processor inside the central PC whether the workstation they are using contains its own processor or not. The AT was intended to be a multi-user system serving up to three users, but because of its poor performance in this respect other multi-user micro manufacturers are attacking this market aggressively even where the customer runs an IBM mainframe. For example, Sperry's personal computer IT is claimed to be able to serve up to nine users with superior performance capabilities.

The key software requirements are a suitable operating system and adapted versions of single-user applications software.

### Operating software
The IBM PC/AT becomes a multi-user computer by plugging PCs into serial ports in the back, and using a multi-user operating system such as XENIX (Microsoft's version of UNIX). The multi-user operating system's basic job is to share the central PC's time between the users.

### Applications software
IBM recently announced its first multi-user software offering in the form of IBM Teamwork, an accounts package written by Pegasus Software. It consists of five modules: purchase, sales and nominal ledgers, invoicing, order processing and stock control.

A key practical implication for management of the increase in power in multi-user systems is that a manager may be one of the users and thereby be able to access up to date management information, resulting from the work of the other users.

## Natural language processing

The ultimate in user friendliness is for users to be able to converse with the computer in everyday conversational language. This would require major advances in the following three areas:

1 Speech recognition.
2 Natural language processing.
3 Speech output.

Although advances are being made in all three areas, it is in the area of natural language processing of text that the biggest impact will be seen in the next few years. This will occur in special application fields rather than in general conversational English which, despite the excessive claims of some advertisers, is still many years away. This is due to the complexity and ambiguity of language and its dependence on situation and context, eg the difficulty in differentiating and understanding the following two sentences:
• 'Time flies like an arrow'
• 'Fruit flies like jam'.

The type of practical situation in which natural language processing is already applicable is fortunately now easy to identify and achieve where a natural language system is used as a front-end to a database in a specific situation where the total vocabulary required to express all reasonable requests for access and application is small. Fortunately, many existing conventional databases are of this kind. Therefore there are considerable market opportunities for new natural language products to exploit advances in natural language processing. An example of a product already on the market which achieves considerable power for its users is CLOUT from Microrim Inc. This allows users to access a variety of data files from standard packages such as Lotus 1-2-3 and dBASEII by converting them to a common format when needed and to request information contained in them by simple English commands, eg: 'List the unscheduled projects and show me the requestors. Sequence them by department and unit'.

CLOUT recognises some 300 words in its basic vocabulary, but the user is permitted to define synonyms and new expressions in terms of existing words, so that there is substantial flexibility.

The potential effectiveness of such focused applications of natural language processing is high. Further extensions are anticipated within the next few years as work currently at the research and development stage is incorporated in new products on the market. The level of research and development work in this area is illustrated by the attention paid to this topic in the Alvey and ESPRIT programmes, and the effort being supplied by the Americans and Japanese is reported to be even greater.

## Expert systems

Expert systems achieved their high profile in the early 1980s due largely to their success in the medical and oil/mineral exploration fields. Transfer of the potential to the business field and management in particular is occurring, although not at the fast rate that had been projected by suppliers. Examples of promising applications in business and management are:
- Finance, eg credit assessment
- Maintenance/diagnostic, eg car engines
- Design, eg aircraft wings.

Expert systems products offered on the IBM PC and AT in 1985 included:
- XI from Expertech of Slough
- TESS from Helix Expert Systems of London
- PARYS from BIT of Bradford.

Complex expert systems require significantly greater processing power and memory than even the IBM AT can offer. However basic expert system shells, small expert systems and special expert system programming languages such as PROLOG and LISP are becoming available on the IBM PC.

A key problem in expert systems development is the knowledge acquisition, ie obtaining expertise from the human specialist and then storing it in the appropriate form in computers. Application of these methods on personal computers offers end users the possibility of developing their own 'expert systems' incorporating the business rules used in their organisation, eg financial control systems. The expert system equivalent of Lotus 1-2-3 is an attractive concept. However it does not yet exist and potential purchasers should be very cautious in believing all supplier's claims. There is now considerable sales' pressure being applied in this field and a cautious approach is likely to be best with only limited initial investment.

## User friendliness and managers — the manager/machine interface

Ideally, the personal computer should be as easy to use as a video recorder; even the harassed executive should be able to operate one successfully.

The issue of user friendliness is important if the personal computer is to be fully effective, particularly regarding management as discussed earlier. A number of trends are occurring which should lead to increasingly user-friendly personal computers, eg:
- Easier to learn software
- Easier to use software
- Easier peripheral devices, eg mouse
- Natural language processing
- Improved graphics
- Better colour facilities.

Although it is difficult to forecast breakthroughs, likely candidates include:
- Amstrad
- Sinclair
- The Japanese.

IBM is unlikely to make an innovative breakthrough but will continue incremental improvement with jumps spurred by competitive advances. A recent extensive research report from Whartons *(HEM3)* concluded that there are significant untapped opportunities for expansion of personal computer use and corresponding increase in the market in the executive sector. This result supports the conclusions developed above.

## Conclusions

IBM domination of the personal computer field is now unlikely to change; indeed it will probably be reinforced by the impact of the IBM token passing network system and greater emphasis by IBM on software sales.

New product launches are likely if IBM tries to exploit the potential of Intel 80286-based machines fully before the advent of more powerful machines based on the Intel 80386.

The use of personal computers by managers is certain to increase. There are many different problems in raising managerial use — for example both to overcome resistance and to increase user friendliness. But basic trends, such as greater computer education in schools, lower prices, new technical approaches including, above all, improved manager/machine interface design and increasingly user-friendly applications software together will inevitably lead to substantially greater use by managers.

# 7: Medium-systems strategy

**A Hughes**

Logica Svenska AB
Stockholm
Sweden

**This paper reviews the products being
marketed by IBM in the medium-systems
range. Defining the medium-systems range
is difficult but in this paper it includes the
lower-end 4300 and the General Purpose
Systems (GPS) as defined by IBM. A brief
history of the products and their evolution is given, with a history of IBM's marketing structure being examined first.
The products that will be reviewed in this
paper (although not in this order) are:
4300 (lower end), System/38, System/36,
the 8100, Series/1, the 5520 and the PC.**

*A Hughes*
Aled Hughes specialises in IBM and its products. He has lectured worldwide on IBM and its strategies and was the architect of a number of major SNA networks in Europe and Australasia. He joined Logica in 1981, having spent nearly 20 years in the computer industry, working with a major bank and one of the large building societies. He has conducted several strategy studies for a variety of clients.

## History of marketing structure

The most significant event in the history of IBM was the introduction of the System/360 in 1964, and IBM enjoyed immense growth during the next few years, primarily by selling mainframes. However, there were a few people at IBM, including senior executives, who were predicting that such philosophies as distributed processing might affect the company's fortunes in the future. To ensure that all sectors of the market were covered, IBM created the Data Processing Division (DPD) and General Systems Division (GSD) in 1969. DPD was still the 'heart' of IBM with key IBM people staying to design, build and sell mainframes, but GSD was given a clear mandate to look after the 'small' computer market and keep companies like DEC at bay.

At about the time that the Carter administration came into power in the US in the 1970s, IBM became aware that it could lose the anti-trust cases. If it lost the anti-trust cases it would almost certainly have been split up, so to provide itself with the potential to overcome this possibility, IBM restructured itself in 1974 into two groups: DPD, which remained much as before, and General Business Group (GBG), which contained two divisions (GSD — also remaining much as before — and Office Products Division (OPD)). IBM felt that if it might be split up, it would at least be according to its own rules. DPD sold mainframes and later the 8100 and the Data Entry System — 5280; GSD sold the smaller machines — initially System/3 but later the System/38 and System/34 — while OPD sold typewriters etc. DPD and GBG had their own development laboratories, plants, administration and salesmen and were frequently to be seen competing against each other for business.

At the end of 1981, when the anti-trust cases were dropped and Reagan was in power, IBM again restructured itself to enable its salesmen to sell all of its range of products to its customers. In the US, there was the National Accounts Division (NAD) for large customers and National Marketing Division (NMD) for smaller customers. In the UK there are Information Systems Account Marketing (ISAM) and Information Systems Marketing (ISM) accounts, the former for the large accounts and the latter for the others. Several European countries have a similar marketing structure and there is no longer the situation where one salesman from DPD competes with a salesman from GSD.

This structure has served IBM well since 1981, but it is an organisation which never stands still: always active and not reactive in its planning activities. (A major philosophy in IBM is planning and much time is devoted to this task by all concerned.) Accordingly, marketing in the US has been restructured with NAD and NMD being merged (October 1985). In their place have appeared two geographical divisions to serve the whole country.

However, a possibly more important move is the expansion in the US of IBM's National Distribution Division (NDD). The NDD's role is to manage its relationship with third parties such as Value-Added Resellers and marketing assistance companies. This restructuring has been organised to take advantage of the fact that hardware is becoming less important than software, and also as part of IBM's drive to contain marketing costs.

This policy is being reflected in Europe with the creation of Information Systems Distribution Marketing Division (ISDMD) in the UK — a mirror of the US NDD. ISDMD is headed by Stafford Taylor who was responsible for the very successful launch of the PC in the UK. (It is worth noting that Taylor spent a period with IBM Europe in Paris along with Tony Cleaver, the new Chairman and Chief Executive of the UK from 1 January 1986.)

There are also rumours that IBM is restructuring the UK and European marketing operation and may merge ISAM and ISM. At the time of writing (October 1985) these are just rumours, but no doubt by the time of publication the new structure (if any) will be in place. A restructuring (if at all) is likely to coincide with Tony Cleaver formally taking over.

## Products

### System 3

The first product from the GSD of 1969 was the System/3 which included major design and concepts of the System/360. It was a small, scaled-down version of the System/360, but designed in such a way as to be incompatible with it. This had advantages and disadvantages. One good aspect was that it avoided affecting System/360 sales but, on the other hand, it also needed highly trained personnel and was, therefore, much less attractive than the DEC minicomputer.

The System/3 was 'upgraded' in 1975 and called the System/32. In 1977, IBM used some of the design concepts from Future Systems (FS) and modified the System/32 to produce the System/34. In effect, it was still a System/32 but with improvements. It proved to be the most popular DP machine in the world with sales in excess of 110 000 (approximately 28 000 in Europe with 2000 in the UK). Many of these machines were leased from IBM, and with the advent of the new System/36, and to a lesser extent the PC, many machines have been returning to IBM. As a result, IBM is offering 'cheap' solutions to some business requirements by selling a refurbished System/34 at prices sometimes as low as £5000. This practice is more common in North America than in Europe.

### System/36

The replacement for the System/34 was the System/36 (see Figure 1) which, despite rumours that it will not be around for more than a few years, is enjoying tremendous success. Orders and deliveries already exceed 40 000 worldwide. This is not hard to understand as it is a very good machine, extremely 'user-friendly' (for IBM), and is very much 'all things to all men' with its Office Systems Architecture (OSA) support and other packages. When first announced, it did suffer from performance problems, but these were quickly solved by doubling the memory and the disk capacity. It does lack a database management function, but this may be addressed in future releases.

Since its introduction, it has grown in memory size to today's 1.75 Mbytes (see Figure 1). Two other members have joined the family: the System/36 Compact was announced in 1984 and was actively marketed to cluster PCs; the more recent Desktop/36 allows a low number (three or four users) to have their own computing power and/or have access to the corporate mainframe. The System/36's communications capabilities also make it a popular machine, and in this respect it can take over some functions from the Series/1. In some countries it is already being used instead of a 37X5 as a front-end processor for an X.25 network. The System/36's office capabilities and functions are much better than those of the 8100 (see below) and as such, it is likely to take its place.

The IBM direction with OSA firmly establishes the System/36 as a major strategic product for a few years to come. It is believed that IBM trebled its marketing force and effort in the UK for this product in 1985. It is also likely that more dealers will be encouraged to sell the product.

### System/23

The first machine to be developed from the 'new' GSD was the 5100, which evolved in 1978 to the 5110, then the 5120 which was probably the undisclosed father of the System/23, announced in October 1981. It was called the Datamaster in the US and was IBM's first product to use an Intel microprocessor chip — the 8-bit 8085. It is interesting to note that the System/23 was the only product

| | | Desktop 36 | S/36 Compact | S/36 |
|---|---|---|---|---|
| Announced | | 6/85 | 4/84 | 5/83 |
| Performance (million instr/sec) | | 0.08 | 0.12 | 0.12 |
| Main memory capacity range (Mbytes) | Min | 0.128 | 0.128 | 0.128 |
| | Max | 0.512 | 1.0 | 1.75 |
| Disk storage capacity range (Mbytes) | | 20-80 | 30-120 | 30-800 |
| Maximum number of terminals | | 4 | 86 | 100 |

*Figure 1: IBM System/36*

introduced after 1974 which did not support SNA. There are less than 100 users in the UK. Unfortunately, it offered no migration path, and the success of the IBM PC effectively killed it, the product being formally withdrawn from marketing in May 1985.

## The 8100

In 1978, IBM announced (and made respectable) the concept of distributed data processing (DDP) by introducing the 8100, which has had a very chequered history. In the mid-1970s, IBM introduced the 3790 as an early version of a shared logic workstation. This machine was a disaster for IBM, probably because it was launched before the software was really ready. However, as always, IBM met this 'challenge' and produced a new product with a dual role — the 8100 (see Figure 2).

The 8100 has always had two operating systems, DPCX for text processing (also allowing the operating system from the 3790 to be lifted into the 8100, thus providing immediate 'relief' for 3790 users) and DPPX for the more traditional DDP users. Unfortunately, the two operating systems were (and still are) totally incompatible and cannot reside together.

The machine was designed to rely heavily on the mainframe for application generation etc and can really only be considered as a satellite processor and not a distributed processor. The 8100 was also used to provide a remote concentrating capability together with network management. The software product Host Command Facility (HCF) allows a host operator to be logically present at the 8100 location and thus run fault diagnosis.

Unfortunately, it has never been considered to be a friendly machine, and an IBM executive is reported, in an unguarded moment, to have described it as having the 'user-friendliness of a cornered rat'. Undoubtedly, it is a 'cumbersome' product, but IBM always stress its network management and central control capabilities, which is IBM's way of controlling the DP strategy of a company.

The amount of operational and program development control that can be obtained centrally for the 8100 is extremely impressive. In the mid-1970s, IBM was worried that if end users were allowed to carry out their

|  |  | 8130 | 8140B | 8140C | 8150A | 8150B |
|---|---|---|---|---|---|---|
| Announced |  | 10/78 | 10/78 | 6/81 | 3/84 | 10/83 |
| Performance (million instr/sec) |  | 0.20 | 0.36 | 0.58 | 0.9 | 1.5 |
| Main memory capacity range (Mbytes) | Min | 0.768 | 0.768 | 1.0 | 1.0 | 1.0 |
|  | Max | 1.0 | 2.0 | 2.0 | 3.0 | 8.0 |
| Disk storage capacity range (Mbytes) |  | 58-64 | 58-516 | 123-516 | 64-1036 | 64-1036 |

*Figure 2: IBM 8100 range*

own DP, they might go to another manufacturer, so the 8100 was designed with this in mind.

Many people have predicted the demise of the 8100, but with over 12 000 machines worldwide, IBM has again shown its ability to make things work. The latest machine — the 8150 range — is new in almost everything and, together with the latest versions of software, it is reported to be making existing users very happy. IBM Germany has had a recent order for 4000 machines from the Bundespost. The 8100 position with System/36 is difficult to predict, but it is felt that the two of them will be retained for some time. One area where the System/36 is weak is in its lack of database management facility while the 8100 has the (host dominated) Database and Transaction Management System (DTMS).

This leads to another IBM philosophy — competition. IBM does not really see any external competition and likes to generate competition from within. Frank Cary, when Chairman and Chief Executive Officer of IBM, once remarked that the System/38 was 'one of the best products we've ever had' but he added that 'the 8100 is our networking product'. This 'competition' could well be the case with 8100 and System/36 and augurs well for the future of both.

## System/38

System/38 (see Figure 3) has always been the unknown quantity of IBM. It was a by-product of Future Systems (FS), a project which was abandoned in the early 1970s mainly because IBM had to protect its existing System/360 user base and considered that FS meant too much of an upheaval even by IBM's standards.

Since its arrival in the marketplace in the late 1970s, the machine has been developed from what one programmer described as a 'nightmare' to a 'joy'. The reason for the programmer's concern was that the traditional methods of programming are not applied with the System/38. The program does not need to concern itself with the location of data; the data is literally left to the machine. For this reason programmers' early reaction to the machine was not enthusiastic — response times were erratic, and there was no way of getting at the data to see if it was held in the main storage or auxiliary storage. However, it is important to note that the first machines were 0.5 Mbyte, while the latest machine — the

|  |  | S/38-4 | S/38-6 | S/38-8 | S/38-18 | S/38-20 | S/38-40 |
|---|---|---|---|---|---|---|---|
| Announced |  | 6/81 | 1/84 | 4/83 | 6/85 | 9/84 | 9/84 |
| Performance (million instr/sec) |  | 0.15 | 0.35 | 0.55 | 0.61 | 0.72 | 0.94 |
| Main memory range (Mbytes) | Min | 2.0 | 2.0 | 2.0 | 2.0 | 4.0 | 8.0 |
|  | Max | 2.0 | 6.0 | 8.0 | 8.0 | 8.0 | 16.0 |
| Disk capacity range (Mbytes) |  | 64-3407 | 64-3407 | 64-6225 | 64-6225 | 64-6225 | 64-6225 |
| Maximum number of terminals |  | 128 | 128 | 128 | 256 | 256 | 256 |

*Figure 3: IBM System/38 range*

Model 40 (introduced September 1984) — is 16 Mbytes and competes in power terms with the top 4361/bottom 4381. However, based on relative transaction throughput, some independent tests have shown the Model 40 to compete with the 4381 MG2.

IBM has doubled the memory every year since 1979 and there is no theoretical reason why the machine cannot grow to 1000 Mbytes. This would make it very attractive as a database machine.

A major benefit of System/38 is that an upgrade does not constitute a new operating system, but merely the installation of a new version of IBM's microcode to which the user has no access. In other words, the user's original programs and data do not have to change. If only mainframes were the same! This reduces (and probably eliminates) the need for traditional systems' programmers and means that the programmer needs little knowledge of the operating system. The latest machines can support up to 256 users, 12 remote lines and 64 X.25 circuits. This latter facility certainly makes it an attractive alternative to a System/370 approach.

When the machine was first introduced it was marketed by GSD, but today it is marketed by all the salesmen, and very actively too. IBM is making significant sales in existing mainframe accounts. Users report a marked reduction in systems and applications programmer effort, and operational support. The recent addition of HCF facilities similar to the 8100s has helped in this respect.

IBM is also selling the machine well to the non-DP environment (eg personnel and payroll) where the System/38 offers extremely good support. There are about 25 000 machines worldwide and sales are predicted to double those for the 4300 in the next few months.

## Series/1

Series/1 has been available for many years, and while extremely popular in the US (20 000 plus), it has never really made an impact on the European market. There have been major marketing drives by IBM over the last few years, but all to no real avail. The area where it succeeds most is its communications ability. It is very powerful as a bridge for non-SNA products to link into SNA. Its range of facilities and packages today is impressive and includes videotex support. There are also regular 'new' hardware products, but despite all this it is felt that it is really a missed opportunity in Europe.

The 7171 ASCII Attachment Control Unit, the 7426 Protocol Convertor, the 3710 Concentrator, and the more recent 3708 Network Conversion Unit can, to a certain extent, take over much of the protocol conversion role of the Series/1. In theory, the System/36 could take over its role, although this is unlikely. Together with the recent Series/1 'on a card' PC, all this may signal the death of the Series/1. It is, however, the backbone of IBM's Audio Distribution System (ADS) — a voice messaging system — although ADS is likely to be replaced soon. This has already happened in the US where the Rolm system has taken its place.

## The 5520

Another GSD product was the 5520 administration system which was loosely based around a System/34. In its time it was a good office automation product but, despite recent announcements, its days must be numbered, particularly as the System/36 is so much better, although secretarial speed keyboard entry is slower on the System/36.

## System/88

In 1985, IBM announced an OEM agreement with Stratus to market its fault-tolerant product as System/88. The System/88 incorporates processors and other components in identical pairs, so that if any component fails, its twin part can instantly and automatically take over the function. With System/88, a failing component causes the computer to diagnose the problem and automatically dials up the System/88 support centre (for the UK this is London). If appropriate, a replacement part is despatched to the customer who can replace the failed part himself.

To what extent IBM will 'grow' this product is debatable. Certainly, there is an increasing demand for fault tolerance, but as other systems hardware becomes extremely reliable, it is difficult to predict the extent of the System/88's growth. It is likely that all IBM's products will one day gain fault-tolerance status anyway. The 8150B already has dyadic processors which, it could be argued, give it some limited degree of fault tolerance.

From a marketing point of view, the System/88 was intended to stem the growth of Tandem. The announcement of the agreement with Stratus certainly affected Tandem and its share price has suffered. It is worth noting that IBM has not announced the System/88 in all European countries.

## IBM PC

IBM was a late starter in the PC marketplace. The problem facing the company was that of predicting what influence the personal computer would have on mainframe sales (around 30 per cent of revenue in 1984 was hardware alone). It was decided that if users wanted personal computers then IBM would enter the market and attempt to dominate it. The development team at IBM was headed by Philip 'Don' Estridge (tragically killed in 1985), and the time between product inception and product launch was only 13 months.

By late 1985, various sources estimated IBM's penetration of the marketplace to be between 40-45 per cent, with an anticipation of 65 per cent by the end of 1986. In 1984, various estimates showed that 10-20 per cent of IBM's business was generated by the PC market.

Today's PC products are diversified and command no less than eight pages in IBM's Systems Handbook Version 2 (compared to two pages a few years ago). The products available are as follows:
- 3270-PC
- 3270-PC/G or /GX
- PC
- Portable PC
- PC/XT
- PC/XT 370
- PC/AT
- PC/AT 370.

(The System/36 PC and Series/1 PC have been excluded.)

The most recent development is the PC/AT which is much faster than the original product. A shortage of stock has allowed room for IBM's competitors, but IBM is again in a strong position. It is rumoured that a PC is coming off the production line at Greenock every six seconds! (IBM is extremely proud of its export figures in this respect.)

The PC can be attached to most IBM products, making it extremely attractive for local and remote usage. It is worth noting that although PCs were initially installed for local processing, more are being linked to mainframes all the time. This in turn means more demand for mainframes, so IBM sales continue.

IBM has consistently argued against multi-user micros, despite the PC/AT which supports up to three users. IBM believes that personal computers should share information and resources in networks, otherwise (so they argue) by definition they are not 'personal' computers. IBM also argues that because of the low cost of the PC, it is better to give each user one of their own. This last argument could be hard for a small company, but IBM always uses the cost of a person, or the loss of production by sharing out etc, as selling points.

## The 4300

Last, and by no means least (in fact potentially the biggest!), is the 4300. The 4300 is the starting point for what is generically called the System/370 line. The 4300 was announced in 1979 and was aimed at the user requiring a small 303X. It used better, smaller technology than the 303X but shared the same System/360 architecture thus making it compatible. A major advantage for the user was that it did not require water cooling, and occupied much less floor space.

As stated earlier, the bottom-end 4300s — the 4361 and possibly the 4381 MG1, are considered as good medium systems (see Figures 4-6).

The 4361 is available in three model numbers, 3, 4 and 5, while the three larger 4381s are available as numbers 1, 2 and 3. The 4361s Model Groups (MGs) 3 and 4 only support DOS/VSE and VM, while the MG5 supports MVS. The 4381 MGs 1 and 2 support DOS/VSE, VM, MVS and MVS/XA while the 4381 MG3 supports VM, MVS and MVS/XA.

They certainly allow IBM to bring the user into the mainframe environment and can enable the user to 'grow' several times. However, the major drawback is support costs, particularly in terms of systems programmers. While SSX/VSE as an entry level operating system could be used, it is not particularly user friendly if any significant growth is required, and the user is faced with a migration to DOS/VSE or MVS or even MVS/XA at a future date.

An advantage of the 4300 is its support for the VM operating system. VM has been around since the early 1970s, and is well liked by users and IBM alike. Not unnaturally, IBM would like to 'standardise' on one operating system, and for several years VM has been a contender. A user of VM is capable of upgrading from a 4300 to a 3080 relatively simply (ignoring for a moment the cost of providing water cooling!), but the user is still forced to pay for another operating system as a 'guest' of VM — typically DOS/VSE.

However, VM does have some other good, likeable products such as Conversational Monitor System (CMS) — considered by many to be far superior to MVS's Time Sharing Option (TSO). It is IBM's own internally preferred program development tool. Another product is Professional Office System (PROFS) which is used by many IBM employees so is unlikely to be replaced by DISOSS in the near future.

## UNIX

A major diversion for IBM came in February 1985 when the company finally announced its move into the UNIX world. The IBM Interactive Executive for System/370 (IX/370) is an implementation of UNIX under VM. While not totally compatible with AT&T's latest offering, it allows IBM to attract users who are keen to have this facility on IBM machines. (There has also been a version of UNIX for

|                                   |     | 4321  | 4331/1 | 4331/11 | 4331/2 |
|-----------------------------------|-----|-------|--------|---------|--------|
| Announced                         |     | 11/81 | 2/79   | 11/81   | 5/80   |
| Relative Internal Performance (RIP) |   | 0.20  | 0.20   | 0.30    | 0.40   |
| Main memory capacity              | Min | 1.0   | 0.5    | 1.0     | 2.0    |
| (Mbyte)                           | Max | 1.0   | 1.0    | 4.0     | 8.0    |

*Figure 4: IBM 4321/4331 range*

|                                   |     | 4341/9 | 4341/10 | 4341/1 | 4341/11 | 4341/2 | 4341/12 |
|-----------------------------------|-----|--------|---------|--------|---------|--------|---------|
| Announced                         |     | 10/82  | 11/81   | 2/79   | 11/81   | 9/80   | 10/82   |
| Relative Internal Performance (RIP) | | 0.4    | 0.7     | 0.8    | 1.03    | 1.42   | 1.59    |
| Main memory                       | Min | 1.0    | 2.0     | 2.0    | 4.0     | 2.0    | 2.0     |
| capacity (Mbyte)                  | Max | 4.0    | 4.0     | 4.0    | 8.0     | 16.0   | 16.0    |

*Figure 5: IBM 4341 range*

| | | 4361/3 | 4361/4 | 4361/5 | 4381/1 | 4381/2 | 4381/3 |
|---|---|---|---|---|---|---|---|
| Announced | | 9/84 | 9/83 | 9/83 | 9/83 | 9/83 | 10/84 |
| Relative Internal Performance (RIP) | | 0.5 | 1.0 | 1.5 | 2.2 | 2.8 | 5.1 |
| Main memory capacity (Mbyte) | Min | 2.0 | 2.0 | 2.0 | 4.0 | 4.0 | 8.0 |
| | Max | 4.0 | 12.0 | 12.0 | 16.0 | 32.0 | 32.0 |

*Figure 6: IBM 4361/4381 range*

the PC for some time, although based on UNIX Version III, but there is no UNIX version on any other IBM offering at this time.)

Conversion from DOS/VSE or its latest version, VSE/SP to MVS or even MVS/XA is not a small step. A recent survey by Xephon showed that several users had reported costs in excess of £1 000 000. Many converted users will naturally refuse to even consider how much they have spent for fear of upsetting the Finance Director!

Developments in Intelligent Knowledge-Based Systems (IKBSs) over the next few years are likely to reduce support costs, but in the meantime the System/370 user is faced with the task of obtaining key staff.

## Key considerations

### Compatibility

Of the key products — System/38, System/36, 8100, Series/1 and 4300, only System/38 and System/36 have a limited degree of compatibility. Migration aids are available to change from System/36 to System 38, and to change from System/34 to 4300 which means that System/36 to 4300 migration aids may be likely in the future (although this may not be the case for commercial reasons).

The 8100 is not compatible with anything — not even itself with DPPX and DPCX.

### Growth path

System/36, when announced, had 0.5 Mbyte of memory and this has already been increased in two stages to 1.75 Mbytes. There are a few 'empty' slots in the machine which indicate that more facilities will be announced in the future, which will undoubtedly give users a growth path. There is already a growth path by going to System/38, but this involves much work, even if using migration aids. As mentioned above, there is potential for some migration aids into 4300 with all its growth aspects and operating systems. There is, in theory, no reason why the System/36 and its operating system System Support Program (SSP) could not be run under System/38 with appropriate microcode (see below for further discussion on this aspect).

The System/38 has consistently grown over the last few years and rumours are rife that IBM is already developing a 15 million instr/sec machine. In theory, and with much new software, there is no reason why the machine cannot grow into a 1000 Mbyte main storage machine, which would be very attractive to customers such as banks with large on-line databases requiring fast response times.

Much in line with the philosophy of System/88, the System/38 may well assume the role of a fault-tolerant system. It is likely that a multiprocessor version of the System/38 will herald this. The System/38 users are known to be concerned about lack of support in the event of a failure.

There is no reason to believe that with its latest announcements for OSA support that the System/38 will not be around for a long time to come.

For 'serious' PC users, the System/36 offers some considerable growth.

Series/1 has little growth path except within itself, as is the case for the 5520. The 8100 has some growth capability, and the 8150B with its dyadic nature offers some fault tolerance. However, in the longer term, the user is faced with multiple machines. This is not a bad thing as it must be remembered that the 8100 was designed to be host dominated anyway. Using HCF will continue to allow the mainframe site to run the 8100.

## The future

Undoubtedly the 'prince' among the medium systems is System/36. Many have already been delivered and IBM is enjoying large orders (around 40 000 installed and on order already). OSA with Document Interchange Architecture and Document Content Architecture (DIA/DCA) is undoubtedly a key to IBM's marketing strategy for the future. All key products either already have or have announced support for DIA/DCA.

The other strategic products are System/38, and the 4300, which may be replaced by another mainframe in the next year or so, but the software will probably be portable to the new machines. Because of System/36's communications capability, this may take over from Series/1 in due course. The System/38 has a limited growth path at its top end but, as stated above, it is likely to be continually expanded for many years to come. Its communications capability over recent months has greatly improved.

The future of the PC is undoubtedly guaranteed. It is likely to expand into specialised marketplaces such as industrial development and retail areas. The PC 'engine' itself will be used in more products.

IBM's own internal philosophy of one terminal per person by the end of 1985/early 1986 as part of its OSA strategy is bound to influence more customers to buy PCs as opposed to the fixed-function (dumb) 3270 terminals. The price difference is low enough to encourage the purchase of PCs with their improved capabilities. IBM's ability to show the benefits of OSA by demonstrating its own office environment will undoubtedly win many customers.

In marketing terms, IBM will continue to sell all the above products — offering the customer a 'choice'. This choice is often confusing to customers, and in the longer term IBM is likely to standardise. Having already declared the need to reduce manpower, IBM has been very careful to add that this must be achieved without a lessening of service.

A major 'drain' on resources is the cost of supporting all its operating systems. It is estimated that MVS/XA is some 16 million lines of code and was jointly written in six countries. However, 'abandoning' any one operating system must expose IBM to criticism from users.

Undoubtedly, it would like to promote MVS/XA as the way forward, but with over 15 000 VM users, and 50 000 DOS/VSE users worldwide, not to mention several thousand MVS users, deciding on a single operating system would not be easy.

Another consideration is 'what next after MVS/XA?'. If one considers that MVS/XA was aimed at the large user who needed more than 16 Mbytes and was approaching this figure in 1980, when will XA with its 2000 Mbytes run out? In hardware terms, user demand is likely to increase requirements by 50-60 per cent per annum in accordance with recent performance. If the same is applied to software (although obviously not strictly realistic), MVS/XA could exhaust its capacity by the late 1990s. Undoubtedly, there will be a need for something new by the year 2000, so IBM has to be prepared for this. In this respect 32-bit addressing may not be enough (MVS/XA uses 31-bit addressing).

A major source of additional workload is undoubtedly going to be the office systems environment. IBM conducted a survey some years ago which showed that 80 per cent of a company's data is textual with 20 per cent being numerical. The traditional DP systems have addressed the numerical aspects of a company so the scope for more use of computers (and hence revenue to IBM) is enormous. The first step towards this 'new business' is IBM's Office Systems Architecture (OSA) which is likely to dominate future marketing and growth.

In order to support all this growth and contain costs, IBM is almost certain to 'standardise' its products and allow a better and more concise growth path for the user.

The following is the author's favourite philosophy in this area. Firstly, although the architecture of the System/38 with its 48-bit addressing is unique to IBM products, the concept can be extended to support the whole range. In addition, it is predicted that a new system will be launched in the next few years to replace all the existing products (see Figure 7).

The new hardware will be based on existing technology, probably using the System/38's 48-bit (or perhaps even 64-bit) addressing, but will offer power from 0.5 million instr/sec to 100 million instr/sec, and possibly more. Use of fault-tolerant technology is likely to be an option. New applications will be developed using Fourth Generation and even Fifth Generation language products. The new operating system will be based on System/38's Control Program Facility (CPF) with improved user interfaces, and will be almost 'transparent'.

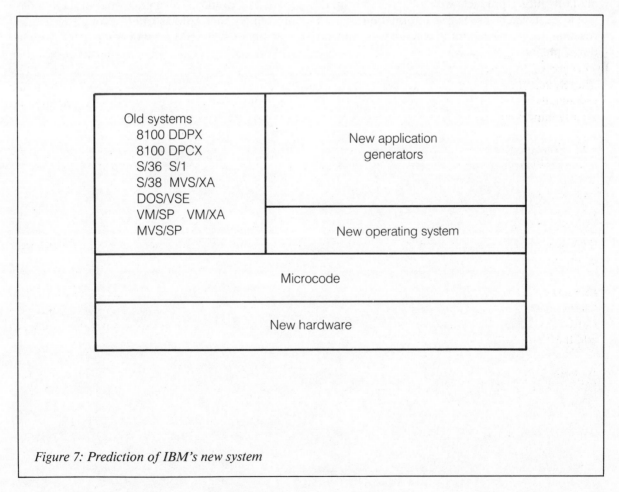

*Figure 7: Prediction of IBM's new system*

The microcode will be the major 'link' component of the whole system. It will allow existing operating systems to run in the new hardware as 'guests', plus supporting the new environment, and when the user wishes to use the new system totally, IBM will merely offer a different version of microcode.

Similarly, when more new hardware is installed, new microcode will also be installed. This concept will allow IBM to offer a 'single' product across the whole range as well as offering support for existing products.

The hardware will, at the bottom end, be small to attract the low-end user, with field upgrades; and modular to attract the largest user with a clear upgrade path. The cost of the hardware is likely to be comparatively low and attractive, certainly at the low end, but the software cost is likely to be high to compensate for loss of earnings from the other operating systems (although initially IBM will earn revenue from both sources).

No doubt after a few years, the support for the existing software products will be withdrawn by using existing practices in this area. Newer products with improved facilities can also take advantage of this structure. Another major consideration for IBM will be the need to keep its development staff happy. By employing this philosophy, no single operating system development team is going to be rejected.

A major influence indirectly supporting this philosophy is that most organisations are likely to need to rewrite their applications in the next few years, and 'packaged' solutions are already much in vogue. IBM will be able to sell the new concept on this basis in that the inevitable major rewrite will be easier using the new environment.

Apart from this philosophy, the real and perceived price of the hardware is likely to continue to come down, although software prices will continue to increase. This will have the added attraction of putting pressure on the competition.

Finally, the user should be aware that many people predict new products from IBM. Often this is based on developments at IBM which never see the light of day. IBM has in recent years been much more 'open' about its future products with key people from development laboratories divulging what in the old days would be termed 'privileged information'. It is far more likely that IBM is often testing user/market reaction to its ideas, for technology is moving so fast that even IBM cannot keep pace with all developments.

# 8: IBM long-term strategy

**J E van Kinsbergen**

Boole & Babbage Inc
Sunnyvale
CA
US

**The IBM Corporation has a strategy of building its future on the office automation link to its captive mainframe customer base. This link will be based on establishing the specific standards as IBM desires them and will encompass the personal computing world, the communications world and the mainframe world. What we are witnessing is the unveiling of a grand strategy that IBM will pursue for many years to come in its battle with AT&T and the Japanese. There is little doubt that IBM will continue to dominate the field due to its single-minded focus and its understanding and control of the marketplace. This paper explores this prospect in some detail.**

*J E van Kinsbergen*
Mr van Kinsbergen has been President and Chief Executive Officer of Boole & Babbage, Inc since May 1980. Prior to joining Boole & Babbage he was a vice president of Citicorp Management Services Inc and a consultant to Citibank management on the use of computers. Before serving with Citicorp, Mr van Kinsbergen was manager of product planning at Amdahl, and earlier manager of the corporate data processing centre of the Hughes Aircraft Company. He had also been a vice president of Programming Sciences Corporation. In the mid-1960s he was a member of the IBM design team that created OS/360; the operating system for the IBM 360, and the basis for all subsequent IBM operating systems. In 1967 he received the IBM Outstanding Contribution Award for his efforts in designing the input/output supervisor for OS/360. His subsequent career has been based on the evolution of the System/360 technology through all its families, with particular emphasis on how to improve its productivity in the user environment.

## Introduction

In 1964 the IBM Corporation launched its System/360 into an unsuspecting worldwide computer industry. At the time, IBM's annual sales totalled three billion US dollars and data processing was confined to the back offices of major corporations. The System/360, 'the big bang', established the standard that has allowed an industry to evolve. This paper reviews IBM's history, assesses its present position and outlines its plans for the future and how it intends to accomplish these plans.

An understanding of IBM is vital for anyone hoping to survive in the DP community. This is because IBM is both the largest customer for electronic components and the most powerful producer of computer systems. IBM's recent internal renaissance is manifesting itself in aggressive and sometimes open relationships with its environment. It has invested heavily in order to defeat the Japanese in low-cost manufacturing and has formed partnerships and alliances with virtually anyone and everyone in the DP community.

Having demonstrated its ability to enter and dominate new markets and to crush challengers at will, IBM has created for itself an aura of comparative invincibility. So furious has been IBM's onslaught and so wide its focus, that it is difficult to make sense of the forces behind the activity.

## History

In 1955, it cost $14.54 to execute a specific set of work that took 375 seconds of CPU time. By 1983, that cost was reduced to $.07 and it took one second of CPU time to execute the same work. It is clear that the history of computer technology has been one of dramatic growth and capability incorporating many technological advances.

In 1952, Sperry-Univac was the leading data processing company, IBM took second place, and nobody else was really in a position to compete. By 1972, it was IBM and the 'seven dwarfs': Sperry-Univac, CDC, RCA, NCR, General Electric, Honeywell and Burroughs. Today it is IBM and five of the seven dwarfs, with newcomers DEC, Hewlett-Packard, Wang and Apple completing the numbers for a 'top ten'. IBM has been by far the most dominant vendor since 1972 and, in fact, has forced major corporations such as RCA and General Electric out of the business.

In 1964, an S/360-65 processed at a rate of .68 million instr/sec. By the 1980s the 3090 processed at 24 million instr/sec. Both of these machines were considered large-scale systems in their time. Historically, both the price and performance of large systems has improved from $7000 per thousand operations per second to about $100 per thousand operations per second. Small computers have accomplished even more as their cost per thousand operations has dropped from over $10 000 to under $20.

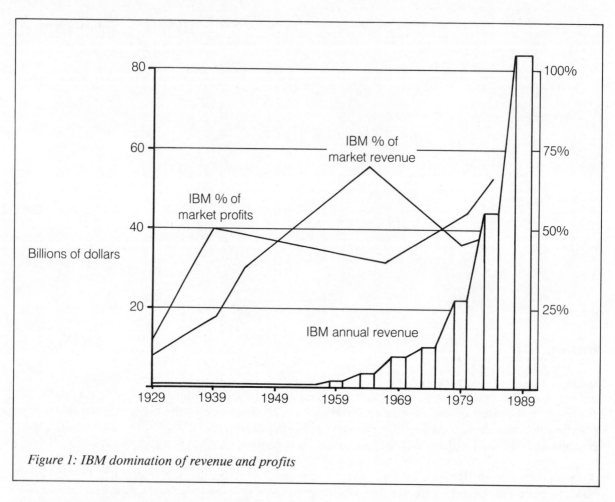

*Figure 1: IBM domination of revenue and profits*

In 1929, IBM was a $19 million corporation; by 1984, it was a $46 billion corporation. This growth represents a doubling in size by the IBM Corporation approximately every five years since 1929. In fact, this trend can be observed from as early as 1914.

In 1939, IBM was a $40 million company and had a 22 per cent share of the calculating marketplace and 49 per cent of the profits. By 1964, IBM had grown to become a $3.2 billion corporation and had 65 per cent of the market but only 37 per cent of market profits. Clearly IBM margins were eroding, and thus the S/360 became a necessity not only for the industry, but also for IBM internal cost controls. By 1984, IBM's overall share of the market was down to 47 per cent but its profits were 70 per cent of those of the industry. (See Figure 1.)

The base of installed large mainframes continues to grow, although not at the same rate as personal computers. As far as million instr/sec operations are concerned, the growth of the installed base is accelerating; that is, the number of systems being installed is growing at a respectable 10-15 per cent per year while the power represented by these systems is growing at a rate approaching 50-60 per cent per year. (See Figure 2.)

IBM is an extraordinarily successful corporation because of its experience, knowledge and aggressiveness. When ex-IBM President Vincent Learson was asked, 'How much of the business do you want?' he was supposed to have responded, 'All of it'. This characterises IBM's attitude. The company intends to sustain an annual growth of 15-18 per cent and the best margins in the business. It moves successfully from one management team to another without a ripple because of the corporate culture and environment it has created. It intends to leave no market niche unoccupied in its drive to continue to double in size every five years for the foreseeable future. It will enter into mutually beneficial relationships with independent software vendors and dramatically expand the software market by expanding and standardising the hardware base. IBM will recapture the DBMS market because it is too important for it not to. In the long term, communication revenue is a prime factor in IBM's ability to continue to grow in the 21st century.

Pressed by a new generation of competitors offering more economical solutions, IBM began to price its

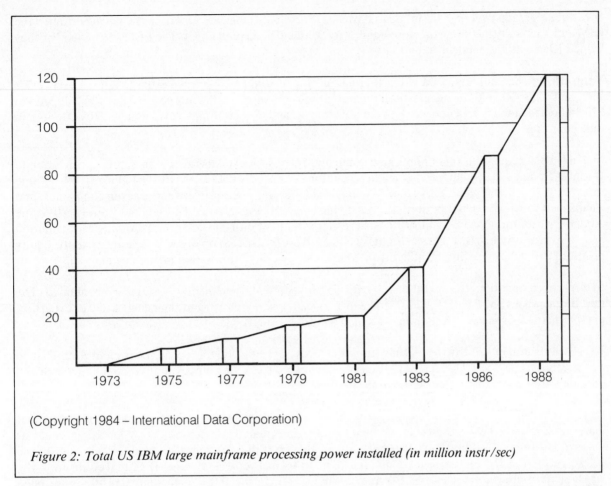

(Copyright 1984 – International Data Corporation)

*Figure 2: Total US IBM large mainframe processing power installed (in million instr/sec)*

products somewhat more aggressively in the late 1970s. As a result everyone was shocked when IBM released pricing details on its 4300 products in 1979. The largest impact was on sales of its large system 303X series product line. Many large-scale users knew that IBM would soon release its H series machines. As a result of the pricing strategy of the 4300, many customers chose to wait for announcements of the H series rather than buy what they perceived to be less price competitive, current system products. The impact on sales of the 'bread-and-butter' 303X product line was severe; customers who needed upgrades either leased or simply waited. At this point IBM seriously set out to convert business from a lease base to a sales base: in 1981 leases represented 37 per cent of revenues; by 1984 they had fallen to 14 per cent. This reflected a deliberate move by IBM to make the terms of sales more attractive than those of leasing.

In 1979, IBM began investing heavily to become a low-cost developer, manufacturer, and marketer of products in order to maintain the large profit margins that it enjoyed. With unparalleled resources and access to capital, IBM expended a total of $7.4 billion in capital investments. In 1979 and 1980, this swelled to $12.6 billion. IBM was modernising, automating, and adding to capacity. Whereas historically IBM had emphasised margins and market share, now it would emphasise volume. Just as the focus on leasing had governed the way IBM did business for decades, a new focus on volume business began to govern IBM's planning.

By converting from a more lease-based business to a sales OEM business, IBM stabilised its revenue stream. At the same time it made great efforts to increase revenue from software products. Since these products are rented on a monthly basis, IBM could begin to develop a stabilising revenue stream to offset the sales strategy for hardware products.

IBM will continue to grow by maintaining control over key large systems accounts. The top 250 accounts are controlled by ensuring that the DP manager is a friend of the corporation. IBM's strategy will be to tie everything, including office automation, into his environment and then control things through this DP manager. Smaller accounts will be dealt with by highly trained salesmen who overmatch the customer. In summary, IBM is aggressive; it is establishing the standards for the industry and no other architecture will crack the IBM world.

IBM wields great power and has influential friends. President Reagan is very friendly, having dropped the IBM anti-trust suit after three previous administrations had been pursuing it. The FBI is very friendly; they helped IBM with the Hitachi 'sting'.

With 725 000 shareholders, IBM is considering splitting several more times in order to approach AT&T's three million shareholders and establish greater grass-roots support. In Europe IBM has 100 000 people, $10 billion in annual revenue, and 25 manufacturing and research and development (R&D) sites in nine countries.

In 1964, IBM acquired a small publishing company. In 1974, it established a joint venture with Satellite Business Systems (SBS). In 1977, it made a deal for Lockheed's CADAM. In 1984 alone, IBM became involved in seven joint ventures in the US and abroad, became a minority owner of seven companies, and established third-party distribution. The latter includes 650 Value Added Resellers (VARS), 40 Value Added Distributors (VADS) and 10 industrial electronic distributors; in addition, IBM runs 20 distribution programs worldwide. IBM is accelerating its pace. By 1987, the company will have many more equity positions and will, in reality, be a family of companies covering information processing markets.

In terms of competition, the old threats — minicomputers, PCMs, and micros — are clearly contained. The new threats that IBM faces — AT&T and Japan — can now match IBM in financing, science, expertise, and production capacity. These threats are much more serious for IBM.

IBM will maintain control by setting the standards, specifically for SNA, Document Interchange Architecture (DIA) and Document Content Architecture (DCA) for office automation, all of which will provide a total workable office automation solution.

IBM has a habit of letting somebody else create a market, then entering it and dominating that marketplace. In the 1960s, Digital Equipment Corporation created minicomputers. When this market was mature, IBM entered it and took the larger share, though it did not dominate that marketplace. In the 1970s, Apple created the personal computer. When this market was mature, IBM moved in, took the larger share, but again, does not yet dominate the market. In the 1980s, data communications has been maturing. Can it be that IBM will take the larger share of this marketplace as well?

## Architecture strategy

The long-term growth of IBM will revolve around office automation and the architecture that IBM is introducing. IBM owns the large corporate marketplace through its success with mainframes over the last 20 years, and it is going to ride on that success by taking office automation and PCs into the large companies. A recent survey of buyers in these large corporations indicates that 72 per cent of the purchases of PCs in 1985 will be from IBM. Until now IBM has shipped 60-70 per cent of the Fortune 500 personal computers but has had little control. IBM's new architecture is going to create a more controlled situation for the corporation.

IBM has a new term, the 'office systems family' representing the results of a four-year effort to link disparate products by editable document transfer. In this family, the System/36 is the hands-down winner as IBM's departmental processor. DIA and DCA will become a *de facto* standard for document transfer.

What we are seeing is a glimpse of a grand strategy which has yet to come to fulfilment. Competitors will not be able to compete with the price of the PC and the System/36. They will have no access to the comparable range of applications, nor will they be able to provide the same homogeneous micro-to-mainframe interface. Finally, they will have difficulties supporting customers to the same degree as IBM. The result will be that, for the first time, IBM will have a single, coherent, document processing and messaging system linking the PC to other office systems, including the host in the back office. The strategy is designed to put IBM back in command and the MIS manager back in control. This will be the first time that IBM has offered a word processing product that expands the entire product line.

IBM's large-scale customers continue to need mainframe processor and storage enhancements even as some begin to question the utility of personal computers. IBM is gambling that increased capabilities achieved through enhancement working the communications features will restore confidence in the personal computer. IBM's argument is that once documents can be exchanged, data freely accessed and voice and data officially removed from both local and wide-area networks, the desktop will prove as valuable to its customers as the 3090 central processing unit or the 3380 disk drive. This leads to the introduction of the office systems family, which will provide the means of uniting all these functions.

The microprocessor has made it far cheaper and far more efficient to put calculating power on every worker's desk. The worker can choose his own programs and run them when he wishes, free of the limitations of a centralised mainframe system. The drawback is that personal computers have limited memory and do not have fast access to the central files stored on the mainframe. In addition, they do not communicate with each other. As John Akers of IBM puts it, 'Everything is connected to everything', however, revolutionary new electronic networks must be developed to interconnect PCs and the mainframes. In order to do this, three basic components are required: a medium to carry the data, software to make the data intelligible to dissimilar pieces of equipment and switchboards to control the flow and direct the traffic. These technologies drive many of the fundamental decisions that might explain IBM's aggressive activity in the communications and software arena.

Corporate planners can expect IBM to try to turn its PCs into workstations as quickly as possible. So far, in 1985, IBM has introduced PC versions of its Series/1 and System/36 minicomputers, as well as 3270 emulation processors, graphics processors and factory automation processors. The key to all of these products is that they are not designed to be stand-alone processors but are meant to function as workstations involved with larger mainframe systems. IBM is simply not interested in selling PCs, except as part of a strategy to sell workstations, connections and, ultimately, mainframes. With the System 36 PC, IBM is providing an attractive upgrade for small businesses, which can ultimately lead to the System/36 minicomputer and the mainframe. For users, IBM's workstation plans mean closer links to the company's host processors and operating systems with emphasis on application software that is available across the IBM hardware product line. IBM's goal is to provide productivity tools that can be used across the hardware line from stand alone to host.

## Future architecture

How is all this power going to be used? IBM's approach to information processing over the next several years is centred around distributed information and office automation. The architecture for information will revolve around the mainframe computer system, which will be tied to departmental level hosts represented by System/36s, which will be tied to personal workstations represented by PCs. The mainframe will be used for major databases and historical data as well as back-up for the distributed departmental processors. The departmental processors will extract from the host databases to maintain local databases and also provide back-up for the personal computing databases. Finally, the workstation's PCs will extract information from the host and the departmental processors in order to create personal databases. (See Figure 3.)

The office of the present (Figure 4) can be characterised by separate stand-alone dedicated systems doing various office processing tasks, eg text systems. IBM's office automation future consists of the three levels of processing described in Figure 5 tied together by standards established by SNA, DCA, DIA, DISOSS and PROFS. Mainframes will be tied to departmental mid-range processors, which will be tied to local clusters of personal computers and workstations. The office systems will then become integrated across corporate America.

This architecture will generate a tremendous demand for desktop systems. Currently there are approximately 22 million in use. The projected figure for 1988 is 76 million, many of which will be in use in the office environment. (See Figure 6.)

Communications is a key area for IBM. The company is making investments in that area, such as increasing its ownership of SBS, offering funding to Sytek for the development of a local area network (LAN), and spending $1.25 billion to acquire the Rolm Corporation. The key areas for IBM are LANs, SNA and the PBX, which is the entry point into corporate America.

The communications battle with AT&T will probably not really surface until the 1990s. In order for IBM to compete in this marketplace, it needs to increase its critical mass significantly. Investments made so far do not accomplish this. Potential targets for IBM to acquire or work with include GTE, Western Union, Boeing Computer Services, Geisco, and ADP.

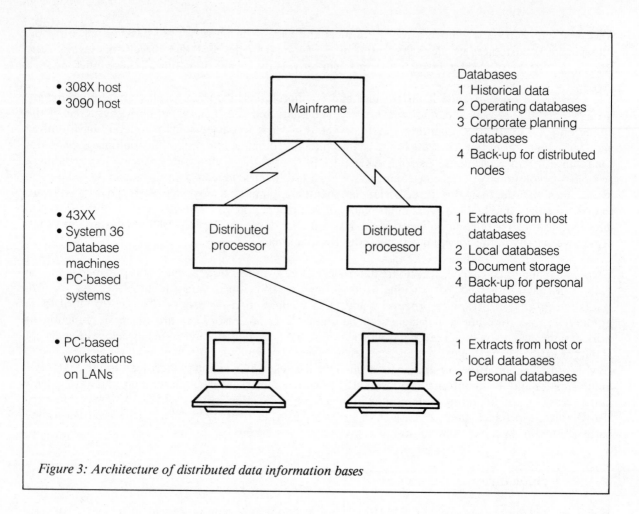

Figure 3: Architecture of distributed data information bases

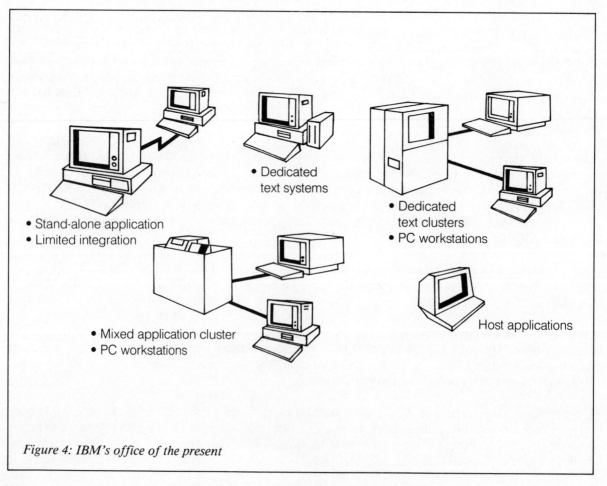

Figure 4: IBM's office of the present

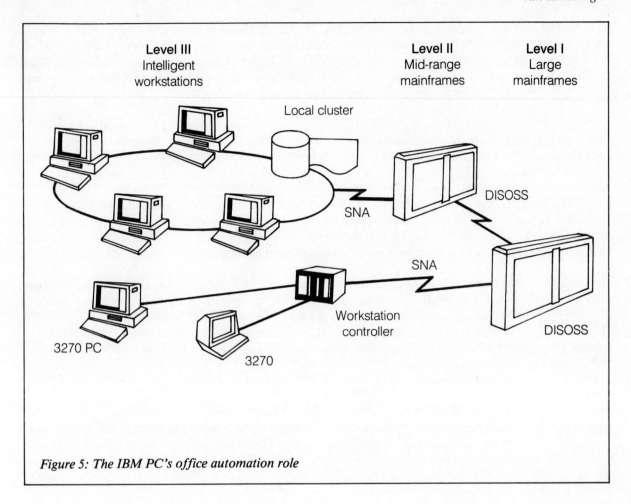

*Figure 5: The IBM PC's office automation role*

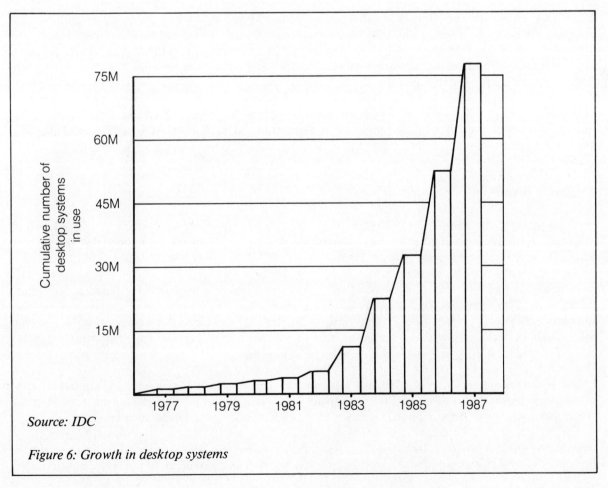

Source: IDC

*Figure 6: Growth in desktop systems*

IBM has taken a $400 million position in MCI in return for turning the assets of SBS over to MCI. MCI needs this help as its finances are fragile, which leaves it in a difficult position to compete against AT&T. IBM hopes that MCI, given access to IBM's Fortune 500 customers, may be able to use SBS's satellites in a way that IBM was unable to do alone. IBM's investments in SBS and MCI show that it believes it must supply data communications support and not just the computers that run user applications.

The acquisition of MCI has angered AT&T. This may be just the action required to push AT&T forward. Potentially, AT&T could acquire a computer firm in order to become more of a full service corporation to compete with IBM. The candidates mentioned most often are Digital Equipment Corporation and the Apple Corporation.

The battle lines are now drawn. IBM's acquisition of MCI gives it access to MCI's 350 000 commercial customers as well as a 20 000-mile nationwide network. This is a crucial ingredient in IBM's pursuit of its integrated architecture. In short, AT&T is no longer the obvious choice for corporate communication customers. In addition, AT&T remains an also-ran in the computer business.

IBM dominated the database business with IMS throughout the 1960s and into the 1970s. Now third-party companies have entered the marketplace and taken a significant market share in middle-range systems. However, 70 per cent of the large systems still run IMS, and that is the bread-and-butter marketplace for IBM. IBM, though, has been forced to introduce DB2 as a relational database system in order to start to address the issues that these middle-range accounts are dealing with. One of the big issues has to do with the complexity and overhead associated with IMS itself. However, it is likely that IBM will recapture DBMS by creating the relational standard with DB2 and Sequel.

In the mainframe area, MVS/XA is clearly the standard and will be for a long time to come. As far as the production of mainframe systems is concerned, the battle is between IBM and Japan. There were 4000-5000 3080x systems sold in the last three years. The recently announced 3090 series is projected to sell 7000-8000 systems in its lifetime. It is also projected that there will be 8000-10 000 4381s sold during its life, 50 per cent of which will be running MVS/XA. Price and performance of these systems will continue to improve at about the same pace as in the past.

All of this revolves around the IBM 3090 series, with VM and MVS/XA the key operating system environments. This has been called IBM's solar system (Figure 7) and satellites in orbit include the System/36 and 4300s. IBM clearly will draw power from its centre, based on the large host system that it dominates, in order to service and support the smaller environments represented by PCs, 4300s, and System/36s in the office environment.

In the 21st century, all of this will be drawn towards a great 'blue hole' of system software: the IBM Corporation will suck everything, including users, applications, data, database systems, and the like, into this incredibly complex environment that will be represented by system software. (See Figure 8.)

## Financial future

IBM will grow to approximately $88 billion in 1989. This growth curve very much fits the pattern of projected user MIS spending in the same timeframe (Figure 9). With this in mind, IBM has only to maintain the market share it has today to double in size by 1989 without any difficulty.

As a result of this direction, the mix of IBM revenue will change. In 1983, IBM was a $40 billion corporation with 48 per cent coming from mainframe systems and 21 per cent from PCs, six per cent from software and 25 per cent from other systems or services. By 1989, as an $88 billion corporation, 33 per cent will come from mainframe systems (recognise that this is 33 per cent of a much bigger corporation), 26 per cent will come from PCs, and software will be up to 16 per cent.

Projected overall annual industry shipments will support this growth in IBM revenue. The area where IBM will increase market share is in the PC marketplace. User requirements and industry projections of the marketplace will support the growth objectives of the IBM Corporation for the next several years.

In order to pursue this marketplace, IBM is accelerating its investment. IBM made a $28 billion investment from 1979 to 1984, which will double over the next five years. The breakdown of the last five years shows

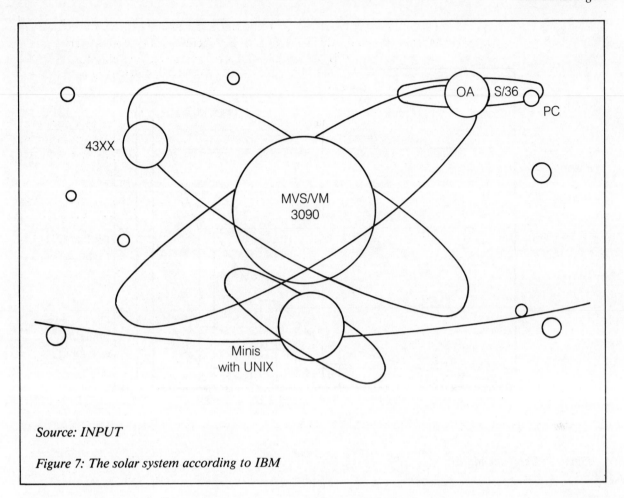

*Source: INPUT*

*Figure 7: The solar system according to IBM*

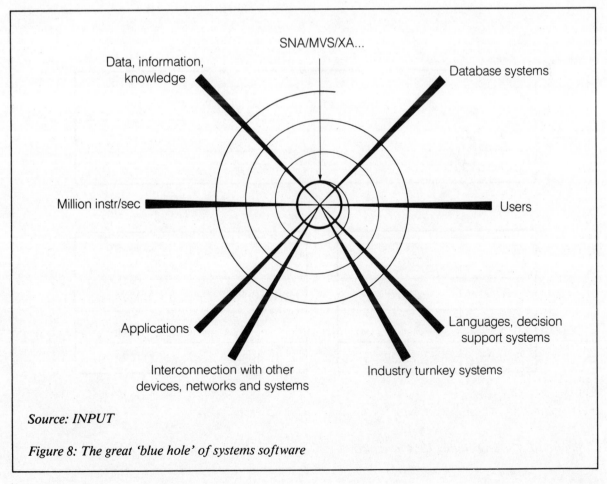

*Source: INPUT*

*Figure 8: The great 'blue hole' of systems software*

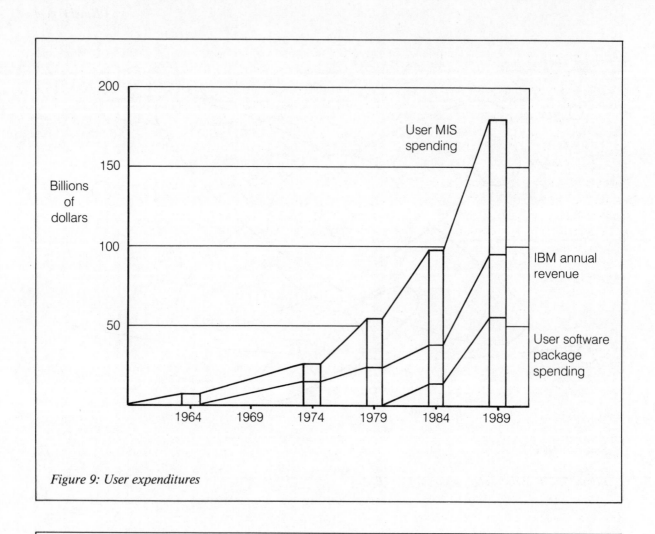

*Figure 9: User expenditures*

| | Investment<br>land/buildings/equipment/R&D/engineering |
|---|---|
| 1979-1984 | $28 B |
| 1985-1990 | $56 B |

| | Investment<br>1979-1984 |
|---|---|
| R&D | $15.5B |
| Capital | $10.5B |
| Software | $2.0B |

| | Software<br>Investment |
|---|---|
| 1979-1982 | $609M |
| 1983 | $588M |
| 1984 | $803M |

*Figure 10: The accelerating IBM investment*

$15.5 billion for R&D, $10.5 billion for capital investment, and $2 billion in software. When the software investment is broken down, you can see that it is accelerating (Figure 10). $609 million was invested in software from 1979 to 1982, while $588 million was invested in 1983 alone, and $803 million in 1984 alone. As you can see, IBM is making a significant accelerated investment in the software arena. Software growth is 30-40 per cent per year. In 1983, US sales for all software companies was approximately $9 billion. IBM had $2.3 billion of this, approximately 60 per cent of the total US sales figure with the rest from foreign sales.

In 1984, IBM generated $20 million in revenue every four hours of each day. In 1988, it will generate $40 million every four hours of each day. IBM will compete in all segments of information processing as the low-cost producer. IBM after-tax profit is $5.5 billion. It is the *most profitable company* in the world, although at revenues of $40 billion it is only the seventh largest corporation in the world.

## Summary

Despite IBM's thrust into the new markets discussed here, mainframes remain its primary sector. Mainframes provide the finance that allows IBM to explore these other areas. The work that goes on in PCs and communications is designed to increase the demand for the mainframe. About 25 per cent of IBM's revenue comes directly from large CPU sales, which account for up to one half of IBM's profits. IBM's competitors in the mainframe area will have difficulty keeping up since their products do not provide the same cash for R&D that IBM has access to.

The impact of IBM on the DP world obviously cannot be underestimated. A major suggestion presented in this paper has been that the office systems family announcement of October 1984 is one of the most significant announcements in the history of the IBM Corporation. It is the unveiling of a grand strategy that will allow IBM to protect its profitable mainframe customer base while pulling together the key technologies represented by personal computers, communications, and software. IBM has a long way to go to make this work, in particular in providing cohesiveness across all of these product areas. Establishing a transparent, clean, user-friendly environment from PC to host is something that will take years to accomplish. Any user or vendor who does not take this announcement seriously will run the risk of being frozen out of the standard information processing environment of the future.

The DP industry has experienced a deceleration in 1985. While many factors certainly contribute to this, including a slow US economy, the author believes that the 1984 announcement of the office systems family has had a severe impact on the minicomputer and personal computer vendors of the industry. I believe that many corporate users have been frozen in place due to the announcement of the office systems family architecture. They are afraid in many cases to make moves that might propel them into an incompatible configuration. While there may come a point when this initial shock will wear off, I believe that many users have in fact been immobilised through the indecision caused by the announcement of the office systems family in October of 1984.

In summary, the IBM Corporation has a strategy of building its future on the office automation link to its captive mainframe customer base. This link will be based on establishing the specific standards as IBM desires them, and will encompass the personal computing world, the communications world and the mainframe world. What we are witnessing is the unveiling of a grand strategy that IBM will pursue for many years to come in its battle with AT&T and the Japanese. IBM will continue to dominate the field because of its single-minded focus and its understanding and control of this marketplace.

# 9: IBM and the future

**F E Lamond**

Independent Consultant
Watford
Hertfordshire
UK

IBM will remain the largest company within the DP industry for the foreseeable future, and its annual sales will continue to grow, but it will never again be able to impose *de facto* standards on the industry as it did with its System/360-370 standard in the general-purpose mainframe market. At best, it may be the king-maker between two rival standards, as when it crowned MS-DOS in preference to CP/M-86 as the standard single user operating system for desktop microcomputers. Since IBM's influence on the minicomputer and personal computer markets does not match its dominance of the general-purpose mainframe market, it is in its interest to expand the System/370 architecture downwards in price to meet the expanding PC performance. This move may enable IBM to regain a larger share of the distributed processing expenditure of its System/370 mainframe customers.

*F E Lamond*
Frederic Lamond studied Economics at Cambridge and the University of Chicago and worked for five years at The Economist Intelligence Unit before joining the computer industry in 1960. Since then he has been a systems analyst at Sperry Univac, export salesman at English Electric Computers, consultant at Leasco Systems & Research and European Editor of the 'Auerbach Reports' before becoming self employed in 1975. He now divides his time between lecturing on DP growth strategies and contributing to 'Datamation'.

## Is IBM's market domination a thing of the past?

The answer to this question depends on what you mean by 'domination'. If sheer size is your criterion, IBM will undoubtedly dominate the DP environment for the foreseeable future. Its share of worldwide DP revenues is variously estimated at between 30 and 33 per cent, six times greater than its nearest rivals: Burroughs and Digital Equipment. Since customers in this exceptionally loyal industry are lost by their suppliers more frequently than they are won by the competition, it would take an uncommon string of crass product and marketing mistakes by IBM to lose its dominant share, and IBM's highly professional committee management rarely makes such mistakes.

But if 'domination' is taken to mean the ability to impose *de facto* standards on the industry, and system and network architectures on users that go against their own initial preferences, then IBM has already lost that kind of domination. It continues to dominate the System/370 architecture — not surprisingly, since it created it — and is the only company that can modify and create new interfaces within it; and that architecture's share of the general-purpose mainframe market is slowly expanding at rival manufacturers' expense. But in the newer minicomputer and microcomputer markets that are growing much faster than mainframes, as well as in the communications and industrial automation markets into which it is diversifying sideways, IBM has no option but to follow standards defined by others; eg UNIX, MAP, ISDN, perhaps soon Pick and OSI/X.25.

## Why IBM dominates the general-purpose mainframe market

IBM's domination of the general-purpose mainframe market with its System/360-370 architecture is an unrepeatable feat due to the revolutionary changes in computer design, manufacturing, distribution and support economics of the last 25 years.

### Distribution and support

At the dawn of the computer era in the 1950s, IBM and its licensees (eg British Tabulating Machine Co in the UK, now part of ICL) held between 70 and 90 per cent of the punched card accounting market, whose users were the first to convert to electronic DP. IBM had achieved this dominance originally through holding the Hollerith patents, but had held on to it by a sales and support network of unparalleled efficiency and reliability.

It was T Watson Senior's genius to recognise that IBM's users were relatively price-insensitive to accounting equipment that represented at most two per cent of their total running costs, but extremely sensitive to any system error or breakdown that could have devastating consequences on their cash flow. By building up a reputation of flawless reliability and support, IBM could charge virtually what it liked, thus earning adequate income to attract the best people for its sales and support network. IBM carried this tradition over into the large mainframe computer-based DP era of the 1960s, and its customers gratefully followed.

## Design and manufacturing

When Gene Amdahl defined the System/360 architecture in the early 1960s, the cost of electronic components and of manufacturing central processors was still very high. The name of the competitive game between manufacturers was to maximise the job throughput obtainable from components by designing a cleverer processor architecture than the competition. That is why System/360 and 370 processors look so different from Burroughs, Honeywell, ICL, Sperry and other mainframes, and neither their operating systems nor their applications software is portable between ranges, even when written in COBOL. Once committed to any particular mainframe computer family, large users thus found it increasingly expensive to convert their applications program libraries to computers with a different architecture. Users choosing mainframes in the 1960s had the choice between a number of manufacturer-designed prisons, IBM's became the largest of these because it had the largest customer base of punched card accounting and 1400 and 7000 series computer users to convert to its architecture.

As computer manufacturing costs and retail prices have plummeted (by up to 700:1 in US dollars for comparable performances and main memory sizes) in the last 20 years, optimising processor throughput has become less and less important compared with saving programming effort. Increasingly, users try to buy applications program packages instead of writing their own, and when they do to program at higher levels than COBOL. The much larger number of System/370, 4300 and 30XX users have written many more applications than other manufacturers' users, and are a much larger potential market for any independent software house with a bright package idea. Thus every year that goes by sees the System/370 compatible program library grow further and dwarf those libraries of rival mainframe manufacturers even more. And every year, it induces a few more Burroughs, Honeywell, ICL and Sperry users to undertake the expensive conversion process to the IBM environment, for the sake of access to that huge, ready-written applications library.

## Towards the portable operating system standard

IBM's — and the independent software houses' — feat in making the proprietary System/370 architecture into a *de facto* industry standard is, however, unrepeatable either by IBM or any other manufacturer. In the newer minicomputer and microcomputer markets, users are moving in ever greater numbers from original proprietary operating systems — DEC's VMS, Data General's AOS, Apple's DOS — to manufacturer-independent portable operating systems, such as UNIX for scientific and engineering multi-user systems, and MS-DOS for single-user desktop microcomputers.

MS-DOS is not another IBM standard imposed on the industry. IBM was no more than a king-maker choosing between the rival Intel and Motorola 16-bit microprocessors and the rival MS-DOS and CP/M-86 operating systems for its PC, both of which were upward compatible with the CP/M-80 that had become the *de facto* standard for 8-bit microcomputers. If IBM had chosen CP/M-86 instead of MS-DOS, that would have become the industry standard; but IBM could not have gained such a large share of the personal computer market with either a proprietary microprocessor architecture or a closed non-portable operating system of its own design.

## Towards Open Systems Interconnection standards

Many people see IBM's Systems Network Architecture (SNA) becoming the industry's new *de facto* standard communications architecture. But SNA is no more than IBM's proprietary implementation of the International Standards Organisation's (ISO) Open Systems Interconnection (OSI) seven-layer model in advance of ISO's slow-moving definition (five out of seven layers have now been defined); other manufacturers have also had to make their own definition. Now that the OSI definition is nearing completion, all other manufacturers are promising an adaptation of their architectures to OSI, while IBM is promising 'gateway' translators for each level.

There are some important conceptual differences between the two. IBM's SNA was originally highly centralised and put into the host computer most of the network control and document distribution and routing functions that OSI puts into network nodes. This makes SNA suitable only for intra-company leased line networks, whereas OSI can be used on these as well as on public data networks for both intra- and inter-company communications. If the European PTTs start levying volume-sensitive charges on digital leased line networks as well as on public packet switching networks, many users will find it more economical to move much of their intra-company traffic to public data networks, and OSI will gain in importance at SNA's expense.

110

Anticipating this and under user pressure, IBM has recently decentralised many SNA functions via SNA Distributed Services (SNA/DS) and the LU6.2 protocol: notably electronic mail, mailboxes and document distribution. As part of the agreed settlement of the European Community's (EC) objections to IBM selling practices, IBM has published the LU6.2 protocol to allow other manufacturers to make their systems as SNA-compatible as IBM's own, and thus deprived itself of a weapon to influence its host computer users' choice of distributed processing and office automation satellites. SNA may continue to evolve and become indistinguishable from the internationally defined OSI both in its openness and the distribution of its network control functions.

## Growth of independent distribution and support

When falling manufacturing costs allowed the much cheaper minicomputers of the 1970s to penetrate a smaller business market previously served by direct keyboard input accounting machines, it became impossible to contain IBM's traditional lavish system support in the sales price and still remain price competitive. The business minicomputer market of the 1970s was thus dominated by younger and smaller firms — DEC, MAI, Nixdorf, Philips, and others — who used independent distributors and systems houses to adapt their systems to the individual users' requirements. Distribution and support were further decentralised in 1978 when the Apple II and other desktop personal computers started being sold through High Street computer shops.

Since 1979, IBM has adapted its distribution and support practices to the markets it serves. Its Personal Computer (PC) range has been sold through the same independent High Street shops as the Apple II and CP/M-80 systems from the time of its launch in 1981 (US) and 1983 (Europe). All its other small systems from System/36 up to the 4361 are sold both through its direct sales force and through independent systems houses that add the value of their applications packages and customer support. Only IBM's largest 4381 and 30XX series mainframes are now sold and maintained exclusively by IBM, but systems support is priced separately from the hardware.

In this way, IBM has managed to bring the hardware prices of all its systems down to competitive levels, but has inevitably lost some of its mystique. The support you get for your IBM PC is as good as the shop from which you bought it, and no better than you would have got for an Apple II, Macintosh, or Olivetti M24 bought from the same shop. The quality of your System/36 software is that of the systems house which wrote it. Nor do these independent systems houses and High Street retailers have the same brand loyalty as mainframe users. More knowledgeable about computer technology, they have a quick eye for the newer more cost-effective systems that would be easier to sell, irrespective of the supplier's identity. If they should change suppliers, they will take many of their customers with them.

IBM's future market share of the personal computer, multifunction workstation, and multi-user departmental and small business systems markets, thus depends now on its ability to offer systems that are more user-friendly, ergonomic, expandable and/or cost-effective than those of its leading competitors. It has all the economies of large-scale production on its side, but has always found it difficult to recruit and retain the truly creative minds that have initiated most of the quantum leaps in computer technology and usage.

### The AT&T challenge

Another factor preventing IBM from dominating the newer minicomputer, personal computer and communications markets is competition from AT&T, the only corporation in the information processing industry possessing a size and finance comparable to IBM's own. Before it divested itself of its local Bell Telephone companies in the US, AT&T's annual turnover was three times IBM's (but its profit much smaller). Since divestiture, the new AT&T is about IBM's financial size, but geographically still largely restricted to the US whereas IBM operates worldwide. To date, the long-heralded fight between the two has been fought with 'wet noodles' as 'Datamation' magazine put it. This is partly because AT&T has been distracted until now by the major reorganisation forced on it by the divestiture of its local US telephone operating companies, and the deregulation of the long-distance communications business that it has been allowed to retain. But it is also the result of an understandable caution on the part of two managements who respect each other, and who see their task as maximising profits for their shareholders rather than engaging in publicity campaigns.

## Unchallenged core businesses

Each of these companies dominates a core business that the other does not intend to challenge. IBM's is in large mainframe host computers, AT&T's in long-distance communications lines and public telecommunications switching exchanges. Each corporation's activities in the other's core business are designed mainly to maintain an open competitive market rather than gain a major market share.

IBM moved into long-distance communications as a co-founder of Satellite Business Systems (SBS) in the 1970s, and has now bought up MCI, the leading independent long-distance communications carrier in the US. These moves were intended as much to prod AT&T to provide adequate long-distance digital communications channels at reasonable prices, which IBM feels its major customers need, as to gain market share.

AT&T has replied by cooperating closely with Amdahl, the leading manufacturer of IBM System/370 compatible mainframe computers, in the development of the latter's UTS version of AT&T's portable UNIX operating system. This move has been designed to ensure that the huge System/370 installed base should have access to a fully up to date version of the UNIX standard. Should Amdahl have further financial difficulties or run short of development capital, AT&T would be ready to step in and either provide additional capital or buy the manufacturer out. The purpose would be to keep the System/370 replacement open and prices reasonable for mainframe host equipment that AT&T itself uses in large numbers.

## Competition for the automated office

The main competitive arena for the two corporations will be the automated office: the terminals, new personal computers and multifunction workstations that are appearing on executive desks to increase their productivity; and the local area networks (LANs) and private telephone branch exchanges (PBX) to tie these together into office networks.

In this competitive fight, AT&T starts with some advantages. It knows far more about telecommunications switching and networking than does IBM, and has a much larger installed base of PBXs than IBM's recently acquired Rolm subsidiary. It is thus as much the first choice of the conservative US telecommunications or office manager, as IBM is of the cautious DP manager. It is better acquainted with the world's telecommunications carriers' plans for single Integrated Services Digital Network (ISDN) user interfaces than IBM, and its Intel designed Starlan standard for departmental LANs is a less costly solution better adapted to most user requirements than IBM's original common cabling specifications and Sytek designed PC-Net.

IBM, however, has a much more dynamic and flexible sales force, accustomed to dictating product policy in the light of perceived users' needs, whereas AT&T product design remains — after a recent internal political fight — engineer dominated. IBM has the larger installed base of synchronous visual display terminals connected to host mainframes, and has succeeded in gaining, in a short time, the largest share of the desktop personal computer market.

The PBX market will be the key to the automated office market, because PBXs will be the integrators of all internal communications lines to interface them to the common carriers' future ISDN interfaces. That is why IBM bought the Rolm Corporation — largest supplier of digital PBXs to the North American market after AT&T — after trying unsuccessfully to gain a major share of the European PBX market in the 1970s with its own design of 3750 and 1750 PBXs. In order to gain a much larger share of this market, where AT&T now has the advantage of experience and installed base, IBM might instruct Rolm to develop an integrated multifunction communications system that combines the functions of the telephone and teletex PBX with those of 3725 communications front-end processing for host mainframes. Such a project would take at least four years to develop, however, and is unlikely to be installed before 1989.

In choosing between IBM and AT&T or European telecommunications manufacturers' PBXs and workstations, users will be looking for adherence to international interconnection standards. That is why IBM has promised SNA to OSI gateways and is implementing its own UNIX versions on the PC, Series/1 and 370-compatible hosts. Whatever relative market shares the main contenders thus win in the developing automated office market, their competition will serve to keep the market open also to smaller more innovative suppliers, and prevent it being dominated by a single giant to the users' detriment.

## Will IBM's small and medium systems converge?

IBM dominates the general-purpose mainframe market with its System/370-compatible 4300 and 30XX series in a manner in which it will never be able to dominate the newer minicomputer, microcomputer, and communications markets. It is thus in IBM's interest to protect the mainframe's position in user installations, and, if possible, to expand its market share downwards at the minicomputers' expense. But IBM's modular MVS and VSE operating systems require a great deal of fine tuning by expensive systems programmers backed by IBM systems engineers to adapt them to each site's requirements, and neither smaller users nor IBM itself can afford this at too many sites.

### The DP centralisation policy that failed

In order to limit its selling and support expenses, IBM tried to persuade its System/370 users in the 1970s to centralise their DP as far as possible on a single site, and kept the entry-level price to System/360 and 370 compatibility stable at around $80 000 for the smallest CPU and $120 000 for the smallest configuration, from 1964 to 1981. Below this price level, IBM introduced smaller and cheaper small business computers — Systems/3, 34 and now 36 — with simpler integrated operating systems requiring little support but incompatible with System/370. As a growth path for these smaller users, IBM announced System/38 in 1978 within the same price range as the 370-compatible 4300 series, but with an integrated operating system that comprises a built-in relational database management system.

The DP centralisation advocated by IBM flew, however, in the face of the industry's changing economics, where falling computer hardware prices make it ever more advantageous to distribute DP systems to all factories and sales offices, to save on leased communications line capacity whose costs are not dropping.

Since 1975, therefore, a growing number of companies have decentralised order entry and many accounting functions to each remote site, using computers of appropriate size. Since IBM's smaller systems were no more compatible with the larger 370-compatible hosts than other manufacturers', but also less expandable, many IBM mainframe users bought their distributed DP and office automation satellites from DEC, Data General, Nixdorf, Philips, Wang and other manufacturers.

### Centralised support for 370-compatible satellites

To encourage users to install 370-compatible satellites without raising their systems engineering support costs to unacceptable levels, IBM has developed a series of tools allowing remote 4300 as well as 8100 series satellites to be controlled from the central host computer site whenever a system software fault occurs with which the local end users are unable to cope. These are the HCF, VM/PTF, NPDA and NCCF programs on 4300 or 30XX hosts complemented in the latter case by OCCF or ROCF running on the remotely controlled 4300 satellite.

### Towards cheaper 370-compatible entry-level systems

The next stage is a gradual reduction in the entry-level price to System/370 architecture. Since 1981, 4321 processors and their 4361/3 successors have been available from $63 000 upwards, a 20 per cent reduction on the previous entry level. Since 1983, the 370-compatible PC/XT 370 desktop single-station system has been available from $9900 and now $8300. A 2 million instr/sec 370-compatible engineering workstation was expected to be announced at around $25 000 at the Computer Aided Design and Manufacturing (CADAM) conference and exhibition in Detroit at the beginning of November 1985, to compete against the highly successful DEC MicroVAX II which brought DEC's 32-bit VAX architecture down in price in a similar manner.

This leaves a price gap between the two single-station systems and the multi-user 4300s that is currently filled by the incompatible System/36 and Series/1. IBM is expected to fill this gap in the course of 1986 or early 1987 by a new 4300 hardware generation that will replace the current 4361s (which were no nore than 'end of life kickers' for the 4331 processors announced and first delivered in 1979).

On each previous occasion when IBM introduced a new hardware generation, this offered a four-fold improvement on the performance/price ratio of the 360 and 370 generation it replaced. At the $63 000 price level of the current entry-level 4361/3, IBM should thus announce a 2 million instr/sec multi-user processor with 31-bit addressing able to support MVS/XA and 4M to 32 Mbytes memory. But IBM is also expected to announce a smaller Intel 80386-based multi-user system — if not in 1986, then in 1987 — that will offer the 4361/3's 400 thousand instr/sec from $15 000 upwards, thus closing the price gap with the 370-compatible single user PC/XT 370 and PC/AT 370.

## IBM small systems convergence

If the next 4300 series' hardware generation becomes available from $15 000 per processor upwards, what will happen to the incompatible 8100 series, System/36 and Series/1 that currently fill the performance/price gap between the PC/AT 370 and the 4361/3?

### *The 8100 series*

The 8100 series has been a sales disappointment on the distributed processing market for which it was designed, though it has done better on the office automation front. Not more than 1000 systems are believed to be installed worldwide. This makes the development of a compatible successor hardware series uneconomic, while its multi-interrupt level architecture is also too complicated to be efficiently emulated on an Intel 80386 or Motorola 68020 microprocessor. This series will thus disappear from the IBM product catalogue when the new $15 000 4300 processor is announced, but the whole 4300 series will, in the future, support the 8100 series' DPPX operating system as a guest under VM, as well as all DPPX compilers, utilities and applications packages; it already supports the 8100 Cross System Product (CSP) generator. The DPCX office automation package DOSF will be converted to run under DPPX, thus most 8100 series users will be bridged relatively painlessly to the 4300 series.

### *System/36*

By contrast, there are more than 110 000 System/34 and System/36 installations with a huge library of applications packages, from both IBM and independent origins, which IBM does not wish to throw away. IBM has thus protected System/36's sales position in advance by the following measures:

1  Adopting the Baby/34 and Baby/36 packages that allow PC/XT and PC/ATs running under PC-DOS to recompile and execute System/34 and 36 RPG II. This brings System/36 down to the $3000 price range.

2  Announcing the new entry-level Desktop/36 office automation file server at $4800 and bringing the larger Compact/36 down to $10 000.

3  Giving System/36 a key role as Office System with DisplayWrite/36 and Personal Services/36, user interface compatible with comparable packages on the PC and 370-compatible systems.

### *Series/1*

With an installed base estimated at 10 000-20 000 processors Series/1 is in an intermediate position. IBM has implemented its architecture on a proprietary microprocessor, used in the desktop 4950 which is both Series/1 and PC/XT compatible. Series/1 has also been chosen as IBM's departmental UNIX system, but there will be no 32-bit Series/1 as that slot has already been filled by the Motorola 68000-based CS 9000 series.

## System/38's future

System/38 was announced in November 1978 in the same price/performance range as the 4300 series when IBM thought it might have to divest itself of the General Business Group to satisfy the US Department of Justice. With an integrated operating system that obviates all the costly system generation of 4300 operating systems, and very powerful and user-friendly program development facilities, System/38 is too strategic a product for IBM to drop, and now has between 10 000 and 20 000 users worldwide.

At the beginning of 1982, therefore, IBM instructed its reorganised System Products (design) Division to develop a new generation of processors in time for 1986 production which would be able to run in both 4300 series and System/38 mode and to multiprogram both 4300 CMS, VSE, MVS and System/38 CPF environments and applications under the VM hypervisor. Observers have noted that the interactive System/38 command language is closer to VM/CMS than are the originally batch-based DOS/VSE and OS/MVS job control languages. CPF would thus be the preferred migration path for small PC/AT 370 and 4300 VM/CMS users, leaving VSE and MVS for large users' distributed DP.

With its very high-level user interface and single-level 48-bit addresses for both virtual memory and user file records, System/38 architecture is probably too complicated to be emulated efficiently on the 24-bit address Intel 80386 microprocessor. The next 4300 entry level model will therefore be able to run in 370, System/36 and PC mode only, with VM/CMS as its main operating system. System/38 emulation will become available side by side with a 31-bit addressing MVS/XA mode on the next model up — namely the two million instr/sec processor that will fill the 4361's current price slot and that is believed to be a Reduced Instruction Set Computer (RISC) of IBM's own design.

# 10: The evolution of the PC

J M D McIntyre

Digitus Ltd
London
UK

IBM's policy of not speculating about possible future products is well known. In an industry with more than its share of 'paper promises' it also makes good sense. Indeed, even this careful policy has not protected IBM from the uncertainties of component supply, which have sometimes left it unable to deliver what it has promised. All of which makes forecasting what IBM is likely to do a hazardous business. However, the aim of this paper is to review the overall IBM direction in order to provide input to the planning process. Given that there is a certain momentum in any major development, the history of IBM's PC programme is probably a reasonable base on which to look ahead. The author's objectives, therefore, are to review the development of IBM's PC family in all its major facets; to discuss the effects of these developments on the user base and to propose a possible direction for the future.

*J M D McIntyre*
John McIntyre joined IBM on leaving the Royal Air Force and launched the IBM PC in the UK. His positions within the corporation included District Manager of the General Systems Division and Personnel Staff Manager. In his present role with Digitus, a new technology systems house, he is responsible for the management and development of the Computer Systems Branch.

**Features of the IBM PC programme**

IBM's preparation for, and entry into the microcomputer business was affected by a number of factors. They characterised the company's approach, and showed more publicly than before IBM's adaptability and market sensitivity — features claimed by critics to have been lacking at times in the company's history. The first factor was organisational freedom for the PC developers. The second was the 'personal' in personal computer, and the third was quite unusual for IBM — it was joining a market, not leading it.

## Organisational freedom

The PC operation — Entry Systems — was set up as the most significant of IBM's Independent Business Units (IBUs). IBM had set up these together with European Business Units (EBUs) in response to the need to move rapidly into new areas of the information industry while retaining its traditional organisation and management system for its day to day business. It had more than 10 such units at the time of the PC launch, and will doubtless continue to use them as tactical business development vehicles. As we have seen with the PC unit, the IBU is like a business 'special force', set up for a specific mission, and re-absorbed into the main organisation once the launch phase is completed. With the PC business the original Entry Systems Unit acquired full IBM Division status, and a broader mission covering all the company's commercial entry-level systems efforts which had previously been spread among the GS, OP and DP divisions. More recently the 're-absorption' has been completed with the removal of responsibility for sales and channel management. Entry Systems is now a traditional IBM product division, with development and product management responsibilities. The management of the dealer channel, which was so vital to the success of the PC, and such an unusual feature of Entry Systems, is now the responsibility of a new division, Information Systems Distribution Marketing (ISDM), which handles all of IBM's third-party marketing channels. These changes recognise two facts of IBM life. Firstly, that the PC family and derivatives are now fundamental elements in IBM's line of products and no longer a new venture in any sense of the words, and secondly, that product sales through third parties have become a major business for IBM and that business sense demands the grouping together of the various channels for management by specialists in that field.

So, going back to the days of the PC IBU, Entry Systems was set up under the late, and much lamented Philip Estridge. With maximum autonomy, minimum staff review and visible top management support, the charter was 'Get us into the personal computer business'. In 13 months from inception to announcement the PC IBU did just that — with a success which is now part of the folklore.

## A computer for personal use

From the outset, the mission of Entry Systems was focused on the development of systems for personal use. Commentators have often remarked on the lack of multi-user capability in the earlier PC family members. Even today, the PC/AT supports, almost reluctantly, only three users under the XENIX operating system when, with its power, it could clearly do more. Indeed the third-party suppliers have produced adaptors supporting over 10 user ports. However, to the Entry Systems people, personal is the key word. Virtually all of IBM's other computers are multi-user at some level — the PC is first and foremost for individual use. From the basic assumption that the PC is a facility for the individual to have permanently to hand it follows that 'multi-user' needs should be met by local area networks (LANs). IBM's response to the multi-user PC question has been that in the context of a personal dedicated machine, multi-user means sharing data rather than sharing computer power. Hence the LAN as the means by which to share data among personal machines. We can expect to see more and more host-connected variants of the PC family, which combine personal use capability with the multi-user cluster control computer or mainframe applications.

## Joining the market

The 'big three' of microcomputing at the time of IBM's entry to the market were, of course, Apple, Commodore and Tandy. They had developed a business area of sufficient size and growth to demonstrate that microcomputers were not a 'false dawn' technology, but a normal extension of traditional computing. Market features were already defined: the 8-bit processor, the CP/M operating system and a large library of application software, the 5¼-inch diskette, VisiCalc and non-traditional prices. IBM's challenge was to produce a market leader with a cost structure that would support a competitive price and an acceptable profit. At no time was the PC regarded as an experiment in this market. Right from the decision to fund the PC programme IBM's mission for Entry Systems was to establish the company in new markets and a new distribution channel. The word 'establish' is uncompromising — no hint of diffidence, of 'what if?', of test marketing. From day one the assumptions about sales, numbers of dealer outlets, about international development were appropriate to a full-blown business operation. Every feature of the design of hardware and software, of development and of marketing was focused on producing a serious entrant for the PC market, embodying the values of quality and competitiveness to which IBM is committed. Then, despite having taken that committed approach to the PC programme, IBM itself was genuinely amazed at the market acceptance of the product. Demand for the PC saw to it that the company's production plans had to be continuously accelerated.

The PC programme itself, as well as the technology, the cost disciplines and so on were, and still are, completely consistent with IBM's overall goals. To be a 'complete' information technology company it aims to have a product range that covers the entire spectrum. To compete profitably in a price conscious market demands cost effectiveness of a high order. Developments in the PC family so far have been consistent — extension of the range and reductions in prices as manufacturing costs have fallen. The future direction is likely to follow the same pattern.

## Marketing

In the case of the PC, IBM adopted a classic marketing approach. Exhaustive research was completed in every facet of the business including:

1 Technology:
- Component development and direction
- The availability of the new 16-bit chip families
- Industry standards
- The top performing peripherals
- All relevant hardware.

2 Software:
- The industry standard operating system
- Evolution and the need for improvements in 'user friendliness'
- Application software
- Leading products in all key areas:
- personal productivity
- business
- education
- entertainment.

3 Competitive products:
- The best features and the deficiencies of all the major competition.

4 Marketing arrangements:
- The reseller business
- Computerland
- The Radio Shack chain
- Independent dealers.

5 End-user characteristics:
- Small business
- Corporate end users
- Education
- The home
- The professions.

6 Other areas:
- Pricing
- Support
- Distribution
- Warranty
- Component supply
- Production processes.

All of the above were studied intensively while product development was proceeding. Discussions with industry leaders in software and distribution were pursued in parallel. The objective was very simple: if IBM's PC was to win market leadership it would have to equal or exceed all the best features available from other brands, run all the best software and be marketed and supported better than the competition. Achieving superiority in all these areas and more was the constant focus of Philip Estridge and his team.

## Open architecture

The architecture of the PC was a major departure from IBM's earlier product philosophy. Maintaining uniqueness had been a reasonable way to gain maximum advantage from one's inventions in the face of the plug-compatible business. The *quid pro quo* was incompatibility with other manufacturers' equipment.

In the personal computer world things were very different. There was no possibility of producing most of the product combinations, let alone all of them. The alternative to the architectural 'closed shop' was 'open house'. IBM designed the PC to accept plug-compatible options, and published a reference manual containing all the necessary information for hardware and software designers. The intention was, of course, to encourage people to put the PC to work in every possible way.

The early effect of the open architecture was to produce a tremendous level of support from both hardware and software developers. Indeed, many new products were released only in their PC versions to start with, and 'ported' to other brands later. The effect was to produce a large and growing library of application software for the machine, as well as adaptor cards with extra functions to cover an enormous variety of needs.

The result has been that the IBM PC is the best supported personal computer in the market. Arguments may rage about which brand has most software to support it, but there can be little dispute over hardware options. One firm alone — Tecmar — which specialises in options and peripherals for the IBM PC, was reported recently to have 50 pages of products for the PC family.

The second effect was the production of several brands of 'look-alike' or 'run-alike' machines. These claimed various degrees of compatibility with the IBM PC, and therefore access to the software supporting it. Actual compatibility varied, some products were not very compatible at all, but one manufacturer claimed that its machine was more compatible with the original IBM PC than IBM's own counterpart to its product!

Although the use of open architecture must be judged a handsome success in terms of the overall support for the product and the number of ways in which it can be put to work, it also places a limitation on IBM in that any attempt to develop away from what is now an industry standard loses the support advantage.

Without doubt this would create a lot of unhappiness among the firms who have backed the PC who would view any such move as damaging their earlier development investment. IBM must therefore stay with the standard, or at least evolve gradually and build compatibility bridges as it goes. The announcements by IBM and Microsoft in the summer of 1985 regarding their continuing joint developments have gone a long way to reassure an industry constantly perturbed by the spectre of IBM 'closing the doors' on the independent software developer. It was speculated when IBM announced TopView that the company was about to launch a proprietary development and operating environment which would end the period of open architecture and shut out non-IBM application software. The author's own view has always been that for IBM to shut out the third-party industry would be an extremely self-damaging move.

A further interesting effect of the open approach was in IBM's own product divisions. Acting exactly like a third-party developer IBM produced options for the machine and initially announced the PC/XT 370 and 3270/PC. The basic utility of the PC family as 'engines' has since been reconfirmed by the release of variants of the PC/XT or PC/AT which include a more rugged version for use in industrial environments and models which function like the IBM Series/1 and the IBM System/36. There is also an IBM 4700 finance terminal version. Doubtless other versions will continue to be released wherever there are good business grounds for doing so.

## PC family evolution

Apart from the development of PC variants by IBM's product divisions, Entry Systems itself has been evolving the PC family continuously since the first model was launched in August 1981. Although one sees comment in the press to the effect that the PC is not particularly technologically innovative, that in price/performance terms the various models of the PC can all be beaten by rival brands, and there are still some inexplicable gaps (especially onboard tape streamer back-up) in the line, the PC family has developed considerably since its initial announcement. The sales and market share of the machines confirm that the good all-round total package can still hold its own against the leading-edge products when it comes to corporate use. The latter area of course will invest with least concern where it sees the apparently boring aspects of reliability, consistency, stability and standardisation. The PC started out with such curiosities as a cassette-tape interface and a 16 Kbytes memory option, not to mention a single low-density, single-sided diskette version. These were rapidly dropped as the market made its comment through its buying pattern. Developments in memory capacity, in diskette density, the fixed disk XT, operating systems improvements and application software followed fairly quickly. The third-party market accelerated the pace enormously and soon the PC could claim to be the best supported range of its kind in the market. The circuit board used in the XT provided more space for yet further increases in memory as well as extra slots for option cards. This has now become the standard basis for the PC.

The PC/AT was announced and, to the embarrassment of IBM and many who were depending on it, eventually appeared in reasonable quantities after an unreasonable delay. Tales of management changes and supplier switches seemed to suggest that powerful corrective action had been taken inside the company to prevent any recurrences of this situation. The two exceptions to the story of general success were the PCjr and the Portable PC. They provide an interesting rebuttal of the view that a product only has to have IBM's name on it for its success to be assured. This view is often expressed to explain the phenomenal success of the PC family, but why did these two products not succeed as their illustrious family did?

## The PCjr and the Portable PC

The author's personal view is that these offerings were not a success because they were both poorly positioned in terms of the function offered for the price asked. The PCjr was designed as a minimal function home computer. The plug-compatible ROM, and 'Chiclet' keyboard clearly identified its target market. Unfortunately, it was not competitively priced. Its specification, which lacked a professional keyboard and a reasonable display, could never have been acceptable for a portable business machine. Later attempts to rectify this situation appeared only to create the impression of a patch-up job which failed to inspire confidence. The PCjr was withdrawn, accompanied by the derision of the press. However, IBM rarely fails to capitalise on its experience, and we can be sure that when it is judged to be the right time for the right product it will extend the PC family downwards into the school and the home.

The Portable PC was a slightly different case. It appeared to be a version of the standard PC re-engineered to be portable but, coming when it did, suffered the fate of comparison with COMPAQ's well-timed launch of a purpose-designed portable which was extremely rugged. COMPAQ had the additional market advantage of releasing its fixed-disk version just when the PC/XT was supply constrained. The overall specification and price of the Portable PC were quite attractive, and maybe offering a fixed-disk version would have made up for the unpopular screen. Certainly portable machines for professional use were almost always required to have fixed disks; this may have been the Portable PC's most serious lack. Whatever the reasons, and no doubt IBM has researched the market thoroughly, the Portable PC seems to be retiring from the fray. There can be no doubt that portability will come as the technology takes us in that direction, and IBM will eventually have a competitive offering in the range. This could be as early as 1986 if there is any truth in the 'PC2' rumour.

## Peripherals

The final area in the PC family is that of peripherals. The current range of displays and printers from IBM make it clear that the company is committed to providing a broad range of own-brand peripherals for the PC family. We should expect to see exciting advances in both printer and screen technology and, no doubt, in voice, touch, plotter and communications as well. The limit to IBM's production of own-brand options and peripherals is more likely to be the level of demand, and hence manufacturing volumes, rather than any lack of technology or interest. Sizable third-party niches are therefore likely to exist for some time to come.

## The effect of the PC on the microcomputer market

It is said that the IBM PC made personal computers respectable. This view was reflected in the welcome its greatest rival, Apple, gave it through its famous advertisement. Certainly, in the corporate environment, the PC convinced the management and staff who had not so far experimented with microcomputers that the personal computer was a practical, serious and available facility. Initial corporate purchases were generally made in small numbers through IBM's PC dealers. These were the evaluation and development machines, but now that the growth phase is at its peak the PC is reaching large numbers of corporate end-users on a planned basis. The natural result has been not only to the benefit of IBM's PC, but has also focused attention on personal computers generally, generated demand for many different brands and created challenges for DP management in coping with the new interest.

From the buyer's point of view this has brought the usual mixture of good and bad news. The good news is that reasonable technical standards have emerged, at least in part, that choice has never been wider and that competition is fierce for the buyer's business. The bad news is that the level of competition has led to levels of price cutting which leave virtually no margin to invest in support and service and have resulted in the downfall of some service-minded dealers. This will not matter if they are not needed. The problem is that many of those giving large discounts have the minimum of support competence. There is also the danger that a few big operators will set prices at levels unsustainable by the smaller dealers, the latter will disappear and those left will be unable to provide the quality and quantity of service required.

In a marketplace which grows daily more complex, where thousands of products are promoted in a riot of claim and counter claim, and where the rate of change is difficult for even the industry to keep up with, there is a growing need for a knowledgeable, serious and service-minded distribution industry. Those who hasten its destruction by seeking only the lowest bid and by believing that they have no further need for advice, assistance and support may find themselves in serious trouble when the end-user base reaches mass proportions. The microcomputer distribution industry is still trying to find the balance between the benefits to customers of low prices which result from vigorous competition, and the ability to survive to service those same customers. The low-cost, high quality, well-staffed dealership is still an objective rather than an achievement for most.

## The PC — engine of the workstation

The architecture of the PC has been used by some IBM divisions to develop adapted PCs of their own; logic suggests that the PC family, as long as the architecture remains 'open', will provide a very flexible basis for a 'converged' workstation. We define converged as the merged end-user functions previously served by 3270-type non-intelligent terminals, by typewriters and word processors and by the PC itself. One could envisage a range of mix-and-match modules which could offer the nearest possible thing to the 'universal workstation'.

Consider a family of system units ranging in power and capacity from a basic PC to the biggest PC/AT and beyond. Add a variety of keyboards, including special-purpose variants; screens to cover every need from word processing to high-resolution graphics; every kind of printer and plotter; industry adaptors; scientific interfaces; barcode, tag and badge readers; all kinds of local and remote networks and on and on.... The possibilities are endless and IBM has the opportunity to produce an unrivalled set of matching workstation modules. We have already seen the effects of third-party developers, and they are likely to continue.

## Convergence of the product lines

The convergence of the end-user workstation functions seems logical. What about the rest of the product line? Here the argument is more difficult. Clearly there is logic in standardising file structures, protocols, interfaces and operating systems. However, the PC is still a personal rather than a multi-user system. Even the PC/AT, with plenty of capacity and power, has an understated multi-user implementation. This may be partly to avoid impacting the System/36, but almost certainly reflects the continuing 'personal' influence. IBM has been consistent in its view about personal computers and the importance of the end user being 'owner' of the computing power. However, the PC Networks, the Cluster and UNIX on the PC/AT all acknowledge the need to share files. Although typically restrained, IBM's announcement of XENIX on the PC/AT, and the PC network are of strategic importance. They not only put the seal of respectability on local area networks, but confirm UNIX as a standard.

It remains to be seen whether the successors to the System/36 and System/38, and even the 4300 series, will support UNIX, and how well IBM will integrate its future processors, operating systems and network architectures with emerging industry standards. Provided that it finds the standards acceptable, and that it has a voice in their development, then it may be that IBM will avoid arguing about the 'track' and concentrate on developing the best 'trains'. It has a major investment in its history however, and building bridges from the present to the future standards environment will be neither trivial nor quickly achieved.

Presumably the ideal processor product line would consist of upwards-compatible modular machines covering the power range from the PC to the top of the 308X series. All would run under the same operating system, use common file management and standard networks. This may sound like nirvana but the technology is available.

The various statements from IBM, AT&T, Microsoft and Intel could lead to some interesting speculation. In summary, AT&T will maintain UNIX V as a standard, Microsoft will ensure object code compatibility between XENIX V and UNIX V, Intel will implement UNIX V on the 80286 chip (and presumably the 80386 and successors), IBM and Microsoft will continue to work jointly on operating system development and IBM has a 20 per cent stake in Intel whose chips power the PC family. On a different tack, IBM has also said that it will build bridges between SNA and OSI. Perhaps the first glimmerings of truly global standards in operating environments and communications protocols are beginning to light the horizon? The next few years promise to be extremely interesting, but these changes would be a step-function difference from the past pattern.

## PC network and multi-user systems

The PC family now supports multiple users via networks and UNIX. These types of use are likely to increase. The most obvious areas for the near future are in office automation (or at least in electronic mail, word processing and information storage and retrieval) and the automation of company management systems, both financial and decision. This is likely to occur through the development of cells or clusters of machines, sharing local files, and later hooking up to company networks.

We are likely to see an acceleration of the trend to disperse computing to the end user, while building a hierarchy of more and more centralised files. This would consist of at least three levels for individual, group and corporate databases. Recent statistics show that more microcomputer power than mainframe capacity was shipped in the US in 1985. By 1987 the installed base of microcomputer power will exceed that of mainframes. A similar effect will no doubt be seen in Europe soon after. The dispersion of computing power is a fact, and the day of the 50 million instr/sec fileserver may soon be at hand!

## Summary

A summary of some of the important factors involved in the development of the PC will provide a basis on which to anticipate its possible future direction.

### Organisational freedom

In the last few years IBM has established several IBUs. These venture groups have been set apart from the mainstream of the business and its day to day operational concerns. Separately funded and resourced, the IBUs have been able to dedicate themselves to mastering new areas of the IBM world. Starting with a virtual *carte-blanche* the only provisos have allegedly been 'to uphold the company's value system and obey the law'!

The IBU approach is in line with the guidance T J Watson Jr laid down in 'A business and its beliefs'. His message was that to succeed in modern business life a company has to be prepared to change everything about itself except its basic beliefs. IBUs have given IBM the best of both business worlds: the scale and coherence of a major multinational company, and the flexibility and speed of a new business 'commando' unit.

We can expect to see the IBU concept used more in IBM's future, and can therefore assume that the company will prove to be very quick and responsive to new technology opportunities.

### Personal computing for individuals

The PC has demonstrated that, regardless of other system developments, IBM is committed to the idea of computing for the individual, wherever the individual is. The success of the PC has proved the thesis. We can expect to see continuing, perhaps increasing, development efforts in this area. The present technological barriers will no doubt be vigorously attacked: displays, touch data entry, voice, software ease of use and function, and communications.

Let us set IBM a target: a powerful (32-bit) computer with 10 Mbytes of non-volatile storage and 10 Mbytes of removable storage, which you can talk to, and connect easily to the public communications networks, all of this to be the size of a telephone directory, to cost less than $1000 and to be produced by the end of the decade. At the present rate of development IBM might not need as long as that.

### Consistent with IBM's goals

Of course we can assume that whatever IBM does, with or without the IBUs, will be consistent with its goals of competing in all areas of the information business and of striving constantly to lead the field in cost effectiveness while achieving the highest quality standards. The PC has demonstrated IBM's ability to compete aggressively on price while not compromising on other values. We should expect to see the pattern set by the PC family continued and extended in price and performance.

High volumes are required in order to achieve competitive cost levels with present production technology. This suggests that, at least in the near term, IBM will concentrate on the high-volume items in the PC family and will therefore continue to look to the industry to produce the shorter run special adaptors, peripherals and the like.

### The marketing approach

The development of the PC family since its launch in 1981 has reflected market experience quite rapidly. The current base configuration of the PC no longer offers features which were not in demand, eg tape interface, 16 Kbytes storage. IBM has 'tuned' the offering to the marketplace.

We should expect to see a continuing sensitivity and adaptability in new personal computer products. Again, the third-party involvement is important — IBM seeks to satisfy the end-user and the distribution channel, and depends on the channel to give the customer service and support. The dealer is seen very much as the guardian of the joint IBM/dealer reputation. Therefore, not only should future PC products reflect end-user needs, but the IBM-authorised distribution channel should be developed, supported and managed to achieve IBM's aim of excellence.

## Open design

As discussed earlier, the open design approach has been a crucial factor in the success of the PC. Some of the elements which affected this were:

- Development access for third parties and OEMs
- Development access for the other IBM product divisions
- Wide acceptance by the software and hardware industries
- Self-reinforcing popularity
- *De facto* standards for the industry
- Compatibility with industry standards.

All these led to optimum demand, ie high-volume standard items from IBM and shorter run options from third-party specials developers.

It is difficult to see how IBM could continue to sell maximum volumes of PCs without the range of options offered by the third-party market. We should therefore expect to see a continuation of the open architecture approach, especially as the company's products move towards the mass markets.

It seems probable that the immediate future will see market development which includes:

1  A steady volume of shipments to large customers, both direct from IBM and via the dealer channel.

2  A rapidly increasing focus on the vertical and small business markets by IBM in support of its dealers, and by the distribution and software industries.

3  Renewed focus by IBM on the education opportunity for personal computers en route to the home by the late 1980s. These two areas are fraught with difficulties. The education business in Europe is of course very different from that in the US, and is not likely to submit to a pan-European approach. The home is a question of really practical applications and the breaking down of attitude barriers. In fact, the full development of home use may only be achieved when the present college generation becomes home owners.

4  A PC family which will continue to develop upstream of the PC/AT and downstream of the late PCjr; the MS-DOS single user and UNIX multi-user standards continuing to evolve; network development both to broaden application and to bridge into industry standards. All of these will of course continue to be augmented by vigorous development by third-party hardware and software companies, and by IBM's other product divisions.

## Conclusion

As information processing becomes a common utility IBM is well placed to develop what might be termed a 'coherent systems environment'. This would consist of a compatible, modular range of products, fully integrated with the international standard communications environment and covering uses in every situation — from the home to space vehicles. The company has a number of features listed below which together provide it with an unique foundation from which to develop:

1  Experience in all areas of the industry.
2  A wide range of current products, and a massive investment in research and development.
3  A multinational customer base covering all industries and interest groups.
4  The technology, both through in-house efforts and through association with Intel, Rolm and SBS.
5  An efficient and coherent management system and structure.
6  Acceptance of industry standards.
7  A proven ability to adapt quickly to the changing environment.

The future will see computing power diffused everywhere. Just as the 'two car family' was a modern phenomenon, so we shall pass rapidly through the 'two computer family' phase to the point where computing capability is as unremarkable as the refrigerator, the television and the oven. Information, subject to various levels of security control, will be an 'electronic utility'. Stored in homes, in libraries, in businesses, in banks, in public and in private services, it will be tapped into, processed and presented to the end user by computer.

IBM wants to be a 'total' information technology company, with no part of the information horizon excluded. It will be competing for its share of the opportunity. Prefixes such as mainframe, mini and micro, personal, and games will soon be irrelevant for normal purposes. Many computers will be as unseen as the insides of appliances, motor cars and fuse boxes. Many of them will have the three letters of the IBM logo on them.

---

## Acknowledgement

This paper is a revised and updated version of J M D McIntyre's paper 'PC developments' published in the Pergamon Infotech State of the Art Report 'Microcomputing' (13:5) 1985.

# 11: IBM and PC software — open or closed?

**J M D McIntyre**

Digitus Ltd
London
UK

**The title of this paper poses a question which reflects an opinion heard increasingly over the past several months — that IBM will move from the early 'open' philosophy of the PC's design to a 'closed' position. This would put an end to third-party development of software for the PC family. The author's view is that the opinion is mistaken, and the purpose of this paper is to explain why and to look at some of the factors affecting the PC application software business.**

## Introduction

Recent (summer 1985) statements by IBM and Microsoft, that they would continue to work together on the development of operating systems, have gone a long way to allaying fears about IBM closing the doors. However, even without those reassurances, there are several underlying reasons why the closed position would be counterproductive for IBM. The fear implicit in those reasons seems to arise from an assumption that IBM has a possessive view of the market. It may feel that way about its customer base. However, certainly as far as the PC business is concerned, IBM had to join a market established and 'owned' by others. Its success is due as much to its 'open' approach, both in design and marketing strategy, as to any other factors. For the sales of the PC, IBM had to rely a great deal on third-party developers and on its authorised dealers — it was not slow to see the opportunities.

## Characteristics of the PC business

There are several basic characteristics of the PC business which are quite different from the traditional pattern:

1  Much of the basic technology is common — processor and memory chips, disk files — the industry uses largely standard raw materials.

2  There are few operating systems providing a more or less standard environment for application software.

3  The vast majority of PCs of all brands are sold through third-party dealers neither owned nor controlled by the manufacturers.

4  Significant changes can sweep through the market very rapidly — there are few secure bastions which can survive for long without changing.

5  The cost of product entry, both hardware and software, is comparatively low. This leads to the constant appearance and disappearance of companies, many with a single product and some with a short life span.

6  The industry has a small number of market leaders and the balance of sales is more evenly spread than in the mainframe and minicomputer businesses.

The effect of these characteristics is to produce powerful standards or common denominators. This reduces the ability of any one manufacturer to capture and hold a significant market share on the basis of product uniqueness alone. Long-term leadership is most likely to be won by those offering the best all-round package of function, performance, ease of use, quality, price, service and compatibility with industry standards. As the information industry becomes truly universal so utility will depend on the ability of computers to use programs, communications facilities and data which conform to accepted standards. The alternative will be the development of barriers every bit as difficult to cope with as the different languages of the world.

The author believes that the above characteristics will become inherent in the computer industry over time and that their arrival has 'broken the mould' of the past — for IBM as for everyone else. Eventually, no doubt, a totally adaptable form of artificial intelligence system will be developed, capable of producing and executing application programs in real-time. Until then 'universal' demand will depend on 'universal' application software. IBM is not, nor can be, economically in the 'universal' business of hardware or software on its own.

## All-purpose for maximum sales

The PC developers in IBM seem to have believed, quite logically, that the best way to generate the maximum demand for the machine was to encourage its use in the greatest possible number of ways. This would depend on application software, and IBM designed the PC as an 'open' system which allowed anyone to develop features and software for the machine. This strategy has been extremely successful and must take much of the credit for the PC's adoption as a standard. It has been continued in successive models in the PC family, with upwards compatibility of software preserved while new versions of the operating system have given access to the features of the new machines.

For the long term, the maximum number of uses for the PC will be limited only by what software can be produced for it. In order to achieve minimum production costs IBM, like any other company, has to concentrate on high volumes of the more standard products. Although in the production sense this applies less to software than to hardware, the development of software imposes similar limits ie the cost of development can only be recovered if the product sells in high volumes, unless it has a very high unit value.

### Application software

An analysis of PC application software shows a very wide spread by brand and function. However, products such as VisiCalc and Lotus 1-2-3 are very rare and make history when they arrive. One might even claim that of these two products only VisiCalc was the real 'new' invention, and that 1-2-3's success was the result of effective development of the concept and powerful marketing. This suggests that automatically producing brilliant and practical ideas in PC software is no more possible than any other form of creativity. For any one company, even IBM, to assume that it can produce breakthrough products on a planned basis would be folly. It is far better to make sure that whenever and wherever such a product is produced it can easily be run on one's own machine. The best proof is that what VisiCalc did for the Apple II, Lotus 1-2-3 has done for the IBM PC — neither software product was produced by the hardware manufacturer.

So the development of the PC business depends, by definition, on the development of application software. The wisest policy to follow for a company which wants the greatest possible sales volumes is to encourage, by any means possible, the general development of compatible software. IBM has done this since the earliest days of the PC. It evolved, with Microsoft, a 16-bit operating system standard and stuck to it — providing a consistent environment for developers. Successive releases of PC-DOS have maintained upwards compatibility. It encouraged software house and individual development of software by its submissions scheme. It marketed software under the joint IBM/vendor logos, openly acknowledging the need to work with the industry rather than against it. Its announcement of XENIX on the PC/AT, thus establishing a multi-user operating system standard for the application software industry, continues this pattern.

Ever since IBM announced its TopView development and operating environment, commentators have speculated on whether IBM will try to 'repossess' its PC market. TopView, in that context, is seen as the vehicle to pull application software back under the IBM covers and shut out the third-party developer. The greater the share of the market IBM captures, the more successfully it could call the tune and monopolise the application software business — so goes the argument. While the market has learnt the risks of trying to forecast IBM's possible directions, there is nonetheless a very considerable industry of 'IBM watchers' which people are happy to pay to pronounce on possible scenarios. It is interesting to note that although individual journalists and commentators have been ready to speculate that IBM is getting ready to 'close the doors', so far none of the major IBM-watching firms seem prepared to agree.

A recent analysis of software sales by application in the UK market for IBM compatible PCs suggested that of some 2500 titles in total, the average sales of truly vertical software packages was six per title — a commercial disaster for authors and publishers alike if true. The reality is probably that many titles do not sell at all, while the average is made up by slightly more successful applications. What seems clear though, is that the vast majority of PC packaged software sold is covered by a comparatively small number of generic applications. These would include spreadsheets and related modelling packages, word processors, graphics utilities, integrated suites, communications utilities and accounting applications. Why should IBM concern itself with offering access to a vast array of little-demanded software? Possibly to offer the PC user the widest possible choice. Even though the selection made is limited, the 'largest library of application software in the business' cachet is reassuring to the buyer — just in case. Possibly too the constant search for new opportunities by the software developers, and the widest cover of possibilities gives IBM the best chance of 'being there' if a new market or niche develops.

## Challenge to software developers

A number of other factors have to be considered by IBM or anyone else with a similar interest in software publishing:

1 Program development is costly and complex to do well.

2 It requires at least two areas of competence — design and programming skills and in-depth application knowledge.

3 It is a difficult combination of art and science. This is less of a problem when programming standard applications than when trying to be innovative and produce bestsellers.

4 Sales of programs do not relate directly to development costs. The corollary is that lack of care in development can produce an unworkable product from a good idea.

5 Some programs will have wide appeal and will sell perhaps thousands of copies. However, this will attract rivals and may lead to aggressive pricing. Others will have specialist appeal and high value, but will require a high level of application and marketing skill.

6 Faced with high development costs, programs need to be designed for easy adaptation to future environments. This feature alone may make the difference between profit and loss in an otherwise sound product.

7 Marketing personal computer software is a new business in which everyone is still pioneering. Some excellent products have hardly sold, other heavily marketed and popular software has proved to be bug-ridden in real user environments, and a liability.

This incomplete catalogue illustrates the challenge faced by software developers, and suggests that for any one company — even IBM — to produce a 'total' set of application programs is impossible. Added to all of these points should be the fact that IBM had to move quickly to join the personal computer business if it was not to miss gaining a vital market niche. It was clearly better to sponsor improved versions of the most popular PC software than to try to develop own-brand versions from new. The company took on the role of being a software publisher to support its own PC family. But if publishing successfully for one's own machines, why not for others as well?

The existence of standards makes it practical to run IBM logo software on any compatible machine. There is also a significant new opportunity area for application software running under UNIX. IBM could follow successful sales of software to its own and the IBM-compatible base by porting application software to other machines — thus addressing the total personal computer software market potential — and not simply limiting itself to its own-brand base. The possibility becomes less important, and less appealing, as more and more of the market adopts the standard and makes IBM's job of reaching all parts easier.

UNIX (and XENIX, Microsoft's version of UNIX) has been another area of major debate about IBM's intention and raises two questions. Firstly, is IBM going to modify its original 'personal computers are for single users only' stance and provide a complete implementation of UNIX/XENIX on the PC/AT? Secondly, what is the company's real attitude towards UNIX as a standard operating system?

## New definitions for computers

The personal computer question is probably academic. The Intel 80386 chip is perhaps only 18 months to two years away from commercial-scale availability. At the same time the equivalent PC/AT will be a four million instr/sec desktop system supporting four operating systems on the chip — rather more flexible than a VAX and with vastly greater virtual storage potential (64 trillion bytes). The terminals for multiple users will, by the same token, be able to contain 'intelligence' at no more cost than today's 'dumb' terminals. So the personal computer will simply have moved one step further down the cascade. We shall soon have to find new definitions for computers. 'Mainframe', 'mini' and 'micro' are losing their distinctions as technology advances, and perhaps 'personal computer' will replace 'terminal' and 'workstation' as the individual's device. In the meantime we can expect to see developments in sharing data via networks and multi-user systems (remember shared logic?) and sharing resources such as plotters and laser printers by similar means. The advantages of networked PCs include system resilience and 'removability' (able to take a system off-line without upsetting other users). The advantages of the multi-user system include cost as perhaps the major element. The initial application programs IBM published at the time of the PC launch were really the minimum necessary. They included a basic set of spreadsheet, word processor, ledgers, asynchronous communications, file and report programs, some training software and some games. Until quite recently the IBM logo library had grown comparatively slowly. It was the announcement in August 1984 of 31 new programs and TopView that caused the flurry of speculation that perhaps IBM was about to reclaim the PC software business and walk away from the third-party developers.

## UNIX

The question of UNIX as a standard operating system is in some ways more intriguing. Aside from the political question of why support and adopt an 'enemy' standard (UNIX is AT&T's), there is the whole debate about proprietary versus industry standards. Standards include the three areas of quality, safety and design. The first two of these are not relevant here other than to state that IBM's commitment to quality and safety are well known in the industry. It is in the area of the standard design that the proprietary versus industry argument arises. There have been suggestions that the traditional computer manufacturers, and especially IBM, may be reluctant to give up the competitive protection of proprietary design and adopt industry standards. The objective user argument is that by standardising such areas as operating systems and communications one is freed from the 'trap' of proprietary hardware. Should the manufacturers worry? Only if their customers feel trapped.

In the past, in the absence of industry standards in the relevant areas, IBM developed its own, as seen for example in the System/360 standard interface and the OS/360 operating system. More recently, as industry standards have emerged and been supported, IBM has acknowledged them. The company's statements on SNA/OSI bridges, on UNIX and on the token ring local area network (which conforms to US IEEE and European standards) are examples. The author believes that IBM will accept and support industry standards when it believes that they are functionally sound, they have sufficient support in the industry and especially if the Corporation can be involved in their evolution. Will IBM join the SVID group responsible for the UNIX standard? It would surely be in the interests of SVID, but would IBM be welcome? It will be interesting to observe the development of the SVID initiative, the growth of UNIX, SVID's acceptance by the industry at large, and IBM's future reactions to UNIX.

IBM has made a fairly bland statement about being customer-driven on the subject of UNIX. However, it has expended a considerable amount of effort in studying the topic and evaluating the product. It is reliably claimed that the company has UNIX running on every system in its product line, so if the signals 'turned green' it could launch a formidable presence in a short time. Several interesting implications arise, particularly in the context of competition. UNIX could provide a unifying thread running throughout IBM's current product ranges. At present the company has four major operating system environments, reflecting the divisionalised development of its systems. Another factor is that adoption of an industry standard operating system moves competition, to use a railway analogy, from ownership of proprietary 'track and trains' to standard 'track' and competing 'trains'. At first glance this may appear to be yielding an advantage to the newly emerging competitive colossus of AT&T. But consider a confident protagonist's view of the situation. A standard 'track' means I can drive my 'trains' into the competition's heartland. There are many 'Ifs' to be considered though — *if* the world settles for the SVID standard, *if* Microsoft is committed to converging XENIX with UNIX System V, *if* Intel is committed to supporting UNIX V and XENIX V on its chips... DEC stole an initiative from IBM and established the minicomputer business before IBM's General Systems Division developed its counter-thrust. UNIX would provide a clear run into the DEC customer base, not to mention the other seven in the X/Open group. There is no inference that adoption or support of UNIX is incompatible with maintenance, at least in the short/medium term, of IBM's proprietary operating systems. UNIX can run as a task under VM. As usual, speculation is rife that IBM is ready to launch a mide-range UNIX 'engine', perhaps for the System/36. This may do many things, including providing the company with a VAX-attack vehicle. Whatever the speculation may say it can be safely assumed that IBM is watching the UNIX situation extremely closely, is maintaining itself at combat readiness and, if UNIX continues to gain acceptance, will be able to field a formidable and competitive offering which will be aimed at superiority in all markets of sufficient size.

The author believes that in developing its range of PC software IBM is continuing its original direction. Nothing has changed as far as the third parties are concerned. The new IBM application programs are the results of the efforts of third-party vendors and those of IBM itself. The company will surely continue to publish joint logo software of the best possible quality. It will want to win a share of the total software business. As a software publisher it might not even have to port its products to non-IBM hardware — if the world adopts MS-DOS and UNIX as the standards.

## No retreat from the 'open' approach

There are several factors which would make a retreat from the 'open' policy counter strategic for IBM, including the following:

1  Limitation of future PC sales opportunities to only those applications supported by IBM proprietary application software, and vice versa. IBM has not done such a thing, even with its minis and mainframes. In fact, with minor exceptions, it has never produced its own application software — it has always depended on customer-written and software house-produced programs.

2  Making obsolete the past investments by IBM itself and the industry — a major waste, not to mention the extremely negative reaction such a move would produce in its customers and the industry.

3  The requirement for application software for personal computers in every environment in the strategic timeframe will take the combined efforts of IBM and the rest of the industry to fulfil.

4  As hardware becomes more and more 'generic' the information industry will depend increasingly on the software. Working with the industry and developing an IBM-quality software publishing capability which can harness the best developments in the software world must be of major importance. To walk away from the third-party software industry at this stage would appear to be self-defeating.

All of this suggests that IBM will continue its 'open' architecture policy in developing the PC family. One could go further and suggest that as the current 'micro' technology moves upstream the need for a sound third-party software industry will become more and more important for all manufacturers.

### A stable environment for efficient development

IBM's open strategy not only benefited its own PC, but by establising standards for application software provided the industry with a reasonably stable environment in which to develop. This undoubtedly focused more effort and investment into the development of program function and utility than would have been possible if software authors had had to spread their efforts across many different environments. If the industry will continue to accept such standards, and ensure that compatibility is maintained as they are developed, then this efficiency will continue to the benefit of all.

IBM can be a major force for or against such a trend. From its past experience with the PC it would seem unwise for it to abandon the open approach which has proved to be such a successful form of modern patronage. Considering the amount of software effort needed to support the future development of the PC it could even take more advantage of its present position.

Companies developing software in specific application areas could be sponsored on a 'no guarantees' basis by the provision of at-cost hardware, a 'developer's pack' of software tools, special support from IBM's PC software group and network connection to IBM facilities for program testing and evaluation, tips and so on. This type of sponsorship could have several benefits including:

- Focusing new development effort on chosen application areas
- Ensuring continued support for the IBM PC across a wide range of applications
- Maximising the chances of developing breakthrough products
- Spreading the business risk
- Building industry support for the company (PR)
- Harnessing specialist knowledge in vertical application areas
- Promoting vendors' products under the 'IBM-sponsored' banner
- Maintaining and improving standards, such as 'IBM-sponsored products meet the following minimum standards....'
- Adaptation to all countries and language groups
- Providing IBM with 'first refusal' on products offered for joint logo publication.

There are several areas due for major expansion where such focus could reap rewards: vertical markets, integration, networks, multi-user systems and ease of use.

## Vertical markets

As the large company market pattern settles down to a period of high volume acquisition of PCs, the majority of its needs are being met by a combination of currently available and in-house developed software. There are probably several areas still in need of development, eg host interconnected applications, but from the dealer's point of view the next area after local area networks for significant value added growth is the small business market. This still needs a great deal of vertical application software although IBM could sponsor this area, perhaps by a more direct involvement than the Dealer Associated Value Added Reseller programme it piloted in the US. Its efforts in the UK software market may be an indicator of future direction.

## Integration

The attempts of the market to increase the ability of programs to interchange data have already produced useful results. Integrated suites like Symphony and Framework have been joined by the integrating programs like Enable and Desq. TopView provides an integrating environment and signals a new direction, as seen also in Windows, GEM, the Apple Macintosh, Taxi and the WIMP approach generally. There is clearly a great deal yet to be done to help established users avoid having to rekey or abandon previously developed files, or attempt risky conversions. The development of integrating software seems to have a bright future.

## Networks

The potential for software in network environments hardly needs comment. The need to be able to interrogate files, store and forward, transmit messages, enquire and update remotely is already clear. In an environment where information services will be provided increasingly over networks, and where more business will be done and more private communication carried out, the need for software to cope more or less invisibly and very simply is crucial to the successful exploitation of the technology.

## Multi-user systems

The establishment of UNIX as a multi-user standard operating system will generate a demand for application software similar to that for single-user software. The growth of multi-user systems will, as in other areas, depend on the availability of application software. There is a major opportunity for the developers of UNIX application software to take an initiative. This applies particularly to software which has so far been identified as 'single user on PCs only'. Multi-user sharing of files, manipulated in personal versions of spreadsheets or word processors, which have been developed on PCs, will be in demand running under UNIX. The PC/AT with multiple users, and itself networked to other PCs, will probably be increasingly common in the near future. Although the requirement for personal computing will always exist, there are clear application needs for multi-user systems even in very small businesses.

## Ease of use

Every possible effort is needed to bridge the man/machine interface. If the computer is to achieve mass acceptance, as it must, then the bridge must be built from the machine to man. The other way is not possible in the mass use context. Tools which assist developers and users to generate menus, write 'help' screens, use single-keystroke macros, interpret touch screens and mice (or whatever interfaces are developed), are essential to the progress of application software. There is the potential for a significant sub-industry in this area alone. It is interesting that despite the development of some fine personal facilities software such as diary and time management, keyboard macro and other applications exemplified by the range of software from Caxton, its mass adoption has not yet begun. This seems to be at odds with the personal computer's essence of being a productivity tool for the knowledge worker. Perhaps we shall see a 'generation skip' and discover such functions as alarm and stop-watch operations in digital wrist-watches embedded in the ROMs of future PCs as standard facilities. By whatever means, their provision to all PC users must surely be desirable, necessary and inevitable.

## Summary

There are several compelling reasons why IBM should continue its original PC development policy, encourage the acceptance of standards and the design and production of PC-compatible software by the third-party industry. IBM itself can be expected to continue its practice of working with software companies to publish joint-logo software. It can also be expected to develop more of its own-brand programs. It can certainly be expected to compete vigorously as a software publisher for its share of the total software market.

# 12: Managing the micro/mainframe environment

**F F McMahon**

The Morgan Bank
London
UK

**The micro has already established itself as a necessary tool to meet the needs of corporate personal computing. Recently its role has begun to evolve as a front-end to the mainframe. A number of reasonable technical solutions are now available which allow the micro to perform all common types of terminal emulation. As corporations continue to increase the number of micros connected to the mainframe, the data processing culture must change to absorb this fundamental technical advancement. This paper provides guidelines for managing the co-existence of these two distinctly different types of computer architecture.**

*F F McMahon*
Freddie McMahon has many years' experience in commercial and financial computing environments. He originally concentrated on the development of IBM mainframe application systems, working for Hoover Ltd, the London Electricity Board and, since 1975, The Morgan Bank. In 1979 he joined the Systems Management Group which provided support to project teams. He was responsible for producing a range of technical practices including on-line design guidelines; software evaluations and implementations to improve productivity; presenting in-house training courses to project personnel and quality assurance reviews. In 1983 he joined the newly-formed Information Centre as Product Manager and assisted in the formulation of an end-user computing strategy. His specific responsibilities and achievements in the IC have included micro hardware and software selection; creation of a mainframe decision support environment with attached micro workstations; fast application development; user training; user standard practices and user support. Since late 1985, Mr McMahon has managed a newly formed Installation Management group which is responsible for capacity and service management of the centrally controlled hardware and software.

140

## Introduction

The micro has already established itself as a necessary tool to meet the needs of corporate personal computing. Recently its role has begun to evolve as a front-end to the mainframe. A number of reasonable technical solutions are now available which allow the micro to perform all common types of terminal emulation. Corporations now face the problem of managing the co-existence of these two distinctly different types of computer architecture.

The micro architecture, for a low cost, has set a high standard for functionality and ease of use. This allows the user to quickly develop a wide range of activities and applications. Only a short training period is normally necessary to make an unskilled user reasonably proficient in using a micro. Another benefit of this architecture is its ready availability and reliable response times.

Mainframe applications are often criticised by the user for their expensive solutions, long lead times and poor operational service levels (ie availability and response times). The mainframe, however, has painstakingly built a good reputation over the years for reliable applications. This has been achieved by having data integrity, application controls, comprehensive security and full back-up/recovery services.

The main demand for connecting micros to mainframes comes from users. This is because they need easy access to data which can then be copied by the micro. Data processing already recognises many of the benefits which can be achieved by linking these architectures. There are also just as many pitfalls for the inexperienced attempting such links. In particular there is a need to maintain data integrity. The stakes are high. Failure to achieve a link which maintains data integrity is likely to be costly, perhaps resulting in a corporation losing its competitive edge. Success will lead to another significant step towards full office automation, helping a corporation to be more competitive and dynamic.

This paper examines the applications, tools, benefits and pitfalls of using the micro as a front-end to an IBM mainframe. It excludes the more advanced application of having a micro able to access any number of different mainframes and minis.

## The benefits of having micro/mainframe links

There are many benefits to be gained from linking the micro to the mainframe. The following categories have been used to identify some of the major ones:

1  Transaction/control/information systems.
2  Decision support systems.
3  Office systems.

## Transaction/control/information systems

There are two important benefits which involve the on-line environments of transaction, control and information systems.

The first benefit involves data preparation. Normally it is only applicable to an application which requires local data preparation. This type of activity can be considered for processing on the micro and works particularly well when there is no dependence on the mainframe for data validation. On completion the data can be batched and sent to the mainframe. Standard activities such as validation and confirmation of the data can still be performed (repeated if necessary) on the mainframe. This benefit provides the user with more flexibility for the micro application to accommodate quickly further local processing requirements for reports, enquiries and investigative analysis.

The second benefit involves reporting and investigative analysis during the on-line day. Traditional teleprocessing systems cannot cope efficiently with these types of requirement. Mainframe applications can often be easily adapted to allow data download to the micro. This provides the freedom for the users to produce their reports and perform investigative analysis locally. Other benefits include saving costly mainframe processing overheads and program development costs which can be more cheaply achieved using micro software.

## Decision support systems (DSSs)

DSSs on the mainframe provide general utilities for professional staff to perform planning, analysis and strategic work. These utilities mainly involve using data enquiry, financial modelling and project management tools. The data enquiries can be the type which have either been programmed by data processing or by the user. Professional staff often require the flexibility to 'play' with the data. This can be accomplished by allowing extracts of data to be copied from the mainframe into the micro. The data needs to be converted to the format of the destination software. Various micro software utilities available today allow the professional to have the flexibility to massage the data in many different ways.

The benefit of having a micro linked to the mainframe DSS excludes the ability to update the corporate database unless it has been a feature specifically designed into the mainframe system.

## Office systems

The micro has already established itself as providing easy to use utilities. The most popular of these utilities are word processing, graphics, and spreadsheets. Similarly the mainframe is increasingly becoming accepted for corporate office system facilities — document distribution, library service, diary and message services. Having an interface between the micro and mainframe provides a good distributed processing balance between personal and corporate office system facilities.

## System design for the micro/mainframe link

The following major goals need to be addressed to establish a successful link between the mainframe and the micro:

1 Install a reliable technical solution.

2 Retain the integrity of the corporate database. This involves having a controlled interchange of information between the two processors.

3 Tighten current mainframe security in recognition of having intelligent workstations instead of the traditional 'dumb' terminals.

4 Ensure user friendliness by providing simple operating activities to cater for the complex interchanges between the two processors.

5 Consider the ergonomic implications.

142

## Technical solution

There are three methods addressed in this paper for connecting a micro to a mainframe as follows:

1 Obtain hardware/software which allows the micro to perform 327X emulation.

2 Use a gateway switch which converts standard asynchronous protocols which can be produced from most micros to a bisynchronous format needed to access the mainframe.

3 Use a micro specifically built for micro/mainframe processing (eg IBM PC 3270).

These methods can be met today by products available from IBM or third-party vendors. The difficulty facing a corporation is to determine which products are appropriate for their needs. The following guidelines briefly assist with this type of evaluation:

1 Determine the type of 327X emulation required (eg the micro needs to act as a graphic workstation).

2 Data transfer between the mainframe and the micro can be catered for by a packaged solution. A good 327X emulation product provides the software for data transfer between the micro and the standard IBM mainframe conversational monitors (TSO, CMS) or the IBM teleprocessing monitor (CICS). Where the mainframe is within an SNA network then one of the more attractive options is to use a packaged solution which allows the micro to emulate an SNA workstation. Using a gateway switch solution will probably require in-house development of the data transfer routines. This also applies to the IBM PC 3270-type micro which normally only caters for data transfer using details from one screen at a time. Another aspect to be considered is the speed of data transfer. Experiments need to be conducted to ascertain which options meet the service levels required.

3 Special consideration is needed to ascertain the type of keyboard to be used. This subject is one which can easily be overlooked though it is often the most difficult to resolve. The keyboard must now meet the needs of the two processors — micro and mainframe. To meet this requirement means having two logical keyboard layouts for the one physical keyboard. The IBM PC 3270 uses a special keyboard. It has approximately 30 per cent more keys than a standard keyboard. These extra keys cater for the specific requirements of both processors. The 327X emulation products overcome this problem by supplying the software which provides the two logical layouts. However, the layouts they choose may not be desirable and in-house modifications then become necessary. These first two solutions provide a 'hot' switch facility which allows the user to alternate easily between each mode. Using any type of micro with the gateway switch option may cause further problems. First, there probably will not be any software supplied with the gateway switch to develop the logical keyboards. Secondly, the keyboards for some micros do not physically have all the keys needed for the mainframe activities (eg examine the capabilities of the micro for supporting function keys and PA keys).

4 Determine the characters needed which are applicable to the country of operation (eg £ sign for the UK). The packaged solution may not meet these requirements.

5 Ideally, when the micro is transferred into a workstation to meet both local and mainframe processing an easy-to-use front-end is built. The terminal emulation solution for connecting the micro to the mainframe should be able to interface smoothly with this front-end.

The costs of connecting a micro to the mainframe are expensive. These costs should include the 327X emulation software/hardware, cabling, controller ports, additional communications equipment (ie line drivers, modems) and mainframe ports. There are various ways by which these costs can be reduced. One option is to consider having a micro local area network whereby only one of the micros acts as a fileserver with the mainframe. Similarly, a mini could act as the interface between the mainframe and a group of micros. The following issues should be addressed when considering the option of using a micro network:

1 Economics. The costs to be considered should include not only the obvious such as the hardware/software purchases but also the support costs — operational, technical, in-house documentation and training.

2 The capability of the operating system in a multi-user environment.

3 Support for software packages especially in a multitasking application.

4 File management capabilities.

5 Response times. These should include the micro using virtual disks.

6 The available menu and password facilities.

7 Ease of use.

8 Ease of adding extra micros.

## Integrity of the corporate database

The most restrictive limitation involving the interface of the micro to the mainframe is data management. Currently it should be assumed that there is no data management software which provides overall management of data scattered between the mainframe and the linked micros. Thus, if a record is updated on the mainframe then it cannot automatically update the data copies resident on the micros.

The effect of this limitation requires the system design to cater for the movement of data between the mainframe and the micro whenever integrity needs to be maintained. This can be likened to the traditional problems of keeping duplicate data by a batch system and an on-line data entry system. An interactive on-line solution can be sought by using the on-line enqueue technique involving synchronisation of the data updates covering a combination of mainframe and micro files. Using this method should be avoided as there are many complex issues at stake which would need to be addressed.

When the corporate data is to be maintained from data sent from the micro it is still necessary for the mainframe to repeat all appropriate validation and confirmation checks. Repeating this process is necessary to ensure the data is validated against the latest information immediately before the update to the database is actioned.

New rules are needed for users who are able to extract data from the corporate database and manipulate it with their own personal utilities. Any presentation of information which has involved the user unofficially changing the data needs to be clearly reported. This ensures the audience is aware that the data being used does not necessarily have the same integrity as that associated with the corporate database.

## Tighten mainframe security

Security systems of mainframe on-line environments were often built for usage by 'dumb' terminals. The design of these security systems may be based on assumptions which are no longer true today, especially as the new terminals added to the system may be intelligent workstations (ie micros). One example involves the security design being based on the assumption that only a limited number of attempts would be made to enter the application illegally. This assumption may no longer be true when a micro can be programmed to attempt hundreds of sign-ons within a few seconds compared to one attempt by an operator. Security systems should be reviewed before micros are permitted to be used instead of the traditional 'dumb' terminals. Remember, the success of 'hackers' today is mainly based on their usage of micros to bypass the security of a system!

## User friendliness

Ideally, the personal computer should be user friendly, thus allowing the user to get on with the job instead of having to waste effort on understanding technical jargon and complications. There are various options for providing user-friendly front-ends:

1 Use an icon front-end with a mouse, either by having this facility built into the computer (firmware) or by purchasing specialised software.

144

2 Purchase an integrated software package which normally has a menu front-end. One potential problem with this method is that it tends to be restricted to the functions provided by the packaged software.

3 Develop an in-house menu environment which is applicable for the needs of the corporation.

## Ergonomic considerations

The following factors need to be considered when installing equipment for users:

1 Generally, when selecting a monitor for infrequent use, colour is preferred unless monochrome is more ideally suited. Consideration should be given to the glare and smudges that appear on the screen.

2 There are many types of input device. All these should be considered against the type of work the user is undertaking.

3 Printers can be noisy for an office environment, therefore special covers for noise reduction should be considered or, better still, the purchase of noiseless printers.

4 If a micro is to be moved about a lot then it should be portable and not luggable, or it should be put on a specially adapted trolley. Make sure the trolley can go through the doors of the office!

5 Standard desks are not ideally suited to micros and therefore special desks, especially modular furniture, should be considered.

6 One of the biggest ergonomic problems involves the amount of wiring needed to support a micro configuration. Again the correct type of furniture and proper electrical circuits should solve this problem.

## Managing the system — the role of data processing

Having installed a micro/mainframe system we need to manage this new type of environment. Data processing departments have traditionally acted as low-profile technical services. To be successful in the new environment data processing will have to learn to communicate effectively with the new breed of end user. This communication is essential to help establish effective control. Accompanying this emphasis on communication is a raising of the data processing profile until it becomes a highly visible service provider. The data processing department of the future will be very different; managing these changes is now a key issue.

## Establish control

The micro/mainframe environment involves a new dimension of complexity for data processing to control. To ensure there is effective control requires careful strategic planning. When the basis of the strategy has been established, it is necessary to refresh it regularly for catering with frequent changes to the user's requirements — especially to cater with personal computing, new demands for capacity, industry trends and legal requirements. This method should ensure the major technical components are always in place to support the continually evolving environment.

To keep pace with this ever-changing computer environment in a corporation requires central control of purchases for all computer hardware, including personal computers, minis and local area networks. These purchases can be vetted to ensure they meet strategic, or where necessary, tactical needs, ensure the purchase is justifiable, check there is adequate capacity available when the purchase is to use existing shared computer resources and finally to obtain the appropriate authorisation. This purchasing control is an effective way to partially manage the integrated micro/mainframe environment.

Another aspect of control involves environment management. This covers control of changes, problem analysis and security control. This latter category involves such things as:

1 Assignment of user identifications and private work spaces.
2 Managing and booking up of user work spaces.

3 Checking password violations and various audit controls.

4 Allocation of processing constraints on users and monitoring their usage of functional and data levels.

## Data processing personnel

Today, when a user makes a request for a new systems application, the data processing department needs to consider the best way to action the request. This may not involve traditional solutions being employed as various types of processors and software could be applicable. Even the resource to develop the requirement may be different. A traditional solution probably requires no change to the resourcing of the project. Using fast application tools may not only include data processing personnel, but could also involve a joint development with the user, or even the user developing his own application.

Traditionally, data processing carefully controls changes to applications. This requirement is obviously still needed but needs to extend where applicable to DSSs and office automation systems which normally involve a micro workstation connected to a mainframe or mini processor.

The new type of computer environment requires data processing personnel to have additional training. This involves all types of personnel from management level to designers, analysts and programmers. Without this training, the data processing consultant is at risk of not being able to advise the user of all the options available to meet a new requirement. As some users are already conversant with the other types of environment, they may be at an advantage over the consultant by knowing some additional computer options which have not been part of the proposal.

## Development considerations

There are various steps involved in developing applications for micro/mainframe applications. A few guidelines are listed below to be considered in conjunction with traditional development methodologies:

1 Define the business requirements. This is the same as for traditional systems development though special orientation classes may be needed for the users to understand the benefits of the micro and its link with the mainframe.

2 Define the system taking into consideration the technical implications of a mainframe/micro link, especially those involving the network and file conversions relevant when crossing software boundaries.

3 The software programming of the system can be performed jointly by data processing and the user when micro or mainframe non-procedural facilities are available.

4 Micro/mainframe systems need to be carefully monitored by capacity management when they are in production. This is because their usage of the computer resources can easily be changed by the user developing his own functionality.

5 The mainframe transaction systems should have their security reviewed to ensure they are still good enough to cope with the new types of connection, such as the personal computer.

6 Effort is required to ascertain the effect of current data legal implications, especially as the user can now develop his own systems.

7 It is necessary to design around potential network failures as professionals become more dependent on the mainframe/micro link.

8 The environment needs to be factored into an implementation plan to ensure there is adequate air conditioning, electrical circuits, facilities for cabling and the ease for adding new facilities.

9 The implementation of micros linked to the mainframe should take into account expected or potential future company reorganisation changes. This is necessary to minimise the cost and time factors for moving a micro which is linked to the mainframe.

## Installation management

The installation management function is responsible for maintaining a reasonable standard for serviceability and availability of computer resources. This function has noticeably grown in complexity with the linking of micros to the mainframe. The effect of this change is not only limited to these new types of user but can also effect the traditional user population when the same computer and network resource is being shared.

The main area of activity involves ensuring there is adequate computer/network capacity to meet the real needs of the corporation and also to agree and maintain the associated service levels. This can be difficult to achieve especially when it involves professional staff using the micro/mainframe link as their usage patterns are more varied compared with those involved with traditional on-line systems.

Capacity management has not been a success story for data processing even though it often only concentrated on a simpler domain compared with the one being faced today. The need to perform capacity management is even more essential than ever before because the micro/mainframe link is likely to be involved with heavy resource utilisation from information systems, DSSs and office systems. Those systems have many facilities which can be used in uncountable numbers of ways, some of which are very high on resource usage.

The installation management concept is based on a new type of data processing group responsible not only for capacity management as described above, but also providing service levels and resource cost services. These functions are planned, monitored and reported to management, users and technicians. It is for this reason that installation management is ideally organised outside the traditional systems programmers group because it needs to be more business oriented, even though a high degree of technical competence is still necessary.

## Information centre

The information centre is a concept which involves a specialised group to focus on the personal computing needs of the user covering micros, office automation systems and DSSs.

It initially needs to formulate, and then maintain, a detailed end-user computing strategy in keeping with the overall corporate strategy. This involves many aspects and includes the following:

1  Create a standard list of supported hardware and software.
2  Develop end-user computing environments.
3  Instigate adequate controls and procedures for the purchase of personal computing products.

The information centre needs to develop a user training program which:

1  Publishes and promotes the use of personal computing products among designated end-user departments.

2  Provides training to management.

3  Trains users to use the micro hardware and selective software. This may involve using a combination of external courses, internal courses, self study and one-to-one training.

In keeping with traditional systems, it is still necessary to have standard practices. The information centre should develop these to cover:

1  Handling corporate data which takes into account any laws associated with the home country and those countries where the user can send or receive data.

2  Application development, especially for systems to be regularly used and produce output upon which decisions are made.

3  Processing of systems, covering the need for operational procedures so that more than one person can use the system, making changes to the 'production' system, and of course back-up/recovery procedures.

147

Additional guidelines should be documented covering how to take care of hardware and diskettes. It is also important to state clearly that copying of licensed software is strictly prohibited.

The information centre should also provide general services such as a 'help desk' so that the user has a contact point for any queries or problems, as well as offering a quality assurance service so a manager can independently review a system that has been built by his own staff. Where users intend to build their own systems, the information centre should assist with the initial development in conjunction with the user until he feels confident to continue on his own.

Another important area for the information centre to be involved with is an administrative function whereby it handles the maintenance and purchase contracts for personal computers. This ensures that the best service, maintenance and discounts are achieved. It should also be its responsibility to liaise with product suppliers concerning queries about potential or already purchased products. The assignment of user identifiers and workspaces for micros, office automation systems and DSSs should also be administered by the information centre. Overall the information centre should provide a good all-round user support and consultancy service.

It is unclear whether the information centre should be within or outside the data processing group. No matter where the information centre is sited it is necessary to define its interfaces with users and data processing, otherwise conflicting standards will emerge, especially with the handling of the micro/mainframe link.

A variation of the information centre help desk can be considered as representing the interests of the whole of data processing. This provides the user with one point of contact to action a request which may be handled by one of any number of groups within data processing. These groups could cover:
- Security control
- Traditional systems development and maintenance
- Fast application development
- Strategy
- Micro applications
- Communications and networks
- Operational processing support
- Professional workstations (micro/mainframe).

By having the one help desk, user requests can be handled either entirely by the help desk or by directing the user to the appropriate group to handle the request. This avoids the user being confused over who should receive the request for work and adds a new level of control which can follow up on the request to ensure it has been handled promptly and correctly.

The micro itself has created various security issues which need to be addressed by the information centre:

1 The hardware and software is portable and therefore could easily be stolen, especially as it is such an expensive commodity.

2 As all micros have diskette drives any person can come along with their own copy of an operating system and reboot the computer. This allows an easy bypass to most security built around micro systems.

3 The ease of access to diskettes means that systems data and software could easily be changed by unauthorised personnel.

The following safeguards can be taken to counter some of these security issues:

1 There need to be clear guidelines on the security measures that should be taken within a corporation.

2 A complete inventory should be kept of all hardware and software. Also appropriate insurance should be taken out against theft and damage.

3 The system unit should be kept locked when not in use or kept in a locked room or secure area.

4 Important data should be encrypted and, where feasible, application software should be compiled or prevented from being read or changed.

148

**Managing the system — the role of the end user**

The end user will be the vital component of any effective micro/mainframe link. End-user support and contribution is essential. However most end users need to be educated in their new role and made aware of the participation of their peers. Keen end users will become the software developers of the future if they are given the right assistance. Data processing operational standards and development standards need to be assimilated if end users are to benefit from their new tools.

## End-user orientation

The first step for users is to ensure they have a good understanding of the computer facilities and options available to them. There are many different ways in which this orientation can be achieved:

1  Orientate managers with the strategy for the convergence of the micro and mainframe environments. This includes describing the facilities which will be made available and how these should benefit the end user.

2  Orientate the staff with a different view of the strategy. This concentrates on providing more detailed information on the use of the new facilities.

3  Demonstrations of hardware and software in action are a must. Until a user can see how quickly a spreadsheet application, for example, can be built and then subsequently changed, it is difficult to comprehend how such a package can be useful. It is also necessary to demonstrate applications which are applicable to the user's work.

4  Having an open day is a good way for the user to informally see demonstrations of the different services and products on offer.

5  Once users have completed their orientation it is necessary to ensure their knowledge is kept up to date. This can be partially accomplished by the open day concept where the latest offerings can be prominently displayed, but also there should be a regular publication of the latest offerings by using leaflets (probably supplied by the manufacturer of a new product), newsletters and posters.

6  Specialised training in the use of a facility can be met by:
   * Interactive training — some of the modern courses make use of a video coupled to a micro
   * Custom-built courses which can be prepared by internal personnel or consultants — these can be presented at live sessions or built as self-study courses
   * Video courses which are increasingly becoming available for micro/mainframe-type activities
   * External courses specially designed for end users covering anything from basic computer appreciation to knowing how to use a specialised software package.

## End-user development

Special care should be taken by users when selecting the tools to build systems. Traditionally, data processing has, for many years, been using Third Generation programming languages. This means using a language whereby the logic is procedural, thus the code has to be written in sequential order. Languages like BASIC are procedural. Though they are relatively easy to learn at a basic level, the complexity of using the language substantially increases when a user stops building functions and starts to build systems.

As the system increases in complexity, so does the risk that the development will not be done properly. Many years ago data processing painstakingly learnt the skills and methods needed to build an application using Third Generation languages. Today, they have overcome the problems of inefficient, poorly designed software and lengthy programming development effort by having their programmer staff trained in using structured techniques for designing, coding and testing. A user should not undertake development work where he will need this level of expertise and skill.

Fourth Generation languages are more ideally suited for end users. This involves building a system without the need for sequenced code. However the user should be aware of the following:

1  Some products are sold as being Fourth Generation when in fact they have only some of those features, such as use of a relational database, but generally use Third Generation procedural code.

2 Fourth Generation languages tend to be very machine intensive and therefore involve an expensive computer processing resource. This is very applicable when they are used on a central processor such as a mainframe or mini.

3 The user should be aware of basic file screen and report design considerations to minimise the effort required when changing the application. Guidelines should be made available from the data processing group.

4 For complex systems, professional support should be sought especially with the design of the application. Any application which supports concurrent user access should be deemed as complex.

When a user has a facility which allows him to build an application on the mainframe or the micro and interchange the software and the data between the two environments, then special design issues need to be considered. This is applicable to financial planning software which can be shared between the two environments mentioned. Some of the considerations are as follows:

1 The speed of transfer between the mainframe and the personal computer can be slow.

2 Batch processing in an on-line environment, such as report production, is machine intensive and should be run either on the micro or overnight on the mainframe.

3 Some of these packages allow the user to have direct access to the operating system. This is not advisable, especially for the mainframe, and therefore a protected environment should be built around the software to prevent access to the operating system.

4 Passwords are allocated both on the micro and the mainframe to protect unauthorised updating of the software and data and to control interaction with the expensive mainframe resource.

## User back-up and recovery

The user needs to give special consideration to back-up and recovery, the latter only being needed in a crisis and therefore must be guaranteed to work. The type of medium for the back-up needs to be selected, such as using diskettes, tapes or disk cartridges. Plans should also be made for when to replace the back-up media as the life expectancy tends to be short with only 40 hours usage for a diskette! The method for back-up is important and three generations of back-up should be mandatory. Where the user data software is contained on a central resource such as a mainframe, then back-up and recovery is easier as it is in the hands of professional operators. However, the user should determine again the frequency of the back-up and what type of recovery facilities should be made available, such as having a file and/or disk restore.

## User procedures

Each department should allocate a person to manage security and procedural control, covering such things as the control of password allocation and the frequency by which passwords have to be changed; determining who can have access to computing facilities, what facilities each person can have, and how much time a person can be allocated at the computing resource; checking that departmental working practices are still followed, for instance that a certain method of calculation is being used, and reporting and investigating security violations or believed irregularities.

## Problem-resolving procedures

The more users are involved with personal computing the more they should have support for resolving problems quickly. After a while it is likely that most problems a user experiences will have actually happened before. Therefore it can be deemed wasteful if time is spent investigating how to resolve the problem when the answer is already known elsewhere. User time spent in resolving computer problems can be minimised by:

1 Ensuring that the user is aware of error messages and solutions documented in the software manuals.

2 Developing an in-house error message manual to cater for messages not previously documented or those which are not easy to find in existing documentation.

3  Developing an in-house problem determination procedure.

4  If the above documentation does not help a user then he/she should be able to contact the data processing help desk or specialist as appropriate.

## End-user awareness

A new problem facing users is when to use computers instead of traditional desk methods. This is not an easy area to address as standard advisory procedures are not available, nor are there monitors to measure the effectiveness of the decision taken by the user. Also there needs to be an awareness of when to contact data processing or to go ahead and develop an application within the user department. As previously mentioned, the user needs to be aware of the hardware, software and network capabilities available. The manager of a department should be aware of the need to effectively control the time spent by his staff using computer facilities. A basic project control system may be needed for applications being built by staff.

## Testing considerations

Care is needed to ensure important systems are properly tested. Traditionally, data processing can have up to five distinctive stages of testing before giving a system production status. However, a user typically only has one stage of testing and this is normally unstructured and not controlled.

## Reports

Care needs to be taken for computer reports produced by users. There is a tendency today to believe the accuracy of information produced by reports generated from a computer. This is based on the confidence slowly built up by data processing for applications they develop. This could be quickly undermined if users produce reports with inaccurate information which is then used for decision making. Some guidelines to follow are:

1  All reports must be properly labelled as to their source (ie the individual who prepared them, systems employed and data used).

2  All reports must be properly labelled as to the authorisation of the content, even to say if there is none.

3  To state the users responsible for identification and authorisation on the source of this report data.

It should go without saying that all reports are properly identified and have a date of creation.

## Additional end-user responsibilities

The user should also ensure that there is a safe environment to protect equipment and software and access to data is protected where necessary and encryption is used for confidential data. It is also the user's responsibility to ensure proper back-up facilities to protect against erasure and that all information generated is correct. Good standard practices should also be documented to protect against misuse of the personal computing environment.

## Summary

The main objective of this paper is to provide guidelines for managing the environment in which the micro and the mainframe co-exist. There are many new danger areas which can be avoided by setting the appropriate standards and guidelines. As discussed, some organisational changes are probably needed to cope with the additional responsibilities and to ensure the right emphasis is being concentrated on the new domains.

The full extent of using the micro as an intelligent mainframe workstation within a corporation is yet to be realised. Generally it is being assumed this type of workstation will be available on every desk in a corporation by the end of this century. As we slowly move towards this goal, we must begin changing the data processing culture now in order to absorb this fundamental technical advancement.

---

# 13: The architecture of the IBM System/38

**M Newman**

Pacific Associates
Basingstoke
Hampshire
UK

**When announcing the System/38 in 1978, IBM intended it to bring dominance of the sophisticated small systems market. For a system of its size, System/38 brought together advanced features never before seen in a single system. This paper analyses the system by examining its architecture, advanced use of technology, Control Program Facility and data management functions.**

*M Newman*
Mike Newman joined the Data Centre Services division of IBM UK Ltd in 1969 when he worked on System/360/65 running OS/MFT, OS/MVT and DOS systems under ASP. He later specialised in the System/3 range of machines and telecommunications systems in particular. He has spent a total of three and a half years in technical education in IBM and two years in systems engineering. He spent most of 1978 in the IBM GSD headquarters in the US on assignment to the System/38 development project, and returned to announce the product to IBM in the UK. He left IBM in 1979 to help found IDS Limited, a software house specialising in packages for System/34, 36 and System/38. In 1985 he left IDS to found Pacific Associates, a new System/38 consultancy and system development company based in Basingstoke, UK.

## A new machine

System/38 was announced on 24 October 1978, as the long-awaited replacement for the successful IBM System/3 range. By this time the machine had been six years in development and was taking far longer than expected. With the marketplace moving very clearly towards workstation systems, IBM's small systems marketing division of the time, GSD, was becoming exposed, and interim solutions had been required. These had included the abortive System/3 model 4 and the highly successful System/34 — a system which had to play a much bigger role in GSD's marketing strategy than was originally planned, and which evolved into the System/36.

System/38 was intended to give IBM dominance in the sophisticated small systems market, and brought together advanced features never before seen in a single system, especially of this size.

## Current implementation hardware

System/38 continues the trend to high integration of components started with the System/32 and System/34. All major parts are contained in the system unit: main and control storage, the minimum required auxiliary (disk) storage and the high-speed channels, all peripheral device attachment microprocessors, and the System Control Adaptor (SCA). In addition, a diskette magazine drive and workstation controller (microcoded control unit for local terminals) are included in the base system unit.

Five models are currently available, giving different performance options. The system is presently evolving from the early model family (models 3, 4, 5, 6, 7 and 8) into the current family (18, 20 and 40). A model 10 and a 60 are expected in 1986. All models have identical structure but use different technologies for control storage and main storage, with different cycle times. Any model can be upgraded on site to any other model (they are all externally identical) giving the System/38 the widest power range of any of IBM's general-purpose computers.

The machine is essentially a multiprocessing system to the extent that there are specially-designed processors to manage instruction execution, virtual address translation and magnetic media attachment. Slower device types are controlled by their own I/O controllers which are microprocessors attached to the channel. There are two channels although currently only one is used. Both are multiprogrammable and have a burst data rate approaching 5 Mbytes/sec.

## Advanced use of technology

A basic premise of the System/38 hardware implementation is that advances in component technology would allow the machine to develop without repackaging. That is, one basic CPU frame would accommodate all models for the life of the product. So far this has happened, and System/38 has made heavy use of some of IBM's most advanced components. IBM's 64 Kbit Metal Oxide Semiconductor Field

155

Effect Transistor (MOSFET) chip and 704-circuit logic chip were first announced with the System/38. The model 40 uses the 256 Kbit memory chip and logic with the same cycle time as on the 308X series; and IBM's one Mbit chip is expected to be implemented first in the System/38 model 60.

## System/38 architecture

## Machine structure

System/38 is designed in several layers in a tight mix of hardware, microcode and software (see Figure 1). The major characteristic of the system is its high-level machine interface in comparison with other machines, such as IBM System/370 or DEC VAX. That is, the lowest level of programming support and the nearest a programmer can get to the hardware — the Assembler level on System/370 — is more sophisticated than on any other machine currently available. This machine interface (actually called MI on System/38) is supported by IBM-written microcode which supports the range of instructions provided at the MI level. Some of the more than 300 instructions are shown in Figure 2. IBM software writers, such as those responsible for the high-level language compilers, write their code using a language called PL/MI (based on PL/1) which incorporates the System/38 machine interface instruction set.

MI instructions are not usually executed directly by hardware. Their functions are interpreted by a layer which IBM calls Vertical Microcode (VMC) which, in turn, is based on a more primitive Horizontal Microcode (HMC). VMC is so called because its instructions tend to be executed in series to perform a specific function. By contrast HMC instructions exhibit a high degree of parallelism, with several circuit-level functions being performed in one instruction cycle. The HMC supports an internal interface level, accessible only to IBM development engineers, called the internal microprogramming interface (IMPI). This IMPI language is what the VMC developers work with.

Below HMC is the logic circuitry of the machine and HMC instructions are directly executed from high-speed control storage by the on-chip machine instructions.

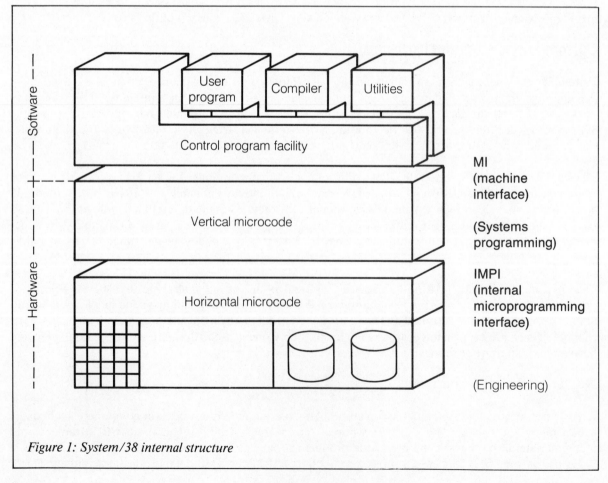

*Figure 1: System/38 internal structure*

```
        COMPUTATION/BRANCHING              PROCESS
           Copy numeric                       Initiate process
           Edit                               Suspend process
           Convert external to numeric        Destroy Process control space
           etc                             EVENT
        PROGRAM                               Monitor event
           Create, Destroy, Materialise program    Signal event
           Activate program               MACHINE
           Call program                       Modify machine attributes
           Store parameter list length     DATABASE
        AUTHORITY                             Activate cursor
           Create, Destroy user profile       Create data space index
           Grant, Retract authority           Delete data space entry
        OBJECTS                               Insert data space entry
           Suspend object                     Set cursor
           Ensure object                   INDEPENDENT INDEX
           Reclaim object                     Create, Destroy independent index
           Lock/Unlock object                 Find independent index entry
        QUEUES                             SPACE
           Create, Destroy queue              Create, Destroy space
           Enqueue, Dequeue                   Modify space attributes
        SOURCE/SINK (I/O)                  MACHINE INTERFACE
           Create, Destroy CUD, LUD, ND       Terminate machine processing
           Request I/O
```

*Figure 2: System/38 machine instructions*

This layered approach to the development of System/38 has a number of benefits — at least to IBM. In the first place it allows IBM to keep the application programmer and the IBM software developer away from details of the actual hardware of the machine. For example, the machine takes care of all access to disk storage — you cannot tell that System/38 uses disks at all; it appears only to have a very large area of main memory. Secondly, it allows IBM to vary the internal implementation details without affecting user programming. This has happened on numerous occasions since announcement, most obviously when the company brought out a new family of System/38 processors, based on different chip technology and component packaging, in September 1984. It also allows the machine's developers to move functions between the various layers to achieve different price/performance tradeoffs. For example, technically it is perfectly feasible to implement large sections of HMC in silicon, or to implement the machine on several parallel processors, perhaps using Reduced Instruction Set (RISC) processor technology. There is nothing in the System/38 MI architecture which prevents this. In fact quite the opposite; there is a lot of scope for parellelism in the MI design.

The third major benefit to IBM is the essentially closed nature of this architecture as far as other manufacturers are concerned. IBM needs to reveal next to nothing about the internals of the System/38 machine, making it very difficult for add-on suppliers or competitors. The 4300 by contrast is extremely vulnerable to this sort of competition.

## Von Neumann or not von Neumann?

There has been some discussion about whether System/38 is the first radical departure from 'von Neumann' computer architectures. Almost without exception, today's computer designs have been based on principles suggested by John von Neumann, a Cambridge mathematician, in the Thirties.

A primitive von Neumann machine has the following characteristics:

1 *A single, sequentially addressable store.* Program instructions and data are stored together and, if storage is not big enough, need to be brought from an external device to storage before the processor can access them.

2 *Program instructions cannot be distinguished from data.* The machine cycles through various phases, controlled by instructions decoded from memory. If, through a programming error, the machine reads data bytes during its instruction fetch, it will attempt to decode these as an operation and execute them. The data characters may even, by chance, represent a genuine instruction and the results are then, as the IBM manuals say, unpredictable. Assembler programmers actually depend on the ability to modify instructions 'in-flight' by treating them as data in some operations.

3 *Data attributes are defined by the instructions, not by the data itself.* Because of this, most commercial computers have a whole range of similar instructions, such as ADD NUMERIC, ADD BINARY, ADD HALFWORD, ADD PACKED, etc. If the data is declared incorrectly, the results are 'undefined'. The compiler or assembler may or may not trap the error. All kinds of nonsense may be generated, eg an instruction may even try to add two instructions together.

4 *No built-in security.* Clearly no help is offered by the machine itself to assist in the multiprogramming environment or even to protect the programmer from himself.

## The System/38 machine interface

At the MI level System/38 looks very different from the classic von Neumann machine. Whereas other systems provide instructions at the machine level to support operations only on bits and bytes, System/38 supports operations on structures called *objects*. Everything stored in the machine is stored as an object of one type or another. Some of these objects may be listed as follows:

- Access group
- Context
- Controller description
- Cursor
- Data space
- Data space index
- Index

- Logical unit description
- Network description
- Process control space
- Program
- Queue
- Space
- User profile.

There are machine instructions (MI instructions) to create, modify, destroy and materialise objects. Thus, to create an executable program, the compiler generates a string of MI instructions from the high-level language code (an intermediate form of the program called IRP) and then issues the CREATE PROGRAM machine instruction. This instruction calls a VMC function called a translator which translates the IRP into microcode. The result, simplifying it somewhat, is a program object. The machine assigns a unique six-byte virtual address in storage, then finds auxiliary storage on disk to store it. The program is said to be encapsulated — that is, its contents cannot be directly accessed or modified and the user is unaware of its location. All objects are encapsulated in this way.

## Object addressability

To manipulate an object such as a program, the user refers to it by name. The machine searches an index held in another type of object called a context (the application programmer refers to this as a library) to find the virtual address of the object. When found, the machine checks to see if the user is authorised to use the object. This authority is indicated in the object's description and in the user's user profile (another object). If he has the necessary authority, addressability to the object is stored in a system pointer (another object) to reduce the time taken to service subsequent requests for the object, and the machine invokes other routines which translate the virtual address to a disk address and page the object into real main memory in sets of 512-byte pages. The user task then has access to the requested object, via the system pointer.

The system distinguishes a pointer through extra 'tag' bits set and tested by the machine itself on the bytes of the pointer. In addition, the pointer also specifies the kind of authority the user has to manipulate the object — to destroy it, for example. It is impossible for any function but the machine itself to set and modify pointers so the integrity of all objects is guaranteed. The System/38 machine thus offers a very high level of security to the user. This accessing of objects via authorised pointers is referred to as capability-based addressing in computer systems theory.

## Dictionary addressing

Instead of having data attributes and values embedded in the program instructions, as on other machines, data is defined in tables separately from the program instruction stream. This allows for *generic* machine instructions (eg there is only one ADD), array support and for late (execution-time) binding of data to the program. One practical result is the absence of a linkage editor on System/38. A program can dynamically call any other program on the system at any time.

Since the object type is defined in the operation itself, the machine can do integrity checks on the validity of the operations. Thus a nonsense instruction is rejected by the machine when the system pointer is resolved. Also, because modifiable data values are stored outside of program instructions, all programs created on the machine are re-usable and re-entrant. That is, they can be shared by multiple callers and only one copy of the instruction stream need ever be active.

## Control Program Facility (CPF)

System/38 machine instructions provide support for facilities normally implemented in the software of operating systems. Built onto this machine architecture is an optional IBM-written licensed program which provides an interface for application developers to the machine. Although it is a chargeable option (the rental charge is currently around £450 a month or it may be bought for a one-time charge of £16 000) every System/38 customer installs it since the alternative would be to code all applications in System/38 machine language. Since the PL/MI compiler is not freely available this would be difficult.

CPF aims to provide an easy to use interface to the basic machine facilities. One of the major ways it does this is through the unified Control Language (CL), a highly modular, command-oriented language. The CPF facilities are the same on all models of System/38 irrespective of hardware configuration, so a system generation is not necessary.

CPF is modified and extended in new releases brought out about every nine months. VMC (and even HMC) changes are also provided when required, as hardware Engineering Changes (ECs) to the machine. These are shipped on diskette. CPF facilities are used by user programs, the high-level language compilers, and the IBM-supplied utilities.

## CPF objects

In a similar fashion to the machine itself, CPF provides the concept of a set of objects from which the user builds his application. Some of these object types are listed below:

- Class
- Command
- Control unit description
- Data area
- Device description
- Edit description
- File
- Job description
- Job queue
- Library
- Line description
- Message file
- Message queue
- Output queue
- Program
- Print image
- Subsystem description
- Table
- User profile.

These objects are based on, but not the same as, the System/38 machine objects. A database file is an example of a composite CPF object which provides an easier way of managing data than with the basic machine objects it is based on (see Figure 3).

Every CPF object has a set of attributes associated with it, such as the name of its owner (this is generally the user who created the object), its type, and the date it was created and last saved off-line, and on which diskette or tape volume. Even if the object (eg a file) is off-line, CPF considers that it still exists on the system and will request signal for it to be restored if it is used in an application.

CPF objects are created with Control Language (CL) commands. This unique CPF language provides over 300 commands to manipulate objects. For most objects, the relevant CREATE command is all that is needed to create the object.

CL commands have a simple verb-noun structure with a variable number of usually optional parameters.

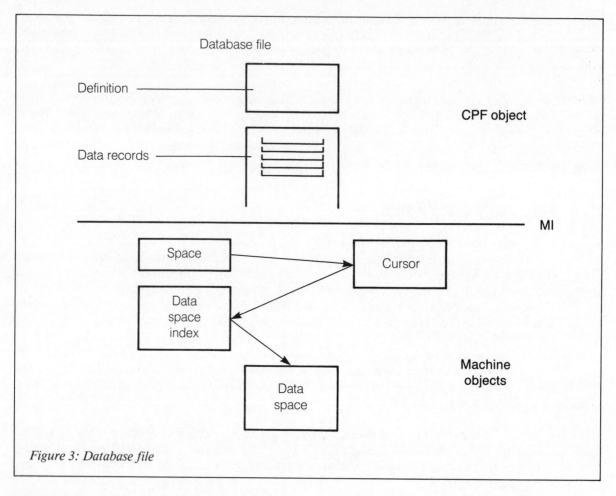

*Figure 3: Database file*

Any available system function is supported through a command. Some examples are as follows:

- CALL                Call a program
- CHGOBJOWN      Change on object's owner
- CNLJOB             Cancel a job
- CRTRPGPGM      Create RPG program
- DLTF                 Delete a file
- DSPFFD             Display file field descriptions
- DUPDKT            Duplicate a diskette
- OVRPRTF           Override print file
- PWRDWNSYS     Power down system
- RLSJOBQ           Release a job queue
- STRPRTWTR       Start print writer.

Since all commands are constructed in the same way, application developers can create their own commands and change IBM supplied commands to suit their requirements. CL statements may also be compiled into CL programs. This gives the function of JCL or OCL procedure calls on other systems, but without the huge overhead of interpreting each statement before execution. It also allows file handling and logic capability.

## Data management

By far the most powerful and useful feature of System/38 is its intrinsic machine-supported data management facility. In fact, System/38 can be fairly characterised as the world's most advanced *data management* machine. Everything in the architecture of the machine is aimed at supporting the definition and management of data, outside of user programming. To CPF, all data on the system is stored in and accessed through files. There are files to define the interface with all attached I/O devices, called device files; and files which define the data stored permanently on the system, called database files. Whatever the type, the user programmer sees all files on System/38 in a similar and consistent way. There are many parameters stored as part of the file on System/38 which are defined within the application program on other systems.

## Database management

Most computer applications have been built around sets of files which store records defined as sets of fields. The concept of files is well understood. However, as data storage and processing demands grew in the Sixties, particularly in on-line, information-oriented environments, manufacturers developed more complicated data management software and the first database management systems (DBMSs) appeared.

The chief goal of early DBMSs was the attempt to separate the user's view of the data and the way it was organised (the so-called conceptual schema) from the physical form. The physical definition of the database and of the logical views which the user or programmer is aware of become the responsibility of an individual called the Database Administrator (DBA). The programmer typically uses a data sublanguage as an adjunct to his application language in order to request database functions.

Unfortunately, a characteristic of almost all commonly-used DBMSs (including IDMS, IMS and DL/1, and TOTAL) is the amount of effort the customer is required to spend in structuring the relationships between data items or fields. It is generally difficult to change the database design once it is developed, and it requires dedicated maintenance. Worse, DBMSs are often closely associated with their implementation on disk-based systems, and make use of pointers and relative address chaining to create the database structure. The result of all this is that most DBMSs require a complete conversion from earlier file-based application designs, through analysis and design before implementation, and a good deal of maintenance for optimum performance. The ensuing huge cost of implementation has made such systems unattractive to all but the larger sites.

## System/38 database files

The System/38 database is seen essentially as a collection of flat files. These have a similar organisation and can be processed in the same way as traditional disk files, with the difference that the file always includes a definition of its stored record formats and the access path to the records, as well as the data records themselves.

Database files are of two types:

1 Physical files actually store fixed-lengths data records of a single record format in *members* of the file.

2 Logical files provide alternate views (different record format or access path) of the data in one or more physical files.

The collection of these files is the System/38 database. There is no concept of separate databases for different applications as there is on many systems.

The user creates a physical file by defining the record format and access path in the Data Description Specification (DDS). This fixed-column form is similar to an RPG coding sheet, but has nothing to do with RPG. Data definition is central to the System/38 and DDS provides the mechanism for the analyst or programmer.

The DDS source statements are keyed in at a screen using an interactive utility to a source file; then the user (generally a programmer) issues the CREATE PHYSICAL FILE command.

The system creates and encapsulates the physical file and assigns it space in virtual storage. It then allocates a minimum amount of disk space (typically 4 Kbytes) and as records are written to the file subsequently more disk space is allocated, not necessarily contiguously and not necessarily on the original disk. Any I/O appears to the programmer to be simply to a disk file.

At this stage, the file is operational but contains no data records. The user has to add a member to the file (he can do this at create time) to store the records. A file can have one or many members; each member would have a unique name. Records can be placed in the member using an application program, a utility or a COPY command.

CPF uses the key specifications of DDS to construct a machine index and associates this with the file. All subsequent operations on the file use this index, and whenever a record is inserted or deleted in the file, the index is dynamically modified to reflect the change. This 'dynamic access path maintenance' is what gives the System/38 database much of its power.

To use the file in a High-Level Language (HLL) program such as COBOL or PL/1 or RPG III, the programmer specifies it by name. At compile time the HLL compiler extracts from the file the details of the stored record format and uses this to define all the data fields to the program. On subsequent GET (READ) requests to the file, the system uses the index to locate the required record in the member, then ensures the data fields map to the desired format before passing the record to the program.

A useful feature allows the programmer to suppress the retrieval of the record format at compile time and instead to define the record format within the program in the traditional way (normally the COBOL programmer would not need to code a data division). This greatly aids conversion from existing systems, since it removes the need to modify working programs in order to use database files — they can continue to run as if with the original disk SAM, DAM or ISAM files.

## Logical files

Logical files are created in a way similar to physical files. That is, the analyst or programmer uses the DDS to define a record format and/or access path which is actually based on the definition of specific physical files. The logical file definition provides an alternative to that in the based-on physical file. Logical files have several other capabilities: fields can be excluded from the physical record or have their data attributes changed; fields can be joined to form a new field (but fields in the physical record cannot be subdefined), and a logical file can give the physical fields different names. The access path (index, if you like) can be based on the ascending or descending values of any field or group of fields in the record, or none at all; duplicate keys can be allowed and presented in first in/first out or the opposite sequence; and records from up to 32 physical file members can be merged or joined to form new records. The logical file access path can also select or omit records based on the value of any fields in the underlying physical record, making it very useful for applications where a 'status' character in a record represents 'deleted order' or 'stock item temporarily allocated' and so on.

There can be any number of logical files based on the physical files, and the machine will automatically update the access paths whenever a record is added or modified. There is never any need to sort the files since the access paths are always maintained in key sequence. The system checks whenever a new logical file is created to see if it can make use of an already-created access path, to minimise overhead. Nevertheless the access path maintenance routines in the machine's microcode are obviously critical to the performance of the System/38, and it is quite astonishing just how fast a properly-configured machine works under operational conditions.

System/38 database is the best IBM data management scheme presently available. It provides virtually all of the facilities of DB2 but, by contrast, it is very easy to define and to use database files with high-level language operations familiar to any programmer. All normal file operations are supported including generic key and relative record processing so the database files are compatible with the disk files supported by most other machines. Dynamic maintenance of the file access path ensures the accuracy and integrity of data for multiple users, and the reformatting and selection capabilities of logical files provide excellent support for concurrent logical views of the database.

Security to the field level can be implemented through logical files and is based on the basic machine/CPF-implemented security. There is no other way to access stored data on the System/38 except through the database so there is a high level of integrity.

The system supports all relational operations including Project and (read-only) Join, but also permits the user to process data as if it was organised hierarchically or as a network. In contrast with other relational-type database systems System/38 supports a large number of operational users, and is not simply a vehicle for online queries.

## Device files

DDS is also used on System/38 to describe the record layout of display and printer *device files*. A CPF command creates a display file or printer file which can then be used by any HLL program, which selects which display or printer record format to read or write in the file by name.

Because the data fields are defined outside the application program, program code can be made independent of data definition. Data description specifications for screen formats can refer to a database file for field definitions, and so not only all database files but also all screen and report formats can use the standard data definitions in the application field reference file. System/38 offers the analyst a degree of data independence in the application which is beyond that offered by most systems (see Figure 4).

System/38 goes even further in submerging the intricacies of communications programming below the machine interface. To the application programmer it is irrelevant whether a screen is local or remote; the system handles all the communications functions. Similarly the programmer is not involved if a user calls a program from a completely different system such as another System/38 or even a 4300; System/38 will establish the SNA communication session and manage the data transference and routing between the machines. The programmer on the System/38 sees the other system through a CPF object called a communications file.

The System/38 approach to integrated data management has the following advantages:

1 Programming is simpler because data definitions are already made and all files are handled the same way as traditional disk files.

2 Data definition is system wide, and typically done only by management or application analysts, not by individual programmers. This improves the integrity of data and simplifies program maintenance.

3 Only one data definition interface needs to be learned, so application development and conversion are speeded up.

4 File reference commands provided in CPF reduce the need for application documentation.

5 Since data is defined to the system, utilities such as data entry application generators (DFU) and Query can be built into the standard system support.

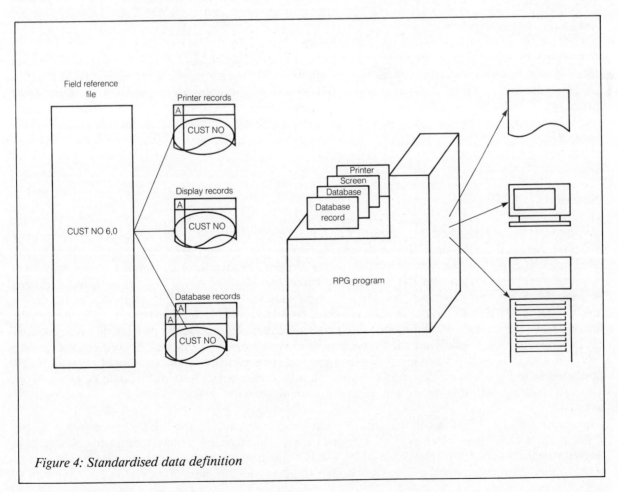

*Figure 4: Standardised data definition*

6 File attributes can be overridden at execution time. For example, a database file can be directed to a printer device file or even a display file. This helps significantly in testing.

## Recent and future developments

IBM had invested over $1000 million in the development of System/38 by the time of its announcement. The early sales performance was disappointing and there have been constant rumours over its future, particularly as it competes very strongly with the traditional 4300 which IBM understands much better. With the demise of the General Systems Marketing Division within IBM in 1982, things looked bleak for a while, but in 1983 the Corporation made a huge new commitment to the System/38 and developed a new family of processors, took the main memory size to 16 Mbytes to support 256 on-line local screens and developed three major new CPF releases.

Characteristic of these CPF versions has been the accent on communications, including SNA support for System/370 hosts and 3270 screens, peer-to-peer coupling of System/38 (and 4300 and System/36) processors and support for X.25, and an even stronger accent on office support under IBM's DIA/DCA rules. The IBM PC is now very strongly supported and all the signs are that this link will be made closer and closer. Evidence of the productivity benefits to IBM's own development programmers of the System/38's high-level machine interface is in the fact that in the space of 18 months about two million lines of extra code was written and tested and delivered, not including the complete implementation of the Graphical Data Display Manager (GDDM) colour graphics code from 4300, function for function. And all of this is part of the basic CPF, and standard on all models of the System/38.

The present level of sales of the machine in the UK is the best ever and the installed base will probably have topped 1000 machines by the end of 1985. System/38 is recognised by the financial people within IBM to be the most profitable in terms of growth once installed, pointing to high levels of user satisfaction. The machine is beginning to be IBM's main competitive account winner and to be gaining credibility with even 'large systems' IBM users as a replacement for IBM's VSE (DOS) operating system on System 370/4300.

It is widely expected that a new top-end processor, to be announced in 1986, will bring 32 Mbytes of memory and 512 local workstations, as well as adding more on-line disk storage and providing IBM's leading edge arrival into truly distributed database configurations. A 16 million instr/sec array processor is planned for later, to take the machine into the critically important manufacturing/ engineering applications area. A new SQL-like query language will be announced, and office support strengthened.

## Summary

It is difficult to imagine a better architecture than that of the System/38 machine for the hugely complex software required in the applications environment forecast for the 1990s and beyond. IBM's only alternative is some evolutionary derivative of the System/370 architecture, running operating system software such as MVS/XA and DB2. System/38 by contrast is designed to support a 64-bit addressing scheme (MVS/XA on the System/370 supports a 31-bit address) which would allow the machine to address every byte of all the disk space ever manufactured. Its architected machine interface implies no specific hardware, so different implementations could make use of parallel processors; provide different memory technologies including optical disk; and support different communications mechanisms and user interfaces through optical fibre and voice/image processors. The application programmer should continue to be insulated from the hardware dependencies through microcode. In fact System/38 would be an excellent point to start implementing the current ideas in knowledge-based systems.

Having said all this, IBM is still very much a marketing company and still heavily committed to the System/370 architecture, which is now, effectively, a world standard. It has a difficult task ahead in reconciling the architectural approaches of its past with the demands of the present and future. It must be very attractive to try to set the computer design standards for the next 20 years, and to continue to dominate the information systems of the world, as it has done so successfully with System/360. IBM's success in these fields is the envy of other manufacturers. System/38 offers IBM an opportunity to repeat the act — but does the Corporation have the courage to take the risk?

# 14: SNA, open systems and IBM

**P Rigg**

Logica UK Ltd
London
UK

**First released more than 10 years ago, Systems Network Architecture (SNA) is still IBM's central communications product. Rapid developments in technology and increased levels of user demand continue to change the market for communications solutions. Using the Open Systems Interconnection (OSI) Reference Model as a framework for comparison, this paper considers the facilities which SNA will need to support over the next five years.**

*P Rigg*
Peter Rigg specialises in SNA, public data networks, office automation developments and their relevance to end-user organisations. He joined Logica UK Ltd in 1973 and has been involved in the design and development of such networks as Euronet and the British Steel Network. He has advised a number of international organisations on various aspects of communications policy, strategy and implementation.

## Introduction

The rate of change in communications is increasing and the following three facts are prominent:

1 Improvements in hardware technology are still occurring at an amazingly high rate.

2 There is enormous scope for using new technology to improve the performance of a large and rapidly growing group of workers, ie office staff.

3 There are two principal limitations to 'progress': firstly, our ability to produce good applications programs fast enough and, secondly, the communications infrastructure. Both are reacting swiftly to the pressures being placed upon them.

The Intel 8086 16-bit microprocessor, already obsolescent, has the raw power of a PDP-11/45 at a fraction of the price; main memory is so cheap that nobody now thinks of building a general-purpose system with less than 128 Kbytes to start with and disk-based backing store comes at £75 per megabyte. We already have personal workstations providing the following features for £3000:
- A 16-bit or, perhaps, 32-bit processor
- Up to one megabyte main memory
- Megabytes of backing store
- A communications link to shared files and large-scale processing power.

Variants with less power and sophistication, right down to the Sinclair ZX81 at £50, are becoming increasingly available. IBM, which only joined the race in 1981, was expected to sell 2 500 000 personal computers in 1985. Office automation and personal computing are considered to be the major market areas of the 1980s and this is one point on which IBM and 90 per cent of all other suppliers appear to be in agreement; what differ are their market solutions.

IBM, together with other traditional manufacturers, is constrained not only by what it offers now but by the attitudes of both its own staff and its major clients. However, IBM has, in the last two or three years, made rapid progress in meeting these challenges and its PC range already has over a quarter of the business microcomputer market. The advent of IBM into this unfamiliar market in 1981 must have been triggered by the success of companies such as Apple.

Everyone is now more or less agreed on the nature of technical constraints on progress:

1 The applications in the relatively new area of office automation are complex — and potentially far more so than for data processing. Combined with the potential for personal (business and home) computing, they offer almost boundless variations which will tax to the limit our ability to analyse requirements and produce software solutions.

2 Computer usage in the 1980s has shifted sharply towards the interactive mode, with the user on-line. Huge increases in communications capacity and sophistication will be needed to support the following:
   • Interaction whenever it is not local to the desktop
   • Access from the desktop system to remote files and programs. The first law of desktop micro systems is that their power is always exceeded by the ambition of their user. Hence the need for flexible, reliable and powerful resource-sharing schemes with access to large databases, mainframes or bureaux, along with the current emphasis on Local Area Networks (LANs).

## Systems Network Architecture (SNA)

In this rapidly changing market, IBM is also making changes — in its product range, how that range is marketed and, above all, in its attitude. SNA is the corner-stone of all strategic IBM products concerned with communications and many new application packages will emerge during the next few months and years which will only run within an SNA environment. Indeed, it could be argued by IBM that it is only because SNA communications modules are already available, offering a practical networking base, that these packages can be developed quickly and efficiently. Without SNA, the overhead of developing a suitable base each time would be too great.

The first release of the architecture and its supporting products in 1974 confirmed IBM's emphasis on star networks based on a central mainframe supporting multiple terminal devices; the only significant concession to distributed processing was that the terminal could be intelligent, perhaps even offering local processing facilities, but it could, within the SNA network, talk only to the central host. With the introduction of SNA 3 in 1978-1979, it became possible for SNA host nodes (mainframes) to intercommunicate and for remote terminals to access more than the single host system. This support of distributed processing did not mean that system control was in any way devolved to the (intelligent) terminal systems; it could only be shared between the SNA host nodes, each of which looked after its own network domain, and one end of each SNA session still normally had to terminate in a host node — terminals could not be linked together (at least not within SNA itself). A recent announcement — the Network Routing Facility (NRF), described briefly below — does, however, offer a partial but specialised solution to this general restriction.

Roughly in step with the SNA 3/4 developments, IBM made great improvements in the field of SNA network control, so that multihost networks can now be configured, monitored and controlled from one or more operator positions without massive user disruption in non-critical failure situations. This kind of management capability is becoming essential, with the number of on-line users growing rapidly during the early 1980s. Having networks with thousands of terminals means that much more attention needs to be given to the question of service availability and network support.

Until recently, SNA support was centred very heavily on mainframes, with unintelligent terminals. This bias is now shifting so that SNA host node facilities of some kind exist also in 8100s, System/36s, 5520s and Displaywriters and the master-to-slave relationship is itself yielding to peer-to-peer communications.

How do SNA and the products based upon it meet the requirements of today? Below, facilities are identified which, it is suggested, IBM and other serious computer systems vendors will need to support over the next five years. The list is expressed in terms of the Open Systems Interconnection (OSI) Seven-Layer Reference Model, which provides a useful framework for analysis. Starting at the bottom, the list is as follows:

1 Physical layer: support will be needed for Integrated Services Digital Network (ISDN) and other interfaces in the 64 Kbit/sec range — voice and non-voice, and preferably through the same twisted pair. IBM will offer something of this kind — on its Rolm-based switch or separately — for specific workstations, along with high-speed (> 1 Mbit/sec) interfaces onto a shared LAN highway. This will not be available for two or three years but will be discussed later in this paper.

2 Link layer: Synchronous Data Link Control (SDLC) will need to accommodate 127-frame window sizes for satellite transmission. Also, there will be a need (especially on a PBX/LAN) for voice communications to mix with data and, therefore, for a priority system and different error control procedures. IBM will cover the priority question with the token-passing access protocol; the link protocol to support mixed error procedures will need different hardware or microcode.

3 Network layer: here the main need is to accommodate both connection-oriented and connectionless (for very short, burst-mode) communications. SNA is efficient at the former but cannot support the latter without significant modification. IBM's solution is likely to be for users to set up SNA sessions between user equipment and then to multiplex separate conversations onto the session as required. This could be either satisfactory or very expensive, depending on the application. IBM, like everyone else, will also have to interface the private switching networks, based currently on 3725s, with the public systems, which are growing in importance. The System Network Interconnection (SNI) Gateway system, described below, is important in this respect. A similar need is emerging to interconnect LANs of whatever access technology with each other and with SNA/SDLC or X.25 wide area networks. IBM has not yet shown its hand in this area, since the high-speed, general-purpose LAN is due either this year or next.

4 Transport layer: this is the crucial layer, represented by the Virtual Telecommunications Access Method (VTAM) Application Program Interface (API) for IBM mainframes and by the recently ratified 'open' CCITT and ISO protocols. Implementation of these protocols should greatly facilitate interworking of incompatible systems and IBM's reaction to OSI-based developments will be critical. In West Germany, IBM announced the Open Systems Network Support program product, sitting on the VTAM API, to allow specific higher-level protocols (non-IBM) to be added by the user. In addition, it announced general support for the ISO transport and session layer protocols, resident above VTAM and made available in 1985.

5 Session layer: as IBM is recognising, the need is for both master-to-slave and peer-to-peer sessions (see the section on LU6.2 below), where the peers can be mainframes, or mini- or micro-based processes. Also, intelligent workstations need to conduct multiple concurrent sessions and to dynamically switch between them. Current PUT.2 SNA products are not built efficiently enough for this and IBM will need to modify products (around LU6.2) quite considerably.

6 Presentation layer: here the main emphasis needs to be on supporting a mix of data, text, image and graphics (and maybe voice annotation) within the same bit stream and output 'document'. IBM is making progress, using the document interchange and content architectures, but is making things difficult for itself by trying to implement the protocols on so many office products. Compatibility with 'open' standards will again be a big problem. It is also desirable, especially now that all user equipment is becoming intelligent, to utilise one standard intra-network data format (for efficiency and reliability) and for each end point, at or above the presentation level, to convert to and from the end user's presentation formats. IBM is not very good at this at present but improvements are likely in the near future — again centred around LU6.2.

7 Application layer: the development of a common end-user interface across different communications services (for example, command formats, error messages) is becoming a high priority. IBM has announced some first moves in this area. Also, there is the need for many 'Level 7' services, such as message store and forward and file transfer where, again, one can foresee a clash between IBM's approach and the CCITT/ISO community (for example, SNADS and X.400).

8 Network management: network users are beginning to demand systems with very high availability as a matter of course, plus easy expansion and reconfiguration. Built-in mechanisms for diagnosis and monitoring are essential. IBM is investing heavily in this area and it is probably where its systems score most heavily against those of other computer vendors. This area also forms the basis for IBM's new ventures into Value Added Network Services (VANs).

In summary, one can say that, as a base for future developments, SNA has proved reasonably powerful and flexible, although some problem areas persist. These are:

1 Connectionless communications: these can be supported but not efficiently.

2 Distribution of network control and management facilities: these are incorporated into SNA host nodes at the moment (VTAM/Systems Services Control Point (SSCP) and the superimposed Network Communications Control Facility (NCCF) products) but there are some problems with putting them onto type 2 or 4 nodes. However, the main restraint is commercial, not technical. The type 2.1 nodes are a first step towards decentralisation but much more will be needed.

Until recently one end of any SNA session had to reside in a host node, in the S/370 context 'behind' VTAM and the SSCP. A session could not be set up between two nodes where neither of them were hosts. To allow point-to-point connection between, say, a pair of word processors without the need to go through a mainframe host — a facility well worth having — IBM introduced a simple session type, called LU Session Type 4.

Much more recently, in an acceptance of the inevitable extension of intelligence down to single-user devices, IBM has introduced the following two facilities:

1 A cluster controller node variant, called PUT2.1, where the device can, using SNA procedures, connect a local user port (LU) to an LU in another PUT2.1 via leased line or dial-up, without utilising a host node's SSCP services. A PUT2.1 contains, instead, a Single Node Control Point (SNCP) controlling sessions with 'downstream' devices which may themselves be 2.1 nodes. The SNCP is, in effect, a minimal SSCP (not before time) and a 2.1 node is a minimal host node.

2 A Network Routing Facility (NRF), where LUs in different non-host nodes can converse through a 3705, ie without a host node LU being involved.

The 2.1 node, which is coupled with the general LU type of the future, 6.2, forms a strategic announcement — which, however, IBM has played down until various other features and services are ready to be announced. NRF is less important. After these announcements, one can easily foresee SNA networks where genuine peer-to-peer communications will be common.

One design aim of SNA is to allow users to request sessions without specifying the destination's network address. This location independence, which is a useful facility allowing resources to move location without all interested parties having to update their address book, is implemented through a table look-up in the SSCP, which resides only in a host node. This is why all session requests, which are made by name, have to be routed to the host node to find the current address. There is absolutely no technical reason why, in a System/370 context, this directory table look-up function cannot be moved out of the mainframe into, at least, the 37X5 front-end; this distribution will probably be preceded by a facility allowing sessions to be set up between users in any node type as part of the PUT2.1 facility described above.

It should be remembered, however, that devolution of this kind means that any 'autonomous' node will also have to implement its own network management facilities, since the (mainframe) SSCP now has no knowledge of what is happening. This is a problem but it is not by any means insuperable: many little nodes can survive without management support. The 2.1 node SNCP is also likely to have a mechanism to inform the SSCP of sessions set up between 'downstream' users and to send status and alarms to any central network management facilities, such as Network Problem Determination Application (NPDA).

Much of the recent development of SNA has gone into the area of network control, in terms of the following:

1 More flexible network configurations: for example, the SNA 4.2 facilities allowing multiple links between 3705s, 37X5s and the remote concentrator 37X5s and 3710s.

2 Built-in monitoring and diagnostic capabilities: from the IBM modems up through the PUT2 nodes, all of the newer devices now contain considerable chunks of monitoring software and the ability to report on status and events to a network control point.

3 Better operator facilities for network control: mainly incorporated in the NCCF and NPDA program products but including facilities to take over the operation of remote host systems automatically.

## Document Interchange and Document Content Architectures (DIA/DCA)

Recognising the need to ship documents of different formats between different IBM equipment and to support a variety of office functions on all this equipment, IBM has defined some common rules and procedures referred to as DIA and DCA. These are Level 7 facilities above SNA.

If one regards SNA as a transport mechanism like the postal system, DIA represents the instructions on the envelope to the computer systems storing and distributing the document. DIA functions cover document distribution, filing and retrieval, and reformatting. DIA also defines a profile for the document, ie its author, subject, date, addressee, circulation list and its filing location; these data elements form a base for subsequent document filing and retrieval. The DIA program logic, incidentally, attaches to SNA through an LU6.2 session.

DCA is concerned with the contents of the envelope. The destination computer must be capable of processing the contents in some way, so certain allowable formats have been (or are being) defined. They are:

1 Final form DCA, where the text is directly viewed or printed, with all formatting commands having been processed.

2 Revisable DCA, where the text has embedded formatting and other commands, so that the destination can undertake the revision before turning it eventually into final form.

Through revisable DCA, text in preparation can be shipped between different IBM text composition systems for shared processing — a powerful facility. In addition, a mixed DCA is being defined to support a bit stream composed of data, image and voice.

DIA/DCA is slowly emerging from the chrysalis stage, with partial implementations on the 5520, DISOSS, the Displaywriter, 8100, DOSF, System/36 and Scanmaster. The power and potential of DIA/DCA, in terms of ensuring product range compatibility over the foreseeable future, are very evident — and yet another example of how IBM's systems approach can easily outstrip the competition, at least in the long term. There is, nevertheless, plenty of opportunity for competitors before the 'long term' arrives, since IBM does not show anything like as much apptitude in addressing the other main issues of the moment: a friendly user interface and an integrated set of office user functions (text creation, spreadsheet processing, business graphics, mailbox, information storage and retrieval, and voice integration). The following three points are worth noting:

1 In spite of this grand architectural edifice, IBM salesmen are still unable to offer some of the basics. Why is there no automatic telex interface on any IBM system, for example? There are, after all, more than one million telex terminals throughout the world and everybody uses the service.

2 It also seems a pity that until quite recently the most common IBM terminal of all, the 3270 display, was not part of the DIA/DCA family: like the PC, it is still not fully integrated.

3 IBM is not the only organisation developing document interchange standards. Some time ago the European PTTs began the Teletex development, to extend the telex service towards communicating word processors. The CCITT Teletex standards (F.100, T.61, T.62 and T.70) approximate to the higher levels of SNA, to DIA and to final form DCA. Teletex did not, in its initial form, include the concept of a revisable document and it defined only graphic characters to be printed or displayed; storage, retrieval and format conversion were considered as local functions, outside the scope of the standard.

Within CCITT and ISO at the moment there are three concurrent developments. They are:

1 Towards an all-embracing Office Document Interchange Facility (ODIF) capable, as with mixed form DCA, of supporting text, data, image and voice in revisable and final form. ODIF is still at an early stage and the ISO working group is waiting with interest to see whether IBM (which is represented on the committee) will offer DIA/DCA as an international standard.

2 Towards 'mixed mode' Teletex, capable of integrating text and image (pictures, signatures, etc) within the same document, transmitted between computer stores.

3 Towards a Message Handling System (MHS) standard, suitable for mailbox store-and-retrieve environments. This is a far more ambitious development than Teletex and could be the basis for general-purpose, interprogram communications in the more distant future. These standards, now referred to as the X.400 series, were ratified by CCITT in 1984.

Teletex and X.400 were developed for document transfer between computers. An X.400 software package within every computer product, including IBM's, may well become a *de facto* standard in the late 1980s.

## LANs

In terms of local connectivity, IBM still relies heavily on individual coaxial connections on many of its devices. In addition, systems like the 4300, 8100 and 3600 Financial Terminal offer a local (and remote) SDLC loop, which uses twisted pairs of wire to interconnect processors and peripherals in a ring topology.

### Loops

The loop configuration has inherent reliability problems because any break in the loop interrupts all data flow. The 8100 system loop utilises two twisted pairs (main and alternate loop circuits) to minimise this problem. Another problem with the current loop configuration is its relatively low speed. The maximum data rate of the SDLC loop is 38.4 Kbit/sec. This low bandwidth and the central polling technique limit the number of devices which can be attached to the loop without serious reductions in system throughput.

It is important to note that distribution of data over these loops (or for that matter, over coaxial cables) is not addressed by SNA. In an SNA environment, the devices that are the ultimate source and destination of data (display stations, printers, etc) are supported by LUs in the device controllers. SNA is concerned with transmission of data between these LUs and not between the devices themselves. For example, in a session between a 3278 display station operator and Customer Information Control System (CICS), SNA concerns itself with communications between the LU supporting CICS in the host mainframe and the LU in the 3274 supporting the particular display station that the operator is using. SNA is not concerned with the actual distribution of data from the controller to the display station. The 3274 employs a special, non-SNA protocol for transmitting and receiving data across this connection. Moreover, SNA is unaware if this connection is via a direct coaxial cable or an SDLC loop.

### Series/1 ring

IBM has developed a ring-based LAN, using Series/1 computers as the individual stations. The system offers 2 Mbit/sec bandwidth, controlled on a register insertion principle by each Series/1. There is no master control station. The Series/1 already offers a wide variety of communications protocols, which are not only IBM proprietary, and can be used with the ring to interconnect foreign devices to IBM hosts, as well as offering IBM proprietary protocol support. The problem with this product must be its cost: a minimal network costs £35 000 (plus £5000 for the software).

### 327X cable networks

Many clients have miles of IBM coaxial cable, connecting 327X screens to 3274/6 controllers, each screen needing a point-to-point line. The Zurich experimental LAN (see below) will be addressing this problem, which can only get worse as on-line terminal use increases. Various suppliers offer a 3270 network LAN-based alternative, which is sometimes more cost effective (especially when installing new devices). IBM itself has recently introduced a stop-gap device, the 3299, which multiplexes up to eight 3278/9 or printer devices onto one cable to the controller. When, in the next two to three years, users have generally moved away from the 327X family to more intelligent workstations, these presumably will be all attached to the general-purpose IBM LAN.

The loop products emphasise IBM's traditional dependence on a star network controller; the loop is driven by a master station. The Series/1 ring moves away from this principle in that all the nodes on the ring can be peers in relation to each other; however, the solution cannot be said to be optimal since each node is a small minicomputer costing some thousands of pounds.

At its research laboratories outside Zurich, IBM has for some years been developing a genuine, distributed control, high-speed LAN. The Zurich LAN is a token-passing ring: IBM is mounting a strong campaign to promote token passing, which, it claims is definitely superior to the CSMA/CD control procedures used on products like Xerox's Ethernet. Whatever the technical merits of this argument (and they are strong), the impression gained is that IBM is basically trying to ensure that CSMA/CD and, therefore, Xerox products do not become a *de facto* standard. IBM, after all, knows the strength of *de facto* standards.

174

It is also fairly clear that the Zurich experiment is not just about the academic niceties of the control method. The LAN is designed for a wide variety of client environments; its basic topology is a ring but each user device attaches, over potentially more than just a few feet, to a shared Ring Wiring Concentrator (RWC). The topology is, therefore, a star/ring combination, with much of the cable passing through the RWCs, which contain logic to test each device when it powers up and can switch control round a failed local device. This last point minimises one of the problems of a ring, where a node or station failure can bring the network down. Multiple rings can be linked together through a bridging node, which performs address conversion; very large networks can be supported in this way and the cable can be installed gradually over time, rather than all at once.

Much work has also gone into features of network operational control and reliability. Cable failures are automatically detected and recovered from by switching to another back-up cable; node failures can be bypassed, as described above. Each node contains a considerable amount of diagnostic microcode and any node can automatically take over the special duties of the ring monitor station, should the designated monitor fail.

IBM also stresses (correctly) that any LAN should be 'open', allowing equipment from different manufacturers to be, in IBM's words, 'intermixed'. Such an admission is a good step forward.

In May 1984, IBM's major 'non-announcement' that this long-awaited LAN would not be available for two or three years took many of the industry pundits by surprise. It should not have, for the following reasons:

1   IBM is a commercial enterprise and is already doing very well in the areas where a LAN could have an impact. In fact, adding full LAN capabilities to the PC, Displaywriter and System 36/5520 range of products could lead to embarrassments in terms of over-demand.

2   At the same time, announcement of a LAN would also mean that IBM would need to announce which IBM systems were going to interface to it. This implied prioritisation — because in no way could all the myriad IBM systems be attached in one batch — and could have a negative effect on the sales of those distributed DP and office systems not scheduled for attachment.

3   IBM's current office systems policy is to encourage applications development in virtually all product areas, the emphasis on rationalisation being mainly on a common document interchange capability between systems. This policy just cannot continue forever and it is quite possible that the two to three year delay quoted for the LAN actually represents the time by which the fundamental applications-level rationalisation decisions will need to be made. By that time the migration aids to help customers off the 'stabilised' products onto the strategic ones (which will be those interfaced to the LAN) should be in place.

4   The delay also gives time for the related developments in the Rolm, PBX, SNA, PUT2.1, LU6.2 and network management areas to mature, so that by 1986-1987 the alternative transport systems (PBX, LAN and various wide area SNA options) will appear as a set of compatible components within the IBM product line.

5   There are many signs that IBM has never placed a high priority upon LANs, the most obvious being that the development contract was placed outside with Texas Instruments (TI) — an organisation not noted for timely production of complex communications circuits or for a particularly accommodating attitude towards customers. IBM could easily have done the job itself: witness the speed with which the 'PC Cluster' system has been produced.

The 'non-announcement', therefore, although probably forced by TI's lack of progress, was likely to have been accepted without any great reluctance by IBM. It has taken care of the immediate marketing problem by announcing a 'cabling system', which customers wishing to wire up new buildings can adopt without needing to wait for the LAN itself.

With this approach, the LAN twisted pairs radiate on, say, every floor from a distribution frame (which will also house the LAN's RWCs once implemented). If the user devices do not have the LAN interface chips, they will need an adaptor box to allow the local signals (eg the 3278 2.3 Mbit/sec data stream) to be carried on the LAN twisted pairs. Until the RWC and interface chips are implemented, the LAN cable functions merely as a physical replacement for a variety of internal IBM standards, such as 3270 coaxial or 5250 twin-ax. Each workstation will talk only to its own controller, so there is no 'shared-resource' concept and, therefore, little or no reduction in actual wiring; in fact, there may be more. Once the interfaces are installed, the routing of the LAN twisted pairs between floors and distribution frames (LAN concentrators) can be altered relatively simply to promote sharing and ease relocation and maintenance. The cabling within a local area remains more or less untouched — to the extent that the workstation controllers are in a different area from the workstations themselves.

With the lack of a full LAN implementation, this is about the best that IBM can do in the meantime. Customers are unlikely to be over-enthusiastic, however, especially if they are faced with moving to this scheme from their present arrangement. By adopting a ring rather than a broadcast bus mechanism, IBM has, of course, not helped itself in terms of ease of installation. The saving grace may indeed be the gimmicky — but valuable — suggestion that voice twisted pairs from PABX to extension can be packaged together in the same sheath as the LAN.

The token-passing mechanism advocated by IBM, and incorporated now in the IEEE 802.5 standard, is theoretically suitable for supporting conversational voice as well as data devices. All the signs are, however, that for the next few years at least, IBM will keep the two streams apart. Data, which may, indeed, include voice annotation of documents and possible voice messaging, will go on the LAN; conversational voice is too expensive for a LAN (especially if IBM is not yet sure about the costs of LAN interface chip development) and will be supported on the digital voice/data exchange to be acquired from Rolm.

## Emerging communications standards

We shall now concentrate on the many and varied developments currently taking place, on a non-proprietary and usually international level, in the area of new and general-purpose, communications-oriented services.

Why should computer system users be interested in this subject? After all, their vendors will usually have their own proprietary standards (SNA etc) so why worry about the rest of the world? Well, one of the messages that should be emphasised to any user in the mid-1980s is that no vendor can, or indeed wishes to, operate in isolation: the wider community, whether represented by the carriers, their competitors operating general-purpose transport networks, or by competitive suppliers of data processing or office systems, can no longer be ignored. The multivendor installation is becoming the norm and the leased line, private network is yielding to a mixture of leased lines and public switched networks, often with value-added services and voice/data integration capability. Such a picture of the near future implies that users need to constantly monitor how far, if at all, their vendors' communications support is in line with non-proprietary service and protocol developments. Developments can be categorised into the following three broad classes:

1 The OSI service and protocols.

2 Various transport mechanism services, generally (but not always) consistent with the OSI model.

3 The special-purpose, end-to-end interworking services, again more or less compatible with OSI.

## OSI

Four or five years ago the prospect of general-purpose interworking between different product families from different suppliers was regarded, even by many of the cognoscenti, as something for the twenty-first century. Since then the picture has changed dramatically. An enormous amount of time and effort has been expended, mainly by product vendors, in developing a general framework to support 'open' (ie unrestricted) interconnection between systems. Whether their efforts have resulted in an unequivocally solid and flexible basis for all future requirements is open to question: however, protocols which can be implemented are now emerging and will continue to emerge over the next few years. Many vendors, including IBM (but with qualification), are now formally committed to implementing these protocols as an integral part of their product support. The few dissenting voices represent organisations who have already invested heavily in their own proprietary systems (but even they, including IBM, are tending to hold their peace rather than disagree vigorously) or who disagree with the OSI view of life in general. They are in a small minority, which should not be ignored, however.

OSI work began in the International Standards Organisation (ISO) with the establishment of ISO/TC97/SC16* some years ago and ISO is the body responsible for the production of OSI standards. However, both ISO and CCITT recognise the importance of reaching joint agreements in the preparation of ISO drafts and the development of relevant CCITT recommendations.

The European Computer Manufacturers' Association (ECMA) is, in comparison with ISO and CCITT, a geographically and industrially limited pressure group. These limitations, however, enable it to reach decisions rather more quickly than ISO and CCITT; in consequence, ECMA work has been of very great value and, in many cases, has served as the basis on which further development proceeds. ECMA prepares and votes upon 'standards', which do not have the authority and recognition accorded to ISO standards or CCITT recommendations but can and do record industry agreements and provide strong input to ISO and CCITT.

End users are not particularly well represented in the standards development process, which is strange when one considers that they have most to gain. Some organisations see fit to allow individuals to participate in some of the various forums and, recently, in the UK the Telecommunications Managers' Association has been active in making input to bodies such as ECMA. There are signs of progress here, in that various user representatives are setting themselves up either as pressure groups (eg the UK IT Users' Association) or, like General Motors in the US, to develop their own 'community' standards, which may or may not be compatible with international developments but at least are not proprietary to vendors.

ISO standards pass through a number of stages in their progress to full international standards. These stages are outlined below:

1  First they exist as technical papers within a particular subcommittee. At this stage their status is a matter of agreement at subcommittee level.

2  When they are felt to be stable, they are issued as draft proposals. At this stage they are given a number that they will retain through later stages. A draft proposal is a document the technical content of which is substantially agreed but points of minor detail and editorial matters may remain.

3  Progress to draft proposal may be by subcommittee vote or by separate national ballot.

4  The next stage is to Draft International Standard (DIS). A DIS should be technically stable — though extensions may, of course, be foreseen.

5  Finally, approval and publication as an International Standard (IS).

For practical purposes, draft proposals may be regarded as very useful base documents and DISs as ISs in all but name.

The OSI developments centre around a reference model, with the now well known seven layers. The ISO Reference Model, defined in IS 7498, differs only trivially from CCITT's model (X.200). Each of the seven layers is, or will be, defined in terms of the 'services' it provides to the layers above it and the 'protocols' it uses to communicate with a peer functional layer, usually at the other end of the network path.

The model definition allocates functions to layers. Its main deficiency, especially in the eyes of many US observers, is the lack of support for 'connectionless' communications; at the moment, everything is centred around 'calls', which have to be established before data can be transferred. Extensions to incorporate connectionless communications, for example, for very short transactions, are due for inclusion in the 1985-1988 period.

*The lower OSI layers (1, 2 and 3)*
A variety of technology-dependent, low-level communications standards is useful, for example to enable common interfacing methods to different LANs, but these need not relate at all strongly to OSI. The level at which OSI becomes important is in linking together 'subnetworks' of different technology to provide a

---

*TC: Technical Committee
 SC: Subcommittee

standard end-to-end network service between the OSI end systems. Over-constraining the low layers would restrict the development of new technology but some constraints must be applied where subnetwork interconnection is required so that a standard end-to-end service can be offered. This is the task of the network layer, now defined in DIS 8348, which is fully compatible with CCITT's X.213.

## The transport layer (4)

This layer offers a basic process-to-process link between heterogeneous systems — over any transport mechanism (given the appropriate supporting layers). As such it is the critical layer and was the first end-to-end protocol to be implemented, in 1984. In fact, the ISO standard (IS 8072 and 8073) includes five classes of service, the simplest of which was added in agreement with CCITT specifically for the Teletex service (F.200 and T.70). The reasoning behind having many classes is that high-performance transport networks will only need a basic transport layer; unambitious networks require a high-class transport layer to compensate. The Transmission Service (TS) classes are as follows:

- 0 — simple (Teletex)
- 1 — basic class
- 2 — flow control class
- 3 — error recovery class
- 4 — error detection and recovery class.

## The session layer (5)

The session layer adds value to the transport layer. It provides services for dialogue control, synchronisation and connection release. The session layer is now reaching standardisation. The offerings currently available as standards are:

- ISO, DIS 8326 (service) and 8327 (protocol)
- CCITT X.215 and X.225
- The ECMA standard, ECMA-75
- The CCITT Teletex standard, T.62.

They are compatible, respectively, with DIS 8072/3, ECMA-72 and CCITT T.70, mentioned previously in the discussion of the transport layer.

## The presentation layer (6)

The nature of the presentation service has been the subject of great debate and has only recently begun to stabilise. The current majority view (of the files and job groups, and of the group on upper layer architecture) is that it should provide general data-type manipulation and negotiation facilities suitable for use by file transfer, message handling, job transfer and virtual terminal components of layer 7. It is not yet clear whether this view is shared by the virtual terminal group, which had previously seen the presentation layer containing many functions specific to virtual terminal operation.

## File Transfer, Access and Management (FTAM (part of 7))

FTAM is now solid enough to have been implemented, at least in part, by some dozen different suppliers since the NCC in 1984.

## Virtual Terminals (VTs) (part of 7)

Progress in VTs has been very slow; the group has been embroiled in architectural aspects relating to the split of functions between layers 6 and 7. The major inputs are from ECMA and the speed of progress of ISO drafts in this area will depend upon the willingness or otherwise of this group to go along with the ECMA approaches. It is believed that ECMA has drafts for scroll and basic page modes that are near internal ratification.

## Management

The management group is concentrating its attention on mechanisms for the following:

- Commitment
- Accounting
- Error reporting.

## OSI implementation schedule

A good order of protocol implementation could be: transport, network (specifically, internet sublayer), session, presentation and applications (for instance, file transfer and electronic mail). Transport is capable of standing alone and is sufficient for a process-to-process communications link between heterogeneous systems. Internet is supplied on a per-system or per-network basis but a common internet protocol is needed to avoid installing an internetwork bridge for each internet protocol used within one local network. Session is the next in importance but it is not a critical protocol in terms of its being required before intersystem communications can take place. A common presentation sublayer will be useful but most applications will be supplying some elements of that layer themselves and the applications are needed as soon as they can be made available.

The best resolved protocol is transport and it will be the first to be implemented. Transport will only offer intermachine/process communications without a session capability but it will provide a common communications technique that a lot of vendors can follow and will find useful. The ability to utilise transport without accompanying session and internet protocols also contributes to its value for early implementation.

Implementations of transport and file transfer have already appeared, for example, the multivendor LAN demonstrations at the NCC in mid-1984. The process has already started and the confidence level is quite high. There is no reason why implementations of internet and session protocols, which are both in specification stages, could not occur at the same time, though the confidence level that either or both might be available by then is much lower. However, transport is all that is needed for a start. It is the key to the communications protocol standards door. In a short time that door will be opened and a wide range of ISO protocols will be revealed.

## Specific transport mechanisms standards

Most activity is centred on the high-speed, distributed control, data LAN, the next major division being between the broadband CATV-based products and the various 'baseband' systems. However, the basic classes which seem to have been identified as candidates for standardisation (CSMA/CD, token and slotted systems) can be found in both these product types.

A vast number of proprietary LAN products already exist in the marketplace. Two independent groups have been set up to study the problem of identifying the elements of any approach. In the US, the IEEE set up project 802 as a development from the instrument bus standard IEEE 488. The first meeting was held in February 1980, since when the work and committee structure have developed considerably. In Europe, ECMA has taken up the work but is a little behind the IEEE in timescale.

The IEEE initially set up three Working Groups — WG1 to investigate 'link-level' access to LANs (layer 2), WG2 to investigate various 'media', for example coaxial cable, fibre optics etc (layer 1), and WG3 to investigate the higher-level issues (layer 3). Shortly after the work commenced, Digital Equipment Co, Intel and Xerox issued their Ethernet specification. It soon became clear that at least two 'access methods' to the physical medium would exist — CSMA/CD and token passing — the latter preferred by manufacturers such as IBM. More recently, the committees have been restructured to take into account both token ring and token bus systems, as well as metropolitan area networks (25-mile radius of network centre, using CATV broadband technology).

The most solid document (802.2) is the Logical Link Control which was drafted in November 1982 and acquired technical committee approval in 1983. Next come CSMA/CD (802.3 and 802.4 respectively) which also have been approved. The token ring documents (802.5) are available in draft form but the metropolitan area network documents are still some way off. Approval by the IEEE Computer Society Standards Board will be needed before the documents are finally passed to the IEEE Standards Board.

IBM's long awaited LAN product was discussed, *inter alia*, in the 'IBM Systems Journal' for June 1983. Its preference for token passing and a ring topology is based, at least officially, upon a desire to support a wide mix of applications, including voice, for which the CSMA/CD probabilistic access mechanisms are not inherently suitable or cost effective. The unofficial reason is that IBM does not want Xerox to take over the whole market with its Ethernet-based CSMA/CD systems. Xerox is still fighting strongly: it has offered, for general implementation by vendors, its higher-level protocols (Xerox Network Systems, or XNS) to be used over Ethernet. These are well tried and are likely to be proposed as at least part of the base for connectionless protocols from the US. Both the Xerox systems and the IBM LAN are said to be open, ie for use by heterogeneous products. A more recent LAN announcement by IBM — the PC Network — is, however, solely for IBM PCs and it is not a foregone conclusion that it will be open in practice.

## PBXs

The proponents of PBXs as the basis for voice and data LANs can claim that the standards scene is much further advanced here than for the high-speed, distributed control LANs we have just discussed. PBXs have, after all, to attach to the public telephone networks through international standard interfaces. However, the PBX has no efficient standard method for linking to computer host systems or to certain terminal configurations and no international standard is being developed. Some coordinated development will be necessary before long. PBXs will, after all, form an essential part of the ISDN but they will need to adapt considerably if they are to offer an efficient, flexible base for computer-based office systems.

## ISDN

For advanced digital services (voice and non-voice) the European administrations (CEPT countries) favour a concept based on circuit switching (or slot switching) at 64 Kbit/sec with out-slot access signalling. This has arisen from the introduction of 30-channel digital voice multiplexors, with separate channel signalling and the provision of equipment within subscribers' premises (telephone sets, PABXs etc). The access to the network can be classified in two types as follows:

1  Out-slot signalling (separate control and information channels).
2  In-slot signalling (same channel for both, for example X.25).

For the ISDN, the current proposals are for a network termination interface providing two basic types of interface channel:

1  b-channel, providing a fully transparent 64 Kbit/sec path between subscribers.

2  d-channel, operating in a message interleaved form, used to carry signalling information for the b-channels or to convey additional types of information (eg low-speed data or telemetry).

The basic line rate will be 144 Kbit/sec. The user access would then be two b-channels, each at 64 Kbit/sec, and one d-channel. Extended access is possible, eg for PBXs, corresponding to multiple b-channels and one d-channel. For example, using the standard 2 Mbit/sec PCM links, there would be 30 b-channels and one d-channel.

The ISDN standards have recently been promulgated in the I-Series recommendations, which will be the subject of significant development in the period 1984-1988. Thoughts, in the UK at least, are that terminals would attach to the ISDN through an Integrated Digital Access (IDA) point, consisting of a basic digital interface (NT1), possibly a multiplexing/signalling system (NT2), plus whatever is necessary to adapt the Data Terminal Equipment (DTE) to these standards. IBM, amongst others, is attempting to ensure that DTE suppliers are permitted to supply as much as possible of their own IDAs without having to rely on the local PTT.

## End-user interworking services

Many relatively new communications services, based on the need to support a wide mix of heterogeneous devices, are being developed more or less along the lines of the OSI model. They address the question of the higher-level, interworking protocols which end-user systems need to adopt.

In the rapidly growing area of electronic mail systems, the two most interesting, non-proprietary developments are Teletex and Message Handling Systems (MHSs), both being developed under the auspices of the CCITT.

### Teletex
This service should, by this year, be offered widely within Europe, and also Canada, Japan and perhaps certain US carriers. The aim is to support document transmission between end-systems which have storage and intelligence, with transmission and reception operating concurrently with local processing. Transmission speed will normally be 2400 bit/sec synchronous, using either the new data networks (circuit or packet) or the Public Switched Telephone Network (PSTN). The character set supported is extensive, covering just about all the symbols used within the Latin-based languages. Support for image (pixel) transmission is being developed.

The Teletex service is defined by CCITT Study Group VIII in document F.200. The protocols defined for a Teletex terminal are at OSI levels 4-6, in documents T.70, T.62 and T.61. Many European vendors are building Teletex terminals or, more interestingly, incorporating the Teletex protocols into their office or DP systems. IBM, for example, has stated that it intends to support Teletex on the Displaywriter and 5520.

## MHSs

Whereas the Teletex service model assumes intelligent end-user systems with storage, communicating across an essentially transparent mechanism, the MHS concept tends more towards an intelligent network with value-added services. The basic aim is to support 'store-and-retrieve' message transfer (text, image and voice) between individuals — to retrieve messages from their personal mailbox files somewhere in the system. The need for a standard has arisen from the recent proliferation of 'mailbox' computer systems, offered either on a proprietary basis or as a value-added service by the carriers. None of these systems currently interwork, since there is no common protocol or message structure.

The MHS service model which was initially developed by IFIP WG65 (see below), defines User Agents (UAs), directly supporting end users and separate Message Transfer Agents (MTAs). The end user, UA and MTA can all co-reside in the same box or they can be distributed in space and offered by different vendors. The protocol between a pair of MTAs is called P1, between an MTA and its local UA the protocol is P3, and a pair of UAs converse end to end via P2. The X.MHS drafts are now the X.400 Series of CCITT recommendations, which include the following:

- X.400: system model; service elements
- X.411: message submission and delivery (P3)
- X.409: presentation transfer syntax.

X.409 defines the presentation transfer syntax used by application layer protocols in MHSs. From an OSI architectural standpoint, a presentation transfer syntax is used to represent the information exchanged between application entities. This syntax defines a representation of various types of data. Data is described by data types and data values. A data type is a class of information (for example, numeric or textual). A data value is an instance of such a class (for example, a particular number or fragment of text). This draft recommendation defines nine generally useful types (such as Boolean, integer and string) from which application-specific data types (for example, the message protocol data units defined in X.411) may be constructed in companion recommendations. Note, however, that X.409 does not attempt to define document format control characters.

Mailbox systems normally allow recipients to be specified by name, which is a highly user-friendly approach. The new international MHS standards, however, require users to be designated by addresses. While this approach requires no directory look-up and is useful now because no international directories capable of mapping names into addresses are in place, addresses (instead of names) are much harder for people to discover and remember.

To remedy this situation, and it certainly needs a remedy, IFIP WG6.5 (which has made enormous contributions to the general MHS development) is trying to propose a more user-friendly naming convention and show how the international directory required to support it can be constructed. In the MHS model, the unit of information transfer is the message, which comprises envelope and content. Each user is represented by a UA when acting as either the Originator (O) or Recipient (R) of messages. A single Message Transfer System (MTS) made up of one or more management domains carries messages between UAs. Messages enter the MTS by means of a submission protocol and leave it by means of a delivery protocol. Each user has one or more O/R names, by which other users know him, and a single O/R address by which the MTS locates him.

IFIP WG6.5 has produced a document in which name, address and route are defined. It describes how names and addresses are obtained from the international directory and records the goals that guided the design of the proposed name form and directory.

Another part of the document identifies the entities (besides users) that require names and proposes forms for those names. A third section presents a functional model of the international directory and indicates how it relates to a layered model, to the MHS model summarised above and to other applications that may use the directory.

The MHS developments are much wider ranging than Teletex and could, indeed, be used as a general-purpose 'block' (file/document/message) transfer mechanism between any pair of computers. The mailbox type of service has enormous potential by itself and an X.400 gateway facility will need to be supported by all serious office systems vendors.

## Office Document Interchange Facility (ODIF)

Neither Teletex nor MHS specify how the contents of a document should be formatted or edited so that sender and recipient can both use the same controls. This is something which IBM's DCA attempts to provide in its DCA revisable format — and now ISO is trying the same thing in developing ODIF. This work, hosted by SC18/WG3, has not yet progressed far but it will be interesting to see the similarities, if any, between DIA/DCA (from IBM) on the one hand, and ODIF, MHS and Teletex on the other.

## Videotex

In the years since the introduction of Prestel, the first interactive videotex service in the world, much work has gone into development of standards for transmission and presentation of videotex frames on videotex (-compatible) terminals. The basic Prestel standards are still used on about 98 per cent of all terminals and the European PTTs have agreed a CEPT standard broadly based on the UK and French alphamosaic graphics. The North Americans have tended to favour the more powerful, and expensive, alphageometric graphics system, now generally referred to as the North American Presentation Level Protocol Syntax (NAPLPS). So, for both interactive and broadcast (teletext) videotex services there appear to be two basically incompatible standards emerging. The crucial question, of course, is when, if ever, videotex is going to revolutionise computer usage from home and office; probably, in Europe at least, we are not going to see any significant impact until the widespread use of cable-based interactive services in the late 1980s and early 1990s.

## Community standards

Various user groups are working together to provide open communications, at least within the community, mainly because they feel unable to wait for OSI standards. The most advanced group, in practice, must be the UK academic community, with levels 2-7 standards of their own, already supporting file/job transfer and interactive access on a wide range of equipment. The Unified Higher Level Protocols (EHKP) implemented in West Germany have much the same aim.

In the desktop and home micro communities one can also see a wide variety of open protocols emerging, most obviously in the area of file transfer between micros. The bandwagon effect of these groups is enormous and must represent some danger (and stimulus) to the mainstream OSI developments. Most of them, however, profess to remain faithful to the ISO model — if not to the ISO protocols.

## IBM's attitude to 'foreigners'

Increasingly IBM is becoming more tolerant with regard to interworking with non-IBM equipment. There are now numerous examples of conversion/adaptor facilities available for equipment supporting non-IBM protocols to access, typically, IBM mainframes. These include:
- Network Terminal Option (NTO)
- The NCP X.25 support package (NPSI)
- The 3710 concentrator, which also supports 'foreign' devices
- The 7171 ASCII interface
- The Open Systems Network Support package available for the German EHKP community
- Support for the ISO transport and session layer protocols
- Support for videotex and Teletex.

From these developments it is clear that IBM is making efforts to interwork with foreign standards — since it is in its marketing and public relations interests to do so. It should not, however, be construed from this that IBM regards this kind of accommodation as a high priority; it intends to sell its own equipment (especially the lucrative mainframes and workstation systems) and will provide gateways/convertors only as fast as the market pushes it to do so. IBM is, for example, supporting the (open) Manufacturing Automation Protocols (MAP) standards for use as an industrial LAN precisely because General Motors insisted upon its support by all LAN vendors. The BT/IBM VAN venture, which rightly failed to receive a licence, required host systems to be SNA-compatible. Therefore, users will need to apply pressure — but they may now find it easier to get their demands met.

182

# Glossary of acronyms and abbreviations

*API:*
Application Program Interface
*ASCII:*
American Standard Code for Information Interchange
*CATV:*
Cable television
*CEPT:*
Conference of European Posts and Telecommunications
*CICS:*
Customer Information Control System
*CSMA/CD:*
Carrier Sense Multiple Access/Carrier Detect
*DCA:*
Document Content Architecture
*DIA:*
Document Interchange Architecture
*DIS:*
Draft International Standard, from ISO (qv)
*DTE:*
Data Terminal Equipment
*ECMA:*
European Computer Manufacturers' Association
*EHKP:*
West German Unified Higher-Level Protocols
*FTAM:*
File Transfer, Access and Management
*FTP:*
File Transfer Protocol
*IDA:*
Integrated Digital Access
*IEEE:*
Institute of Electrical and Electronic Engineers
*IFIP:*
International Federation for Information Processing
*IS:*
International Standard, from ISO (qv)
*ISDN:*
Integrated Services Digital Network
*ISO:*
International Standards Organisation
*LAN:*
Local area network
*LU:*
Logical Unit
*MAP:*
Manufacturing Automation Protocols
*MHS:*
Message Handling System
*MTA:*
Message Transfer Agent
*NAPLPS:*
North American Presentation Level Protocol Syntax

*NCC:*
National Computer Centre
*NCCF:*
Network Communications Control Facility
*NPDA:*
Network Problem Determination Application
*NPSI:*
NCP Packet Switching Interface (X.25 support package)
*NRF:*
Network Routing Facility
*NTO:*
Network Terminal Option
*ODIF:*
Office Document Interchange Facility
*OSI:*
Open Systems Interconnection
*PABX:*
Private Automatic Branch Exchange
*PBX:*
Private Branch Exchange
*PCM:*
Pulse Code Modulation
*PSTN:*
Public Switched Telephone Network
*PTT:*
Post, Telephone and Telegraph authority
*RWC:*
Ring Wiring Concentrator
*SDLC:*
Synchronous Data Link Control
*SNADS:*
SNA Distribution Services
*SNCP:*
Single Node Control Point
*SNI:*
System Network Interconnection
*SSCP:*
Systems Services Control Point
*TS:*
Transmission Service
*UA:*
User Agent
*VAN(S):*
Value Added Network (Services)
*VT:*
Virtual Terminal
*VTAM:*
Virtual Telecommunications Access Method
*WG:*
Working Group
*XNS:*
Xerox Network Systems.

# 15: IBM and Pick

**J St John Bate**

Digitus Ltd
London
UK

**The IBM user searching for a flexible operating system may find the attractions of Pick irresistible. Not even IBM offers an operating system which can be used on such a variety of IBM hardware as Pick does. But is this the user's only reason for choosing Pick? What other attributes make it an attractive alternative? This paper examines the facilities offered by the Pick operating system and its various implementations in the IBM environment.**

*J St John Bate*
Joseph St John Bate is Product Manager at multi-user Digitus Ltd. His 15 years of experience in business and computing includes involvement with software, systems, hardware selection, computer applications and training. His career developed in the gas industry where he was responsible for selecting and implementing a wide range of office automation equipment and systems. His particular interests include the industry standards, UNIX, Pick and MS-DOS.

## Introduction

To some people it might seem that the last thing the dedicated IBM user wants is a portable operating system. Since he is unlikely to want to use any other supplier, why should he choose an operating system that can run on other machines? One answer is that Pick's portability offers more choices within IBM. There is not an IBM operating system that will run on the variety of IBM hardware that Pick operates on. Pick runs on the XT, AT, the Series/1, System/36 and the 4300s, up to 3XXXs.

However, most users choose Pick for other reasons, the main one being that it gives the end user, especially those without computer experience, impromptu access to their data. The only other way this could be achieved would be with paper and an army of clerical workers. Pick combines this facility with a formidable computing power, making the writing of applications so simple that it can result in considerable cost savings of programming staff. It also means that the applications can be written quickly and, therefore, when required.

Before we examine the various implementations on the IBM range it is necessary to explain some of the facilities that Pick offers.

## The Pick operating system

The Pick operating system is, first and foremost, a database management system (DBMS) and secondarily an operating environment. It is this fact that differentiates it from virtually all other operating systems. As an operating system upon which to base a distributed data processing strategy for both large and small organisations, it meets the requirements of data-driven systems and provides the tools necessary to allow the manipulation of data into information.

Dick Pick, the designer, first implemented a query-type database system on an IBM System/360 at TRW. Once the potential had been realised, he worked with Microdata in California to implement the system on a microprogrammable microcomputer — the M1600 — the 'REALITY' was launched. By implementing most of the system in microcode, a balance of functionality and performance was achieved.

Dick Pick left Microdata to found Pick and Associates and then went on to form Pick Systems. In addition to the Microdata range, several other Pick implementations have appeared and the system is now available on IBM, Honeywell, DEC, Prime and HP systems, as well as Intel, Zilog and Motorola chip-based micros. Since the system was first developed on an IBM machine there is an element of poetic justice in the fact that Pick is now available on a wide range of IBM hardware. Not only is it available, but in many cases it is preferred to the proprietary operating systems. Once the facilities that Pick offers are understood this preference is obvious. There are a number of aspects of the Pick operating system that need to be understood, and one of the main ones is the system architecture.

## Operating system architecture

The key to an understanding of the Pick system is its database structure, since the heart of the Pick operating system is its relational database. In Pick, the DBMS is an inherent part of the operating system and not a utility or an add on. No single element of the file structure is constrained in number or real length: the database has any number of variable sized files, each comprising variable length fields. This is implemented in a non-hierarchical, delimiter-oriented structure. The Pick system file structure is managed by a comprehensive series of data dictionaries — implemented in a hierarchical structure — which provides a true relational database capability. Each file or set of files in the database has an associated data dictionary which logically defines the structure of the data file. This data dictionary may easily be changed and complex data interrelationships may be defined without affecting the actual data stored in the file. This can be achieved quickly and without recourse to experienced DP staff.

At the highest level is the system file which contains user information (eg passwords, access and security codes), as well as pointers to the user's data files in virtual memory. The first file associates each user with his master dictionary which contains his personal vocabulary. It includes the following:
- Commands (or 'verbs' to use Pick parlance) such as 'edit', 'list', 'copy'
- File names that the verbs operate upon, such as 'personnel', 'stock'
- Verb associated words (connectives), such as 'with', 'heading'
- Procedures which can be used to interactively prompt, display, update or pass control.

Every file is structured in the same logical manner — even though the physical organisation is different. This means that ACCESS, the system query language, can provide a report on any data in the system, provided there is authorisation. ACCESS is designed to make it simple to turn data into information. It is easy to use and allows answers to be obtained to very complex questions.

Each data record or item has a unique key for that file and can be up to 32 Kbytes long. All fields — attributes, values and subvalues — are of variable length and type. The only system-generated data pertinent to an item is a code for its length, along with the system delimiters used to signify field intervals. Data files are structured through a hashing algorithm random access technique, using the item name (or item-ID) as a key. This allows efficient retrieval of any file record, no matter how large the file grows. Other than the primary file space, which is user defined at file creation, the data in a file may be located in any available disk space, even if this means the data spans multiple disk drives.

These 'low-level' details of the file structure are entirely managed by the virtual memory and database firmware routines. They are totally transparent to the user and the application developer. The user only 'sees' the database at the logical level. Apart from the occasional requirement to change user access or update lock codes, the database is truly self-maintaining and will operate indefinitely without user involvement.

## Pick performance

The real task of a computer in a management context is to change data into information and to help people to manage their business by having up to date information available. As a measure of the difficulty of developing systems to achieve this state of affairs consider the number of times the DP department confuses data with information, resulting in it processing data instead of managing information.

Data includes such things as invoice number and customer addresses, price lists and commodity codes. Information provides an answer to such questions as: 'Is the company profitable or losing money?', 'Have the manufacturing division got enough material to produce what is scheduled for next month?', 'What is the sales pattern for a particular product?', 'Does the company have anyone who is over 35 years, has a degree in engineering and can speak French?'. The answers to these questions are information that can be used to run a commercial organisation.

However, on most computer systems, machine needs and not the user needs predominate. Instead of helping the user to squeeze information out of the real world, the computer tends to trap the user in an unreal world conditioned by its own structure. This uncommercial structure is all too readily re-enforced by dedicated DP staff. This state of affairs is not entirely their fault since they are conditioned by the operating system and the programming languages with which they have to work. One could argue that the IBM operating systems and COBOL are not the ideal combination for a fast-moving commercial environment. There are many, however, who would say that Pick and its language is ideal for the commercial environment.

If the computer industry were to start afresh would there be pressure to design a computer to match the needs of a commercial user and to provide a structure to enable the database to be accessed in a user-friendly and efficient manner using a language of files and fields, record lengths and search keys? If this were not demanded by the DP department then at least it should be by the users.

This highlights a problem, namely that the end user operates in a changing environment and the DP department prefers to operate in a static environment. In the commercial world not only does the data change, but the relationships change too. New ways of doing things are developed, new people join the business, responsibilities change, even the rules and laws that govern the operation may change. The computer's structure should be able to adapt to these changes as they occur. However, this is not the case and in many instances company data is not turned into information that would be of value to the organisation.

## Pick is a virtual-memory multi-user operating system

The Pick operating system represents one attempt to meet this challenge. Pick is a virtual-memory multi-user operating system specifically designed to help the user to get the information required out of the system.

Although it is an extremely sophisticated system, Pick is easy for non-programmers to use. In a few minutes the Pick English-like query language can be learnt well enough to begin answering complex questions about data stored in the built-in relational database.

Other parts of the operating system include an English non-procedural query language called ACCESS — a compiled version of BASIC with major enhancements for business and data management; PROC — a stored-procedure processor that allows the user to write and store elaborate command sequences, much like scripts in UNIX; a command processor called Terminal Control Language (TCL); a print spooler and a number of other utilities.

Most of the utilities associated with microcomputer operating systems are either invisible or non-existent in Pick. Tasks like file handling and memory allocation are done by the operating system, allowing the user the freedom to concentrate on the information that can be obtained from the system. In addition Pick is rich in utilities related to information handling.

## Software structure

Underpinning all this is an elaborate and complex software structure. Pick is implemented as a virtual machine with limited, carefully optimised connections to the underlying hardware through a section of code called the monitor. Pick's inventors started out by designing the best possible computer on paper they could imagine for managing information. Then they wrote an operating system to emulate their design on real computers.

The Pick virtual machine has its own internal structure and even its own pseudo-assembly language, all designed for data management tasks.

On a microcomputer, these features are implemented in software, right down to the virtual memory management system. One result of having a virtual machine implemented in software is a high degree of applications portability. Any Pick machine will run almost any piece of Pick software. The only difference between an IBM PC/XT and an IBM 4300 mainframe is that the application will probably run slower on the PC/XT.

The usual penalty for having such an elaborate software superstructure is a loss of speed. It would be expected that Pick would be slow, especially on something like the 8088 microprocessor in an IBM PC/XT, but this is not the case. The PC/XT implementation is noticeably slower than Pick on 68000-based microcomputers; to those used to microcomputers, Pick can appear somewhat slow because most Pick implementations are designed to work with terminals via serial I/O ports rather than the kind of memory-mapped video used on most microcomputers.

Processing speed, however, is exceptional especially on searches and sorts. The Pick operating system contains many commonly used functions, such as database management and the high-level BASIC language. Since these functions are so tightly integrated with the overall operating system they enable the machine to run fast.

## Pick executes a machine-language code

There are other reasons why the processing speeds are so impressive. One is that Pick executes a machine-language code on whatever machine it is running on. Other operating systems that use the virtual machine concept are usually interpreted or compiled/interpreted. Another reason is that Pick is carefully optimised for each implementation to be as fast as possible.

Pick is not an operating system that can do everything, it is not, for example, a number-crunching system. There are better operating systems for scientific and engineering work, or for anything else that requires a lot of calculation. Pick will score poorly on a computational benchmark such as the sieve of Eratosthenes.

On the other hand, Pick will shine in an information-management test, particularly one with a lot of complex data manipulation. This is because the database is relational and because of the way in which the system stores information, it can usually retrieve any piece of data with one or two disk accesses. It is for this reason that Pick is often ported to the IBM range of hardware.

## Strength in the file structure

There is tremendous strength in the file structure of the Pick operating system. Everything is contained in a file and the files are organised hierarchically. There are three kinds of file in Pick, but only two of them are of immediate use — these are data files and dictionary files. The third, binary files, hold compiled code and stored lists. Both the data and the dictionary files are structured in the same manner. The distinction between data and dictionary files is that data files hold the data and dictionary files establish and maintain relationships between the data.

## Dictionary files

In Pick there is only one type of data file, but there are three types of dictionary file. The master dictionary for each user defines the user's vocabulary, while data dictionaries describe the data and define the relationships. One of the beauties of this separation of data and dictionary files is that it makes it easy to change relationships without affecting the data, and *vice versa*. Dictionary files can be edited, updated or changed completely without disturbing the data entries to which they refer. In the same fashion, data can be edited and updated without making any modifications to the dictionaries or disturbing the relationships already created. This gives the flexibility to change the system as the real world changes. This is the kernel of the Pick operating system — the element that makes it so useful in a changing, fast-moving commercial environment.

## The ACCESS query language

One of the genuine user-friendly aspects of the Pick operating system is the ACCESS query language. ACCESS is designed to make it simple for the user to turn data into information. It is easy to use and lets the user obtain almost immediate answers even to complex questions. The simplicity of ACCESS stems from three things:

1  It makes use of words or universally recognised symbols (such as $+, >, <, =$) to express concepts.
2  It requires the minimum of extraneous information from the user.
3  It works in the same manner in which the user thinks.

One result of these powerful concepts is that the inexperienced user can be taught to use ACCESS very quickly and feel at home with the system in a short space of time. The fact that they can formulate questions in a perfectly natural way and then ask those same questions in almost the same format develops enthusiasm for the system and therefore ensures that the power is used to develop the business by people who might otherwise be apprehensive about using computers.

Commands in ACCESS are called verbs. They are action words like 'Select' or 'List'. The usual sequence of ACCESS command is verb, filename, (selection criteria, sequence criteria, report output attributes and modifiers). However, the user can develop any sequence that seems comfortable as long as it starts with a verb.

These facilities enable both the experienced user and the novice to turn the data in the system into information. This is a very powerful facility and, in many cases, unusual. This is because many computer systems turn information into data by telling the user more than he wishes to know. Computer systems are so unwieldy that they often produce reams of paper with vast amounts of data contained within the pages, instead of the information required by the user or department: confusion by facts.

## Obtaining the information from data

Everyone in a company requires pieces of information, either for decision making or some other purpose. The information required might be how many parts are in stock, or the cost of a particular item, or the rate at which an item was being used, or the amount of an item on order, or the name of the suppliers of a particular item, or the amount owed by the company to the supplier of a particular item, or when the next shipment is due, and perhaps one hundred other things. All this information is in the database, but to give all of it to any questioner would be unnecessary and counter-productive. This is why many traditional computer systems are not used or are not useful. They make work instead of making work easier. This makes the decision maker's task harder not easier. This could explain why the relationship between the DP department and the end user ranges from cold acceptance to open warfare.

Pick solves this problem by allowing the user, through ACCESS, to specify selection and output criteria. The system will then display the information that is of interest to the user. The rest of the information remains invisible and, in fact, may not be accessible to a user as a security measure.

## Virtual memory

There are other aspects to Pick that speed up the system, virtual memory being one of them. The operating system allows the user to address the entire range of available disk space as if it were memory. Consequently, any number of users may execute multiple processes without regard to the actual amount of system memory. The memory is arranged in 512-byte pages or frames. When a frame is needed for processing, the firmware determines if it is already in memory. If it is not, then the monitor automatically transfers the frame from disk, with the least recently used frame being backed out of disk if there is a need to create a space. Since these operations are also hidden from the user there is no requirement for the user or the system builders to concern themselves with optimisation, 'locality of reference' or other virtual memory handling techniques. The system takes the strain and allows the user to be an information worker and not a computer programmer.

## Multi-user capacity

The Pick system is designed as an interactive system capable of communicating with multiple users simultaneously. Users communicate with the system through terminals. Each terminal creates a 'process', an interruptable operation that is controlled by the operating system. There are two types of process — 'virtual' and 'monitor'. Each process has a Primary Control Block (PCB) which contains its software CPU — accumulator, registers, etc. The monitor PCB is permanently memory resident while the virtual process PCBs — which are after all only data elements — are paged into memory as required.

When running, Pick assumes the availability of a CPU per process, using its PCB. The machine must maintain the pretence by manipulating dedicated fields within each PCB as if they are address registers or accumulators, etc, thus providing the environment in which the processes can be executed. Each process attached to the system has a Process Identification Block (PIB) which contains information about the status of the process with which it is associated.

## Memory map

Virtual memory is configured into five primary areas, plus an overflow pool. These areas are as follows:

1  Executive area.
2  Work area.
3  Low workspace area.
4  Pre-allocated terminal workspace.
5  File area.

The executive area starts at the first frame and extends up to 511 or 1024 frames (manufacturer dependent); it contains base system software and user/manufacturer assembly language programs. The work area is an area of 32 frames reserved for each process and the PCB. Beginning immediately after the work area is the low workspace area which consists of a set of numbers of workspace frames per process and is used for additional process workspace. The file area is the remainder of virtual memory and is made up of user data held within the relational database. Any unused storage is allocated to the overflow space pool and is used for additional process workspace when requested. The allocation of this space is controlled by the overflow space management processor. As files expand and contract or terminals log on and log off, frames are taken from or returned to this space. Obviously, the space becomes fragmented over time and a logical file save/restore process is necessary to recreate a contiguous overflow area. This demonstrates the need for prudent housekeeping.

In the Pick operating system, disk space is treated as one contiguous volume. All references to virtual space under Pick are by frame numbers (or FID) and a relative displacement from the first byte in the frame. Frames may be linked together to accommodate larger records.

### The languages of Pick

Traditional Pick implementations support only three languages. They are:

1  PROC.
2  English.
3  DATABASIC.

The first two are unique to the Pick operating system; the other, being BASIC, is a misnomer since it is an enhanced version of the standard Dartmouth BASIC. It is probably only as a result of the micro boom that BASIC is becoming more widely acceptable. The larger mainframe and minicomputer market has been COBOL-oriented for so long that Pick's lack of a COBOL compiler has reduced its acceptability. However, now that this market is widening its view and recognising the position of BASIC, the limitation will not seem so severe — not that it stopped the spread of Pick during the mid-Seventies to mid-Eighties.

### Terminal Control Language (TCL)

The TCL is the main method of interaction between a user and Pick. Hundreds of standard system utilities, menus and procedures may be invoked from the TCL environment, as well as an unlimited number of user-defined procedures. TCL allows the copy, addition, deletion and modification of any predefined system procedure name, thus providing the ability for each user to create an application environment or installation-specific 'vocabulary'.

The syntax is simple. The first word in a TCL sentence has to be a verb or a command. The system software handling that verb or command will then parse the rest of the sentence for anything that it requires, for example file name, and process the command if it can. There are many powerful facilities available using the Pick operating system and that is why it has been ported onto the IBM range.

### Advantages of Pick in the IBM environment

There are many advantages of using Pick with the IBM family of machines, not least of which is that Pick runs on the IBM PC, AT, 4300 and the 30XX as well as System/36. This provides an extensive growth path without the problem of changing operating systems or porting to a larger machine. Pick also allows an added function to the IBM environment since, where appropriate, applications development tools are available. A large number of spreadsheets, calculators, text processors and application generators are available from Pick software suppliers to speed up the provision of applications.

## Developing software

The IBM XT can be used in stand-alone mode to develop Pick applications which will run without modification on the mainframe. This can provide the DP department with a very cost-effective method of developing specialist applications for the end user without involving expensive mainframe resources. This facility is enhanced by the fact that the Pick relational database with its high-level languages and powerful query facilities allows rapid program development and, in many cases, can be carried out by non-technical personnel.

There are a number of sites where relatively complex programs that have been developed by non-DP personnel are running on IBM mainframes under Pick. This would be nearly impossible in any other operating system. There are, no doubt, many DP managers who would think that this facility is undesirable. However, the DP staff have to realise that they are only a resource that is available to an organisation and unless they are efficient there is no reason to continue using that resource.

## The IBM PC implementation

On the IBM PC, Pick requires a 10 Mbyte hard disk and 256 to 640 Kbytes of RAM. No hardware modifications are required and the system uses stock IBM PC expansion boards. The second and third users are supported via RS-232C ports and serial terminals.

The first user is supported with the computer's screen and keyboard treated as an intelligent terminal with memory-mapped video. In this mode, the IBM PC version of Pick offers underlining, half intensity, protected fields and, if the graphics card is installed and colour monitor used, selectable colour. All these features are supported by commands that are an integral part of the operating system.

The hard disk is required partly because the Pick operating system is big and partly because it needs the read/write of the hard disk to function effectively. Since Pick does not have to take up the entire disk, the user can keep other operating systems and their files on the disk as well and switch back and forth between them. However, only one operating system at a time can be used.

The way the Pick virtual memory operates makes it impractical to use the ROM BIOS routines on the IBM PC for disk I/O. The expanded PC BIOS on a PC/XT takes control on a disk seek and read, keeping control until it is done. This works perfectly well for a single-user machine, but is not efficient in a multi-user environment. To get around this, Pick Systems wrote its own hard-disk I/O driver.

## Implementation of Pick on the IBM 4300 and 30XX

The implementation of Pick on IBM 4300 and 30XX series processors is under VM, Pick runs as a guest operating system and as such happily co-exists with DOS, VSI and CMS systems. Data transfer between Pick and other systems is via the Reader/Punch mechanism and is an integrated facility.

Multiple Pick systems can run side by side on the 4300 and 30XX series machines under VM — this enables several Pick environments to be generated (ie test, develop, operational or a split by application) all running on the same processor.

The entire range of facilities of VM's networking products is available to give access to Pick via RSCS, PASSTHRU and the terminal network, including SNA. This means that communications with remote screens, other machines and networks including SNA can be carried out within the IBM environment.

Through VM, the network and all peripherals can be manipulated on behalf of Pick to give absolute flexibility. Performance can be monitored and controlled through VM's monitoring tools and utilities; various options can be utilised to give Pick preferential resource availability as and when required.

## Summary

This brief overview is an introduction to the many features offered by the Pick operating system which can change the complexion of a computer environment, even an IBM environment. The change is very fundamental and should not be underestimated. The Pick operating system allows the end user, however inexperienced, to use the computer as an information tool without becoming enmeshed in the clumsy mystique of traditional computing. Pick makes the computer work for the non-DP user without the use of the traditional DP staff and offers a high degree of freedom even within the IBM range.

## Further reading

1 Sisk J E, 'The Pick pocket guide' (Pick Systems Inc, Irvine, CA, 1982).

2 Bate J St J and Wyatt, 'The Pick operating system' (Collins UK, 1986).

3 'Overview of the Pick operating system' (General Automation, Anaheim, CA, 1982).

4 Bellinger A, 'The Pick operating system, the computer industry's best kept secret' (Pergamon Infotech State of the Art Report, 'The software development process', Series 13 no 2 pp 3-15, Pergamon Infotech Ltd, 1985).

# 16: IBM and the UNIX operating system

**B Salama**

Sphinx Ltd
Maidenhead
Berkshire
UK

**What has caused IBM to release operating systems based on a product developed and owned by AT&T, the company destined to become its largest rival in the DP industry? Does IBM (or perhaps its customers) think that UNIX is superior to VM? Is IBM trying to confound AT&T's move into the computer market by releasing a variety of different UNIX versions into the marketplace, thus confusing it? To answer these questions this paper will look at IBM's involvement with the UNIX system with particular emphasis on its products for this operating system, its strategy for UNIX and the likely benefits and dangers.**

*B Salama*
Ben Salama is one of the key commercial UNIX specialists in the UK. He has been a consultant at ICL on the UNIX-based Perq system and prior to this he spent over two years with Bell Telephone Laboratories, US, where he was a member of the world's largest team of UNIX experts. His present company, Sphinx Ltd, specialises in products relating to this operating system.

## Introduction

In Dallas on 14 August 1984, IBM announced a new addition to its hugely successful personal computer product line — the IBM PC/AT. Architecturally, the AT represents a natural migration from the existing PC/XT, offering extra memory, higher capacity diskette drives, a 20 Mbyte hard disk and a switch to the Intel 80286 microprocessor chip. Not surprisingly a new version of PC-DOS, DOS 3.0, was announced for single-user use, allowing migration of existing PC software to the new machine. The announcement of a multi-user operating system for the AT was also no surprise, given the anticipated performance of the 80286 chip. However, the fact that this operating system was based on AT&T's UNIX and not an IBM proprietary system was certainly unexpected.

The Dallas announcement has subsequently been overshadowed. In February 1985, IBM announced IX/370 — a version of UNIX System V (the latest release of UNIX from AT&T) running as a guest operating system under VM for 370 architecture machines.

## IBM's UNIX products

As we shall see, UNIX is not new to IBM. Its involvement with the operating system goes back to the late 1970s. Today, IBM offers UNIX on most of its product line (System/36 being the major exception).

UNIX is available in the following forms from IBM:

1 XENIX. Developed by Microsoft and based on AT&T's UNIX System III, IBM is offering XENIX on the PC/AT as a three-user system and on the System 9002 as a multi-user option aimed primarily at the scientific and engineering markets.

2 PC/IX. Developed for IBM by Interactive Systems and also based on UNIX System III, PC/IX is available as a single-user UNIX system for the PC/XT and PC/AT. Rather confusingly, therefore, there are two competing products available for the PC/AT — the single-user PC/IX and the multi-user XENIX.

3 Series/1 IX. Based on AT&T's System V, Series/1 IX is available for the Series/1 Model 4956.

4 VM/IX. A UNIX System III derivative, developed for IBM by Interactive Systems, VM/IX is compatible with the PC/IX product. It is also available to run as a guest operating system under VM on 370 architecture machines.

5 IX/370. The first UNIX release developed 'in-house' by IBM (actually by IBM Germany in Boeblingen), IX/370 offers full UNIX System V capability with a number of additional features to be found in VM/IX and PC/IX.

IBM's UNIX offerings are, therefore, very varied. This total lack of cohesion in the UNIX products offered by IBM indicates that not only is IBM's UNIX strategy immature at the present, but many different internal forces have been at work, pushing out products when required on different (and sometimes the same) machines. The current UNIX offerings and the implications for the future are best examined in the order that the various products were released.

## History of IBM's involvement with UNIX

UNIX was originally developed inside AT&T's Bell Laboratories as a multi-user, interactive, timesharing system designed for use in software development environments. In the late 1970s, UNIX running on DEC PDP-11 minicomputers was an ideal and cost-effective vehicle upon which dozens of software development groups within Bell Laboratories based their work. For the first time these groups were able to free themselves from the constraints of mainframe computing. PDP-11s and UNIX were well within their individual departmental budgets and allowed them total control of their computing resources and consequently their development cycles. UNIX provided powerful tools for software development and text preparation, allowing software design, coding and documentation to co-exist on one machine and to be accessed from any terminal.

Almost as quickly as UNIX spread within Bell Laboratories and PDP-11s mushroomed in every corridor, the development groups outgrew their hardware. UNIX was quickly ported onto the new 32-bit machines (the Interdata 8/32 and DEC VAX 11/780) but these were still inadequate for very large project teams and jobs within the Bell Telephone operating companies, where mainframe computers dominated the DP environment.

The desire for mainframe versions of UNIX was so strong in the late 1970s that Bell undertook two further UNIX ports: one to the Univac 1100 and the other, in close collaboration with IBM, to the IBM 370 series. The product, named TSS/UNIX, ran in native mode in the 370 and was front-ended by a Series/1 minicomputer acting as an asynchronous terminal handler. This product has never been made commercially available and was never licenced by AT&T outside the Bell System. It was, however, IBM's first entry into the UNIX world and was a significant indicator to the future. It was possibly the first example (but certainly not the last) of major account pressure for the UNIX operating system on IBM hardware.

Early interest in UNIX was not confined to AT&T and Bell Laboratories. Many universities, both in the US and Europe, eagerly installed UNIX systems during the 1970s and early 1980s. UNIX was an ideal teaching vehicle as well as a solid research and development system and the majority of academic sites installed Digital Equipment minicomputer hardware for their UNIX systems.

Commercial interest in UNIX also began to develop slowly at this time. The interest was, primarily, from very large self-supporting organisations since AT&T sold UNIX in source form only and as a totally unsupported product.

## UNIX for Series/1

The IBM Series/1 minicomputer was the next IBM machine to receive attention from the UNIX community. A port of UNIX to the Series/1 was carried out jointly by researchers at the University of Ohio and Rutgers University. The product was called CPIX and was adopted for sale by IBM's Telecommunications Group in October 1982. It is also available outside IBM under the name of SERIX through Computerised Office Services in the US. The SERIX product has been enhanced over time and upgraded to UNIX System V compatibility. This new version was announced by IBM in 1985 under the name of Series/1 IX and is available for the Series/1 Model 4956.

## UNIX for System 9000

IBM's first real UNIX product was announced in September 1983 for its System 9002 minicomputer. The 9002 is based on the Motorola MC68000 chip set and is sold through the IBM Instrumentation Division, aimed primarily at the scientific and technical markets. The version of UNIX chosen for the System 9002 was XENIX, a UNIX V7 derivative from Microsoft Corporation.

198

## UNIX for the PC/XT

In 1984 a dramatic increase in UNIX activity was seen within IBM. In January of that year IBM's National Accounts Division announced PC/IX which was developed especially for IBM by Interactive Systems Corporation, one of the first companies to sell commercial implementations of UNIX in the late 1970s. This announcement, coinciding with the National Accounts Division being allowed to sell the PC in the US, revealed a number of facts which indicated that the product emerged as a result of major account pressure on IBM. Firstly, PC/IX was only available through IBM's National Account Division and National Marketing Division. It was not available through IBM's traditional PC distribution channels, namely its dealers. Secondly, PC/IX is supplied as an entire UNIX distribution on 19 diskettes and occupies over 6 Mbytes of disk space — hardly ideal for a 10 Mbyte PC/XT configuration. Thirdly, even though UNIX is a multi-user, multitasking operating system, and the PC/XT is capable of supporting two additional serial ports, PC/IX is only licenced as a single-user, multitasking product.

All the indications are, therefore, that PC/IX is aimed squarely at IBM's major accounts — those corporations with a large investment in hard disk PCs and an active interest in software portability, standardisation and, consequently, UNIX. It is interesting that the IBM Information Systems Group UNIX product for the PC/AT is based on Microsoft XENIX and not PC/IX. Indeed, it is not compatible with PC/IX.

Interactive Systems Corporation has now upgraded PC/IX to enable it to run on the PC/AT in full 286 mode, but again only as a single-user product. Therefore, IBM offers, rather confusingly, two UNIX-based products for the PC/AT — one is the single-user PC/IX from Interactive Systems Corporation and the other the three-user XENIX from Microsoft.

## UNIX for IBM mainframes

IBM followed up the PC/IX announcement with a version of UNIX for its 4300 mainframe series. VM/IX is a UNIX System III port produced, once again, by Interactive Systems and runs as a task under VM/SP 3. It is only available as a 'controlled release' product — a PRPQ (Programming Request for Price Quotation), without source, and must be specifically ordered.

VM/IX has a restricted status because it requires a specially modified version of the VM operating system to run on. The product is only available, therefore, to organisations capable of supporting themselves to a large degree. It also requires a dedicated Series/1 running special front-end software to provide ASCII terminal support. 3270-style terminals are not supported.

However, since the release of the generally supported IX/370 in 1985, it is unlikely that VM/IX has much future.

## UNIX for the PC/AT

### *XENIX*
XENIX for the PC/AT is IBM's latest PC UNIX offering. It allows the AT to run as a multi-user system supporting up to three users. XENIX requires a 20 Mbyte hard disk and a minimum of 512 Kbytes of memory, though up to 40 Mbytes of disk and 3 Mbytes of main memory may be supported. The AT disk can be partitioned to allow for a PC-DOS file system to co-reside with the XENIX file system and utilities are provided for transferring files between the two environments.

XENIX has been 'unbundled' for the AT and is available as distinct modules. These are:
- XENIX Runtime Operating System
- XENIX Software Development System
- XENIX Text Processing System.

The basic Operating System module contains the UNIX kernel and most of the standard UNIX utilities. The Software Development System module provides a C language compiler, assembler, run-time library, debugger and version control system. The third module, the Text Processing System, contains a text formatting package, editors, spelling checker and numerous technical documentation tools. In this form, users who are interested in running third-party software need only obtain the basic Operating System module, saving a great deal of disk space and more than halving the cost.

PC XENIX is capable of supporting a total of three users — one via the main PC console screen and two others via any ASCII terminals connected through the AT's two built-in RS232 ports.

The three user restriction on the PC/AT appears to be a marketing decision rather than a technical limitation. Most suppliers of UNIX systems that are using Intel 80286 chip sets (including all of the PC/AT clones) are supporting more users — some are claiming the ability to drive up to a dozen terminals off such a machine.

PC XENIX is now available in many countries through IBM's PC dealer networks. IBM states, quite categorically, however, that 'PC-DOS continues to be the strategic operating system for the IBM PC/AT'.

## UNIX for 370 architectures

The IBM Interactive Executive for System/370 (IX/370) offers a full UNIX System V implementation for the IBM mainframe range from the 4331 through to the new 3090 systems. Unlike the earlier VM/IX product, available only for the 4300 under PRQR status, IX/370 is provided with full IBM service and support across the System/370 processor line.

IX/370 executes as a VM/SP guest system on any 43XX or 30XX machine supported by VM/SP Release 3.0 or later. Unfortunately, the announced version of IX/370 only supports ASCII terminals and requires a dedicated Series/1 to act as a front-end terminal controller. Interestingly, IX/370 does support 3270 terminals since it requires a 3270 operator's console, but these are not offered for general use. However, it seems highly likely that future IX/370 releases will feature full 3270 terminal support as well. In addition to full UNIX System V compatibility, IX/370 includes a number of additional features that exploit characteristics of VM including:

1  Virtual memory support. Currently not a standard part of UNIX System V but available on a number of commercial implementations. IX/370 offers an 8 Mbyte virtual address space regardless of real processor size.

2  Multiple IX/370 virtual machines. This feature permits several IX/370 systems to co-reside on the same processor, allowing groups of users to be divided between virtual machines for greater security. Series/1 front-ends cannot be shared between IX/370 virtual machines, though each IX/370 machine is capable of supporting several Series/1s.

3  Access to VM systems printers. This allows the use of enhanced printing and spool queue facilities which are not provided within standard UNIX System V.

Additionally, IX/370 incorporates a number of utilities taken from Interactive System's PC/IX implementation, such as enhanced electronic mail, full screen editor and machine-to-machine communication facilities. These features make IX/370 more accessible to PC/IX users and comply with the IBM philosophy of using PCs as front-ends to mainframes.

Installation of IX/370 carries an additional one-time charge of between $10 000 and $75 000 depending on the number of users to be connected to the system. Clearly, IX/370 does not replace either MVS or VM. It offers the IBM product range to the UNIX community and not UNIX to the IBM customer base.

### Third-party UNIX products for IBM hardware

Even though IBM's commitment to UNIX has been slow and inconsistent, a number of UNIX products have emerged from third parties for IBM equipment. Three other versions of UNIX for the PC/XT and PC/AT are available: XENIX V was produced under licence from Microsoft by Santa Cruz Operation and is distributed in the UK by Sphinx Limited, VenturCom Corporation has produced its own UNIX version called VENIX, and a Motorola MC68000 plug-in-board with UNIX is available for the XT from Sritek.

At the mainframe end, IBM plug-compatible manufacturer Amdahl has put its weight behind UTS, a UNIX derivative that runs on 370 and 4300 compatibles under VM. At present over 170 UTS sites have been licenced worldwide, many on non-Amdahl equipment. The main use of UTS appears to be in education, software development for communication products and in the military and aerospace fields.

200

Amdahl and AT&T have been working together for more than a year to provide a series of 'mainframe extensions' to the basic UNIX V product — upgrading it to accommodate some of the features expected by users of mainframe operating systems that have been lacking in UNIX to date. The Amdahl UTS product is also being re-marketed directly by AT&T under the name of UNIX/VM and this cooperative venture will ensure long-term availability of UNIX on IBM mainframe hardware.

UTS is based on UNIX System V and a native mode version (capable of running directly on 370 architecture machines without the need for the VM operating system) is due to be released early in 1986. Clearly, there is a large perceived demand for UNIX systems on IBM hardware.

## IBM's UNIX strategy

At first sight it appears that IBM does not have a real UNIX strategy. Certainly, IBM does not (yet) have a cohesive strategy for UNIX, but it is committed to entering every computer market in which it believes there is money to be made and, furthermore, which it can dominate. IBM must believe, therefore, that the UNIX market is, or will become, a viable one.

In most markets IBM waits for rivals to demonstrate their viability before it moves. In the case of UNIX IBM has been forced to act sooner than, perhaps, it would have liked. Many US Government agencies and major corporations are more committed to industry standards than they are to IBM. This has been demonstrated in recent months by several extremely large US Government computer contracts (the US Army and the US Internal Revenue Service for example) that have been awarded to suppliers of UNIX-based hardware. Indeed, UNIX was a prerequisite in order to even bid on these government contracts, so to remain in this lucrative market IBM must offer a UNIX-based solution on its hardware. This explains completely IBM's involvement with UNIX on its mainframe systems. IX/370 is IBM's attempt to attract and win over companies looking for larger and more powerful UNIX systems. It is not designed to replace VM or convert contented users of IBM proprietary operating systems.

In the small multi-user marketplace, UNIX (and XENIX in particular) dominates as the *de facto* industry standard operating system. Manufacturers like Tandy and Altos are offering viable multi-user alternatives to networked personal computers. Again, for this reason, IBM is offering XENIX on the PC/AT. Its alternative PC offering, PC/IX, is a single-user UNIX for PCs and its compatibility with VM/IX and IX/370 appears to be IBM's answer to the demands of the corporate market for Personal UNIX. It seems that IBM's current products are a reaction to the marketplace rather than part of a cohesive strategy.

Will UNIX ever be available on System/36? Probably not. System/36 is extremely successful in specific multi-user vertical markets and existing users do not appear to be asking for UNIX. Additionally, System/36 is based around a 16-bit architecture — not the best environment for the newer, larger and more memory-hungry versions of UNIX.

But are there markets in which UNIX offers IBM an offensive rather than a defensive position? The answer is definitely yes. IBM would dearly love to dominate the scientific and engineering markets where it has traditionally lost out to companies such as Digital Equipment, Prime and Data General. It is in this marketplace, and in the areas of high performance, single-user scientific workstations, that UNIX is being most demanded. An IBM product offering aimed at this area would undoubtedly have to offer UNIX in order to succeed, but such an offering could provide IBM with the key it needs to unlock this marketplace. The hardware for such a market is unannounced but has been rumoured for some time.

Two final factors indicate that IBM's interest in UNIX is not a temporary one. Firstly, IBM has signed 'long-term' cooperative agreements with both Microsoft and Interactive Systems, its current suppliers of UNIX operating systems, and secondly, IBM has recently announced a series of third-party application products that it will resell under XENIX and IX/370 — a sign, perhaps, that it is beginning to make its move into the UNIX market in earnest.

## Benefits and dangers to IBM

What does IBM stand to gain by offering UNIX on its equipment? The PC/AT represents a new standard in personal computing. The Intel 80286 chip set is powerful and can easily support multiple users. UNIX has successfully emerged as a *de facto* standard multi-user operating system for the latest generation of microprocessor-based hardware — the so called 'departmental systems'. In supplying XENIX for the PC/AT IBM has adopted an industry standard multi-user environment and will be able to exploit the wealth of third-party software currently available and being developed for UNIX.

On IBM mainframes, UNIX running under VM provides an attractive combination to end users, enabling them to retain existing investments in mainframe software and systems while allowing easy communications between mainframes and newly installed departmental systems already running UNIX. For the first time, users will be able to run the same package on a range of machines from personal computers to mainframes while allowing complete transportability of data between vastly differing architectures.

By providing UNIX systems on its hardware, IBM may successfully defuse some of the interest that is being shown in AT&T's current and future hardware product line. Even though AT&T 'owns' UNIX, its historical lack of support for the product combined with the large number of manufacturers offering UNIX derivatives on their hardware, means that AT&T will have to fight very hard to control UNIX development. IBM could, and perhaps will, set the UNIX standard for the entire industry, removing from AT&T its most powerful weapon.

There are a number of potential pitfalls that await IBM if it pushes strongly down the UNIX route. Firstly, the very feature that makes UNIX so attractive to end users, namely software portability, is also the most dangerous for the hardware suppliers. IBM UNIX may eventually provide users with a migration path away from IBM hardware. Secondly, if AT&T is successful in controlling the UNIX standard in the future, will its hardware not always have an edge in the marketplace running the latest, most advanced versions of UNIX?

## Conclusion

Whatever IBM's final position may be, a number of factors are apparent. UNIX will never replace IBM proprietary operating systems on mainframes — at best it will be supplied as a virtual machine under VM. On supermicros UNIX will play an important role, either as a native operating system on machines like the AT or as an industry standard operating environment (alongside PC-DOS, perhaps) running on top of a proprietary IBM operating system. In either case one thing is clear — the UNIX operating system running on IBM hardware makes a very powerful combination in the marketplace.

# 17: The PC/AT and XENIX

**O G Saurin**

**R C Burgess**

Digitus Ltd
London
UK

A number of implementations of UNIX on the IBM PC have appeared from various suppliers. However by far the most important of these is IBM's own version of XENIX (the Microsoft adaptation of UNIX), intended for the PC/AT, since it is the only one which gives a realistic multi-user system. This paper presents an initial appraisal of IBM PC XENIX, including benchmark results which show that as a multi-user system it compares extremely well with other UNIX systems, some of them much more expensive.

*O G Saurin*
Olivier Saurin was educated in France and worked in adult education before entering the computing business as an administrative organiser, acting as a link between users and the computer department for CEBAL in Paris. He later set up and taught a range of computer-related courses: accounting, data entry and merchandising, and subsequently worked in software support in charge of the BASF 7100 systems range of micros. Within Digitus he is a Managing Systems Engineer, with training and consultancy responsibilities for communications and UNIX. He has also worked on process control and been responsible for a project scheduling system as well as playing a major role in the development and implementation of subsystems for Gatwick Airport's flight information system.

*R C Burgess*
Ross Burgess holds degrees from Oxford (Philosophy, Politics and Economics) and the Open University (Mathematics). Most of his 16 years' computer experience has been with systems houses, as a programmer, systems analyst, project manager and consultant. He has led design teams on a wide range of systems, including accounting, on-line seat reservations, payroll, stock control and tea blending. His consultancy assignments have included library systems and a major 'office of the future' study. Within Digitus he runs the Consultancy Group, and is responsible for evaluation of software products, and quality control and standards for consultancy projects. He has taken a major role in several Digitus consultancy assignments, including a study of the management information requirements for an airline terminal, and a strategy study for a major City institution. He was one of the originators of the Digitus management seminar 'Managing office automation', and has given talks on office automation and other subjects. He was joint author, with Joseph St John Bate, of 'The automated office' (1985) and 'Office automation using the IBM Personal Computer systems' (1986), published by Collins. He was editor, and a principal contributor, for 'The UNIX report' published by Digitus.

204

## Background

## Introduction

Two standards have emerged in the microcomputer world over the last few years: firstly, the IBM PC set the standard for single-user computers, and secondly the UNIX operating system, on a host of different machines, set the standard for multi-user systems. The convergence of these two standards, in the form of an IBM-label version of UNIX for the PC/AT, is a crucial event indeed.

## UNIX and XENIX

To begin with, a word of clarification is necessary about the often misunderstood relationship between XENIX and UNIX. UNIX is of course a multi-user, multitasking operating system originated and sold by American Telephone and Telegraph (AT&T). Currently AT&T is actively marketing UNIX, but for a long period it was prevented from doing so by legal constraints. During this period a number of other companies bought the original source code for UNIX from AT&T and added their own enhancements to make it more viable for commercial purposes. One of these companies was Microsoft, which called its version XENIX. When introduced it had a number of additional features compared to standard AT&T UNIX, including the following:

- Hardware error recovery
- Automatic file repair after crashes
- Power-fail and parity error detection
- Shared data segments
- Improved inter-process communication.

A number of these features have subsequently been incorporated, not always in the same form, in other UNIX versions.

At the same time as XENIX was being developed, other companies produced UNIX-like operating systems from scratch, without buying a source licence. These have included such names as Cromix, Coherent and UNOS. It is now clear that there is little future for these 'look-alikes'. XENIX is thus a 'true' UNIX version, not one of the 'look-alikes' — indeed it is by far the most successful version of UNIX in terms of the number of copies sold. However, the situation is slightly complicated by the history of UNIX and the various versions it has gone through. In short, the important official AT&T versions have included Version 7 (1979), System III (1981) and System V (1983). System V represents a much more definitive standard than the earlier versions and is the first one to be actively marketed by AT&T.

XENIX was introduced in 1980 and surprisingly was based on Version 7. More recent releases of XENIX, including IBM's, are equivalent in functionality to System III. There were two ways in which

Microsoft could have achieved this: firstly, by upgrading the original Version 7-based XENIX, and secondly, by buying a new System III source code from AT&T and enhancing it to make it compatible with earlier versions of XENIX. Internal evidence in today's XENIX, in the form of a few relics from Version 7, suggests that Microsoft has taken the first of these two routes, and upgraded the original system. It will be interesting to see how it has implemented its new System V version (announced by Microsoft but, as we write, not yet available from IBM).

Part of the confusion about UNIX and XENIX may be blamed on their respective suppliers. For instance, if you read the documentation for IBM's XENIX, the words 'UNIX' and 'AT&T' are (almost) nowhere to be found. Certainly IBM is not keen to publicise its arch-rival AT&T. Remarkably, AT&T does not insist on licensed products acknowledging their origin — in fact it restricts the use of the world 'UNIX' in the name of software supplied by one of their licensees (hence the confusing plethora of names — XENIX, Venix, PC/IX, Uniplus, Zeus, and so on). They merely *permit* the licensee to say that it is 'derived from UNIX System III under licence from AT&T' *(SAU1)*. IBM appears not to have taken advantage of this permission.

## UNIX and the IBM PC

The success of the IBM PC and the popularity of UNIX made it inevitable that PC versions of UNIX would appear, and there have been a number of versions for the PC/XT with hard disk — a twin floppy PC with UNIX is just not a practicable proposition. Among the XT versions we may note are:
- Venix from Venturcom
- XENIX from the Santa Cruz Operation (developed by Microsoft)
- PC/IX from IBM (developed by Interactive Systems).

PC/IX differs from the others in being not only an IBM-label product but a single-user implementation.

All of these versions of UNIX for the PC have had some success amongst users who want a UNIX machine on their desk, but they all have performance problems. This is inherent in the architecture of the PC, and particularly its microprocessor chip, the Intel 8088, which is not fast or powerful enough for multi-user systems. The inevitable complexity of a multitasking system means that even in single-user mode, PC UNIX systems are decidedly slow compared to DOS, which has much less to do. Probably most users of UNIX on the PC/XT (not merely PC/IX users) have used it as a single-user system, thus sacrificing part, but by no means the whole, of the benefits of UNIX.

A more satisfactory PC UNIX system became possible with the advent of the PC/AT, whose Intel 80286 is specifically designed for multitasking systems. AT XENIX (or to give it its official title, IBM Personal Computer XENIX) is the system which fills this gap.

## XENIX on the PC/AT

IBM's PC/AT (Advanced Technology) is a major advance on the basic PC and PC/XT. Many of its features make it much more suitable for running a multi-user operating system such as UNIX. In particular the Intel 80286 microprocessor is faster (about 2.5 times faster by our tests) and more powerful than the 8088 used in previous PCs, and has memory management and protection features specially designed for multitasking. The standard hard disk can now hold 20 Mbytes of data and is supported by a larger capacity diskette (floppy disk) drive — 1.2 Mbytes per diskette rather than 360 Kbytes as previously.

There is no theoretical limit to the number of user terminals that could be attached, but there is a physical limit imposed by the fact that there are only two serial ports available. The maximum number of users is therefore three: one using the 'console' (the standard keyboard and memory-mapped display screen) and one each on two external VDU terminals.

IBM Personal Computer XENIX (the word AT does not appear in its title) comes packaged as three modules or products. The prices below were correct as at October 1985:
- Operating system £352
- Software development system £407
- Text formatting system £132.

This gives a total price for the three modules of £891; a lot more than the price of DOS at around £60, but very cheap for a fully featured multi-user operating system.

## XENIX in use

### Notes on the evaluation

On receiving a copy of the XENIX software we carried out an intensive evaluation, including the running of a number of benchmark tests. The hardware used for this evaluation comprised an IBM PC/AT with 512 Kbytes (half a megabyte) of memory, one 20 Mbyte Winchester disk, and one high density floppy disk drive. We then repeated the tests using 1 Mbyte of memory. A colour/graphics monitor was attached, as well as a Wyse terminal on the first asynchronous port. All three modules of XENIX were available for this evaluation, although we concentrated mainly on the base module.

Before evaluating this implementation of XENIX on the AT we had, for some time, used the Santa Cruz Operation (SCO) implementation of XENIX for the IBM PC/XT. Some of the following points refer to the differences between IBM XENIX and SCO XENIX. The overall impression is that in some respects SCO did a more complete job than IBM in the actual implementation, although the differences in total are not substantial.

### Use of the hard disk

XENIX, like all forms of UNIX, is essentially a system for use with hard disk machines. The PC/AT provides for 20 Mbytes of hard disk storage, normally as a single physical device. Nearly all PC users however will make some use of DOS, so if XENIX is in use the disk needs to be divided into several partitions, or logical devices, one of them reserved for DOS. Different implementations of XENIX use the hard disk in different ways. For instance, SCO XENIX has just one XENIX partition on the XT's 10 Mbyte disk. This partition is treated as the 'root file system' in UNIX terms, and contains all the XENIX files and directories, other than those on floppy disks — the floppy drive allows for the mounting of separate file systems.

IBM XENIX on the PC/AT uses two file systems on the fixed disk, each being a partition, and thus requires a minimum of three partitions of the hard disk, compared to SCO's one. The three IBM partitions are for the root file system, the user (/usr) file system and the BBT (Bad Blocks Table). The BBT requires a partition even though it is only one cylinder long — a peculiarity of this implementation. XENIX thus accounts for three out of the four possible partitions on the AT disk, leaving only one available for DOS or another operating system. It would thus not be possible to have, for example, DOS, XENIX, and CP/M-86 all loaded.

SCO XENIX can run with 6.6 Mbytes and is thus small enough to share an XT's 10 Mbyte disk with PC-DOS, provided that the partitioning is two-thirds for XENIX and one-third for DOS. IBM XENIX requires much more space — a minimum of 9 Mbytes for the root file system plus 6 Mbytes for the user file system, giving a total of 15 Mbytes or three-quarters of the AT's standard disk.

### Installation procedures

The installation procedures for PC versions of UNIX tend to be rather tedious because of the large number of utilities included in the operating system, and hence the large amount of data to be loaded. Whereas the essential parts of DOS are contained on a single floppy, PC/IX (not a very full implementation) comes on 19 diskettes.

IBM XENIX takes advantage of the AT's high density floppy disk drive so that the 'base' of the operating system is contained in three floppies, compared to eight for SCO XENIX. In total there are eight floppies supplied for the full IBM XENIX system as follows:
- Operating system        (three floppies)
- Text formatting          (one floppy)
- Software development  (three floppies)
- Installation disk          (one floppy).

The installation procedures on both IBM and SCO implementations take the user into a program called hdinit, itself calling fdisk to set disk partitions. The SCO fdisk is similar to that for DOS, except that it uses q instead of ESCape to return to its menu, and that upon exit it asks you if you want to save to /dev/hd00. IBM's fdisk is completely different. Firstly, the name of the raw device for the hard disk must be given upon invocation of the command, and secondly, fdisk is not menu driven, but command driven. One of the commands is a help. Other possible commands including the following:

- c to create a partition
- d to delete a partition
- p to print the partition table
- w to write the modifications back to the disk
- q to quit.

The help message mentions q,x to quit, but x gives a message telling you that it is an invalid option and reminds you that ? will give you the list of valid commands — which includes x, of course!

Another innovation is that IBM's fdisk will not let you write back the partition data and quit without shutting down the system automatically, even if there is no change. The IBM XENIX installation puts the operator in a state of confusion when it asks for a number of blocks to allocate to each partition while displaying the partition data in cylinders. The operator is left to work out the number of blocks in a cylinder.

## Special features of IBM XENIX

As the hardware has a battery backed-up clock calendar, and XENIX knows about it, the user is not prompted for time and date at boot time. Instead, the current time and date are displayed on the screen. It is possible to change the system with a setclock(M) command.

There is a shell script to assist the system administrator in changing the log-in shell type for a user: chsh(C). This will edit the password file and copy the default initialisation files for the specified new shell. It will not remove existing initialisation files for previous shells. Special features include the following:

1  pwadmin(C) — a super-user command to deal with password ageing.

2  setkey(M) — a command to load the IBM PC's keyboard function keys.

3  setclock(M) — a command to set the battery-powered clock. This is also available through reading and writing /dev/clock.

4  cmos(M) — a command to display and/or set the values in the CMOS database. This is also available through reading and writing /dev/cmos.

## Multitasking aspects

In the office environment, a multitasking computer system can be very useful. XENIX, like all UNIX systems, is of course multitasking, but not every method of implementing multitasking is equally user friendly. A standard way of initiating multiple concurrent tasks is to set off background programs (easily done by adding the & character to the end of a command line). This is convenient for tasks such as printing a report, which require no further interaction with the user. Multitasking may also be involved when a number of processes are piped together, but again this is mainly suitable when the various programs do not require further input.

A different type of multitasking arises when there are several interactive tasks running concurrently, for instance by having each linked to a different 'virtual terminal'. This is the concept behind Digital Research's Concurrent DOS. The SCO version of XENIX implemented multiple (10) terminals on the same memory-mapped screen and keyboard, with the ability to flick from one virtual terminal to another with ALT and a function key. For instance, this enables you to respond quickly to the interruptions that are part of office life. While typing a document with a word processor, you can break off and use another program such as a calculator or a database without needing to close the current file, halt the program, and load a new program.

Another function of multiple virtual terminals is particularly useful on this size of machine, where most users are bound to be also super-users. When starting the machine you log-in as root on the console, then as a normal user on the next screen. That way, you can work in safety (super-user privileges are dangerous to live with all the time) and do your super-user tasks at the flick of an ALT function key.

SCO's virtual terminals are real users: tasks are not suspended while the terminal is not current (unlike programs such as MemoryShift, and the 'pop-up' programs including SideKick, available with MS-DOS). IBM XENIX did not implement this very useful facility: we would hope it may be implemented later, either on a 'virtual terminal' basis like SCO XENIX, or perhaps using windows, as Microsoft, IBM and others, have provided with DOS.

## Problems and bugs

Surprisingly, the IBM implementation of XENIX as delivered in the UK does not take into account the UK keyboard layout. The result is that symbol keys are somewhat mixed up. This is a nuisance, particularly when skipping constantly between DOS and XENIX. However, consider the problems endured by French keyboard users with the additional complication of the AZERTY keyboard layout, plus a few accented letters.

SCO XENIX knows that a good proportion of IBM PCs run with a colour/graphic screen, and provide a setcolor command to allow you to select your preferred foreground and background colours (the colours on different virtual terminals can be different). IBM XENIX does not provide this facility to set the colours on the terminal, although it is not difficult to write a shell script to do this.

Both SCO and IBM implementations know that DOS exists, and even that it can share the hard disk. They both allow the disk to have a non-XENIX partition and both have a series of dos commands:
- doscat (display DOS files)
- doscp (copy to and from DOS)
- dosdir (get a directory of DOS files in DOS format)
- dosls (get a directory of DOS files in XENIX format — file names only)
- dosmkdir (create a DOS directory on the DOS disk)
- dosrm (remove a DOS file)
- dosrmdir (remove a DOS directory).

SCO's DOS commands allow you to perform all these operations with DOS floppies and the DOS partition on the hard disk. IBM limits the operations to floppy disks. Moreover, with the default permission sets on the device drivers, any write to the DOS floppies in 48 tracks/inch mode (for standard IBM 360 Kbyte diskettes) can be achieved only by the super-user!

It also appears that SCO's doscp allows you to copy from DOS to DOS, which IBM's version refuses to do. When the IBM hot line was interrogated on this subject, part of the answer was that it bought XENIX from outside (we knew that, and SCO bought it from the same suppliers) and that, anyway, XENIX was not a strategic choice for IBM but was merely supplied because people asked for it! The same comment has been reported widely in the press.

IBM changed the name of the familiar incremental dump program (dump) into backup, but it works in exactly the same way. If IBM want the same name as in DOS — with a different syntax, that does not seem like the best idea — why did it not just link backup to dump so that we, the users who were in UNIX before IBM knew what it stood for, can use our standard tools with their standard names?

Of course, the user can create such a link, but he should not have to. Incidentally, backup still writes the last dump dates into /etc/ddate which stands for dump date. backup takes its default disk and 'tape' from a file in /etc/default, which is a XENIX convention, unknown to standard UNIX.

IBM's implementation of vi (visual editor) made use of the cursor keys of the PC keyboard, which SCO's did not. However, there is a problem: when moving the cursor too fast to the right with the cursor key, or past the end of the line, a part of the line — sometimes the whole line — is deleted (not just disappearing from the screen). This is very distressing. Experimentation reveals that the undo function (u) restores the deleted line. The problem does not arise when using the letter 'l' to move the cursor right, which is the convention for keyboards with no cursor keys.

As a last noticed bug, more and vi reset the highlight bit when they display a reverse-video message on the screen. Unfortunately, this is due to the screen controls: there is no specific code to reset reverse. The same code (ESC [ O m) is used to reset reverse, highlight, and so on, and there is no way of knowing which attributes were set before.

## Other points

SCO XENIX has a strange way of dealing with auxiliary ports for modem control or three-wire connection: for each of the two physical ports it declares two logical ports; one for three-wire connection and one with full modem control. IBM XENIX has a one to one mapping of logical to physical ports. There does not seem to be any specific command to declare which ports have and which do not have modem control handling, and the documentation does not send the reader to the stty command which can set or reset the clocal mode.

On the subject of terminals, another point is worth noting: the console is the memory-mapped PC screen and the PC keyboard. Logically it is addressed as an ANSI terminal, with speed set to 9600 baud. However, the data transfer is achieved through memory instead of through the RS-232 interface. The result is that the console is nearly twice as fast in displaying data as an external terminal running at a true 9600 baud.


## Documentation

### Manuals supplied

The full documentation consists of eight A5-size manuals. They come in rigid boxes without notches, making it difficult to extract a manual from its box without tipping the box forward — this can be difficult if you stack them! Here is a list of the manuals:

1  Operating system:
   - Installation guide, visual shell, system administration
   - Basic operations guide
   - Command reference.

2  Software development system:
   - Software development guide
   - Software command reference [surely all commands are software!]
   - Programmer's guide to library functions, C compiler reference
   - Assembler reference.

3  Text formatting system:
   - Text formatting guide.

In addition to these eight manuals, an advanced user is referred to the 'IBM Personal Computer AT technical reference manual'.

### *Documentation structure*

In most UNIX manuals as supplied by AT&T (including the on-line manual supplied with certain versions), the documentation is organised in sections, as follows:
- 1: User commands
- 2: System calls
- 3: Subroutines
- 4: Special files
- 5: Files and conventions
- 6: Games
- 7: Program support files
- 8: System administration.

References within the documentation make use of these sections, for instance 'chmod(1)' means see the entry for 'chmod' in section 1. The modular nature of IBM XENIX has meant that this scheme is somewhat modified: commands normally in section 1 of UNIX manuals are here in section 'C' (base package), 'CP' (programmer's package) and 'CT' (text processing package). There is a section 'S' for system calls and subroutines, a section 'F' for file descriptions and a section 'M' (as usual) for system administration.

## Comments on the documentation

We were disappointed by the lack of references, in particular to the customisation of the system. Sentences like 'At some installations an option may be invoked ... ', in the description of login(M), leave you wondering how you can invoke the specific option (in that case a secondary password).

Reference manuals broadly assume that you are using the Bourne shell and make hardly any provision for C shell users. For instance, Bourne shell initialisation files are always mentioned as if they were the only possibility. This may be very misleading indeed as a user is told that modifying something in /etc/profile will have an effect on his environment, which is not true for a C shell user. The 'About this book' section in the 'Software development guide' says that, 'Chapter 10 ... explains how to use the C shell, a command interpreter that provides greater flexibility and more power than the standard XENIX shell, sh'. If the C shell is so good, it is perhaps surprising that IBM does not do more to encourage its use.

XENIX reference manuals are of the same level of clarity as the standard UNIX reference manuals — much jargon and few good examples. There is no equivalent of the 'User's guide' supplied with DOS, which guides new users easily through the basic housekeeping tasks with the aid of cartoons. Clearly the expectation is that XENIX will not be used by naive users: users will start with DOS, and graduate to XENIX only when they have learnt a good deal about the practicalities of personal computing. This is a valid assumption at present, but as more application software becomes available we can expect that XENIX systems will be supplied by systems houses to end users, packaged with the appropriate software for the job in question. In this case a simple manual, detailing the basic housekeeping functions, would be highly desirable.

## Errors in the documentation

We discovered a few errors in the XENIX documentation, as follows:

1  In the default (from release floppies) /etc/ttys, the console speed character is set to C. This speed is not in the list of valid options for getty(M).

2  setkey(M) is a command to assign function keys. The one page entry does not contain all the necessary information: it does not tell you what the size limit on the string is; it also does not tell you that it is only for the console (IBM PC/AT's monitor and keyboard). XENIX is supposed to be a multi-user operating system and the two possible additional users need only VDUs. Indeed the command is in the 'M' section meaning that it is for use with root log-in only, but you can log-in as root on an external VDU. When tried on a VDU, setkey returns an error message saying, stdout must be /dev/console. Logically, the operation of setkey should at least be extended to any ANSI terminal — testing not the terminal port but the terminal type.

3  The setkey command reference description also exemplifies meaningless and mind-boggling examples. The following is a quotation from the manual: 'The string can contain control characters, such as a newline character, and should be quoted to protect it from processing by the shell. For example the command setkey 2 "pwd;lc" assigns the command sequence "pwd;lc" to function key 2. Notice how the newline character is embedded in the quoted string. This causes the command to be carried out when function key 2 is pressed. Otherwise, the Enter key would have to be pressed after pressing the function key.' Unfortunately, the command as stated does not have an embedded newline. If you type what the manual says, you still have to press Enter. After some trying, we realised that Enter before the closing quotation mark gives the secondary prompt (if you are a Bourne shell user, of course) to which you can give the closing quotes and Enter to terminate the command sequence. So it works, but not as per the example. A C shell user can achieve the same result by typing setkey 1 "pwd;lc followed by a space, a backslash, a newline (enter key) then a quotation mark, then Enter.

4  There are at least two other mistakes in the setkey(M) entry alone:
   - setkey should not be in the 'M' section, as it is not restricted to the super-user but to the console (a confusion that should have been avoided)
   - The example for pwd;lc has two spaces surrounding the ;. These spaces are just a waste. Furthermore, the following text says that the string pwd;lc is assigned to function key 2, which is wrong. Also, the example intends to load pwd;lc<Enter>.

5  The tset(C) command is also wrong when it states that options -e[c] and -k[c] set the Erase and Kill characters respectively to Ctrl-C, although this looks more like a bug in the system than in the

documentation. What actually happens is that Erase and/or Kill are set to the character specified, rather than the corresponding control character.

## The other modules

Most of this evaluation has concentrated on the base module of IBM XENIX, but many of its potential users will find the other modules, text formatting and software development, of considerable interest.

### Text creation

The text formatting system contains the following commands:
- col (filter reverse line feeds)
- cut (cut out selected fields of each line)
- cw (prepare constant width text for troff)
- deroff (remove special characters and formatting instructions)
- diction (check for bad or wordy diction)
- diffmk (mark differences between files)
- eqn (format mathematical text)
- explain (correct bad diction)
- hyphen (find hyphenated words)
- man (print entries in the manual)
- mm (print documents formatted with the 'memorandum macros')
- mmcheck (check usage of mm macros)
- mmt (typeset documents using the mm macros — equivalent to troff -mm)
- nroff (formats text files for output to line printer or daisywheel printer)
- paste (merge lines of files)
- prep (prepare text for statistical formatting)
- ptx (generate a permuted index)
- soelim (copies included files within a text file, thus eliminating the .so directive)
- spell (find spelling errors)
- style (analyse document for readability)
- tbl (formats tables for troff or nroff)
- troff (typesets text).

In addition to the above, XENIX also contains, as part of the basic operating system module, a number of more general-purpose utilities such as grep (search a document for a pattern), wc (count words, lines, and characters), and sort (sort a file, line by line).

### Office automation

XENIX, like other UNIX implementations, comes with certain 'office automation' facilities. In particular, it includes the mail and calendar facilities in the basic price.

The mail program, originally an enhancement of the University of California at Berkeley, gives you a basic electronic mail service. The XENIX version has a number of additional features compared to the standard UNIX version. It allows you to send mail to another user who need not be logged onto the system — he will be told 'you have mail' when logging on. You may also use mail to read a message sent to you, then delete it, keep it, forward it with annotation to another user, or reply to it. Mail may be sent to a number of users at once, by means of the distribution list facility, and you may be prompted for additional complimentary copy (cc) distribution.

The calendar program looks in the user's calendar file and lists events occurring today or tomorrow. A further option allows this to be done once a day, and notify all users of events in their calendar files, by means of the mail facility.

### Software development

The software development system contains two main programming languages:

1  The C language compiler, together with the standard C library routines for input, output, and so on, the

special curses routines for screen handling, and facilities for using such UNIX features as pipes, semaphores, and shared data segments.

2 An assembler language for the Intel 8086, 80186, and 80286.

There are also some 'programmer's workbench' facilities such as:

1 lint — for checking the syntax of C programs beyond what the compiler does.

2 make — for automating the compilation of large programs, for instance involving many source language and other files, some dependent on others.

3 lex (lexical analyser), and yacc (compiler-compiler) — for sophisticated manipulation of source programs.

4 adb (debugger) — for use with both C and assembler programs.

5 sccs — the source code control system.

Together these facilities give very powerful tools to the programmer — far in excess of those found in most non-UNIX systems. The sccs program in particular is useful not only for program source code, but for any document which goes through multiple versions, and for which it is important to be able to preserve the latest version, and also recreate the history of previous versions.

## The shells

UNIX systems are generally supplied with more than one 'shell' (command processor): principally the Bourne shell (sh), part of AT&T standard UNIX, and the C shell (csh) from the University of California at Berkeley. SCO XENIX offers you the C shell in the base package. From IBM's pre-release documentation, and in some parts of the released documentation, it is mentioned that the C shell comes with the second package, the software development system. We were surprised to find the C shell within the base package. The only thing missing is the C shell documentation, correctly included in the development kit. Also included in the base package is the visual shell (vsh), a Microsoft innovation.

### Networking and Micnet

IBM XENIX (like SCO XENIX) uses Micnet, the Microsoft Network, for networking XENIX machines. Micnet is a limited network scheme — it does not require additional hardware as it uses RS-232 ports — but this has the consequence of a limited transfer rate (maximum 9600 baud). Moreover, RS-232 ports are in short supply on the IBM PCs; the architecture limits them to two. An IBM PC connected in the middle of the linear network therefore cannot have more than one user (on the console). Only end-of-line machines can have one additional terminal attached. So, with Micnet on IBM PCs we are talking mostly about networking single-user UNIX machines.

Micnet allows the following operations across the network:
• mail: when Micnet is set, the XENIX mail command allows mail to be addressed to remote users
• rcp: a remote copy utility which copies file by file
• remote: execution of commands on a remote machine.

Micnet limitations are:

1 Wild card characters are not expanded on the remote machine.

2 Commands which can be executed on a remote host are defined in a system file on each host (executeall specifies that all commands can be executed), but there is no restriction on users.

3 Files to be copied from a remote host must have public access (because there is no user validation).

4   Network user names must be unique across the network and different from machine names.

5   Output of remote commands cannot be redirected to the local machine.

Micnet is in no way as versatile as the Altos network Teamnet. It is mainly intended for occasional file transfer between machines. Moreover, because of its lack of user validation (if a command is available for remote execution for one user, it is available for all, if a file is accessible to one user, it is accessible to all), it opens security breaches which are likely to be incompatible with many installations' requirements.

Perhaps surprisingly, IBM XENIX does not provide facilities to connect to the IBM PC network — DOS (version 3.1) is required for this.

## General points

### The implementation

It is a little disappointing to realise that IBM did not go as far as SCO to deliver a fully tailored version of XENIX. However, the system runs smoothly and seems resilient, so the overall impression is what one would expect from an IBM-label product.

### Software availability

At the time of writing, several months after the introduction of the IBM PC/AT, and nearly two months after the release of XENIX for this machine, there is very little available in the way of off-the-shelf software packages. Indeed, the success of XENIX on the AT will be closely related to the number of packages available, and this number will be closely related to the success of the operating system, and so on.... This situation is usually unblocked by external factors, such as the forecast of the success of the operating system by software suppliers.

Of course, since IBM has declared that XENIX is not a strategic product, software suppliers can be pushed only by the market. Their response will determine whether XENIX on the AT will be an operating system to recommend or whether to follow the still-born PC/IX.

### Hardware restrictions

The AT has a hardware restriction which places it in a class of its own as far as UNIX systems are concerned: since there only two RS-232 ports, the number of users is limited to three, one of them using a privileged memory-mapped screen. This limitation is lifted with third-party offerings such as the AST-FourPort/XN board which adds four ports to the AT and comes with the corresponding TTY drivers. Two of these boards can be used in the AT — making it an eleven-user system, which is probably a little excessive if these users intend to do anything at all with the computer.

## Benchmark tests and results

### Comparative test results

The benchmark tests carried out were those published in 'Byte' magazine *(SAU2)*. The results are shown in Figures 1 and 2. Figure 1 shows the results of single tests, while Figure 2 shows the results of 'multi.sh' which attempts to simulate a multi-user system by running several tasks in background.

The results for one machine alone would not be significant: what matters is the comparison of the same tests across several different machines. The machines used were:
- Altos 986, 1 Mbyte, 40 Mbyte disk, running XENIX (System III)
- Altos 486, 0.5 Mbyte, 20 Mbyte disk, running XENIX (System III)
- IBM PC/AT, 0.5 Mbyte, 20 Mbyte disk, running IBM XENIX (System III)
- IBM PC/AT, 1 Mbyte, 20 Mbyte disk, running IBM XENIX (System III)

214

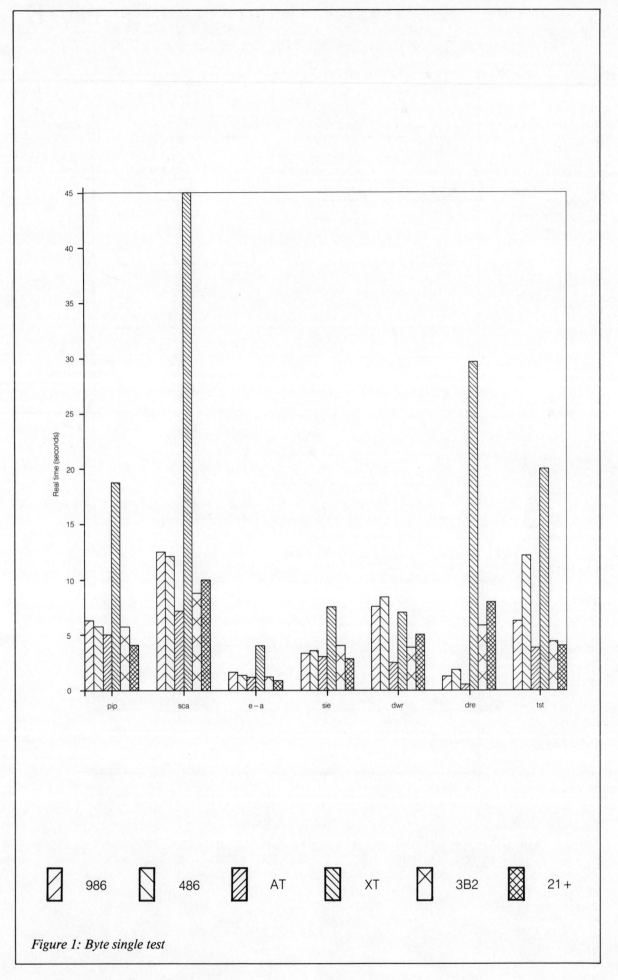

*Figure 1: Byte single test*

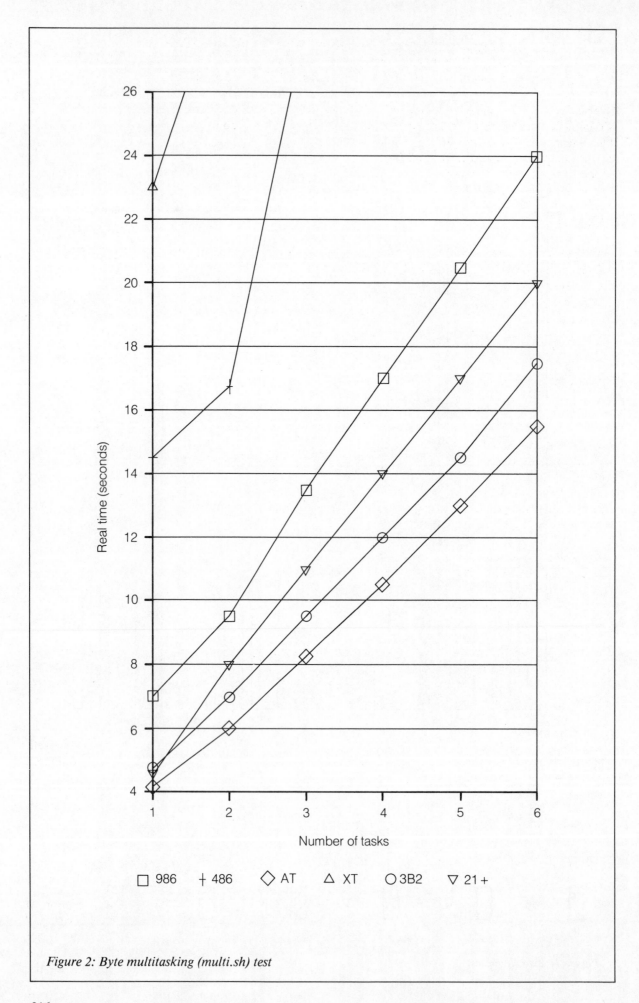

Figure 2: Byte multitasking (multi.sh) test

- IBM PC/XT, 0.5 Mbyte, 10 Mbyte disk, running SCO XENIX (System III)
- Olivetti/AT&T 3B2/300, 1 Mbyte, running UNIX System V
- Zilog System 8000 model 21+, 50 Mbyte disk, running Zeus 3.2 (System III).

Overall we were impressed by the results obtained by AT-XENIX. The poor performances of the XT implementation were left far behind, and the AT had a very good position in the cluster of 'feasible' UNIX machines. Of course there are faster machines on the market, but all the machines used for the comparison (apart from the XT) have been successfully sold as UNIX engines. Being well positioned in this cluster, for a fraction of the price of the competition, gives the AT a very good level of acceptability.

## Test details

The various tests carried out were as follows. In most cases there was little difference between the two AT machines — with 512 Kbytes and 1 Mbyte respectively — but the difference is shown very clearly in the 'multi.sh' test.

### Pipes (pip)
This test assessed the performance of the system using pipes, which are an essential part of the implementation of a UNIX system. The AT came second after the 21+, with a short lead on System V 3B2.

### System calls (sca)
This test performed a system call 10 000 times. The AT, even with only 0.5 Mbytes, was by far the best performer.

### Function calls (e-a)
This test was the result of the difference between a program calling a function and the same program without the function call, in order to isolate the time taken by the function call from the time taken by the program loop and assignment to a variable. The AT came second, together with the 3B2, after the Zilog. There was not much difference between the AT and the Altos machines but the XT needed more than twice the time.

### Sieve (sie)
This test was a CPU-intensive test, based on the sieve of Eratosthenes (a method of computing prime numbers). It also reflected the efficiency of the compiler. Apart from the XT, which again took its time, all machines achieved close performances, with a slight advantage for the AT and the 21+.

### Disk write (dwr)
This test assessed the speed of the disk for write operations. The AT's disk performed extremely well under the test conditions but the advantage of System V on the 3B2 — System V is bound to be faster on disk access — does not make up for the difference. This was also the only test in which the XT did not achieve the worst results — it actually outperformed the Altos machines.

### Disk read (dre)
This test assessed the performances of random reads from the disk. The AT performed remarkably well, while the XT took more than 60 times as long! The Altos machines also performed very well, compared with the AT&T and Zilog, although the faster of the two Altos machines took more than twice the time of the AT.

### Application mix (tst)
This test attempted to give a mix of applications. The AT came first, together with the Zilog 21+, but not far from the 3B2/300. Not surprisingly, the XT was far behind.

### Multitasking (multi.sh)
This test ran the tst test in background up to six times in an attempt to simulate multi-user operation. It should be noted that the number of tasks did not directly represent the number of users, as in real conditions each user can run several tasks. Attention should be given to the shape of the curve, together with its position. The performances of the XT — and the Altos 486 to a lesser extent — were so poor that it was not possible to show them in full on the same graph and still be able to show the results for the other systems clearly.

When we ran the AT with half a megabyte, it was the fastest up to three background processes, but then the curve took a steeper slope and crossed that of the three remaining machines: with 512 Kbytes, the AT did not take the load that well. Our first reaction on seeing this was that IBM's restriction of the AT to three users was for performance reasons, since the performance with more concurrent tasks dropped off so soon. However, on monitoring the accumulated swapping time, we realised that the system started swapping tasks in and out of memory much more heavily at the point where the multi.sh curve started to bend upwards. It was clearly not fair, in this case, to compare a 512 Kbytes AT with machines with one megabyte. Therefore we ran the tests again after upgrading the AT to one megabyte. We then had an entirely different picture: the AT outperformed all the other test machines throughout the test, as Figure 2 shows.

Clearly the AT continues to be an impressive performer with a reasonable number of users, although one would obviously need to provide a sufficiently large memory. With 3 Mbytes potentially available, this is not too much of a problem. It would seem that IBM's restriction to three users is for strategic reasons (perhaps to avoid competition with System/36). We can therefore welcome third-party manufacturers who will release the power of the AT with multi-terminal cards.

## Conclusions

### Performance

The benchmark tests show that the AT is a much more 'serious' machine than the XT when it comes to running UNIX. It is even a serious competitor to higher price systems which have been accepted as UNIX machines. It should be noted, however, that:

1 The Altos machines were running with a kernel providing for the sophisticated Teamnet network, which slows down their operation by an unknown, however small, factor.

2 Zilog and Altos now have faster systems than those used for the comparison; AT&T have a higher performance model, the 3B2/400.

The AT definitely has two advantages besides its speed:

1 It bears a well known three-letter logo.
2 Its price is extremely competitive.

As far as price is concerned, the AT with half a megabyte of memory, a 20 Mbyte disk, a 1.2 Mbyte diskette drive (also capable of reading DOS 2 floppies), a screen and a keyboard, with full XENIX operating system (the three modules) costs less than £6000. With a full megabyte of memory, the price is still less than £7000.

An AT&T 3B2/300A with half a megabyte of memory, a smaller disk (10 Mbytes), a smaller capacity diskette drive (720 Kbits), two serial ports and no parallel interface costs £9000.

The Altos 486 with half a megabyte of memory, 20 Mbyte disk and double-sided diskette drive, costs nearly £7000: for that price, you have five serial ports plus a network (RS-422) port but no parallel port.

The AT can have up to three parallel ports and XENIX-accessible memory can be expanded up to 3 Mbytes on a single slot with the AST 'Advantage!' card, or using all eight slots with IBM memory cards.

At the moment, the AT with XENIX lacks application software. However, we can expect that many hardware and software manufacturers will follow the trend and make the AT with XENIX a successful product. But if someone with enough credibility was to offer PC-DOS running as a task under XENIX, users would not have to make a choice between the two rival operating systems — they could move slowly to XENIX while still using all the software they acquired for their XTs. An American software house has produced a product which allows DOS applications to run as tasks under UNIX. The product runs under PC/IX, but attempts to make it run under XENIX have failed. Another solution could be a future version of the PC using the Intel 80386, which is specifically designed for switching easily between environments such as DOS and XENIX.

Meanwhile, there is a vast amount of application software available to run under other versions of XENIX and UNIX. As soon as a market is demonstrated — and this should not be difficult given the very impressive price/performance ratio of the AT with XENIX — this software will be made available very quickly. The C compiler and a COBOL compiler already exist on the AT, and an increasing number of applications packages are now written in one or the other.

Another interesting possibility is the use of IBM XENIX running on some of the IBM-compatibles, such as the COMPAQ 286, which promise substantially greater speed and capacity than the AT.

We can also hope that somebody will provide a better networking scheme, of the Teamnet kind, or better still the IBM token passing network, to replace the limited Micnet. Unfortunately, that kind of network means a modified kernel — a risky undertaking for a third party. Meanwhile we can await the appearance, in due course, of the 'streams' facility promised for a later version of UNIX System V.

## The future

The future of XENIX depends very much on two developments — one short term, the other long term. The short term development is the convergence of XENIX with AT&T UNIX System V, which is now established beyond question as *the* UNIX standard, which all other implementations will be measured against. It will be fully compatible both with standard System V and with current versions of XENIX. IBM has not yet announced a System V version of PC XENIX, but it will surely come.

The longer-term development, also in the hands of Microsoft, is the convergence of XENIX with the single-user operating system MS-DOS (which is itself the basis of IBM's DOS operating system, generally referred to as PC-DOS). Today's MS-DOS is much more UNIX-like than the earlier versions, with directories, pipes, and redirection, but it is still a long way from compatibility. If and when DOS/XENIX compatibility arrives, it will open up the enormous number of DOS application programs, giving XENIX the ready-made basis of software which it lacks at present.

Microcomputer applications have developed along two paths, based respectively on UNIX and MS-DOS, and the types of software that have evolved in the two cases are rather different, but in some ways complementary. The two paths have been coming closer together as more and more software houses write their packages in C and offer them both on UNIX and on DOS: the Informix database management system is a case in point. IBM's XENIX could be the vehicle to finally bring these two paths together and offer the best of both worlds for small business applications and personal computing.

# 18: The strengths and weaknesses of IBM

**R J A Woods**

Independent Consultant
Northwood
Middlesex
UK

This paper begins with a consideration of IBM's strengths, tracing their derivations and developments, and emphasising how the company has managed to build its own individual technical and computer business environment within which its own standards of technology and commercial practices normally apply. We then discuss the company's (often relative) weaknesses, several of which are the antithesis of its strengths, placing these within a general context so that they can be measured in a realistic manner.

*R J A Woods*
John Woods has been an independent consultant for more than 10 years and has concentrated on a mixture of management and design advice on complex data processing and office automation systems. His career in computing dates back to 1956 and his specialisation in communications and transaction processing to 1964 when he was involved in the BEACON seat reservations system. He also worked on several real-time computer systems in the US and Australia. He is the author of a technical and marketing study into local area networks in Europe.

## Introduction

IBM is undoubtedly the Colossus of the computer industry. Its domination is based on a great breadth of product line, a massive user base which is especially strong among major organisations, a huge cash flow, an unequalled profit ratio among all large organisations irrespective of industry sector, gross revenues that equal those achieved by the next 15 largest companies in the business, profits that are roughly double those earned by the remainder of the industry, a staggeringly large research and development (R&D) budget and an enviable corporate culture that percolates through the entire international operation.

IBM is truly a multinational corporation — although it is still clearly controlled from its US-based headquarters — whose product developments and marketing decisions continue to be dominated by the demands of its domestic market which brings in about half the annual revenues, and usually a higher proportion of profits.

The company's success is rooted in its history, by the manner in which it first came to control the punched card market, then — after a false start — managed to control its transition to the computer era. Over the years the company has maintained a consistently high degree of competence in marketing and planning that would be the envy of any business organisation. Fundamental to IBM's progress, has been the remarkable quality of its management, and the extent to which it has nurtured the inherent loyalty of its workforce by very enlightened personnel practices. Likened by some to a modern version of a medieval monastic order, the company has been able to establish, maintain and enhance a remarkable corporate culture that transcends language, race, nationality and technology, as well as its own (occasional) product and market lapses. This basic business ethos undoubtedly underlies its success.

Nevertheless, even IBM's great size and broad resources cannot wholly obscure a number of weaknesses, some of which might be considered as fundamental. Whereas most of the company's competitors might delight in having such failings, nevertheless when present on such a scale, and spread over a very large and international user community, their adaptation and correction are major tasks. In the meantime their presence gives fresh opportunities to companies that are faster and more flexible in operation, are little constrained by the inertia of a major customer base, and who do not constantly have to worry about competing strongly with themselves.

## IBM's strengths

The company's strengths are multifaceted and depend upon an extensive current market position; a very comprehensive, although only partially coherent, product line; consistently high-quality marketing aided, of course, by the power to implement these strategies; the existence of broad third-party markets which see the IBM community as constituting by far the largest available for their associated products and services; great financial and technological resources; and — by no means least — an enduring and consistent corporate culture that has been sustained and developed remarkably well both over time and across international boundaries.

## Standards

These major attributes have enabled the company to impose, upon much of the data processing market, standards of price/performance, servicing, data communications protocols and — in both the mainframe and personal computer market sectors — system architectures, which include the key hardware and software interfaces. These standards have, however, evolved on a *de facto* basis. With the exception of pricing and performance, as well as marketing and support — where competitors must regard IBM as the archetype to be surpassed in some way — these other technical standards bear only the validation of extensive use, and not (in general) the approval of international authorities.

## Market position

Most of these strengths are only too apparent in the marketplace. They are based upon a very powerful position in *the medium to large-scale mainframe business*, which becomes stronger as one rises up the performance scale. Worldwide, the company holds around 75 per cent of this business: close to 80 per cent in the US, nearer 70 per cent in Europe, but only 40 per cent in Japan.

However, the strength of this posture is intensified by the support of the so-called 'plug compatible computer' suppliers — behind whom stand Fujitsu and Hitachi in Japan — so that the System/360/370 mainframe computer architecture now has serious pretentions to becoming the international *de facto* standard — at least from the mid-performance point upwards. Some take the existence of the Plug Compatible Manufacturers (PCMs) as being disadvantageous to IBM, in that other suppliers can 'slipstream' in the company's wake and benefit from its education of the market and its basic architectural designs. This commentator takes precisely the opposite view, despite the presence of major forces such as Fujitsu and Hitachi. IBM benefits enormously from having good and reliable second sources for most of the equipment that it provides. In this important respect it is alone among all the major computer system suppliers.

Together IBM and the PCMs have the ability to turn most of the mainframe market 'blue' and — provided that competition remains intense — the customer will benefit. In comparison, non-IBM mainframe suppliers are to some extent locked into their own proprietary designs, they have neither the incentive or the resources to take major new initiatives and their role, for the most part, is now concerned with retaining and further exploiting their existing bases. Much of this has now to be accomplished with alliances, leaving them too little time to pay attention to developing the more rapidly expanding sectors of the industry.

In contrast, IBM's position in *the smaller business system market* is much less satisfactory. This is due to the far more diffused nature of this major sector, the substantially lower market entry cost and the difficulties that larger organisations with their high sales and overhead costs have in handling smaller customers profitably. As a comparison, IBM's share of this systems market is nowhere much higher than 20 per cent — mainly because of a relative weakness in the less than eight terminal market — and somewhat lower in Europe and Japan. Indeed, in recent years, the company has been losing market share here, a process which is probably only now being slowly reversed due to the more effective use of Value Added Resellers (VARs) of various types, and the greater number of smaller systems being sold into large accounts.

Possibly the most dramatic expression of IBM's inherent strength is the way in which it has truly revolutionised *the business personal computer market* in only three years. Although a latecomer to this particular market, the company was able to benefit from the fragmentation of this market sector, where it applied its very considerable planning and educational capabilities, successfully introducing order and discipline into what had become a very confused environment.

The manner in which this was achieved — by overthrowing many of the principal tenets of its own business dogma — is now history but it demonstrates the company's resilience and adaptability (neither having been very obvious previously) to the new market requirements. As a result IBM now holds around 45 per cent of the North American market for business personal computers, and nearly 35 per cent in Europe. *De facto*

16-bit PC standard hardware and software architectures have been established, and though to this extent the company has lost full control of its direction, the example of the PC/AT and the formation of a whole new IBM support industry and series of distribution channels are major gains.

## Inherent financial and technical strengths

IBM has shown itself to be a company with consistently high profits. Indeed, its net profits represent a larger proportion of revenues than those of any other major organisation. It is financially conservative, although always prepared to invest very substantial sums in new plant, methods and R&D. R&D expenditures, despite much overlap, certainly greatly exceed those for the rest of the industry combined. During the last eight years nearly all the company's plants have been completely refitted and modernised in pursuance of the objective of making it the lowest-cost producer in the business. Furthermore, senior officials have publicly stated that the investment plans of the next five years will involve twice the expenditure of the previous five. This gives the company almost complete control over its own product and systems direction, even though at times this may not always be totally beneficial.

Ultimate direction is exercised from the US, but R&D and product manufacture (of hardware and software, but the latter to a more limited degree) is carefully spread around the company's major markets. This permits the use of international talent, often leading to certain countries or laboratories being given specific target roles. In manufacturing terms the aim is to preserve a general balance of imports against exports in all principal markets. As a result, IBM is often a more important contributor to national economies than locally owned computer industry suppliers.

## IBM's weaknesses

IBM's weaknesses — many of which would be regarded by its competitors as being relative strengths! — can conveniently be divided into the following three broad categories relating to:

1 The difficulty of properly controlling the sheer size of the operation and of instituting changes in its business objectives and market attitudes.

2 The inertia of the existing product and user base with much of the former being, if not actually obsolete, at least inappropriate for the next decade.

3 The problems of converging and enhancing existing major products so that they can be suitably placed into a new strategic design — an immense and extremely time-consuming task.

The trouble stems from IBM's extraordinarily broad product line, most of which has its antecedents in the 1960s or early 1970s — a time when quite different types of computer were produced to meet each major perceived market sector. Even the company's success (in the late 1960s) in being the first to turn its mainframe computer range into a single architecturally compatible line has subsequently been dimmed by the inherent contradictions in such an approach. (Although to be fair, other companies — notably Burroughs — have perhaps been more successful in this aim.)

The variations in requirements, and indeed also in ability and resources, on the part of large and small customers ensured that the former System/360 soon separated, in practice, into two rather different products. The low end, stressing an altogether much simpler operating environment with a need for relatively limited on-site technical support, uses the Disk Operating System (DOS)-derived Virtual Storage Extended (VSE) operating system, while the mid to high range, having an altogether much broader range of requirements, needs the very complex Multiple Virtual Storage (MVS) and its subsequent Extended Architecture (XA).

### New market sectors

Historically IBM has always been a mainline data processing supplier, earning only a relatively modest share of its revenues from typewriters and copiers on the one hand, and PABXs on the other. Even so, these PABXs were restricted to European markets and have been little enhanced in recent years. In the US the company has also been active in parts of the medical equipment sector, although not to any significant extent.

225

## Telecommunications

The slow but steady long-term convergence between computing and telecommunications has recently started to accelerate; a trend which will continue strongly for the next decade and beyond. This seminal development is bringing IBM into competition with very well-entrenched telecommunications equipment suppliers. In the US this means principally AT&T which, since deregulation and divestiture in 1984, has formed AT&T Information Systems (ATTIS) in order to enter the computer business from which the company had previously been excluded by law.

While all American eyes may have been directed at how these two companies will face each other in open competition, the situation in Europe — as indeed through most of the remainder of the industrially developed world — brings IBM face to face instead with national legal monopolies whose often narrow interests have been pandered to by their governments for years.

These PTT organisations (Post, Telephone and Telegraph — a no longer always accurate summation of the facilities they usually provide) jealously guard their rights, which are usually entrenched in national law. As a group they form the CCITT, the Geneva-based authority under whose guidance communications' (a term which they are endeavouring to expand with the market) standards are established in the form of so-called 'Recommendations' which are, in fact, almost invariably applied throughout the world with the exception of North America.

CCITT is now extending its scope beyond the mere physical characteristics of interfaces and equipment interworking towards the logical relationships between systems when they are connected by communications facilities. Consequently, they lay claim to functions which historically have fallen into the realm of computer companies' network architecture designs.

It is no secret that CCITT is a strong force in the development and progress of the Open Systems Interconnection (OSI) model. Many of IBM's major computer industry competitors as well as certain market sectors in government, the European Economic Community (EEC) Commission and the PTTs, would like to see the OSI model eventually supplant, or perhaps absorb, IBM's SNA. This latter objective is wholly impractical and quite unlikely, if for no alternative reason (and there are many others) than the fact that a very high (and still growing) proportion of the world's major computer users have based their system installations upon SNA. These clearly represent enormous and continuing investments in both financial and operational terms. However, this situation means that, in the non-North American telecommunications market at least, IBM is, for the first time, meeting other organisations that together have the strength, authority and possibly also the ability to impose their own standards on at least part of the market.

The company's response to developments of this nature has been typical. Disinterest soon gives way to interest, followed by active participation as the process advances, concluding with partial if sometimes grudging and belated acceptance. This cycle has already been seen in respect of the X.25 standards relating to packet-switched systems in Europe, and it is now being repeated for OSI, although to be fair IBM always does take a full part in the international standards process, even if at times it seems to be more an observer than a fully genuine participant.

IBM's difficulty has been that it wishes to destroy these embryonic standards before they can truly emerge. However, this cannot be done openly and instead the company does little until (and if) the standard has received considerable support and its own customers start to demand that it be provided. This reluctant countenancing of non-proprietary alternatives until they have been well established is probably unavoidable if SNA and its derivatives are to retain their pre-eminence in the market. However, this approach does not endear the company to national governments, certain market sectors and even to many of its own users.

IBM has attempted to enhance its own internal telecommunications developments first by an abortive alliance with Mitel, followed by a major share purchase in Rolm, soon followed by its total acquisition. Important time has, however, been lost in product development terms, while in the fragmented national markets of Europe, where monopoly still usually reigns, major stumbling blocks exist for the company.

The main difficulty is the intensely nationalistic nature of European voice markets and the entrenched position of both the PTTs and their principal local suppliers. Of the latter only Siemens — and to a lesser extent Philips and Ericcson — from among the telecommunications equipment suppliers has any

226

real presence in data processing. An equivalent to AT&T is clearly absent. For this reason the weakness of IBM's position here is not serious, at least in straight competitive terms, and the difficulty is more that of how to penetrate these new markets.

## Office automation

Historically IBM was arguably the major force in the clerical and secretarial office. Its electric — particularly the Selectric — typewriters had captured well over half of the heavy-duty office typewriter market by the late 1960s. Subsequently the company coined the term 'word processing' and the early Selectric-based magnetic tape and card equipment first launched the concept of automating the text entry, storage and output functions using computer-based elements. However, the three-way divisional split of the early 1970s which lies at the base of the company's varied and incompatible product lines and market approaches, gave the principal word processing franchise to the Office Products Division (OPD). General Systems Division (GSD) eventually produced the System/34-based 5520 Administrative (shared-logic) System, while Data Processing Division (DPD) introduced mainframe-based software to handle these functions.

Not until well into the 1980s were serious attempts made to redress this highly fragmented approach and, in the meantime, several competitors — mainly the super minicomputer manufacturers, such as DEC, Data General, Wang and Prime — have been able to obtain substantial amounts of business from larger IBM accounts, principally because the company has been unable to offer a distributed office automation system. This position is being redressed now that System/36 has been established as the preferred departmental computer, with the introduction of support for DIA and DCA, plus the tying in of the IBM PC into the three-level hierarchy with System/36s and host computers, plus support for DisplayWrite and Personal Services software across these levels. Indeed, IBM's ability to provide a greater degree of integration — however distant — is likely to turn an early major failing into a distinct advantage.

It may be noted that the delay in IBM's local area network (LAN) plans and their implementation has not been mentioned here as a weakness. Certainly the company would have been in a stronger position had these delays not occurred, and surely the (modest) momentum built up for Ethernet and its derivatives would have been less. However, IBM will certainly impose its new token-passing method on the bulk of the data processing market, although other techniques can be expected to survive and indeed prosper at the PC departmental level. Regrettably perhaps, there is simply no other major supplier — or even groups of suppliers — capable of instituting and establishing key standards of this nature in the market.

## Factory automation

This is a sector where — with the significant exceptions of Honeywell and Siemens, marginally also Olivetti — none of the computer manufacturers have any great experience. IBM is aided by its strength in corporate data processing centres, but DEC's position, for example, is probably much more relevant here.

IBM has extended into the market for intelligent robots, while also producing rugged 'factory floor' versions of the PC range. Significant developments are the way in which third parties in the graphics and CAD/CAM sectors have been moving on to IBM computers, introducing a substantial measure of competition for the DEC environment.

Factory automation — probably unlike office automation — will be much less influenced by the views of the data processing department. Much of the market will be directed through VARs and OEMs of various types, thus giving IBM rather less influence, since the sheer variety of applications and associated equipment to be connected will be very great indeed.

## The 'chains of history'

Ironically IBM's greatest problem, and hence a serious weakness, is the direct inversion of its major strength — the size and scope of the company's customer and product base. Such a statement might appear — at first glance — to be obtuse. Nevertheless the immense investments made by IBM's users in both hardware and software precludes the company from making many of the changes that it would prefer.

The example of the 'Future Series' (FS) during the mid-1970s dramatically proved this point. During this period IBM spent a substantial proportion of its R&D budget on the development of a fundamentally new type of mainframe computer architecture. Aimed at providing an escape from the already mature System/360 and System/370 design, this was to act as a more effective basis for interactive and database operations and make it easier for users (as well as third parties) to develop applications programs. In the event, the 48-bit System/38 with a relational database management system integrated with its operating system appeared having some of these characteristics — very much as a 'clean sheet' design. IBM's good marketing sense was soon to be demonstrated. System/38 suffered major gestation difficulties and it was several years before the computer received the high reputation that its innovative design really deserved. Had IBM 'bet the company' on FS, rather as it had done with System/360 in the late 1960s, then customer fall-out to other suppliers might have been substantial.

Hence, to a significant extent, IBM is constrained in its movements by its need to offer graduated and relatively trouble-free migration to new systems. This would be no great problem had the computer system product line not become so very diverse and diffused. This leads naturally to the next important IBM weakness — the fragmented system product line from above the PC to the low-end 4300 mainframes.

## A (too) great variety of choice

IBM's current product line — for the reasons stated above — betrays the effect of its marketing policies since the mid-1970s. The two basic philosophies were first to 'fence off' the mainframe market from other systems in price/performance terms, and secondly to develop specific systems for each major type of activity. At the time this method of market segmentation by the use of non-compatible products was very sound and extremely successful. However, its inherent disadvantages only really became apparent — and extremely troublesome — during the later 1970s as it became necessary to converge these various products into fewer basic designs, or at least to ensure that they could intercommunicate effectively. Since IBM usually manages to sell a considerable number of even its less successful products — often to its own larger users as well — its problems are rather greater than they might be for many other suppliers.

Examples of this approach are particularly numerous in the small to just below medium range of performance:

1 The IBM PC: fortunately for the company this has established itself as a nearly international standard and a product which is flexible enough to act as the basis for many different designs and uses.

2 System 23: the maximum four-terminal System/23 had previously taken over from the 5100 series at the very low end of the small business system market. It was never provided with an upgrade path, and was effectively killed by the PC, its place being later taken by the Desktop/36.

3 System/36: this system naturally took over from the System/34 but is now being repositioned into the 'departmental computer' role for larger users, acting as a local applications processor for PCs and terminals, a LAN controller, and a gateway to other networks and to host computers.

4 System/38: this is now the 'competitive knock out' machine at below the $400 000 price level. Its presence, however, causes the company some problems at its upper levels where it competes rather too effectively with the 4361 and 4381, especially in transaction processing environments.

5 The 8100: as the original 'distributed mainframe' computer the 8100 provided support for distributed functions and applications, but remained closely tied to the host. It became the principal conduit for distributed DISOSS support, a role which is now being transferred to System/36.

6 Series/1: is the company's general-purpose minicomputer, but it is also frequently utilised as a communications processor, and is now also available as a PC and node controller.

7 The 5280: a low-end distributed data entry and processing system, also sold as a small business system which, in effect, has now been discontinued.

8 The 5520 Administrative System: is a System/34 dedicated to office automation operations. It also has been discontinued, and is now supplanted by System/36 in a more general-purpose departmental computer role.

Ironically with all this wealth of choice when IBM came to select a design which would act as the basis for its departmental computing philosophy — systems that were placed between PCs and host computers — it found that none of these was fully suitable. The choice eventually fell upon System/36 which, while clearly representing the nearest match, is nevertheless deficient in performance and storage capacities compared with almost all of its rivals.

## Product cannibalisation

Any dominant market position, particularly if the products concerned are not integrated into one grand design which has clearly marked migration paths, lends itself to the major dangers of cannibalisation. By this we mean that the introduction of new products is made difficult because many otherwise attractive moves will severely impact the existing user and installed base, and possibly even lead to lower rather than higher revenues.

Certainly IBM has carefully been selling off its installed rental base during recent years, and this minimises the direct risks of such cannibalisation. Nevertheless important existing customers can easily be offended — some still remember the truncated lives of the 370/155 and 370/165, while current users of 3080Xs might also qualify — by too rapid product replacement cycles, especially when new directions are taken or major improvements are made. The situation is of course seriously exacerbated unless good — and certainly compatible — migration is available.

## Conclusion

It has become a habit of the computer industry press to make much of IBM's apparent shortcomings and its weaknesses. Perhaps these are more comforting topics than a consideration of its undoubted major strengths! The trouble with this approach is that such comments are rarely put into a true perspective.

IBM is certainly a 'super tanker': very large in size; relatively slow to react; concerned for the impact that its movements might have. However, these characteristics are changing. The formation of Independent Business Groups — one of which spawned the PC — is evidence of how even giant organisations can preserve something of the entrepreneurial spirit. The key fact to be remembered is that market forces rule. Probably only IBM can fundamentally sway the market, but even then only at (more or less) the pace and in the direction that it wishes to take. In this respect the company has the truly formidable advantage of having the major share of the business from large and key users in most national markets. Its inherent range of resources and integrated methods of control dwarf those of all its competitors overall, although not in every market or product sector that exists. Hence the company is able, to a considerable extent, to set both the pace and direction in which the market is to go, guided certainly by its perceptions of self interest, but also by the wishes of its customers.

*HEM1*
'PC producktvergleich '85'
(PC product comparison)
ADV/ORGA Research GmbH
Wilhelmshaven
West Germany

*HEM2*
*Mintzberg H*
'The manager's job: folklore and fact'
Harvard Business Review
(Aug 1975)

*HEM3*
'The UK personal computer market: its
beginnings, the present, the future'
Wharton Information Systems
(1985)

*SAU1*
*Yates J*
'Software licensing —
the UNIX operating system'
In 'The UNIX
system encyclopaedia'
Yates Ventures
(1984)

*SAU2*
*Hinnant D F*
'Benchmarking UNIX systems'
Byte vol 9 no 8
(Aug 1984)

Analysis

# 1: Background

IBM has effectively dominated the mainframe computer market for many years. It failed to achieve the same dominance in the minicomputer market but has clearly learnt from this experience. Despite very important research and technological resources, the main strength of the company has always been in marketing. In this Section, we examine the way in which IBM's marketing skills have been applied to secure dominance in the personal computer market and a strong position in small business computers. There are many strands of continuity in IBM's approach over the years, but from about 1979 there has been a new aggressiveness which leaves IBM poised to extend its dominance still further.

## Introduction

IBM dominates the computer industry in a way that few companies have been able to achieve in any market — especially one so central to the shape of industrial and commercial life in our age. Its dominance has been measured in many ways, but in profit terms it leads not only the computer business but also American and, indeed, world business as a whole.

> *Woods (001):*
> *In 1984 IBM ranked sixth in the US 'Fortune 500' in terms of revenue size, but first when measured by net profits. Although Fortune tends to disregard the world outside the US, the top American-based companies outrank those in the remainder of the world. This makes IBM the most profitable major company in the world, measured by volume although not by margins....*
> *When compared on purely a European annual revenue base IBM would appear at perhaps position eight, and probably again come first in terms of profitability.*

In the computer industry, IBM has dominated the mainframe business since the 1950s. It has dominated the personal computer area since 1983/4. In the area between the two, the mini and 'small business computer market', it has never achieved the same dominance. To see how it has reached today's position, we need to look back a little into history.

## The nature of IBM

Among the vast range of business organisations in today's world, two types have been identified: marketing-led and technology-led companies. In the computer industry in particular, there is a tendency to concentrate on the technology: it is after all technological advances that have enabled the whole industry to come from nowhere to enjoy the enormous influence it has today. But technology merely makes success possible — it is marketing which makes it happen.

> *Drucker (002):*
> *There is a common belief abroad that it is new technology that creates sales and with them jobs and industries. But new technology is only a potential. It is marketing, and especially innovative marketing, that converts the potential into actuality.*

IBM, throughout its history, has been a marketing-led organisation. Technology has been pursued indeed, but not for its own sake. The company has long been undertaking and sponsoring technological research, not all of it directly related to its own lines of business.

> *Woods:*
> *R&D expenditures, despite much overlap, certainly greatly exceed those for the rest of the industry combined. During the last eight years nearly all the company's plants have been*

*completely refitted and modernised in pursuance of the objective of making it the lowest-cost producer in the business. Furthermore, senior officials have publicly stated that the investment plans of the next five years will involve twice the expenditure of the previous five. This gives the company almost complete control over its own product and systems direction, even though at times this may not always be totally beneficial.*

*Ultimate direction is exercised from the US, but R&D and product manufacture (of hardware and software, but the latter to a more limited degree) is carefully spread around the company's major markets. This permits the use of international talent, often leading to certain countries or laboratories being given specific target roles.*

However technology has not been allowed to dictate the direction of the company, which has always been determined by a judgement of what the market would require.

Elsewhere in the computer industry, this lesson has not always been understood. There have been many instances of technological breakthroughs which have not proved a market success, or which have been successful only when taken up by companies other than their originators. Of the companies which have had a major impact on the shape of information technology, two stand out as leaders in the purely technological sense: Xerox and AT&T; both have provided examples, for different reasons, of a failure to follow through a technical advance into the marketplace.

In the past AT&T (American Telephone and Telegraph) was primarily known as 'Ma Bell', the parent of most of the American telephone companies, and a larger company even than IBM. Its contributions to information technology have been fundamental, including major work (by Bell Laboratories) on the invention of the transistor, from which the microchip age has sprung. Government action in the US has split up the AT&T empire, but at the same time made AT&T itself able to take a much more aggressive role in world markets. For example Bell Laboratories devised the UNIX operating system for its own internal use, and it crept out to become a world standard with little help from its originators. Now that AT&T has started actively selling UNIX, its future seems assured. We have seen AT&T, and especially its computer arm, change from a totally technology-led company to one which will be aiming more and more for market dominance — and providing a strong threat to IBM in the process.

Xerox is still best known for its pioneering work with photocopying — still often referred to generically as 'xerox copying'. It has branched out into other areas, for instance word processing and microcomputers, and the Ethernet standard for local area networks. It also had a short period of attempting to enter the mainframe market, but it is the work of the Palo Alto Research Centre (PARC) that is most relevant here. The contribution of Xerox PARC included the Alto computer and the Star electronic workstation, which have given computing and office automation a whole variety of new concepts: the 'mouse', the 'icon' and the 'window'. Despite inventing these new concepts, Xerox has not actively pursued them in the market. The Window/Icon/Mouse Presentation (WIMP) approach to the display screen has indeed made a name for itself, but associated with the name of Apple and the Macintosh, rather than Xerox and the Star.

Throughout most of its history IBM has been a marketing-led company *par excellence*. Despite its enormous investment in research and development, some of it of a fundamental nature, it has seldom been the source of a crucial innovation in information technology. Rather, the company's approach has been to let others explore a market and map out its main features, and then enter from a position of strength and seek to dominate. It would be difficult indeed to imagine IBM inventing a concept, as Xerox did with WIMP, and leaving it to others to make it into a runaway success.

Of course there have been times when IBM itself has not maintained its marketing-led philosophy. Indeed, Sobel maintains that it was a falling away from this approach that gave DEC and others the opportunity to establish a lead in the mini market.

*Sobel (003):*
*During the post-war period Tom Watson and his father* [Thomas J Watson Senior] *had argued about the relative roles of salesmen and scientists. Tom, who had maintained that IBM had to stress technology, had achieved a major part of his objective. By the late 1960s the company was in the forefront in several areas of research and was involved more in pioneering than had been the case a generation earlier. In the process however the influence of salesmen had weakened*

*somewhat.... In Watson Senior's time, when a salesman would report that customers would require a new kind of data processing capability, the managers would consult the technicians on how the request might be met. After the 360 experience, Watson and Learson would learn of an innovative technology and then plan to introduce it into the next generation of machines, adapting them to customer requirements as expressed by sales personnel. Perhaps this was to have been expected, given the different kinds of business and technological atmospheres occupied by father and son in their primes. Still, IBM was less customer-oriented by the late 1960s than it had been in earlier periods.*

*This helps explain why Watson failed to move promptly into the minicomputer field.... DEC's growth was no secret, but because it was taking place outside IBM's historic markets, it was permitted to continue without a direct challenge. ... in retrospect, the failure to act promptly in this area may turn out to have been Tom Watson's greatest error in business judgement.*

## IBM and its approach to business

IBM UK, in its Annual Review for 1985, has neatly summarised the company's philosophy in terms of a concept called 'Three, four, five'.

*Nixon (004):*
*'Three' represents our basic beliefs which have stood us in good stead for many years, and which, more than anything else, account for our continuing success:*
- *Respect for the individual*
- *Service to the customer*
- *The pursuit of excellence as a way of life.*

*'Four' represents our business goals:*
- *To grow at least as fast as the industry*
- *To maintain technological and product leadership*
- *To be the most efficient high-volume, low-cost, quality producer, marketer and administrator*
- *To generate sufficient profit to sustain our growth.*

*'Five' represents our responsibilities to our stakeholders who all benefit from our achievements:*
- *The shareholders*
- *The employees*
- *The customers*
- *The suppliers*
- *The community at large.*

We thus have a picture of a responsible and mature corporation, conscious of its duties within society rather than seeking profitability at all costs. While making due allowance for the source of the quotation, there seems little reason to doubt that the company philosophy is as Nixon describes it, and the company's basic beliefs can be seen as an element of continuity in an industry which has been subject to enormous changes in scale, in the market and in the nature of the products.

The continuity and cohesion of the IBM approach to business are perhaps related to the way it has grown up. IBM is unusual in the world's major companies in having grown mainly by expanding its operation rather than by acquiring additional companies. After the initial creation of Computing-Tabulating-Recording by C R Flint, out of a number of smaller companies, and its reshaping by Thomas J Watson Senior into International Business Machines, there have been extremely few acquisitions. There have, meanwhile, been a number of joint ventures, such as Satellite Business Systems (SBS) and the DiscoVision venture in optical disk storage.

One notable acquisition has been the Rolm telecommunications company; the purchase of Rolm fitted in very well with IBM's need to gain a foothold in the PABX market, following the lack of success with its own products in this area. Surprisingly for a company with little track record for acquisitions, the Rolm take-over has been hailed as a 'textbook case on how to acquire a company', and much of the special character of Rolm has been preserved within the overall framework of IBM policy. Certainly a presence in this area, and maybe a separate corporate style, is needed if IBM is to start competing with AT&T on its own ground.

Other takeovers by IBM have been much smaller in scale — for instance it has secured itself a foothold in the scientific instrumentation industry. More significant in the medium-term future, however, may be its stake in the Intel semiconductor company, giving an element of vertical integration at the 'mining' end of the information technology business.

While there is certainly a basic continuity running through the history of IBM, there have been some quite fundamental changes in the way in which it actually operates. Dorn has identified just such a turning point.

*Dorn:*
*The IBM of the past no longer exists. It is hard to pinpoint exactly when the change occurred but it is likely that it started in 1979 when the then chief executive officer, Frank Cary, decided that IBM was going to win the long running US Government anti-trust litigation. The decision ... was correct and led to a set of decisions and major changes within IBM. These included:*

*1 Immediate entry into the soon to explode microcomputer business.*

*2 Announcement of a steady stream of new products without worrying about legal implications or the impact of the announcements on competitors.*

*3 A restructuring of IBM, permitting the development of a group of smaller, more fast moving organisations, equipped to deal with emerging technologies.*

*4 A change in philosophy to emphasise buying necessary components, rather than building everything in-house.*

*5 Use of IBM's vast cash reserves to acquire companies in businesses in which it wanted to participate.*

*6 Accepting the changes in IBM marketing required by the rising cost of a sales call and reduced product price: leading to dealerships, distributors and joint venture arrangements.*

*7 Continued heavy investment in new plant and facilities to create the most modern, highly automated production facilities in the industry.*

*8 Shortening of product cycles, which greatly reduced the second-user marketability and life-cycle of IBM systems.*

*9 Movement away from short-term rentals to long-term leases and outright sales, generating immediate cash at the expense of a revenue base.*

*10 Creation of the IBM Credit Corporation to provide leasing capabilities and to recapture some of the revenue base 'lost' in the sale philosophy.*

*11 Increased emphasis on having customers do more system installation, testing and first-level diagnosis, even on comparatively complex systems.*

*12 Entry into the retail business.*

*13 Vastly increased advertising budgets, utilising expensive nationwide television, as well as traditional media.*

*14 Development of a 'consultant industry' network to aid and support consultants rather than treating them as 'non-persons'.*

*15 A new press policy which, while still short on information and hard facts (especially pre-announcement), nevertheless opened channels for discussion and permitted appropriate events and entertainment.*

*16 Development of a series of 'statements of intent', suggesting to customers the directions in which IBM was proceeding without announcing specific products.*

## IBM and the anti-trust laws

A key factor which has clearly affected IBM's tactics and strategy, in different ways at different times, is the threat or possibility of regulatory action by the US authorities under the anti-trust legislation.

The authorities themselves have appeared to change their attitude over the years. At one time it was believed that competition of itself would achieve socially or economically desirable benefits, and that it was therefore essential to ensure competition as such, rather than enquiring into its merits in a particular case. More recently, however, a more pragmatic approach has prevailed.

> *Scott (005):*
> *The underlying philosophy of anti-trust laws is preservation of competition, based on the theory that competition is a socially desirable goal.... Unfortunately, in more recent years, there has been a concerted effort by conservative economists to re-orient the anti-trust laws. Under their philosophy, anti-trust laws should be used to preserve competition only when such competition can be justified from an economic viewpoint, ie, when the complaining party can prove that the defendant's actions are not only anti-competitive but would also result in an immediate and substantial increase in prices or decrease in availability of products.*

For much of its history, IBM was dogged by litigation under the US anti-trust laws — litigation inspired sometimes by government, often by its competitors. As a consequence, it was always very careful to act in such a way as to avoid the opprobrium of the authorities. Indeed, some have recognised an almost obsessive carefulness to avoid any hint of certain types of activity which the authorities might consider objectionable. This concern has reinforced, no doubt, the underlying philosophy of being a good corporate citizen. Additionally, it has led to a certain rigidity in its procedures.

> *Dale (006):*
> *IBM is, probably more than any other company, bound up in bureaucratic procedures — much of it self-imposed to appease those looking for an excuse to legislate against a company which they believe is guilty of abusing its allegedly dominant market position.*

This bureaucracy has meant, for instance, that IBM's standard contract terms have been so carefully worked at by IBM's army of corporate lawyers that any attempt to vary them in a particular case is almost bound to fail. Another effect, at a certain period, was that IBM had to live with the thought that the company might have been forcibly broken up into several components, and no doubt made contingency plans for this eventuality. It is sometimes surmised, with little real evidence, that the reason for the sharp divergence between Data Processing Division (DPD) and General Systems Division (GSD), still reflected in the IBM product range, was part of a contingency plan with such a break-up in mind.

> *Hughes:*
> *At about the time that the Carter administration came into power in the US in the 1970s, IBM became aware that it could lose the anti-trust cases. If it lost the anti-trust cases it would almost certainly have been split up, so to provide itself with the potential to overcome this possibility, IBM restructured itself in 1974 into two groups: DPD, which remained much as before, and General Business Group (GBG), which contained two divisions (GSD — also remaining much as before — and Office Products Division (OPD)). IBM felt that if it might be split up, it would at least be according to its own rules.*

While this view has something to be said for it, a more solid reason was surely the need to reinforce sales of the medium-range machines, which might otherwise have been lost sight of in the natural concentration on the more lucrative mainframes business.

## IBM and the competition

IBM's position in the marketplace is very special — whereas other manufacturers need to provide IBM emulation or compatibility, IBM has no need to reciprocate. However, once a standard has been widely adopted there may still be pressure on IBM to support it — witness IBM's recent announcements of support for UNIX and for Open Systems Interconnection (OSI).

A company with the market dominance of IBM has no need to break the law or resort to fraudulent or blatantly unfair tactics in order to put its competitors at a disadvantage. The mere announcement of an impending product is enough to cause confusion in the market and deter potential customers from buying other companies' products, even when these may be better than the IBM product and available today rather than next year. A case in point is the local area network scene — a market full of competing products, with no very clear standards, and one in which IBM's long-awaited token ring has merely served to spoil the market for other technologies such as Ethernet which might otherwise have become a standard. The effect is that competition in new areas may be stifled until the point at which IBM decides that its own product is ready to be launched. Similarly, van Kinsbergen believes that the announcement of IBM's office systems family has had a paralysing effect on the market.

> *van Kinsbergen:*
> *The DP industry has experienced a deceleration in 1985. While many factors certainly contribute to this, including a slow US economy, the author believes that the 1984 announcement of the office systems family has had a severe impact on the minicomputer and personal computer vendors of the industry. I believe that many corporate users have been frozen in place due to the announcement of the office systems family architecture. They are afraid in many cases to make moves that might propel them into an incompatible configuration.*

Competing with IBM is thus fraught with hazards; there are various stages of the game, and it is vital to know which stage the game has reached, and be prepared to switch tactics or indeed leave the field altogether, depending on which direction IBM decides to take.

One stage is a market before IBM has become established. For instance, at the time when the IBM PC was launched, the general shape of the personal computer market was already becoming fairly clear: the typical machine would be 16-bit, probably using the Intel 8086 processor, and probably running an operating system such as CP/M-86. A number of companies entered the market on this basis, some of them with better machines than the IBM PC (such as the DEC Rainbow) but with little actual compatibility between them. The market opportunity for these machines lasted for a year or so until the IBM PC had become so well established, and the availability of software so IBM specific, that the competitive machines were reduced to effective obsolescence. A similar effect can be seen in the case of the mainframes, where the 'seven dwarfs' of the industry offered 'Third Generation' computers broadly comparable to the 360 and 370, but not compatible. The seven, now reduced to the five comprising the 'BUNCH'*, have retained a minority share of the market and have their own devotees, but are, in a sense, outside the mainstream.

> *Lamond:*
> *When Gene Amdahl defined the System/360 architecture in the early 1960s, the cost of electronic components and of manufacturing central processors was still very high. The name of the competitive game between manufacturers was to maximise the job throughput obtainable from components by designing a cleverer processor architecture than the competition. That is why System/360 and 370 processors look so different from Burroughs, Honeywell, ICL, Sperry and other mainframes, and neither their operating systems nor their applications software is portable between ranges, even when written in COBOL....*
>
> *As computer manufacturing costs and retail prices have plummeted (by up to 700:1 in US dollars for comparable performances and main memory sizes) in the last 20 years, optimising processor throughput has become less and less important compared with saving programming effort. Increasingly, users try to buy applications program packages instead of writing their own, and when they do to program at higher levels than COBOL. The much larger number of System/370, 4300 and 30XX users have written many more applications than other manufacturers' users, and are a much larger potential market for any independent software house with a bright package idea. Thus every year that goes by sees the System/370 compatible program library grow further and dwarf those libraries of rival mainframe manufacturers even more. And every year, it induces a few more Burroughs, Honeywell, ICL and Sperry users to undertake the expensive conversion process to the IBM environment, for the sake of access to that huge, ready-written applications library.*

---

*Burroughs, Univac (now Sperry), NCR, Control Data, and Honeywell; of the original seven, General Electric sold out to Honeywell, and NCR to Univac.

Another niche that may open while IBM is establishing its presence may come from the slow availability of the IBM product. Thus from the time the IBM PC was launched in the US, 18 months elapsed before it was officially available in the UK. During this time, the ACT Sirius (otherwise the Victor 9000) gained a substantial share of the personal computer market, but as soon as the IBM product became available the main reason for buying the Sirius disappeared, and its incompatible (even though technically superior) disk format has sealed its fate.

When IBM has established itself in the market, the task of competing becomes more difficult. There are really only two alternatives. One is to offer a quite different machine, differently marketed and presented, and thus generate a special submarket which it will take IBM a long time to enter. The classic example of this is the Apple Macintosh, which has achieved much publicity and enthusiastic support, although only a moderate success in the marketplace. The danger with this approach is that as hardware becomes more powerful, more sophisticated software can be supported, so that one machine can take on the personality of another. Thus Digital Research's GEM, offering a Macintosh-like presentation on the IBM PC, could give the user the best of both worlds (subject of course to such limitations as the poor IBM display screen). IBM itself has adopted a similar tactic on occasion; thus faced with the established success of mini suppliers such as DEC, IBM's response was to produce the System/3 family, to be succeeded by the line of machines from the System/32 to the System/36, designated and marketed as 'small business computers', and projected as being something quite different from a traditional mini.

The other alternative, when IBM has become dominant, is to go for full compatibility, as COMPAQ has done with some success in the micro market, and Fujitsu and others in mainframes. Of course to make any headway at all in competition with the magic three letters, such look-alikes need some edge: they must be cheaper, or faster, or have more capacity, or all three. This is a market for short-term profits on a particular line, and suppliers must be prepared to move very quickly when IBM reacts, as it surely will. If we remember that one of the professed business goals is 'to be the most efficient high-volume, low-cost, quality producer, marketer and administrator', and if we consider the enormous economies of scale from IBM's worldwide operation, it should be clear that competing on price with IBM is a hazardous undertaking, particularly when IBM is reducing its prices to clear stocks for a new product. Of course, IBM itself is not constrained by 'IBM compatibility' in the narrow sense. After years of the competitors emulating the worst features of the PC keyboard, along comes the PC/AT with the faults corrected.

The final role for a competitor is to find an area which IBM will not compete in — or at least not until it is too late to set a new standard. The mini market is the best example: IBM's 'naked' mini, the Series/1, was too late to pose an effective threat to DEC and Data General. As we have seen, this was a rare example of a failure by IBM to respond adequately to a change in the shape of the market. It would be rash to expect IBM to let another such opportunity go past in the same way.

## Internal competition

Looking at the IBM product line, particularly in the medium systems area, it is clear that a number of the products on offer are in competition with one another.

IBM's policy in this respect has not been consistent. At times it has deliberately restricted the capability of certain products in order not to spoil the market for others, but in a free market this can only be a relatively short-term approach. If there is a market opportunity, then outsiders will step in if IBM does not. Indeed, in areas where the external competition has been weak, IBM seems at various times to have fostered competition within its own organisation.

> *Hughes (007):*
> *A major point about IBM is that it does not really perceive or acknowledge any competition. This can be seen from several examples, such as CMS versus TSO. Both are developed in different plants in the US and are marketed on the basis that they give the user choice, but the real reason is more likely to be that this system encourages the plants to develop the more user-friendly product.*

A point to be remembered is that IBM is so vast an organisation that there are likely to be several groups of IBM workers in different parts of the world working on the same problem, and a whole host of technologically advanced projects being developed of which only a few will actually see the light of day, as and when the market opportunity is right to launch them. Indeed, as Hughes explains, the existence of such projects is a likely source of unfounded rumours about new products.

> *Hughes:*
> *… the user should be aware that many people predict new products from IBM. Often this is based on developments at IBM which never see the light of day. IBM has in recent years been much more 'open' about its future products with key people from development laboratories divulging what in the old days would be termed 'privileged information'. It is far more likely that IBM is often testing user/market reaction to its ideas, for technology is moving so fast that even IBM cannot keep pace with all developments.*

The tension between internal competition and protection is well illustrated in the early days of the IBM 'small business machines'. Originally the System/3 was held back by the fear that it would take the market away from the mainframes.

> *Sobel (003):*
> *The System/3 was, in reality, a scaled-down version of the 360 and as such might have appealed to those who found the bigger machines too powerful for their needs. Armonk [IBM headquarters] understood this and, to prevent 'downgrading', constructed the System/3 in such a way as to make it incompatible with the 360s and 370s.*

One of the achievements of Frank Cary as President of IBM was to realise that this kind of approach was holding back the System/3, and to reorganise the company so that GSD, as part of a General Business Group (GBG), was set up parallel to DPD, and given responsibilities for small computers and distributed processing.

> *Sobel (003):*
> *For the first time in its history IBM encouraged divisional rivalries — what was known as the General Motors pattern. The lower end of the DPD line would come head-on against not only Burroughs, Digital Equipment, and the others, but also the upper end of GBG's machines and services. Salesmen for each division would compete against those from the other. This was yet another method Cary used to stimulate innovation and keep the company alive to new opportunities.*

The structure which Cary set up has since been swept away, and today one IBM salesman will sell all ranges of IBM machines. However the range itself has its origins in that period, and the tradition of internal competition has, to some extent, persisted ever since.

## IBM and the user community

IBM has a special relationship with its large customers. The IBM salesman and the systems engineer provide a continual service to the mainframe user, which helps to make the decision to buy again from IBM the 'natural' one, and the choice of competitive hardware as an exceptional option needing to be specially justified.

> *van Kinsbergen:*
> *IBM will continue to grow by maintaining control over key large systems accounts. The top 250 accounts are controlled by ensuring that the DP manager is a friend of the corporation. IBM's strategy will be to tie everything, including office automation, into his environment and then control things through this DP manager. Smaller accounts will be dealt with by highly trained salesmen who overmatch the customer.*

However, this comfortable relationship can be a dangerous one for the user.

> *Scott (005):*
> *In negotiating with IBM, one fact is paramount. You must have the option of walking away from the table if IBM will not meet your needs. If your organisation buys only IBM equipment, and IBM knows it, you might as well not even bother negotiating. You have no leverage and will have to take whatever IBM is willing to give.*

Through its close relationship with users, IBM builds up a picture of what the market is demanding and what the competition is offering, and this information has often expressed itself in new product developments. For instance, IBM's public attitude to UNIX is that it is not a strategic product, but one that is offered merely in response to user demand. If the demand from the users is great enough, then a product will cease to be peripheral and be brought into the IBM strategy.

The traditional users of IBM products have, of course, been large companies, and IBM has been very comfortable in building up good relations at all levels within the major organisations. With the growth of the personal computer market, however, IBM computers have found their way into much smaller businesses and the company has been forced to use a different approach, relying on distributors and dealers. However, this approach means that there is no longer direct contact between IBM and the ultimate customer, and hence no opportunity for IBM to push its other products and pursue its strategic objectives. Clearly, where IBM can deal directly with corporate customers and bypass the distributors, it may still be in its interests to do so.

## IBM and its products

IBM made its name as a supplier of mainframes. In this market it came to dominate not only by being the biggest supplier, but also by effectively imposing its own standards on the rest of the industry. In the other markets which this Report covers — the small business computers, the networked and distributed products, the personal computer family — we shall show that the history has been very different.

> *Lamond:*
> *IBM's domination of the general-purpose mainframe market with its System/360-370 architecture is an unrepeatable feat due to the revolutionary changes in computer design, manufacturing, distribution and support economics of the last 25 years.*

Throughout this Analysis, we will see the interaction between the two factors — the technology and the market — together producing the changing mix of IBM products and strategies. As always in IBM, the technology will be the raw material that the company utilises or discards in its approach to maintaining and increasing its share of the market.

We should note that neither the market nor the technology exist in isolation from what IBM itself does. The technology includes not only the current state of developments in magnetic media, but also the existing product ranges and architectures which IBM has developed over the years. The market means not only the general market for tools to satisfy information processing needs, but also the more specialised market (competed in by others as well as IBM) of existing IBM users with specific equipment and software which new products need to be tailored to.

IBM has been nothing if not inventive in adapting the technology to the market, and in so doing changing the face of both. Large questions still remain as to the company's attitudes to external standards, or the development of *de facto* (hence IBM) 'industry standards'. IBM's market-oriented approach to business has often led it to position a product for solely market-determined reasons, rather than on the basis of technology alone. Thus the first successful IBM PC, with a more powerful processor than the PC which succeeded it, was marketed as a word processor — the Displaywriter — and its subsequent history has been not to become a general-purpose micro, as some predicted, but to help define the software standard which may yet unify a wide range of different hardware.

At the same time, old-established products tend to be offered in new guises. Thus the Series/1, not an outstanding success as a minicomputer to compete with the likes of DEC and Data General, appears in such specialised roles as a front-end to a mainframe, enabling it to converse with asynchronous terminals in a UNIX environment. Similarly the PC is now being pushed by IBM as a general-purpose terminal, and the basis of a large number of different product developments.

Again when the minicomputer market was becoming important, IBM devised a new concept, the 'small business computer', and was effectively able to dominate this market by defining the parameters of what such a machine should provide in such a way that the established mini makers could not compete on the same ground.

## IBM and new market areas

When the time came for IBM to enter the personal computer market, the change in approach was quite dramatic. The PC did not fit within the corporate approach from many points of view. In order to make a success in such cases, a new organisational structure is often necessary.

In the computer business there are a number of companies with a well-established product line, which they can develop over the years to provide a continuing source of profitability. There are many more companies which develop a single product, right for its time, but with a limited life, and then struggle to find a successor. Perhaps such companies would be best advised to cash in their chips and retire on the proceeds when the sale of their breakthrough product falters, rather than seeing the profits of their early years drain away in efforts to follow it up. IBM, with its dominant position in the market, needs to cover both types of activity: to be a solid supplier of long-term money spinners, and also to be able to exploit new opportunities when they occur.

> *Drucker (002):*
> *We need to build* [the ability to innovate] *into an economy in which we have, as the nineteenth century did not have, large, permanent, managerial organisations....*
>
> *More and more companies have, for instance, learned that it is futile to expect the truly new to come out of the existing product divisions within the company. The new needs a separate 'development' division which is responsible for it until it is no longer 'new' but an established successful business.*

Within IBM this idea is the basis of the Independent Business Units (IBUs), which have been set apart from the mainstream business of the company and devoted to exploiting new areas such as the personal computer market. McIntyre has described the way in which the IBU concept helped IBM to secure the success of the PC.

> *McIntyre:*
> *The PC operation — Entry Systems — was set up as the most significant of IBM's Independent Business Units (IBUs). IBM had set up these together with European Business Units (EBUs) in response to the need to move rapidly into new areas of the information industry while retaining its traditional organisation and management system for its day to day business. It had more than 10 such units at the time of the PC launch, and will doubtless continue to use them as tactical business development vehicles. As we have seen with the PC unit, the IBU is like a business 'special force', set up for a specific mission, and re-absorbed into the main organisation once the launch phase is completed....Entry Systems was set up under the late, and much lamented Philip Estridge. With maximum autonomy, minimum staff review and visible top management support, the charter was 'Get us into the personal computer business'. In 13 months from inception to announcement the PC IBU did just that — with a success which is now part of the folklore.*

With its family of established products across the range, and its ability to innovate where the circumstances are right, IBM's dominance of the computer business looks set to continue. However, as we shall see, the computer business can no longer be considered in isolation as it could in the past.

# 2: Hardware and technology

In the small and medium systems area, IBM has a confusing mixture of products. However, we can now see that many of these are nearing the end of their life and we can identify the few products that are strategic for the future. The System/38 was to have been the foundation of a new range of mainframes: today it has a very solid following in its special market and plenty of potential for further development. The System/36 seems established as the departmental machine in the IBM office, although some might dispute this claim. Finally, the expanding PC range has an apparently unchallengeable position not only as a personal computer in the strict sense of the term, but increasingly as the general-purpose office workstation, linking into IBM systems of all types.

Looking at the history of IBM products, we can discern two conflicting tendencies: one leading to greater diversity and fragmentation; the other to standardisation and unification. At times one of these, at times the other, has appeared to predominate. Today the dominant tendency is towards unification, in response to the need for the exchange of information between different types of machine, which is now greater than ever before.

When IBM first entered the computer market, it developed different types of system for different purposes, all of them incompatible with one another. Then came the System/360, which aimed to provide a unified architecture and operating system right across the spectrum of computing as it then was. This aim was not completely fulfilled — the old division between OS and DOS/360 has been reflected in main-frame operating systems down to this day — but the intention was clear, and it exemplifies a philosophy that has persisted to some extent ever since.

In these early days, the mainframe was the whole of the computer world (apart from the supercomputer area, in which IBM soon found it unprofitable to compete). But from the mid-1960s new smaller types of computer began to appear from new suppliers, such as DEC, and a response to these could not be fitted into the old 360 architecture.

> *Hughes:*
> *The most significant event in the history of IBM was the introduction of the System/360 in 1964, and IBM enjoyed immense growth during the next few years, primarily by selling mainframes. However, there were a few people at IBM, including senior executives, who were predicting that such philosophies as distributed processing might affect the company's fortunes in the future. To ensure that all sectors of the market were covered, IBM created the Data Processing Division (DPD) and General Systems Division (GSD) in 1969. DPD was still the 'heart' of IBM with key IBM people staying to design, build and sell mainframes, but GSD was given a clear mandate to look after the 'small' computer market and keep companies like DEC at bay.*

So, we saw the beginnings of a second diversification of the IBM product line, in the form of the 'small business computers', followed by a basic mini (the Series/1) and a number of more specialised machines, such as the 5520, 8100, and so on.

The final new product to appear was the IBM PC. Again IBM was entering a market which others had pioneered, but in this case particularly it has since come to dominate it.

## Medium systems

The number of different IBM machines and architectures in the medium systems range has often been commented on. The following are available:

- System/38
- System/36
- 8100

- 5520
- 5280
- Series/1.

Additionally, there is now an overlap with the top end of the PC range (the AT) and the bottom end of the mainframe range (the 4300 series).

*Hughes:*

*Of the key products — System/38, System/36, 8100, Series/1 and 4300, only System/38 and System/36 have a limited degree of compatibility. Migration aids are available to change from System/36 to System 38, and to change from System/34 to 4300 which means that System/36 to 4300 migration aids may be likely in the future (although this may not be the case for commercial reasons).*

*The 8100 is not compatible with anything — not even itself with DPPX and DPCX.*

The short life of the General Business Group (1975 to 1981) saw the birth of most of these machines, at a time when IBM, under the potential threat of the anti-trust laws, was encouraging the various divisions to be self sufficient in marketing and management, and in the range of products on offer. Even so, it is remarkable how many different and incompatible products came from this one source. Perhaps we may explain this in terms of the perception of the market at that time, with different products very closely defined for specific markets. Thus the 8100 was the distributed processing machine and the 5520 the office automation system; today's needs to interconnect, mix and match, were not so clearly defined.

## Small business computers

*Hughes:*

*The first product from the GSD of 1969 was the System/3 which included major design and concepts of the System/360. It was a small, scaled-down version of the System/360, but designed in such a way as to be incompatible with it. This had advantages and disadvantages. One good aspect was that it avoided affecting System/360 sales but, on the other hand, it also needed highly trained personnel and was, therefore, much less attractive than the DEC minicomputer.*

The System/3, with its 96-column cards, is now of historical interest only, but it was the starting point for a range of machines which is still with us, just as the 360 was the foundation of the current line of mainframes. The parallel with mainframes, however, is not exact. We have seen fundamental changes in the architecture of the small business computers, but the continuing factors have been those visible to the user — a concentration on 'business-oriented' applications, and the use of non-procedural languages such as RPG and its associated utilities.

The System/3 was followed by a new generation of machines, based on the then innovative 8-inch diskette — first the System/32, then the System/34 (withdrawn only in 1985) which was one of IBM's most successful machines ever.

*Hughes:*

*The System/3 was 'upgraded' in 1975 and called the System/32. In 1977, IBM used some of the design concepts from Future Systems (FS) and modified the System/32 to produce the System/34. In effect, it was still a System/32 but with improvements. It proved to be the most popular DP machine in the world with sales in excess of 110 000 (approximately 28 000 in Europe with 2000 in the UK).*

The System/38 was presented as part of the same family, but is really a very different type of machine. The System/36 is much more of a true descendant of the System/34.

*Hughes:*

*The replacement for the System/34 was the System/36 which, despite rumours that it will not be around for more than a few years, is enjoying tremendous success. Orders and deliveries already exceed 40 000 worldwide. This is not hard to understand as it is a very good machine, extremely 'user-friendly' (for IBM), and is very much 'all things to all men' with its Office Systems Architecture (OSA) support and other packages.*

## System/38

The System/38 (announced in 1978, with full deliveries starting early in 1981) represents a radically different, 'object-oriented', computer architecture.

*Newman:*
*Whereas other systems provide instructions at the machine level to support operations only on bits and bytes, System/38 supports operations on structures called objects. Everything stored in the machine is stored as an object of one type or another....*

*There are machine instructions (MI instructions) to create, modify, destroy and materialise objects. Thus, to create an executable program, the compiler generates a string of MI instructions from the high-level language code (an intermediate form of the program called IRP) and then issues the CREATE PROGRAM machine instruction.... The result, simplifying it somewhat, is a program object. The machine assigns a unique six-byte virtual address in storage, then finds auxiliary storage on disk to store it. The program is said to be encapsulated — that is, its contents cannot be directly accessed or modified and the user is unaware of its location. All objects are encapsulated in this way.*

This approach also occurs in a rather different context of windowed screen presentation.

*Healey:*
*Given the display concepts of virtual screens and windows, object-oriented processing can be carried further into processing commands and data via the display. The concept of object-oriented processing is amusingly referred to as WYSIWYG (wizziwig) — What You See Is What You Get. The origins stem from the Xerox research programme which defined the operating environment Smalltalk....*

*What then is object-oriented processing? Basically, commands and data I/O are performed by reference to physical screen locations. Commands can be issued via the use of 'pop-up' menus. On entering command level, a window is presented containing an appropriate set of icons, pictorially defining the process required. The cursor is then moved until it lies over the appropriate icon, the corresponding procedure then being initiated.... Technically the computer software uses the cursor X-Y coordinates to identify the particular icon selected and, via look-up tables, causes a jump to the appropriate processing program.*

The point of the 'object-oriented' approach in the System/38 context is that files, programs, and so on are known by their names rather than physical addresses, making possible a much greater degree of security, and much more in accord with today's 'layered' approaches to hardware and software design.

*Newman:*
*This layered approach to the development of System/38 has a number of benefits — at least to IBM. In the first place it allows IBM to keep the application programmer and the IBM software developer away from details of the actual hardware of the machine.*

*The third major benefit to IBM is the essentially closed nature of this architecture as far as other manufacturers are concerned. IBM needs to reveal next to nothing about the internals of the System/38 machine, making it very difficult for add-on suppliers or competitors. The 4300 by contrast is extremely vulnerable to this sort of competition.*

The architecture was originally conceived as a replacement mainframe system, and could no doubt have fitted into this role had not the 360 architecture been so well established. Mainframe software, dating as much of it still does from a period when assembly language was the vehicle of choice for system software development, is very hardware specific, so that a radical change in approach would have been very difficult. The fact that GSD was able to present the System/38 as part of the same family as the System/32 and System/34 has much to do with the presentation of the latter as 'small business computers', with software development in very high-level languages such as RPG. This means that the underlying computer architecture is much less significant: a program written in RPG II for the System/32 or System/34 can be recompiled to run on the System/36. With some restrictions, an RPG II program can be converted to RPG III to run on the System/38.

Despite its original positioning in the market, the System/38 has been enhanced considerably since it first appeared, and now clearly competes with the low end of the mainframe series.

> *Hughes:*
> *Since its arrival in the marketplace in the late 1970s, the machine has been developed from what one programmer described as a 'nightmare' to a 'joy'. The reason for the programmer's concern was that the traditional methods of programming are not applied with the System/38. The program does not need to concern itself with the location of data; the data is literally left to the machine. For this reason programmers' early reaction to the machine was not enthusiastic — response times were erratic, and there was no way of getting at the data to see if it was held in the main storage or auxiliary storage. However, it is important to note that the first machines were 0.5 Mbyte, while the latest machine — the Model 40 (introduced September 1984) — is 16 Mbytes and competes in power terms with the top 4361/bottom 4381. However, based on relative transaction throughput, some independent tests have shown the Model 40 to compete with the 4381 MG2.*
>
> *IBM has doubled the memory every year since 1979 and there is no theoretical reason why the machine cannot grow to 1000 Mbytes. This would make it very attractive as a database machine.*

## The future of the System/38

The System/38 sits rather uncomfortably in the IBM product line, overlapping with the mainframes at one end and the System/36 at the other. Its remarkable features have made it much liked by those users and systems houses who have got to grips with it, and it could still have the potential to be moved much higher up in the mainframe area. The architecture, with its built-in relational database, and its object-oriented approach, agrees very well with one strand of current thinking as to what a multi-user computer should be like. Perhaps a key to its future lies in the ability, by the use of microcode, to make it into something very different from what it is; perhaps a new machine will appear which will be capable of emulating System/36 and System/38 and the mainframes, with UNIX thrown in for good measure.

> *Hughes:*
> *... although the architecture of the System/38 with its 48-bit addressing is unique to IBM products, the concept can be extended to support the whole range. In addition, it is predicted that a new system will be launched in the next few years to replace all the existing products.*
>
> *The new hardware will be based on existing technology, probably using the System/38's 48-bit (or perhaps even 64-bit) addressing, but will offer power from 0.5 million instr/sec to 100 million instr/sec, and possibly more. Use of fault-tolerant technology is likely to be an option.*
>
> *New applications will be developed using Fourth Generation and even Fifth Generation language products. The new operating system will be based on System/38's Control Program Facility (CPF) with improved user interfaces, and will be almost 'transparent'.*
>
> *The microcode will be the major 'link' component of the whole system. It will allow existing operating systems to run in the new hardware as 'guests', plus supporting the new environment, and when the user wishes to use the new system totally, IBM will merely offer a different version of microcode.*
>
> *Similarly, when more new hardware is installed, new microcode will also be installed. This concept will allow IBM to offer a 'single' product across the whole range as well as offering support for existing products.*
>
> *Lamond:*
> *At the beginning of 1982, ... IBM instructed its reorganised System Products (design) Division to develop a new generation of processors in time for 1986 production which would be able to*

*run in both 4300 series and System/38 mode and to multiprogram both 4300 CMS, VSE, MVS and System/38 CPF environments and applications under the VM hypervisor.*

## System/36

The System/36, despite appearing on the market after the System/38, is much more similar in its general architecture to the old System/32 and System/34. There is admittedly some compatibility between the machines, in that System/36 programs will run on System/38, but experience of trying this is that performance suffers considerably. System/36 is nonetheless very much a mainline IBM product at present, and is IBM's preferred vehicle for office automation systems of a certain size, particularly as the hub of a network of PCs.

> *Hughes:*
> *Undoubtedly the 'prince' among the medium systems is System/36. Many have already been delivered and IBM is enjoying large orders (around 40 000 installed and on order already).*

The larger members of the range are clearly minicomputers with multiple processors, each with its own memory. However, just as the System/38 has been expanding up market, so the System/36 range has been expanded downwards, to the point where it touches the top end of the PC range. The smallest member of the System/36 family, the Desktop/36 (also referred to as 'System/36 PC'), represents a convergence between some of the PC concepts and those of the older System/36 models. The PC element is shown, for instance, in the desktop packaging, and the use of 5¼-inch diskettes. The Desktop/36 uses a PC (or PC/XT or PC/AT) as the system console, but the PC can also act as a System/36 workstation or a stand-alone PC. Up to four workstations can be supported.

The Desktop/36, straddling as it does the two worlds of minis and personal computers, has proved difficult to categorise, and even IBM seems not to have clarified its marketing approach.

### *The System/36 in the marketplace*
The situation at present with regard to the System/36 has been well described by Wilkins.

> *Wilkins (008):*
> *IBM's strategy relating to how the System/36 is sold can be most accurately described as confusing, if not confused. Its relationship with 'third parties' is unclear. There exists the provider of complementary marketing assistance, the agent and the territory agent and, of course, its own direct sales force.*
>
> *The 'agent' was first envisaged as a company that participated in the selling process, and has been subsequently redefined as the party that managed the implementation.*
>
> *One thing is for sure, IBM's gross margins are under pressure and to maintain profitable growth it needs to reduce the cost of sales. The way to do this is to increase the marketing force without commensurately increasing the sales overhead. IBM's ambivalence in appointing third-party companies to achieve this end stems from a concern to maintain quality and control, and an ill-defined relationship between the agent and its own direct sales force.*
>
> *Another problem seems to be IBM's perception of a conflict of interests between the agent and the dealer. However, to implement a Desktop/36 both the agent's skills on System/36 and the dealer's expertise on PCs are required.*
>
> *The whole issue is most confusing for the customer. IBM supplies System/36, the agent supplies implementation skills, and the dealer supplies the personal computer. IBM itself and its retail centres are also able to supply PC products, but cannot offer the same level or range of services and products as most competent dealers.*

## The IBM PC

IBM's entry into the PC marketplace was a new departure in more ways that one. A novel feature (for IBM) was the use of a great deal of bought-in technology, both hardware (including the processor itself) and software (including the operating system, discussed in Section 3). The processor, memory, diskette drives, fixed disk and printer were all 'available' technology. The screen was made in Taiwan and shipped to Florida direct. IBM's main original work was in the colour card and power supply.

By the time the IBM PC appeared, it was clear that a 16-bit microprocessor would be at the heart of any new personal computer system. IBM had used the Intel 8086 in the Displaywriter word processing machines, and this chip might have seemed an obvious choice. In fact the PC, when it appeared, was based on a lower-powered version of the 8086, the 8088, which is a 16-bit processor internally but has an 8-bit external interface. The design of the PC has been widely criticised, and a number of companies produced machines with similar features but higher performance. However it was the IBM PC which became the accepted standard, which competitors had to imitate if their machines were to be able to run the latest software. It set a standard for competitors, and has also provoked other parts of IBM to use it as the basis of more specialised boxes.

The IBM PC was thus by no means the first in its market, and it is certainly not the best, but it has set a *de facto* standard not only for the operating system, but also for the layout of the keyboard (much criticised), the disk format, the use of the VDU screen and so on.

Another reason for the importance of the IBM PC has been the existence of multiple expansion slots (five on the PC, eight on the XT) which can be used for plugging in a wide variety of extra devices, either IBM or third party. This expandability has meant that the PC has, in many installations, become much more than a personal computer. With networking, external communications of all sorts, and in particular the latest announcements of voice and telephone management systems, the PC now has the potential to become the 'multifunction office workstation' which commentators a year or so ago were widely predicting. PCs are now being used not only as telex machines and word processors, but increasingly as the standard terminals to larger machines — IBM or others — the extra cost compared to a 'dumb' terminal being compensated for by the ability to manipulate the data downloaded from the host locally.

*Hughes:*
*The future of the PC is undoubtedly guaranteed. It is likely to expand into specialised marketplaces such as industrial development and retail areas. The PC 'engine' itself will be used in more products.*

*IBM's own internal philosophy of one terminal per person by the end of 1985/early 1986 as part of its OSA strategy is bound to influence more customers to buy PCs as opposed to the fixed-function (dumb) 3270 terminals. The price difference is low enough to encourage the purchase of PCs with their improved capabilities. IBM's ability to show the benefits of OSA by demonstrating its own office environment will undoubtedly win many customers.*

## PC developments

The market at which the PC was originally aimed was not exactly the same as that in which it has had most success. Early publicity material featured it as a home or educational computer, and it had such features as BASIC in ROM, and an interface for an audio cassette, features generally associated with the home market. In fact, of course, the PC was always too expensive to compete in this area — the Apple and Tandy/Radio Shack machines had captured the bulk of the market in the US and much cheaper home-grown machines such as those from Sinclair and Acorn were to do the same in the UK. IBM's later PC Junior, specifically aimed at the home market, was unsuccessful and soon withdrawn.

*McIntyre:*
*The PCjr was designed as a minimal function home computer. The plug-compatible ROM, and 'Chiclet' keyboard clearly identified its target market. Unfortunately, it was not competitively priced. Its specification, which lacked a professional keyboard and a reasonable display, could never have been acceptable for a portable business machine. Later attempts to rectify this situation appeared only to create the impression of a patch-up job which failed to inspire confidence.*

IBM claims not to have abandoned the home market entirely, but it is one which it seems not yet to have understood.

254

The IBM PC has, rather, become the effective standard as a personal computer for business purposes. Not so much in the very smallest companies, for whom the purchase price may still be a deterrent, but in medium size and especially large companies, it has been bought in increasingly large quantities.

The PC was supplemented after a decent interval by the PC/XT, redesigned internally and with additional expansion slots. The XT was originally distinctive as the hard disk member of the family, but a twin-floppy XT has since appeared, and is set to replace the original PC; the XT is now cheaper to produce than the original version. Other variations include the PC/3270, which combines in one unit the functions of the normal PC and the IBM 3270 terminal, and the XT/370 and AT/370, which provide a 'desktop mainframe', able to run mainframe software under the VM operating system and designed for software development in the mainframe environment.

> *van Kinsbergen:*
> *Corporate planners can expect IBM to try to turn its PCs into workstations as quickly as possible. So far, in 1985, IBM has introduced PC versions of its Series/1 and System/36 minicomputers, as well as 3270 emulation processors, graphics processors and factory automation processors. The key to all of these products is that they are not designed to be stand-alone processors but are meant to function as workstations involved with larger mainframe systems. IBM is simply not interested in selling PCs, except as part of a strategy to sell workstations, connections and, ultimately, mainframes.*

One area in which IBM has made little headway is that of portable computers. The old Osborne micro pioneered what has become known as 'luggable' computers — those with the disk drive, keyboard and display screen integrated into a unit which can be carried around, and useful for professionals to put in the back of their car when going on site visits. The COMPAQ company made its name with an IBM-compatible machine in this class, and IBM's own Portable PC, following on later, was unable to secure very much of the market, and seems likely to be withdrawn.

> *Hemsley et al:*
> *The Portable PC faced a superior competitive product from COMPAQ which led to significant price reductions in mid-1985. Until then the Portable PC cost virtually the same as the standard one and therefore it was perceived as expensive.*
>
> *Another reason for the relative failure of the portable model was its advertising image, as an aid to the travelling executive, because it now appears that a major contribution to sales of the portable will come from firms that require mobile machines within their office.*

Perhaps the situation will change as 'true' portables become available, lighter in weight and without the need for a mains power supply so that they could be used on a train or in an aircraft. Such machines exist, but will not become totally successful until the technology allows a more legible flat-panel display screen compared to today's LCDs.

The current phase of PC evolution features networking and multi-user applications — the PC is moving towards a position of the 'standard' multifunction workstation as part of an integrated office system, with mainframes and minis also playing their part.

There have been reports in the press that IBM is preparing a 'PC/2' to replace the current version. One report even suggested that there were large stocks of these waiting to be launched on the market. However, the official IBM line is that no such machine exists. Not content with the PC/2, IRD has predicted a PC/3, to be launched in 1987. It is predicted to have 'multiple personalities', offering three operating systems, a version of MS-DOS, a version of UNIX and a proprietary IBM operating system. Clearly, IBM must be working on a replacement for the PC. However, there is still plenty of life in the existing range, and the market meanwhile is still absorbing the impact of the current top-end machine, the PC/AT.

## The PC/AT

The later development of the PC has (for the time being at least) bypassed the obvious move to a faster version of the same thing using the 8086, and gone straight to the newest technology. The PC/AT is based on the Intel 80286 processor. The 80286 is a member of the same family and can run the same software, it is, however, a much more powerful device. The main differences between the 8086 and 80286 include an increased instruction set, many ancillary devices included on the main chip, memory management and protection, pipelined architecture for additional speed and a maximum address space of 16 Mbytes instead of 1 Mbyte. The 80286 is rated at 1.5 million instr/sec as against the 8086's 0.3 million instr/sec.

The AT can be run in two different ways: either as a straight replacement for the PC or XT, running the same operating system (normally MS-DOS) and the same application software, but two and a half times as fast, or as a multi-user, multitasking machine, with up to three users, running a multi-user operating system (XENIX being the one supplied by IBM).

> *Wells (009):*
>
> *The 80286 was designed to be more 'aware' of the complex problems it has to solve. For example, multitasking is a software-intensive solution to many types of problem but represents significant overhead to a CPU that has no knowledge of what a task is and how to support it. The 80286 provides an implementation in hardware of task switching and a protection model that recognises attempts to violate protection criteria and monitors the transfer of control within the system. Virtual memory support was also fully integrated within the 80286 to avoid reliance on external devices.*
>
> *To provide additional flexibility, the 80286 operates in two modes. Following power up or a system reset, the 80286 is in real address mode, supporting a 1 Mbyte real address space.... In protected mode, the 80286 supports a 16 Mbyte real address (24-bit address) and a virtual address space (32-bit address) of up to 1 Gbyte.*

Despite its considerable potential, sales of the AT have not been dramatic. Perhaps its advantages over the XT have not been sufficiently understood.

> *Hemsley et al:*
>
> *Following an initial period during which demand outstripped supply, the AT has been slow to sell. According to dealer reports insufficient effort has been made by software developers to exploit the machine's expanded memory potential or multi-user features under Microsoft's XENIX. A Dataquest analyst termed the AT as follows: 'It's just a big fat PC'. The installed AT base as of autumn 1985 was only 175 000 versus some 4 000 000 PCs and XTs, according to an Intel source. Software developers are more likely to direct their efforts at the latter major installed base unless there are good prospects of strong 80286-based markets. Although it is rumoured IBM will launch another 80286-based machine in 1986 in order to encourage software development and sales, it is now questionable whether these 80286 machines will make a major impact on the market. The crucial issue is the size of the market window for the 80286 chip from Intel. Its successor, the 80386 introduced in October 1985, is much more powerful and is expected to be the processor on which IBM will build its next PC generation.*

## Microprocessors and IBM

Historically, IBM computers have always used IBM-designed and manufactured CPUs. However, with its entry to the personal computer market IBM followed what had become the standard approach for such machines, by using a bought-in microprocessor as the CPU.

Among third-party suppliers of microprocessors, three names have long been predominant: Intel, Motorola and Zilog. A new competitor has entered the market in the form of AT&T with its Western Electric WE32000 series. This part has of course formed the basis of AT&T's own UNIX-based 3B range of microcomputers and is beginning to be adopted by other manufacturers. Perhaps the most striking pointer to its future progress is the fact that Zilog itself has adopted the WE32100, rather than its own 32-bit chip, the Z80000, as the basis for its next range of computers.

IBM has flirted with Motorola processors on occasion, but the main bought-in microprocessors have come from Intel (not surprisingly perhaps given IBM's part ownership of the company: the 8088 in the PC and PC/XT, the 8086 in the Displaywriter, the 80286 in the PC/AT.

All the IBM PCs have versions of the Intel 8086 family as their processor. The original 8086 is a full 16-bit microprocessor, and is used in a number of other micros, and also the IBM Displaywriter word processor.

The 8088 is virtually identical to the 8086, except that it is a '8/16-bit' machine — in other words the internal data bus is 16 bits, the external data bus is eight bits, thus making it easy to interface with the many 8-bit ancillary devices that were in existence when it was first introduced.

Following on from the 8086 were two, more advanced, 16-bit processors: the 80186 and the 80286. The two have rather different purposes.

*Banks (010):*
*The 186 has been designed to integrate predominantly I/O handling functions on the chip. This means that it should be ideally suited to those applications requiring constant and heavy I/O utilisation.*

*The 286, on the other hand, has been designed primarily with memory management functions in mind. It therefore has a comprehensive memory manager built into the chip with the processor, and is best suited to those applications where controlling the storage on a very large memory system is the most important task.*

These differences, Banks considers, are the key to understanding the future of the PC range. A future 186-based machine, he maintains, would be not too dissimilar to a replacement for the PC itself: a machine intended for use with many types of peripheral device: voice, mice, touch-screens, multiple printers and communications facilities.

*Banks (010):*
*This smacks of a predominantly stand-alone machine with lots of I/O options available.... It would probably have some form of multitasking operating system with networking, but probably not multi-user capabilities.*

To launch such a machine prematurely would not fit with IBM's marketing approach at present, as long as it can continue to sell the existing PCs in large numbers. The PC/AT by contrast was aimed at a different market area, as a multi-user machine which could extend the PC range of products without killing off the XT. A 186-based machine remains a possibility, for the rumoured 'PC/2'.

An indication of possible longer-term directions must be the Intel 80386, the most powerful member of the range. The 386, launched in October 1985, is a full 32-bit processor with a performance of between three and four million instr/sec, thus comparable, on this one rather simplistic measure at least, with the top of the 4300 range or the bottom of the 3080s. It now has the staggering total of 275 000 transistors on the one chip, twice the number on the 286. It can support 4 Gbytes of RAM and 64 Tbytes of virtual memory, or far more than any IBM mainframe. Indeed with single-chip general-purpose processors of this power available on the market for under $300 (and predicted to fall below $10 during the 1990s) one wonders how long it will make sense for computer manufacturers, even of the size of IBM, to continue making specialised processors for specific machines.

Clearly the 386 could be the basis of a much more powerful PC in a few years' time. It may be significant that its design includes the ability to switch between environments such as MS-DOS and UNIX. System V UNIX, and Intel's own real-time operating system, iRMX, will be the first operating systems offered.

## Other products

The IBM PC has received so much attention that one might imagine that it was IBM's only microcomputer. However, mention should be made of the 9000 series industrial computers, developed by the large autonomous IBM Instruments organisation. The 9000 is interesting as yet another IBM computer running UNIX, but it has not been released in Europe.

The 8100, IBM's 'distributed processing' product, was launched at a time when 'distributed processing' was the vogue concept, but the nature of what is meant by the term seems to have changed in the intervening period, with the emphasis today being much more on the individual workstation. The dual personality of the 8100, with two different and incompatible operating systems, makes it an awkward machine to categorise.

*Hughes:*
*The 8100 has always had two operating systems, DPCX for text processing (also allowing the operating system from the 3790 to be lifted into the 8100, thus providing immediate 'relief' for 3790 users) and DPPX for the more traditional DDP users. Unfortunately, the two operating systems were (and still are) totally incompatible and cannot reside together.*

*Unfortunately, it has never been considered to be a friendly machine, and an IBM executive is reported, in an unguarded moment, to have described it as having the 'user-friendliness of a cornered rat'. Undoubtedly, it is a 'cumbersome' product, but IBM always stress its network management and central control capabilities, which is IBM's way of controlling the DP strategy of a company.*

The 8100 seems likely to disappear.

*Lamond:*
*The 8100 series has been a sales disappointment on the distributed processing market for which it was designed, though it has done better on the office automation front. Not more than 1000 systems are believed to be installed worldwide. This makes the development of a compatible successor hardware series uneconomic, while its multi-interrupt level architecture is also too complicated to be efficiently emulated on an Intel 80386 or Motorola 68020 microprocessor. This series will thus disappear from the IBM product catalogue when the new $15 000 4300 processor is announced....*

The 5520 was IBM's 'office automation' system for organisations of a certain size, but now seems, like the 8100, to be too specialised a concept in an age when general-purpose machines like the PC and the System/36 (and even the mainframe) are becoming office automation machines by the process of adding software and networking.

*Hughes:*
*Another GSD product was the 5520 administration system which was loosely based around a System/34. In its time it was a good office automation product but, despite recent announcements, its days must be numbered, particularly as the System/36 is so much better, although secretarial speed keyboard entry is slower on the System/36.*

The Series/1 has had a long but rather undistinguished history. In Europe, particularly, it has never really become popular. As a general-purpose minicomputer it has cropped up in several different guises as part of other IBM products. It still has a place within the IBM scheme of things, as shown by its appearance in two desktop versions based on the PC/XT and AT.

## The shape of the product line

Looking at the IBM product line today, can one make any sense out of the different machines offered? At one time, one could certainly say that IBM was fostering alternative competing product lines deliberately; Sobel has described such a contest in the days of Frank Cary.

*Sobel (003):*
*Cary made certain that no favouritism was shown in the contest. Whenever he praised the products of one division, he took good care to say something positive about those of the other. He called System/38 'one of the best products we've ever had because it is so easy for the customer to use'. On the other hand, he said that 'the 8100 is our networking product'.*

In the IBM of today, with its tendency to convergence of the various product lines, it seems much less likely that such an overlap will be encouraged. What then is the relationship of the different product lines?

*Woods:*
*IBM's current product line — ... betrays the effect of its marketing policies since the mid-1970s. The two basic philosophies were first to 'fence off' the mainframe market from other systems in price/performance terms, and secondly to develop specific systems for each major type of*

*activity. At the time this method of market segmentation by the use of non-compatible products was very sound and extremely successful. However, its inherent disadvantages only really became apparent — and extremely troublesome — during the later 1970s as it became necessary to converge these various products into fewer basic designs, or at least to ensure that they could intercommunicate effectively. Since IBM usually manages to sell a considerable number of even its less successful products — often to its own larger users as well — its problems are rather greater than they might be for many other suppliers.*

A key concept of today's computing scene, as office automation and networking become more important, is that of the *workstation*.

Office automation includes two types of function: those which are used by an individual, such as word processing, and those such as electronic mail which only make sense when the use of them is shared by several people. For word processing and other individual services, an intelligent device or workstation such as a personal computer is often the most satisfactory solution. For electronic mail and other shared facilities, we clearly need a multi-user system. Thus for office automation, the traditional data processing solution of a large mainframe or minicomputer is just not satisfactory or cost effective: we need individual workstations with the power to provide a good response in screen-intensive applications, and access to fileservers with multi-user facilities for centralised filing, mail and communications. For smaller departments, or small groups of workers with shared interests, a small multi-user system can be the answer.

*Wilkins (008):*
*Currently, IBM's computers are designed around four distinct architectures:*

| Architecture | Machine |
|---|---|
| 370 | 43XX/30XX |
| System/38 | 38 |
| System/3 | 36/34/32 |
| PC | PC |

*There are no simple conversion paths between these architectures and the costs associated with, say, conversion from System/36 to System/38 or System/38 to 4300 are exceedingly high....*

*It has always been IBM's marketing policy to drive its customers 'up the range'. It is difficult to see how this might be achieved given the present disparities between architectures. However, if one listens carefully to IBM's latest range of 'buzz-words', I believe that there are clues to be found:*

| Term ('Buzz-words') | Product strategy |
|---|---|
| 'Information centre' | 370 |
| 'Departmental solution' | System/3X |
| 'General-purpose workstation' | PC |

*Thus the 370 becomes the large corporate central resource, the System/3X becomes the departmental satellite (or the central resource in the small- to medium-size organisation), and the PC becomes a general-purpose intelligent terminal.*

*In this strategy, convergence becomes less of an issue and is replaced by an emphasis on connectivity with types of architecture being overlaid to imitate an organisational hierarchy.*

## Display technology

To the user, the most visible piece of computer hardware is of course the display screen. IBM users, particularly on the PC, have not always been well served in this respect.

*Healey:*
*Despite its success, the IBM PC is a very low-specified product. In many areas it is below the desired minimum level and only IBM's superb marketing machine could have moved such a*

*product; without IBM's name it would have been unsaleable…. When characters are displayed on the colour screen they are nearly unreadable and surely below any health standard recommendations.*

The IBM PC comes with a choice of monochrome or colour displays. The colour display adaptor is needed to show graphics, it was left to the makers of third-party boards, and compatibles such as COMPAQ, to provide graphical output on a monochrome screen.

As with virtually all personal computers today, the IBM PC has a 'memory-mapped' display — each pixel on the screen corresponds to an area of main memory. The operating system provides routines for updating the appropriate parts of memory, but it is possible to bypass these and let the application program address screen memory directly; this technique gives marginally better performance, but at the expense of making it difficult to interact with other programs such as the windowing products (discussed in Section 3) that are currently appearing.

The IBM screens can be used in text mode (25 lines of 40 or 80 characters) with a ROM-based 256 character set. The colour and monochrome versions are not the same however: in monochrome each character uses a seven by nine dot matrix, in colour seven by seven, so that underlining, for instance, cannot be shown in colour. In graphics mode the resolution of the screen is $640 \times 200$ pixels, or $320 \times 200$ in full colour.

For many graphical applications, this sort of display is just not sufficient, and the Enhanced Colour Display and its adaptor have been introduced to provide greater resolution in graphics mode: $640 \times 350$ pixels, and the ability to display 16 colours on the screen at once, selected from the 64 available.

These limits still fall far short of what is currently expected from CAD workstations, but do go some way to making the PC competitive with other machines in its class in terms of graphical displays. The new displays also seem to have overcome the annoying 'snowstorm' effect produced by certain software on the older display screens.


## Peripheral equipment

The later 1980s will see major advances in peripheral technology, as optical data storage and flat-panel displays become more of a realistic proposition. Meanwhile, the main advances taking place are in the area of networking, communications, operating systems, and standardisation generally, rather than in the basic technology.

Of course there have been advances in older technologies such as magnetic storage: the PC/AT with 1.2 Mbytes on a 5¼-inch diskette is an example of this. It is noteworthy that the smaller sizes of diskette have still not achieved a major breakthrough, except for the Apple Macintosh and a number of portable machines. With their smaller size and improved protection against rough handling, the 3½-inch diskettes might have been expected to advance further than they have. No doubt it is the lack of support from IBM which is preventing them from becoming a standard.

One area in which a predicted change does seem to be taking place is that of hard copy, with the laser printer rapidly becoming the standard output device from a wide variety of situations. The impact matrix printer still has its place as a cheap device with reasonable print quality, but for letter-quality output the daisywheel printer must be regarded as essentially obsolete. In terms of speed, print quality, flexibility and low noise level, the laser printer is far ahead. Prices of laser printers continue to fall as their performance increases, and the possibility of sharing a printer amongst a number of users via a local network means that they are now within the reach of virtually any organisation.

# 3: Operating systems

In considering the various types of computer system which IBM supports, it is not sufficient to look at the hardware. The operating system which is running on a computer can totally transform the way the machine is presented to the programmer, the operator or the end user. Indeed, it is the operating system, far more than any details of the bare hardware, which constitutes the 'personality', if one may so describe it, of a computer system. In this Section, we consider the various IBM-generated operating systems and the main third-party alternatives, and also examine some of the functions that a modern operating system needs to provide.

## Today's operating systems

## Introduction

As with other aspects of computing, definitions vary as to what exactly an operating system is, but we can take it as constituting a level of software which runs alongside, or 'beneath' any particular application program and looks after the most hardware-dependent aspects of the system, so that individual programs do not need to concern themselves with such matters.

The type of operating system required depends very much on the size and complexity of the computer system. A key distinction is between single-stream and multiple-stream systems.

Single-stream systems are those in which only one program or job is running at a time. While the job is running the operating system functions passively, responding to specific calls for hardware resources, but otherwise having little to do. At the end of a program, the scheduling function of the operating system is awakened and takes action to load the next process, perhaps awaiting an input from the operator. Simple systems of this nature were the norm in the First Generation of computing, but also reappeared at the start of the micro age, CP/M on 8-bit micros being the classic example.

Single-stream operating systems are insufficient for most of today's computer systems which usually require a number of programs to be running simultaneously. This is to satisfy several different needs, for example:

1  Multi-user systems allow more than one user to share concurrently in the computer resources.

2  Background processing allows a time-consuming task, such as printing a report, to be carried on without making users wait until it is completed.

3  Many systems now provide true multitasking so that a single user can have more than one program running simultaneously.

Multitasking fits well with the way that people work.

> *Bailey:*
> *Few of us work like computers, so the sensible arrangement is to make computers work more like us. It is a fact that most people who do not work on a fixed production line interrupt their current work to perform other tasks which become necessary from time to time…. Until recently, personal computers could not fully support this human creative pattern. Micros were either running the program you needed or they were not: to break out of a word processing package or a spreadsheet to enter a financial model or a graphics presentation program, the user had to save*

*current files, swap diskettes, and load the new program and any necessary files. This is extremely trying, especially when pressure is high.*

As soon as we have more than one program running at a time, the operating system is bound to take a much more active role. It must allow each process a 'fair' amount of time on the processor; it must arbitrate between different processes requiring access to disk drives, I/O devices or other limited resources; it must give each process a part of main memory and ensure that other processes do not trespass in this area. More generally, it must protect each user from the actions of others, for instance by trapping errors and limiting potentially destructive updates to shared data files.

> *Hatch, Geyer and Prange (011):*
> *Acting as the machine's policeman, the operating system segregates users from one another, and protects itself, the rest of the machine, and other users. In this way, effects of an error are confined to the user who initiated the error.*

Thus, the operating system in a modern computer does three different things:

1  It provides the low-level input/output routines on request from an application program.

2  It schedules the beginning and end of programs and provides the operator with a language to control this.

3  It manages the access to shared resources in a multiprogramming situation.

> *Hatch, Geyer and Prange (011):*
> *At the very least, the operating system must hide hardware interfaces from the user and present a more generic, machine-independent face to application programs. To accomplish this, three basic functions must be provided: hardware resource management, runtime services, and command language processing. The operating system allocates and de-allocates main memory, I/O devices, disk space, and CPU time, and should allow programs to run unaware of the details of the hardware used. For example, programs are not tied to a specific memory location or single disk unit.*

Thus any operating system must provide some degree of hardware independence: the user and the application programmer can concentrate on the problem rather than the details of the hardware and do not need to know the precise characteristics of different devices. A logical extension to this concept of hardware independence is a programming environment which is hardware independent in relation to the actual processor or make of computer. A number of today's operating systems are hardware independent in this sense, in that they can run on a number of different types of computer, even those of different manufacturers.

A key aspect of most of today's operating systems is the management of the files on the disk and the compilation of directories to them.

## Utilities

As well as the basic functions discussed above, an operating system may come packaged with many other facilities. Facilities are nearly always provided for copying, renaming and deleting files, and (in a multi-user system) for adding or deleting users and passwords. Some operating systems, moreover, come 'bundled' with a variety of other more specialised utilities, as follows:
* Language compilers and interpreters
* Transaction processing features such as transaction logging, checkpointing, back-up and restore
* User interface programs (menus, windows, etc)
* File organisation and access facilities such as indexed sequential
* Database management software
* Enquiry languages
* Graphics facilities
* Networking and communications
* Text editing programs
* Distributed processing.

264

The importance of these utilities varies considerably from one operating system to another: those provided with MS-DOS are rudimentary, but other systems offer much more — so much so that the choice, for instance, of UNIX as an operating system has often been influenced by the large number of utilities which come with it.

## Machine-independent operating systems

Over the years a number of machine-independent operating systems have been developed. CP/M on 8-bit micros, MS-DOS on single-user 16-bit micros, UNIX and Pick for multi-user systems, are the best known examples.

UNIX was originally developed for internal use within Bell Laboratories, the research arm of American Telephone and Telegraph (AT&T). It was widely adopted by universities and subsequently adopted for business use. The history of UNIX can be summarised in three phases:

1  In the first phase, UNIX was bought on its merits as a flexible and powerful environment for building systems. It was very expensive (except to educational establishments) and AT&T provided no support.

2  In the second phase, UNIX was developed by third parties, and sold on many machines under a variety of names. People now began to buy it because it offered a common standard over many types of hardware.

3  In the third phase AT&T has taken the initiative. Having been split up and deregulated by the US authorities, AT&T is now willing and able to support UNIX worldwide. The new System V is beginning to draw the various versions together, offering the best of each in a unified package.

The history of UNIX has thus been very different to what it would have been had IBM invented it. Having brought UNIX into being, AT&T abandoned its rights so soon that others had a decisive hand in its development. As the product approaches maturity, AT&T is trying to regain control — with some success so far but, as Salama explains, there may be problems ahead.

> *Salama:*
> *By providing UNIX systems on its hardware, IBM may successfully defuse some of the interest that is being shown in AT&T's current and future hardware product line. Even though AT&T 'owns' UNIX, its historical lack of support for the product combined with the large number of manufacturers offering UNIX derivatives on their hardware, means that AT&T will have to fight very hard to control UNIX development. IBM could, and perhaps will, set the UNIX standard for the entire industry, removing from AT&T its most powerful weapon.*

UNIX is not the answer to every need. Its method of sharing time between tasks, and its lack of good interrupt handling, mean that it is not appropriate for certain real-time systems which need to respond to an external stimulus in a short and clearly defined time. However, some UNIX systems have appeared with real-time enhancements.

In the commercial arena, UNIX has not been widely used for heavy transaction processing loads. This is no doubt partly due to its relative newness as a serious commercial offering. Moreover, aspects of the file buffering mean that it can be difficult to ensure the precise state of the latest transaction if a hardware failure occurs. The privacy and data integrity features of UNIX were designed for a research environment, rather than for the commercial world, and there have also been performance problems in certain implementations. Despite these problems, there have been moves to provide a true transaction processing environment within UNIX, and the latest enhancements to System V have made it much more of a realistic proposition.

For nearly every other type of processing — scientific or commercial — on machines from the largest supercomputers to the personal micro, UNIX can provide an effective solution. The main importance of UNIX is its status as an 'industry standard', available on most important types of machine. There are however gaps in this availability: the System/36 and System/38 are among the most important of these gaps.

# IBM and UNIX

IBM has an ambivalent attitude to UNIX. Officially, UNIX is not a strategic product, but merely offered in response to user demand; certainly we should not expect to see UNIX toppling say MVS from its pedestal. But it is difficult to believe that UNIX is not strategic for the PC/AT: the AT is surely a strategic product; it is a multi-user, multitasking computer, and XENIX (a version of UNIX) is the only IBM-supplied operating system which can take advantage of the machine's capabilities.

> *Salama:*
> *On supermicros UNIX will play an important role, either as a native operating system on machines like the AT or as an industry standard operating environment (alongside PC-DOS, perhaps) running on top of a proprietary IBM operating system. In either case one thing is clear — the UNIX operating system running on IBM hardware makes a very powerful combination in the marketplace.*

The fact that IBM is not actively pushing XENIX is no doubt due to the need to protect the market for the System/36, but the market pressure could well override this decision.

> *Salama:*
> *The three user restriction on the PC/AT appears to be a marketing decision rather than a technical limitation. Most suppliers of UNIX systems that are using Intel 80286 chip sets (including all of the PC/AT clones) are supporting more users — some are claiming the ability to drive up to a dozen terminals off such a machine.*

When IBM launched its reduced instruction set computer, code-named 'quicksilver' (not a main-line product, but nonetheless the fruit of long development within IBM, from concepts developed by IBM itself) a version of UNIX was the operating system supplied. UNIX-based operating systems are now available from IBM at the top and the bottom of the product range.

For the mainframes, IX/370 is a new implementation developed within IBM from UNIX System V. It is announced as 'offering the IBM product range to the UNIX community' (but not *vice versa*!). To allow ASCII terminals to use the system, a Series/1 is required as a front-end processor. 3270 terminals cannot as yet be attached (except as system console) but this is expected in the near future.

> *Salama:*
> *IX/370 executes as a VM/SP guest system on any 43XX or 30XX machine supported by VM/SP Release 3.0 or later. Unfortunately, the announced version of IX/370 only supports ASCII terminals and requires a dedicated Series/1 to act as a front-end terminal controller.... However, it seems highly likely that future IX/370 releases will feature full 3270 terminal support as well. In addition to full UNIX System V compatibility, IX/370 includes a number of additional features that exploit characteristics of VM....*

UTS, the UNIX version provided by Amdahl, allows 3270 connection directly to the host. The latest version of UTS can run as a 'native' operating system, rather than as a task under VM, thus potentially freeing some Amdahl users from their dependence on IBM system software.

At the other end we have the various PC versions of UNIX, with IBM XENIX for the PC/AT clearly the front runner.

> *Saurin and Burgess:*
> *Overall we were impressed by the results obtained by AT-XENIX. The poor performances of the XT implementation were left far behind, and the AT had a very good position in the cluster of 'feasible' UNIX machines. Of course there are faster machines on the market, but all the machines used for the comparison (apart from the XT) have been successfully sold as UNIX engines. Being well positioned in this cluster, for a fraction of the price of the competition, gives the AT a very good level of acceptability.*
>
> *Microcomputer applications have developed along two paths, based respectively on UNIX and MS-DOS, and the types of software that have evolved in the two cases are rather different, but in some ways complementary.... IBM's XENIX could be the vehicle to finally bring these two*

*paths together and offer the best of both worlds for small business applications and personal computing.*

## Pick

Pick is the 'other' multi-user operating system, with key advantages for certain types of application.

> *Bellinger (012):*
> *The Pick operating system is first and foremost a database management system and secondarily an operating environment. It is this fact that distinguishes it from virtually all other operating systems, with the exception of ICL's CAFS. As an operating system upon which to base a Distributed Data Processing (DDP) strategy for large organisations, it meets the requirements of data-driven systems and provides the tools necessary to allow the engineering of data into information.*

Like UNIX, Pick is now available to run on a wide range of IBM computers, and IBM has now endorsed it as the first industry-standard operating system to run on the System/36.

> *St John Bate:*
> *There are many advantages of using Pick with the IBM family of machines, not least of which is that Pick runs on the IBM PC, AT, 4300 and the 30XX as well as System/36. This provides an extensive growth path without the problem of changing operating systems or porting to a larger machine. Pick also allows an added function to the IBM environment since, where appropriate, applications development tools are available....*
>
> *The IBM XT can be used in stand-alone mode to develop Pick applications which will run without modification on the mainframe. This can provide the DP department with a very cost-effective method of developing specialist applications for the end user without involving expensive mainframe resources.*

Pick is unlikely to achieve the same sort of acceptance as UNIX — it is much more of a specialised system and it provides little that could not be provided by a combination of UNIX and selected packages. However, its specialisation accords very well with the needs of a large class of business users and it will no doubt continue to flourish in its own market.

## IBM computers and their operating systems

The question of the choice of operating system arises much more with some of IBM's current range of computers than with others. At the mainframe level there are a number of IBM-supplied operating systems competing with one another, each with its particular benefits and disadvantages. At the personal computer end we have IBM PC-DOS as the main operating system, but with alternatives available from other suppliers; IBM PC XENIX is a second IBM-supplied product which has yet to establish itself (although XENIX is very well established on non-IBM machines). On the IBM medium-size machines, the System/36 and System/38, the operating systems are packaged with the hardware and, on the System/38 in particular, it would be very difficult for a third-party operating system to be implemented without IBM's assistance.

Much of the success of the IBM mainframes was due to the fact of a standard operating system — OS/360 and its various descendants — over a wide range of machines. Admittedly this universality was limited by hardware constraints, and DOS/360 came into existence as a second best; the difference between OS and DOS (or their respective successors) and the cost and trouble of changing from one to the other, is a source of concern to DP managers to this day.

The 'seven dwarfs' of the mainframe world developed their own operating systems; but lacking IBM's market dominance, none of these achieved any importance outside its own sphere of influence. The next generation of mainframe companies, Amdahl, Fujitsu, and others, recognised the fact of the 'industry standard' and made their machines IBM compatible with a view to running IBM software. This development has of course reinforced the position of IBM as the market leader which other suppliers can only follow. It also helps IBM by adding to the increasing proportion of its revenue that comes from software licence fees.

*Economist (013):*
*Operating-software price inflation, which may now be running at 30-50 per cent a year, thrice benefits IBM. First, because it makes up a little for the iron rule that prices of computer hardware decline by 15-20 per cent a year. Second, because it re-introduces some of the stability of earnings that IBM has lost in shedding hardware leases....*

*The third, ironic, benefit is that each piece of hardware sold by its hated plug-compatible competitors swells IBM's coffers. If you buy a mainframe computer from Hitachi anywhere but Japan, you will be paying IBM ever-increasing licensing fees for the operating system needed to make Hitachi's computer run.*

## Software for the System/36

The System/36 operating system, System Support Program (SSP) is a development of that used on the System/34. It is a full multi-user multitasking system. Security features are provided to protect users and resources.

The Operation Control Language (OCL) is used to interact with the operating system, and with the use of Procedural Control Expressions (PCEs) can be used to build up complex command sequences including decision logic and substitution of filenames at runtime.

OCL is remarkable for the extensive help facilities which are available. Hierarchical menus are provided, enabling the user to perform functions by menu selection as an alternative to using actual commands, and to progress from one menu to another to select further options. Using the screen-design aid, screen formats can be set up as help text for user menus, and the application help utility allows programmers to define the use which an application program will make of the help key. The layered structure of SSP makes it very suitable as a system catering for users at widely differing levels of skill.

The System/36 software is generally compatible with that of the System/34, so that programs can merely be recompiled and will then run. There are, admittedly, a few differences in the Assembler language, but IBM does not encourage the use of the assembler in any case.

The success of the System/36 as a packaged product has meant that there has been little perceived benefit in offering third-party operating systems to run on it. Pick is available, but a System/36 UNIX implementation is nothing more than a rumour.

## System/38

System/38 is unique in that the operating system hides the actual hardware from the user very effectively. The operating system comes in the form of microcode, and takes up to 100 Mbytes of disk. Many of the features are superficially similar to those on the System/36, but the underlying structures are quite different.

*Newman:*
*System/38 is designed in several layers in a tight mix of hardware, microcode and software. The major characteristic of the system is its high-level machine interface in comparison with other machines, such as IBM System/370 or DEC VAX. That is, the lowest level of programming support and the nearest a programmer can get to the hardware — the Assembler level on System/370 — is more sophisticated than on any other machine currently available.*

As with the System/36, the IBM-supplied operating system on the System/38 faces no effective challenge from 'industry standard' operating systems. Indeed the close agreement between the hardware and the software, and the evident suitability of the total system for its intended marketplace, make it much less likely that third-party suppliers will enter this area.

*Newman:*
*System/38 machine instructions provide support for facilities normally implemented in the software of operating systems. Built onto this machine architecture is an optional IBM-written licensed program which provides an interface for application developers to the machine. Although it is a chargeable option (the rental charge is currently around £450 a month or it may*

*be bought for a one-time charge of £16 000) every System/38 customer installs it since the alternative would be to code all applications in System/38 machine language. Since the PL/MI compiler is not freely available this would be difficult.*

*CPF aims to provide an easy to use interface to the basic machine facilities. One of the major ways it does this is through the unified Control Language (CL), a highly modular, command-oriented language. The CPF facilities are the same on all models of System/38 irrespective of hardware configuration, so a system generation is not necessary.*

On the other hand, the underlying flexibility of the system, and the extensive use of microcode, would make it very easy for IBM to provide the machine with a totally different personality.

## Software for personal computers

Before the IBM PC and other 16-bit micros appeared, there was one standard for micro operating systems — CP/M. Admittedly CP/M was not a 'universal' operating system — it ran only on the Z80 and 8080 microprocessors — but these covered nearly all the serious business micro market, apart from Apple, and even Apple users could buy a hardware board with a Z80 in order to run CP/M. When the PC was developed, IBM and Digital Research failed (for whatever reason — the stories differ) to agree, and CP/M-86 thus failed to become the standard operating system for PCs. Instead, IBM went to Microsoft (then mainly known as a supplier of language compilers) and its MS-DOS became the basis of IBM Personal Computer DOS, which is generally, but without official support, referred to as PC-DOS.

*Harrison:*
*MS-DOS started life with a small company called Seattle Computer Products, which produced a single board S100-bus microcomputer based on one of Intel's 8086 microprocessors, and decided to write its own operating system for it. The system Seattle Computer Products produced was known as 86-DOS and was clearly based on CP/M....*

*At about the same time IBM decided to enter the microcomputer market and set up its entry systems division. Lacking experience in this field, IBM chose as a partner Microsoft, which had been involved with micros since 1974 and was known mainly as the producer of the standard BASIC interpreter.*

*... when IBM asked Microsoft what it should do for an operating system, Microsoft sent IBM to DRI. There are many rumours about what happened next, but it is clear that Digital Research was unable to make a deal with IBM. Instead, IBM returned to Microsoft and asked it to supply an operating system. Having no in-house expertise, Microsoft promptly bought 86-DOS from Seattle Computer Products and a few months later, in August 1981, 86-DOS had been transformed into PC-DOS 1.0 and the IBM PC was launched.*

MS-DOS and PC-DOS were, in their origins, very CP/M-like, although somewhat less cryptic in their command language (you copy files by means of COPY, rather than PIP), and hence extremely primitive in comparison with operating systems on larger computers. Successive versions of DOS have provided more advanced facilities, many of them imitations of features found in UNIX. For instance MS-DOS/PC-DOS now provides subdirectories, pipes and redirection of I/O files.

However MS-DOS is still far from an ideal operating system, even given that it is only intended for use on a single-user basis. We can see this by the number of utilities which have appeared from third-party suppliers to remedy some of its main failings. For instance we have Smartkey, Prokey and so on, which intercept keyboard input and can substitute one character for another, or even generate a whole string from a single key depression: in this way you can tailor your application packages to be more consistent in their use of the keyboard or set up macros for frequently-used input strings.

*Healey:*
*By failing to improve the whole concept of PC-DOS with Version 3.X, IBM has created a millstone for the computer industry. It is now time to move on to a full operating system, of which DR's Concurrent DOS is a definitive example. Such a system must provide true multi-tasking support with a task scheduler and memory management; it must also provide a message-passing intertask communication mechanism....*

269

*If the user needs to run only one program in an exclusively stand-alone mode PC-DOS is adequate. If he or she is used to a mainframe terminal and has not experienced the user friendliness of a multitasking OS then there will be few complaints. There are, however, major aspects of corporate usage that need rethinking, most of which revolve around the need to communicate with other resources.*

Other limitations of MS-DOS include the totally artificial maximum of 640 Kbytes of memory available — a limitation which is partly overcome with the expansion board developed by Intel and Lotus, with an eye specifically on large spreadsheets.

The announcement that IBM and Microsoft have renewed and formalised their 1980 joint system software agreement looks like confirming the special position of MS-DOS and its IBM variant as the standard operating system for PCs. Another pointer is the fact that IBM has stopped supplying CP/M-86, and at the time of writing does not sell any Digital Research products.

*McIntyre:*
*The various statements from IBM, AT&T, Microsoft and Intel could lead to some interesting speculation. In summary, AT&T will maintain UNIX V as a standard, Microsoft will ensure object code compatibility between XENIX V and UNIX V, Intel will implement UNIX V on the 80286 chip (and presumably the 80386 and successors), IBM and Microsoft will continue to work jointly on operating system development and IBM has a 20 per cent stake in Intel whose chips power the PC family.*

## Technical issues and future prospects

## Memory management

In a multi-user or multitasking environment, managing the use of memory is an important function. One task has to be separated from another, and each provided with an area of memory which it can regard, at least for the time being, as entirely its own property. Older operating systems, such as DOS/360, achieved this by having main memory rigidly divided up into a number of partitions, but the state of the art has moved on far beyond this to the point where some form of dynamic storage allocation is the norm.

The other key task of memory management is to permit the running of programs whose total size (either individually or collectively) is greater than the physical memory available. At one time this was performed by the programmer, dividing the program up into 'segments' and arranging for them to be 'overlaid'. The concept of 'virtual storage' (one of the many additions which IBM has made to the English language, and which has started a fashion among computer people for virtual this, that, and the other) supersedes overlaying in this sense, and makes memory management a function of the operating system, so that it can occur without the application program needing to take any action.

In a virtual memory environment, a program will be allowed a large 'virtual address space', far larger than the actual physical memory. Whenever a program calls for a memory location, the operating system will examine a table to translate this address to a physical address. If there is currently no physical location corresponding to the virtual address (that is, the data in question is not currently in memory) the necessary area is loaded in from disk and the address table updated.

Two different methods of arranging virtual storage are commonly met with: paging and segmentation. In 'paging' systems, virtual memory is arranged as blocks of a fixed size, and a virtual memory address consists of two parts: a page number and a displacement. In 'pure' paging systems, each program is limited in size to a single page, although this restriction does not always apply in practice. In 'segmentation' systems, the memory blocks may be of different sizes and there may be several of them for a single program, not necessarily contiguous in main memory.

In multi-user systems it may well happen that several users are running the same program concurrently, and operating systems often have the ability to take advantage of this.

*Deitel (014):*
*In multiprogrammed computer systems, especially in timesharing systems, it is common for many users to be executing the same programs. If individual copies of these programs were given*

270

*to each user, then much of primary storage would be wasted. The obvious solution is to share those pages that can be shared.*

*Sharing must be carefully controlled to prevent one process from mnodifying data that another process is reading. In most of today's systems that implement sharing, programs are divided into separate procedure and data areas. Non-modifiable procedures are called* pure procedures or re-entrant procedures. *Modifiable data clearly cannot be shared. Non-modifiable data (such as fixed tabular information, for example) can be shared.*

Different operating systems approach the subject of memory management in different ways; moreover, this is increasingly a function of the hardware.

In the System/36 SSP, main storage is considered as a pool of 2 Kbyte blocks, and these can be allocated dynamically to programs on a best-fit basis. Programs are swapped to and from disk as required, so that the total memory required by programs currently in the mix can exceed the physical memory size.

Another approach to multi-user systems is also available on the System/36, in the form of Multiple Requesting Terminal (MRT) programs. An MRT program can be used, for example, when a number of different users are concurrently updating the files using the same program: only one task is active, and it goes round each of the terminals in turn. This avoids the need to have multiple copies of the program loaded at once, and effectively gives a multi-user facility within a single program, as compared to the more usual approach (for instance in UNIX) of having a number of tasks scheduled via the operating system.

Memory management facilities on the System/38 include a Virtual Address Translator (VAT), allowing addresses within the 48-bit virtual address space to be related to 512-byte pages in real memory.

*Newman:*
*... the machine takes care of all access to disk storage — you cannot tell that System/38 uses disks at all; it appears only to have a very large area of main memory.*

Pick is essentially a virtual memory system.

*Bellinger (012):*
*The operating system allows the user to address the entire range of disk space as if it were memory.... Memory is organised in 512 byte pages ('frames'). When a frame is needed for processing, the firmware determines if it is already in memory. If it is not, then the monitor automatically transfers the frame from disk, with the 'least recently used frame' being backed out to disk if there is a need to create space.*

UNIX is not a true virtual memory system, although it does provide equivalent functions. In UNIX, each process has an 'image', which is swapped to and from main storage. An image comprises three logical segments: a procedure segment, a data segment, and a stack segment. The procedure segment is re-entrant, in other words it may be shared between processes, and is not modifiable. Tables within the operating system maintain the location of the various segments in main memory and on disk.

*Deitel (014):*
*Processes are swapped to and from secondary storage as needed. Both primary and secondary storage are allocated using a first-fit storage placement strategy. If a process needs to grow, it requests more storage. It is given a new section of storage sufficiently large to hold it, and the entire contents of the old storage are copied to the new area. The old storage is then released. If insufficient primary storage is available at the moment for the expansion, then secondary storage is allocated, the process is swapped to secondary storage, and is swapped back into primary storage (with its new size) when a sufficiently large hole becomes available.*

MS-DOS, not being a multitasking system, has no need for any specialised memory management scheme, although certain large programs are organised in a fairly basic fashion in the form of overlays. However, the nature of personal computing and office automation tasks is such that it can be very useful to have more than one program in memory at once. This is not multitasking as such — the various co-resident programs are merely 'parked' awaiting to be reactivated — but it does give some of the benefits of multitasking. Typical examples of co-resident programs are Sidekick, which pops up on command to give instant facilities on the screen, such as a calculator, notepad or calendar, and Smartkey, which intercepts keyboard input and can be programmed to substitute different characters or strings to assist with data entry. At a slightly more ambitious level, MemoryShift allows memory to be split into up to 10 partitions, with a program residing in each. Only one is active at a time, but the user can jump from one to another by a single keystroke, and can transfer applications between one and another.

None of these utilities comes near the facilities that UNIX offers, but their popularity indicates that there is a suppressed demand for something approaching multitasking.

## Database management

Database management is an area which overlaps to some extent with operating systems. Today's applications require data to be organised, structured and accessible. A full database management system will provide tools to take much of the work of doing this away from the programmer.

The operating systems available on IBM small and medium systems vary enormously in the amount of support they provide in this area. At one extreme, UNIX, MS-DOS/PC-DOS and the CP/M products provide no specific database facilities at all. UNIX indeed has taken it as a basic principle that data files are unstructured as far as the operating system is concerned.

> *Ritchie and Thompson (015):*
> *A* [UNIX] *file contains whatever information the user places on it.... No particular structuring is expected by the system. A file of text consists simply of a string of characters, with lines demarcated by the newline character.... A few user programs manipulate files with more structure; for example, the assembler generates, and the loader expects, an object file in a particular format. However, the structure of files is controlled by the programs that use them, not by the system.*

In order to provide database management facilities, a number of third-party products have appeared to run under UNIX and/or MS-DOS. C-ISAM, supplied by Relational Database Systems Inc, provides index sequential access for files in either DOS or UNIX, and can be accessed from high-level languages such as C and COBOL. There are a number of database management systems available, as will be discussed in the next Section.

System/36 SSP, by contrast, provides a number of data management features as part of the operating system, including:
- Sequential access
- Direct access
- Indexed access
- Generalised Access Method (GAM) to allow both keyed and non-keyed processing.

Alternate access paths are available to the same data file.

CPF on the System/38, and also Pick, go further and provide a full relational database as part of the operating system. In the System/38 this is of course implemented at a fundamental level of the machine's architecture.

> *Newman:*
> *System/38 database is the best IBM data management scheme presently available. It provides virtually all of the facilities of DB2 but, by contrast, it is very easy to define and to use database files with high-level language operations familiar to any programmer. All normal file operations are supported including generic key and relative record processing so the database files are compatible with the disk files supported by most other machines.*

## The user interface and window products

Operating systems provide, as we have seen, a standard interface between an application program and the machine. However, another area where a standard interface is very much needed is between the application and the user.

*Hemsley et al:*
*Ideally, the personal computer should be as easy to use as a video recorder; even the harassed executive should be able to operate one successfully.*

*The issue of user friendliness is important if the personal computer is to be fully effective.... A number of trends are occurring which should lead to increasingly user-friendly personal computers, eg:*
- *Easier to learn software*
- *Easier to use software*
- *Easier peripheral devices, eg mouse*
- *Natural language processing*
- *Improved graphics*
- *Better colour facilities.*

In the past, a user interface was not considered to be an inherent part of an operating system, but rather a separate layer of software, running 'on top of' the application whereas the operating system runs 'beneath' it. However, a number of developments are making the question of user interfaces more and more critical in the choice of computer systems. One of these was the effect of the work of Xerox's Palo Alto Research Centre (PARC) on developing what has been called Window/Icon/Mouse Presentation (WIMP). The idea is simple: rather than having to type commands or select an option from a menu the user is presented with an ideographic screen display showing a number of little pictures ('icons') and the cursor is pointed at the one in question using a non-keyboard input device such as a 'mouse'. Other features of this type of presentation include 'pop-up' or 'pull-down' menus which appear only when requested, and partitioning the screen up into a number of windows, often partly overlapping, in analogy to papers lying around on a desk; each window represents a program or task in progress, or a document being processed.

*Bailey:*
*The basic ergonomic research underpinning the iconic user interface was carried out in the early 1970s by Xerox at its Palo Alto Research Centre. The Xerox work determined that most computer users found visual interaction with screen objects more satisfying than the use of commands or menus. The Xerox iconic interface was implemented in the Smalltalk environment on the Xerox Star machine....*

*A further contribution to the spread of the iconic user interface to popular personal computing has been the recent advent of low-cost, high-performance, pixel-mapped screen graphics, which enable the fast drawing of icons and object-oriented screens.*

The WIMP approach, although devised by Xerox, owes its popularity to Apple, whose Macintosh personal computer (following on the overpriced and ill-fated Lisa) has made this type of presentation very popular. Even so, the commercial success of the Macintosh has been much less convincing than that of Apple's previous offering, the Apple II. Perhaps this is connected with application availability: the original Apple's success was very largely due to its association with VisiCalc, then a revolutionary product as the first electronic spreadsheet; VisiCalc gave the business user something that he could immediately make use of and that would help him directly in his business; the appeal of the Macintosh is much more immediate, but less substantial: it looks very attractive, but the real business application software is lacking compared to the IBM PC and its clones. Perhaps Microsoft's Excel software will provide the boost that the Macintosh needs.

At all events, the impression that the Macintosh has made on the market has spurred a number of imitations. The closest imitation, in the IBM PC environment, has been Digital Research's GEM. Unfortunately Apple was not flattered by the imitation, which has been so close as to prompt Apple to legal action, and GEM at the time of writing was being withdrawn for cosmetic surgery to make its icons less Apple-like. Other windowing products so far announced have included Windows from Microsoft (itself withdrawn and then relaunched), Taxi from Epson (not previously known as a software house), Desq from Quarter Deck, and of course TopView from IBM itself. Another contender, VisiOn from Visicorp, seems to have disappeared.

This plethora of windowing systems can hardly continue. Application software developers will find it difficult to support all these environments and will need to choose one or at the most two. TopView, as the IBM product, is of course in one sense the favourite, since it has the IBM logo.

*Unquestionably, TopView's current performance limitations are a serious impediment, but with the total commitment of IBM behind it, it will undoubtedly become a market leader, albeit only with the next (graphics, expanded memory support) release. TopView 2 plus PC-DOS will be, effectively, a proprietary IBM operating system. DR and Microsoft must provide GEM and MS-Windows upgrades to make them TopView 2 compatible as soon as the specification is known.*

## The battle for the multi-user PC

The PC has always been presented as a single-user machine — the very name *personal computer* rather implies that after all. Past attempts to make it multi-user, via XENIX, BOS or Concurrent PC-DOS, were always doomed to failure for performance reasons: the PC is slow enough to be irksome at times as a single-user machine; a multi-user PC was really intolerable.

All this changed with the advent of the PC/AT. Not only was the processor itself much faster (about two-and-a-half times on typical DOS applications and up to five times in special circumstances) but the memory management features of the chip provide in hardware much of the protection between one task and another which would otherwise need to be done in software, and thus impose a further burden on the processor.

IBM has not specifically aimed the AT at the multi-user market.

*Hughes:*
*IBM has consistently argued against multi-user micros, despite the PC/AT which supports up to three users. IBM believes that personal computers should share information and resources in networks, otherwise (so they argue) by definition they are not 'personal' computers. IBM also argues that because of the low cost of the PC, it is better to give each user one of their own. This last argument could be hard for a small company, but IBM always uses the cost of a person, or the loss of production by sharing out etc, as selling points.*

The AT, although not principally marketed as a multi-user machine, clearly has the ability to become one, and it would bring multi-user computing within reach of a whole new class of user.

*Digitus (016):*
*There are over a million small organisations in the UK, of whom a large proportion will want to buy small multi-user computers or networks but have not so far been able to afford them. The advent of a three-user system from IBM, in the form of the PC/AT ... means that this prospective marketplace can at last be satisfied.*

The question is, which of the various multi-user operating systems will prevail? Realistically, there are two general-purpose systems, Concurrent DOS-286 and XENIX, while Pick is a possibility in more specialised cases. A multi-user version of MS-DOS/PC-DOS has been rumoured, but Microsoft has denied it. Why should there be a multi-user version anyway? Microsoft has its own multi-user operating system with XENIX, and it would undermine its potential market and confuse its customers to make MS-DOS multi-user.

For the user, the main attraction today of MS-DOS is the wealth of application software available; far more good *personal* software than is available for any other environment.

Ideally, many users would like the possibility of running MS-DOS application software with the other facilities of UNIX. A US company called Uniform Software has produced a package called 'The Connector' which allows MS-DOS to run as a task under UNIX; when the user types in a command, the software first looks for a program in the UNIX directories; if it cannot find it it then looks in the DOS directories, and if necessary runs it as a DOS program, returning to UNIX afterwards. Unfortunately the program is limited in the versions of UNIX which it will work with; it runs correctly with PC-IX, but attempts to make it run under XENIX have so far failed. AT&T, meanwhile, has announced a product called OS Merge, which will allow its PCs to switch from MS-DOS to UNIX and back at will, while this sort of 'context-switching' is one of the key design aims of the Intel 80386, the latest addition to the family which has, because of the IBM PC, become the clear leader in the microprocessor market.

*Harrison:*

*When MS-DOS 1 was released, there was no compatibility between it and XENIX. Clearly it was in Microsoft's interests to bring the two environments closer together, and a number of steps have already been taken in this direction. MS-DOS 2 adopted many of the features of XENIX, including the directory structure and file system, although not always in a totally compatible manner. Utilities have been added to XENIX to allow it to access MS-DOS disks, and a range of cross-development software has been produced. It should soon be possible for MS-DOS and XENIX machines to run on the same network sharing a common server, and Microsoft has hinted that a XENIX version of Windows may be on the way.*

*All of these things help to increase the level of compatibility between the systems, but they do not achieve the ultimate goal of running the same binary on both XENIX and MS-DOS. This could, perhaps, be the major benefit of the dynamic linking feature of MS-Windows, for it will now be possible to write a program in, say, C and distribute it without linking it to the C library. When the program is run, the dynamic linking mechanism would link it to the appropriate C library for the operating system. If Microsoft's intention is to achieve compatibility in this way, the realisation of this benefit will depend on language developers and software producers, so we may still have to wait some time before the average user can buy a single copy of a software package to run on both operating systems.*

For the small business, the prospect of cost-effective, small, multi-user systems is now better than ever. IBM may or may not decide to push XENIX more actively — and the availability of a System V version will, in any case, make it more attractive. IBM seems rather to have decided to concentrate its efforts on the System/36, which now substantially overlaps in power with the AT. Either way, the user is likely to benefit. This is one sector of the market which is set for substantial growth.

---

# 4: Networks and applications

The various IBM machines need to be examined in the context of the applications they are used for. While the mainframe retains its traditional role as a DP engine, the smaller machines are increasingly finding new, less structured applications, of which office automation is attracting a great deal of interest. A common factor in these new applications is that they rely on networking to connect the individual's workstation and the corporate or departmental host. In IBM terms this networking takes two forms — SNA as a standard linking the many machines together, and the local area network (LAN) as the physical expression of a certain kind of peer-to-peer connection. Today, after years of conflicting standards, the LAN picture is becoming less cloudy and reveals IBM's token-passing ring as the long-term standard.

## Computer applications today and tomorrow

Computers today are used for more varied applications than in the past. In the early days of computing the main applications were for research and scientific purposes. Computers were then adopted for commercial data processing and it was at this time the most common applications were very clearly defined. They were intended to fulfil a specific purpose: producing the company's payroll; printing its invoices; analysing the accounts etc. As computing power has become cheaper, so it has been utilised for new classes of application which are much more open-ended in nature: tools for optional use, rather than 'systems' to be fitted in with.

Gradwell has described the degree to which a business function is structured as one dimension in a classification of applications.

> *Gradwell (017):*
> *At one end are rigidly structured applications, for example payroll applications, where all transactions are known completely; at the other end is a very loosely defined structure, for example deciding who to promote.*

It is these less structured applications that we will be considering in particular. Office automation and personal computing, together with factory automation, are widely expected to be the major market areas of the 1980s.

## Office automation

The term 'office automation' has meant different things at different times. It seems at one time to have been used to mean the automation of clerical and administrative tasks by data processing. Office automation in this sense was extremely successful — in most large companies today the computer carries out many of the tasks which would once have been done by clerical workers. The phrase 'office automation' seems then to have disappeared from view for a number of years, to reappear in a new guise in the 1970s. By this time the idea of automating clerical work had become commonplace, and the need was to assist other classes of office workers — the secretary, the manager and the professional worker.

### Word processing

Office automation today generally starts with word processing and text creation, but these terms cover a range of different packages which are suited to different classes of user.

IBM is said to have invented the term 'word processing' and certainly it pioneered electronic assistance for typists. As a leading maker of typewriters, first manual and then electric and later with more sophisticated features such as error correction and memories, IBM was, of course, closely in touch with the typists' needs. The inventors of the 'golfball' could be expected to be ready with new products in this area when the time came.

In the IBM scheme of things, there has, in the past, been a very distinct gulf between word processing and other applications. Like other word processor manufacturers, for a long time IBM offered word processing in the form of closed systems: a specially packaged and expensive desktop computer, which ran only one program. There were several generations of IBM word processing systems, but the most successful dedicated word processor — likely also to be the last — was the Displaywriter. The success of the Displaywriter effectively set a standard for word processing (even for names — hence the Wangwriter and others) and established the floppy disk and microprocessor-based, relatively low-cost, stand-alone machine as the typical word processing product, effectively wiping out the older 'shared logic' systems.

Based on the Intel 8086 microprocessor, the Displaywriter could have been developed into a general-purpose personal computer system, and perhaps would have been, had not the PC been developed along slightly different lines, with the 8088 rather than the 8086, and with 5¼-inch rather than 8-inch disks.

The Displaywriter, despite its similarity to personal computers at a superficial hardware level, reflects the more traditional IBM approach at a software level. Thus essentially all microcomputers, and indeed minicomputers, use the ASCII standard for representing various characters as bit patterns. ASCII is a 7-bit code, with different implementations using the eighth bit of each byte either for parity or for various extensions to the character set. IBM, on the other hand, has for many years (at least since the introduction of the 360 series) used EBCDIC, a full 8-bit code. An indication of the gulf between the Displaywriter and the PC is that the Displaywriter uses EBCDIC as standard, the PC a version of ASCII.

One of the characteristics of the special-purpose word processors was that they had a number of special keys on the keyboard, specially marked as 'file', 'paragraph', 'reformat', and so on — the precise arrangement always differing from one manufacturer to another. Of course the software made use of these special keys, with messages appearing on the screen such as 'press END TASK'. Such a message is clearly not appropriate to a keyboard that has no END TASK button.

The opposite pole of word processing software is represented by the programs that grew up on the early personal computers such as the Apple II and the various CP/M machines. These tended to have very restricted keyboards, often with little more than the normal typewriter keys plus Ctrl and Esc. Consequently a totally different type of word processing software grew up, which used combinations such as Ctrl-E to go up one line, Ctrl-X to go down a line, and so on.

### Word processing as software
By the early 1980s it was becoming clear that word processing should be regarded not so much as a specialised job requiring specialised hardware, but as a software function which in principle could be run on any standard micro. Early personal computers had word processing software available, such as WordStar. However, such packages could not be regarded at that time as true competitors to a dedicated word processor. This was partly because of hardware deficiencies such as poor keyboards, and partly because of the lack of functionality in the software: a maximum address space of 64 Kbytes does not favour large programs, particularly given the need for a reasonable amount of text storage. However, in many smaller establishments a micro with a word processing package gave most of what was expected from a word processor.

Since those early days, word processing software for micros has become ever more sophisticated. WordStar itself, while still not every secretary's dream system, has features far beyond those of its first version, and there are many newer and better systems now available.

Today, more and more word processing is being performed on personal computers such as the IBM PC. Such machines have more keys on their keyboard than the First Generation of microcomputers, but these are general-purpose keys rather than specifically for word processing. For such machines we can see two main types of software, namely:

1 Descendants of the original micro systems: WordStar in its recent versions being the prime example.

2 Adaptations or imitations of software originally written for special-purpose word processors: particularly DisplayWrite 2 (IBM's PC version of the software used on its Displaywriter), Samna and Quadratron, a third-party Wang look-alike.

IBM's own word processing offerings on the PC have not been among the most highly regarded. The initial offering, Easywriter, was poorly received and the running has been made by third-party suppliers.

The principal IBM-label offering must now be the DisplayWrite family, giving the same facilities as on the Displaywriter. IBM's DisplayWrite family of products is clearly intended to provide compatible word processing over a wide range of hardware. However, the products in the range are not always the most attractive. For the IBM PC we have two products, DisplayWrite 2 (the version actively promoted) and DisplayWrite 1. DisplayWrite 2 is a recompilation for the PC of the Textpack 4 software for the Displaywriter (which of course uses an Intel 8086 and is similar, to the PC). DisplayWrite 1, on the other hand, is specially written for the PC and writes its files in ASCII, unlike DisplayWrite 2 which uses EBCDIC. DisplayWrite 1 also has remarkably good (for a word processor) graphics abilities. Other versions of DisplayWrite are now offered on the mainframe and the System/36, although with some differences in the user interface and the precise way in which the programs work.

## Further office automation functions

Office automation needs a little definition.

> *Brett:*
> *Essentially, therefore, OA is a grouping together through electronic or automated means of all the activities performed in a conventional office. Given such a broad definition, the next problem is to assess exactly which facilities need to be supported in terms of interworking and communication across both users and systems.... At BIS, we have identified the following key factors:*
> * *Ability to meet office (application) requirements*
> * *Physical characteristics*
> * *Cost....*
>
> *In summary, characteristics which are invariably in existence in today's manual (human) offices and are, therefore, required in automated office systems, may be defined as follows:*
>
> *1 Reliability: systems may fail only if alternatives exist which meet the need to 'keep functioning'.*
>
> *2 Simplicity: all staff — whether junior or senior, technical or non-technical — must be able to comprehend and use 'systems' without distraction, discomfort or difficulty.*
>
> *3 Flexibility: the office is a real-time, event-driven 'system' with people responding to a wide range of events, many of which are unpredictable.*
>
> *4 Accessibility: information must be readily to hand and obtainable.*
>
> *5 Expandability: requirements change and both expansion and contraction must be achievable. In practice, offices expand — and it is one of the objectives of OA to increase throughput without a proportionate increase in cost.*
>
> *6 Effectiveness: the office must accomplish its objectives.*

A study carried out for a major manufacturer of office systems has identified the minimum requirements for an 'automated office' as follows:
* Internal electronic mail (within an office building)
* Automatic diary keeping and meetings' scheduling
* Centralised filing of documents, available from any terminal
* Personal computing facilities
* Ability to communicate with other systems
* Ability to interface with data processing systems.

Other suppliers have offered packages combining all or most of these functions. DEC's All-in-One and Data General's CEO are examples, while Quadratron's Q-Office products (for UNIX and MS-DOS) are perhaps the best known independent offerings. The picture in the case of IBM, however, is less clear. It has been truly said that no other supplier can match IBM for the range of products, and no other supplier has such a problem of integration.

> *Brett:*
> *... a substantial problem arises when examining what IBM can provide because of the multiplicity of products....*
>
> *The variety is vast, even dazzling. The choice is, superficially, bewildering — and some argue that even IBM is puzzled.... While the list [of IBM products] may appear Gargantuan, in practice there are significant omissions and the way these products or systems link together is enough to cause those thinking of turning to IBM, for OA, considerable concern.*

## IBM office automation products

Most of the IBM office automation products have been based around the concept of a host machine — a mainframe or special-purpose mini — with dumb terminals. Thus, on the mainframe, we have DISOSS and PROFS (two very different concepts, on different operating systems and unable to communicate easily with each other), on the 8100 we have DOSF, while the 5520 has its own specialised software.

This host-based approach to office automation is insufficient in two ways: firstly, it does not allow for the full use of the intelligent workstation which is becoming the key element in office automation; secondly, its hierarchical approach (paralleled in Systems Network Architecture (SNA)) does not give full peer-to-peer communications. Admittedly, as Brett points out, IBM is fond of talking about peer-to-peer communication, but at present this has been implemented in a very limited fashion.

> *Brett:*
> *What is peer-to-peer communication? It is certainly not full networking in IBM's current offering. An S/36 cannot interact with another S/36 (or S/38) as though it is a remote screen onto the second system. It can only initiate pseudo-interactions which are, in fact, file access and transfers. This is only effective if the name of the sought after file is known. In the office the user will be searching for informal, or 'soft', information, the filing structure of which will inevitably be oblique. In this respect, IBM's current 'peer-to-peer' is quite unsatisfactory for practical OA.*

According to Brett, the two most significant factors in the total office automation picture are the user interface and the need for a 'seamless' interface between the individual elements so that information can be readily transferred from one to another.

A move towards greater consistency in office automation is IBM's announcement of its Office Architecture. However, for the time being, this is an architecture with little specific content. A few common strands, however, can be discerned. SNA is clearly intended as the networking approach which will link the various machines and systems together. Within SNA, Document Content Architecture (DCA) and Document Interchange Architecture (DIA) will define the format of documents and text, allowing for revisable as well as final-form text to be exchanged between previously incompatible systems.

> *Brett:*
> *DIA/DCA can realistically be regarded as an IBM solution to an IBM problem. While this is a valid viewpoint, it completely underestimates the quality and thoroughness of the thinking which underpins these architectures. This is manifest in the implicit inclusion of not only text and image — Scanmaster images are stored under DIA/DCA within DISOSS — but also the potential for voice....*
>
> *DIA and DCA represent a structure upon which, or within which, OA can be built. The architectures surpass any of the research performed by other vendors. That is confirmed by the army of vendors who are adopting DIA/DCA (or at least some elements of the architectures). These include Wang, Digital Equipment and Data General. The scale of IBM's research can be assessed with one example. On average a word processor uses about 30 or 40 control characters: DIA/DCA have over 256 defined.*

As far as the user is concerned, DisplayWrite in its various forms will provide the word processing interface, and Personal Services (again in various forms) will provide other facilities. It will be a long time, however, before these disparate elements are truly welded into a seamless whole.

> *van Kinsbergen:*
> *IBM has a new term, the 'office systems family' representing the results of a four-year effort to link disparate products by editable document transfer. In this family, the System/36 is the hands-down winner as IBM's departmental processor. DIA and DCA will become a de facto standard for document transfer.*
>
> *What we are seeing is a glimpse of a grand strategy which has yet to come to fulfilment. Competitors will not be able to compete with the price of the PC and the System/36. They will have no access to the comparable range of applications, nor will they be able to provide the same homogeneous micro-to-mainframe interface. Finally, they will have difficulties supporting customers to the same degree as IBM. The result will be that, for the first time, IBM will have a single, coherent, document processing and messaging system linking the PC to other office systems, including the host in the back office. The strategy is designed to put IBM back in command and the MIS manager back in control. This will be the first time that IBM has offered a word processing product that expands the entire product line.*

## IBM as a user of office automation

Among the companies making use of advanced office automation products, IBM is well in the forefront. IBM UK is implementing a new system called National Office Support Services (NOSS) which aims at total replacement of conventional mail by electronic mail. Most electronic mail systems in other companies have the limitation that they are used only for internal memoranda or as a telex substitute for communicating to a limited number of regular outside contacts. NOSS goes much further in that the mail received by IBM offices every day will be keyed in by a team of typists and appear on executives' VDU screens rather than in their in-trays. IBM's justification for NOSS is based on productivity increases alone: studies in IBM offices in the US have found that correspondence using paper costs 70 cents for every document used, compared to 20-25 cents for a screen. NOSS will use PROFS running on mainframes under VM as its main vehicle.

## Software development

More and more of a company's information processing needs can be met today by the use of standard packages, but there is still a place for the development of special software and it seems unlikely that this will ever disappear altogether.

Traditionally, programming languages have been divided into two categories: high-level languages such as COBOL and FORTRAN, and low-level languages such as 360 Assembler. High-level languages were regarded as problem oriented in that the programmer could concentrate on the application rather than the details of the hardware, while low-level languages were machine oriented, specific to a particular make and model of processor and closely related to that processor's instruction set.

In today's situation this clear distinction no longer obtains. We have seen the arrival of 'ultra high-level' languages, referred to variously as 'program generators', 'application generators' and 'Fourth Generation languages'. In comparison with these, COBOL and its ilk seem very low level. On the other hand, new types of 'intermediate-level' language have appeared, of which C is the classic example. C is 'low level' in providing ready access to data at the bit and byte level and a range of instructions which translate easily to machine language in most current types of machine; it is 'high level' in that it is machine independent (more so than a number of traditional high-level languages) and provides all the control structures necessary for good programming techniques.

IBM has not had a great deal of success in promoting its own languages as industry standards. PL/1, seen as *the* high-level language, making both COBOL and FORTRAN obsolete, has been taken up enthusiastically by certain mainframe installations, but in others COBOL and FORTRAN still reign supreme. RPG in its various versions has been the main programming language on the System/3X family but has never spread much beyond it, perhaps partly due to the lack of a single standard and partly to the complications of using it outside the type of program it was originally intended to handle. The inherent restrictions of the language are eased considerably in RPG III on the System/38, with its ability to support conditional branching, multiple occurrence data structures and control structures outside the normal RPG cycle, but these enhancements are at the expense of incompatibility with RPG II on the System/36 and earlier machines.

BASIC, the language which comes as standard with the IBM PC, shows signs of fading away as a serious development tool. BASIC is an interesting case. Originally designed as a simple language to teach programming (but often regarded as highly unsuitable for this purpose as its unstructured nature easily leads to bad habits) it became the main language for home computers, and it is no doubt from this basis that it was originally supplied with the IBM PC. Even today, BASIC can be regarded as the 'native language' of the PC in a sense — after all, it is partly supplied in ROM — and certain hardware and software add-ons have hooks into BASIC and nothing else. Interestingly enough, BASIC (in the form of DATABASIC) was for a long time the only programming language in the true sense offered with Pick.

There are now many tools which can simplify the work of program development. In particular, database management systems, whether included with the operating systems as with Pick or the System/38, or supplied separately as packages, can supply query and report languages and routines for updating files and creating indices. Many of these are now available from third-party suppliers for the major operating environments, for instance:
- Informix (UNIX and DOS)
- Mistress (UNIX)
- Dataflex (DOS)
- Unify (UNIX).

Nearly all such packages today are described as 'relational' databases, following the philosophy which Codd defined some years ago but which IBM has only recently begun to take seriously. Meanwhile, the older 'language-type' products such as dBase II are still widely used.

## Personal computing

The concept of personal computing covers all those applications which an individual uses for his own purposes rather than as part of a wider system. As such, it is not exclusively carried out on personal computers; indeed the mainframe user has good 'personal computing' facilities of a rather specialised nature under VM.

Personal computing as normally thought of includes relatively few applications, of which the spreadsheet is the prime example. Just as the first spreadsheet program, VisiCalc, is said to have accounted for the success of the Apple II, so its present-day successor, Lotus 1-2-3, has prompted a large proportion of the sales of the IBM PC.

Spreadsheets are an example of a program which relies heavily on the resources of the PC, particularly the memory-mapped screen. In order to get the maximum performance out of the machine, the software has often been written to address the screen memory directly, without going via the standard operating system calls. This is good for performance, but bad for portability: Lotus has (so far) resisted the temptation to port 1-2-3 onto UNIX, and using such programs with TopView or the various windowing environments can be difficult.

The next step beyond 1-2-3 (itself claimed as being three programs in one) was the true integrated package, for example:
- Lotus's Symphony: based, not surprisingly, round a spreadsheet
- Ashton-Tate's Framework: based on a series of nested 'frames' with a windowing presentation
- Smart: from Innovative Software and centred on a database.

The integrated package approach has much to be said for it — it overcomes the difficulties that can arise with multiple different packages, such as different user interfaces and difficulties with transferring data.

The integrated packages have also had their detractors. Healey predicts that their days may be numbered with the advent of environments such as TopView.

*Healey:*
*The major effect of TopView is to force software houses back into writing program modules rather than monolithic integrated systems. In this way IBM fragments the PC software houses and regains control. A major advantage accrues to the end user in that software houses will at last write to a common interface standard and the user can choose the module he or she likes best, building an integrated system from a 'Chinese menu' of modules.*

The whole concept of the integrated package follows fairly logically from the power and the limitations of MS-DOS. Given a very large memory (by comparison with the 64 Kbyte that was so recently the norm), a memory-mapped display and a totally single-tasking environment, it is logical to write very large programs with a multitude of different functions and a special built-in user interface. The tendency with UNIX-based systems, on the other hand, was quite different. UNIX by its very nature both permits and encourages the writing of small programs, each with a limited and clearly-defined function, and to have them linked together, running concurrently if need be, through the mechanism of pipes and redirection.

*Ritchie and Thompson (015):*
*A number of maxims have gained currency among the builders and users of the UNIX system to explain and promote its characteristic style:*

1  *Make each program do one thing well. To do a new job, build afresh rather than complicate old programs by adding new 'features'.*

2  *Expect the output of every program to become the input to another, as yet unknown, program. Do not clutter output with extraneous information....*

It will be interesting to see which of these two approaches prevails in the future; but there are some signs of a reaction from the very large programs which were all the rage about a year ago.

## Networking

Many of today's applications, and office automation in particular, require some degree of networking. However, the precise nature of the connection required will vary from one organisation to another.

*PC Management (018):*
*One reason why people link personal computers with office automation is that they both involve a single individual performing his own work items (and on his own data) at any given time. Only at specific points in his work pattern would he wish to interact with other elements in the system (say to receive or transmit a document or data file). All of the functions within OA are of this semi-solitary nature, as are PC functions, and this helps to distinguish personal computing and OA on the one hand from mainline DP on the other.*

In the area of networking, we need to look at several different types of network: the local area network, linking typically peer-to-peer, and the broader concept of SNA.

## SNA

In IBM's scheme of things, SNA is the concept which will ultimately allow all the various machines and systems to talk to one another.

*Brett:*
*The importance of SNA in the office is absolute — it provides the physical and logical backbone for communication — but it is not the preserve of the user. If the user is aware of SNA itself, then the user friendliness is not available.*

*Rigg:*
*SNA is the corner-stone of all strategic IBM products concerned with communications and many new application packages will emerge during the next few months and years which will only run within an SNA environment. Indeed, it could be argued by IBM that it is only because SNA communications modules are already available, offering a practical networking base, that these*

*packages can be developed quickly and efficiently. Without SNA, the overhead of developing a suitable base each time would be too great.*

SNA was originally developed in an environment of mainframes and dumb terminals and has been slow in allowing communication between intelligent devices. In an office automation network where all the devices are likely to be intelligent workstations this could give rise to considerable difficulties.

IBM's Advanced Program-to-Program Communication protocol (APPC) addresses this need. The PC version (APPC/PC) allows PCs to communicate on a peer-to-peer basis, and additionally to talk to other machines such as System/36, System/38, Series/1 and mainframes. As yet the whole concept is very new and rather restricted in its scope — for instance mainframe communication will only work with CICS/OS/VS Version 1 (release 7). APPC, corresponding to LU6.2 under SNA, will provide a much more sophisticated level of communications than has been available with 'fileserver'-type networks.

> *Healey:*
> *Using LU6.2 an application on one processor can directly coordinate and execute with an application on another processor. The user only conceives one program, despite the use of two CPUs. The 'program' comprises two separate tasks on two machines joined by LU6.2.*

APPC seems likely to be the key to communications at the application level in the future, but in the short term implementing it will require considerable specialist skill.

> *IBM (019):*
> *To market APPC/PC successfully, it is necessary to fully understand the impact of such an environment on the host processor. It is unlikely that this product would be sold without high-level understanding, by both the customer and the supplier, of the implications of using APPC.*

SNA Distribution Services (SNADS) gives SNA a store-and-forward capability for the first time. Data can now be sent around a data network by being passed from one node to another without the need to set up a complete connection from start to finish.

The communications standards area has long been seen as one of conflict between *de facto* standards set by IBM and the international standards which bodies, such as the ISO, are attempting to promote. IBM has moved some way towards the international standards with the announcement of Open System Transport and Session Support (OSTSS) which partly implements levels four and five of the OSI model.

> *Lamond:*
> *Many people see IBM's Systems Network Architecture (SNA) becoming the industry's new de facto standard communications architecture. But SNA is no more than IBM's proprietary implementation of the International Standards Organisation's (ISO) Open Systems Interconnection (OSI) seven-layer model in advance of ISO's slow-moving definition (five out of seven layers have now been defined); other manufacturers have also had to make their own definition. Now that the OSI definition is nearing completion, all other manufacturers are promising an adaptation of their architectures to OSI, while IBM is promising 'gateway' translators for each level.*
>
> *As part of the agreed settlement of the European Community's (EC) objections to IBM selling practices, IBM has published the LU6.2 protocol to allow other manufacturers to make their systems as SNA-compatible as IBM's own, and thus deprived itself of a weapon to influence its host computer users' choice of distributed processing and office automation satellites. SNA may continue to evolve and become indistinguishable from the internationally defined OSI both in its openness and the distribution of its network control functions.*

## Local Area Networks (LANs)

The LAN market has seen plenty of products but few standards over the years. However, the scene is becoming clearer in the wake of various announcements from IBM.

LANs can be regarded in two different ways: as a means of linking together a number of workstations so that they can exchange data and use common services; and as an alternative computer architecture giving the power and functionality of a mini or mainframe but in a modular fashion. In the past, LANs could be divided into two categories: 'open' networks, capable of running many types of workstation, and 'closed' networks (much the more common) designed for use with one type of workstation only. An example of a closed network is the Xionics system using specially designed office automation terminals.

With the increasing popularity of the IBM PC, it is less and less likely that the closed networks will find popularity, except those which are closed in using only the IBM PC. Even IBM's new token-passing network is 'open', in that it is specifically designed to be able to take non-IBM workstations.

Another trend that has become more marked recently is the unbundling of the hardware and software elements of commercial network offerings. As an example, the IBM PC Network uses IBM software running on top of DOS 3.1 with network hardware supplied by Sytek. The Tapestry system, devised by Torus but marketed by IBM, uses the same hardware as the PC Network system but with special software, including an icon-based user interface. The Icon system, supplied by Torus, is essentially the same software as Tapestry (which it preceded) but running on special hardware.

## Types of network

A LAN, unlike a traditional computer system, has no single central machine controlling what goes on. There is, therefore, a need for some system of arbitration in case several stations try to use the network at once. Three technologies have been important in the progress of networking so far:

1  Carrier Sense Multiple Access with Collision Detection (CSMA/CD): a station can transmit at any time when the line is free, merely taking corrective action if it detects that it and another station have tried to transmit simultaneously.

2  The Cambridge Ring, in which a number of packets of information circulate, some full, some empty. Any station can put a message into an empty packet.

3  Token-passing networks, in which there is one and one only 'token' giving the right to transmit which is passed from one station to another.

Each of these technologies has different performance characteristics and technical merits (CSMA/CD is understandably the most efficient when the traffic is low) but the choice between them will ultimately be on the basis of support in the market rather than technical considerations. At one time Ethernet, embodying the CSMA/CD approach, and supported by a number of major manufacturers, seemed the best established, and most likely to prevail. IBM, however, announced its support, in principle, for the token-passing approach. Little more was heard of this for some time, and many companies (including IBM in the form of PC Network) brought out networks using other approaches. But in October 1985 IBM announced the token network as a product, and the rules of the game were suddenly changed.

IBM is addressing all aspects of networking, starting with the physical cabling.

> *Brett:*
> *The importance of the LAN to IBM was demonstrated by the May 1984 'Cabling System' announcement. IBM does not wish other vendors to capitalise on its current weakness. Cabling the office for OA is expensive and is not an exercise to be repeated lightly. The concept of the 'data expressway' to enable differing IBM hardware to interface with those resources — including voice connection — is critical in achieving the penetration of the OA market that IBM wishes.*

Today, IBM offers several different networking systems.

> *Brett:*
> *IBM's history with LANs has not been noted for its success. There are several significant intentions — each with troublesome implications because of the lack of sufficient information.*
> *The key products are:*
> * *PC Cluster*
> * *PC Network*
> * *Token-passing LAN.*

*Of these, the PC Cluster is the least important. It is a convenient low-cost method of pulling together a number of PCs but without special qualities. The PC Network has far greater implications. As a broadband network it has the potential for many more activities.*

*Novell Inc (020):*
*The PC Network Program is a quantum improvement over existing diskserver networks. By embracing the fileserver approach and adding certain features, such as a concurrent workstation/ server, IBM has made obsolete a large number of products from would-be competitors.*

*In terms of functionality and performance, however, the PC Network Program offers a series of mixed signals.... The adoption of broadband technology indicates that the product is aimed at large corporate users who might need the greater capacities of broadband.*

*Yet the performance of PC Network Program is severely limited. This translates to a practical limit on connected nodes, far below that sought by most corporate users.*

## The token ring

The case of the token network is an indication of the relationship between IBM and international standards. It was largely at the insistence of IBM that the token-passing approach was approved as an international standard in parallel to the Ethernet-type approach, but this was a standard that found few adherents. The actual announcement by IBM of a token-passing ring as a product (available later) led, on the other hand, to an immediate flurry of announcements from other manufacturers (except for DEC, which will probably still promote Ethernet as a standard) that they were supporting this standard. No doubt a key factor is the fact that the standard has now crystallised in the shape of hardware. The control and interface chips (made by Texas Instruments) are being made available to other manufacturers. The objective must be to get the standard widely adopted in order to avoid the accusation of it being purely an IBM proprietary product, while still giving IBM the lion's share of the market.

*Hemsley et al:*
*Over 40 other companies were provided with the samples from Texas Instruments, manufacturers of the chipset to implement the token ring, including IBM's major competitors. This should ensure a large number of compatible, competing and complementary products leading to the domination of the LAN market by IBM in the same way that its introduction of the IBM PC led to its domination of the personal computer business.*

*Rigg:*
*The token-passing mechanism advocated by IBM, and incorporated now in the IEEE 802.5 standard, is theoretically suitable for supporting conversational voice as well as data devices. All the signs are, however, that for the next few years at least, IBM will keep the two streams apart. Data, which may, indeed, include voice annotation of documents and possible voice messaging, will go on the LAN; conversational voice is too expensive for a LAN (especially if IBM is not yet sure about the costs of LAN interface chip development) and will be supported on the digital voice/data exchange to be acquired from Rolm.*

The two principal IBM networking products compare as follows:

| IBM PC Network | IBM Token-Ring Network |
|---|---|
| Broadband | Baseband |
| Cable TV-type cable | IBM Cabling System (two grades) |
| Maximum 72 devices | Maximum 260 devices |
| IBM PCs only | IBM or non-IBM devices |
| Tree topology | Star-wired ring |
| 2 Mbit/sec | 4 Mbit/sec. |

## Networks and operating systems

Networking requires support from the operating system to be effective. At the PC level, this is shown by the special facilities provided in PC-DOS/MS-DOS 3.1.

*Novell Inc (020):*
*The importance of Microsoft's DOS 3.1 cannot be overestimated. It directly addresses the two major impediments to the growth of networking: the need for applications and the need for quality throughout the industry.... DOS 3.1 has many fundamental multi-user functions built in as high-level network primitives.... Software developers can write one version of a network application for all DOS networks. No longer must they face the high cost and speculation of writing a separate version for each LAN.*

This mention of multi-user functions in relation to DOS should not go without some comment. DOS is of course a single-user operating system. The functions in question do not mean that DOS can now support multiple users on a single PC in the way that XENIX or Concurrent DOS permit. What they provide instead is facilities for file and record locking.

*Harrison:*
*File and record locking are essential for true multi-user software. Without these features, attempts to use the network to provide a database server will fail when several stations attempt to update the same record in the same file simultaneously.*

*Some people believed that Microsoft would be unable to provide true file and record locking facilities without a multitasking server. Microsoft has proved them wrong by implementing a locking scheme which is considerably better than that offered by its main rival, DR-Net.*

## Mainframe links

Micro/mainframe links are of various types. Outside the IBM area, the most usual approach — cheap and simple — is to connect the micro directly via RS232. In IBM houses, on the other hand, the link is more often by an expensive and specialised hardwired coaxial cable link to a 3274 cluster controller; the PC with the appropriate hardware emulator can act as a 3270 terminal. Used purely in this way it is an expensive terminal: it makes more sense when the PC is also used for local processing, or to manipulate data received from the mainframe or about to be sent to it.

Among communications protocols, SDLC is the most popular for PC users, although BSC overtakes it in a VM environment.

*McMahon:*
*There are three methods addressed ... for connecting a micro to a mainframe ... :*

*1 Obtain hardware/software which allows the micro to perform 327X emulation.*

*2 Use a gateway switch which converts standard asynchronous protocols which can be produced from most micros to a bisynchronous format needed to access the mainframe.*

*3 Use a micro specifically built for micro/mainframe processing (eg IBM PC 3270).*

Special versions of the IBM PC are offered specifically for micro/mainframe links. The 3270 PC is essentially a PC and a 3270-type terminal combined, with a hybrid keyboard.

*McMahon:*
*The keyboard must now meet the needs of the two processors — micro and mainframe. To meet this requirement means having two logical keyboard layouts for the one physical keyboard. The IBM PC 3270 uses a special keyboard. It has approximately 30 per cent more keys than a standard keyboard. These extra keys cater for the specific requirements of both processors.*

The XT/370 and AT/370 offer the ability to emulate mainframe software, but only under a VM/CMS environment. Unfortunately, one of the main groups of CMS users, those using it for financial analysis with ADRS, cannot use it readily because the machine does not support the APL character set. The XT/370 is therefore most suited for software development and scientific purposes — its data security features are not really good enough for general commercial use.

A curious feature of the scene is that to link an IBM PC to an IBM mainframe, a non-IBM device — the

289

Irma 3270 emulator board — is effectively the *de facto* standard. Perhaps for once the IBM marketing department has failed to recognise an opportunity, or perhaps it is a case of IBM trying to preserve the market niche for the 3270-PC.

Micro/mainframe links are implemented in many companies as part of an Information Centre — a concept which has changed its nature considerably since IBM first introduced it in the 1970s. Originally the emphasis was on mainframe-based tools to enable end users to get access to the data stored in their corporate files. Today, much more use is made of personal computers, but problems of allowing users to manipulate data locally on these while still preserving the necessary safeguards of privacy and integrity of data, remain to be addressed.

> *McMahon:*
> *The most restrictive limitation involving the interface of the micro to the mainframe is data management. Currently it should be assumed that there is no data management software which provides overall management of data scattered between the mainframe and the linked micros. Thus, if a record is updated on the mainframe then it cannot automatically update the data copies resident on the micros.*
>
> *The effect of this limitation requires the system design to cater for the movement of data between the mainframe and the micro whenever integrity needs to be maintained....*
>
> *Security systems of mainframe on-line environments were often built for usage by 'dumb' terminals. The design of these security systems may be based on assumptions which are no longer true today, especially as the new terminals added to the system may be intelligent workstations (ie micros).... Security systems should be reviewed before micros are permitted to be used instead of the traditional 'dumb' terminals. Remember, the success of 'hackers' today is mainly based on their usage of micros to bypass the security of a system!*

## Specialised networks

Production control is likely to be an increasingly important area in the future. An indication of its interest here is the announcement by IBM of an add-on board for the PC/AT, to give compatibility with the newly adopted Manufacturing Automation Protocol (MAP), developed by General Motors. In areas such as this, IBM may be forced to follow the lead of its customers more than in the past.

Parallel with MAP is the Technical and Office Protocols (TOP) standard, again supported by General Motors, but this time originated by Boeing which has one of the world's largest privately managed data networks. Like MAP, TOP is an application-specific subset of the OSI protocols, but in this case for networked office applications. Unlike MAP, TOP is likely to have a much harder task in achieving acceptance, by IBM and elsewhere, being much more in competition with other emerging standards.

> *Economist (013):*
> *Part of IBM's power in the computer market has come from the timidity (or prudence) of buyers. Automation buyers are already using their muscle to put all suppliers on an equal footing. GM's MAP and Boeing's standardisation effort for its computer-aided design and engineering machines are examples.*

# 5: Futures

Looking to the future, a number of questions suggest themselves. How will IBM fare against its competitors, particularly AT&T? What is IBM's attitude to 'industry standards' — will the open architecture of the PC and MS-DOS continue, reinforced by a real commitment to UNIX, or will IBM return to its traditional policy of 'closed' systems? How will IBM cope with the coming technological changes? In this Section we consider the new technologies of voice and image processing and the new types of computer architecture, such as the reduced instruction set computer (RISC) which has long been an IBM research project and is now appearing at last as a practical product.

## The future of the computer market

During 1985, the computer market experienced one of its periodic downturns, however, there can be little doubt that the underlying trend is still upwards. We saw earlier that it is one of IBM's stated aims to 'grow at least as fast as the industry'. Kinsbergen believes that the market is growing so fast that IBM can keep its present market share, or even lose ground somewhat, and still double in size over the next five years as it has done in the past.

*van Kinsbergen:*
*IBM will grow to approximately $88 billion in 1989. This growth curve very much fits the pattern of projected user MIS spending in the same timeframe. With this in mind, IBM has only to maintain the market share it has today to double in size by 1989 without any difficulty....*

*In 1984, IBM generated $20 million in revenue every four hours of each day. In 1988, it will generate $40 million every four hours of each day. IBM will compete in all segments of information processing as the low-cost producer.*

The marketplace in the coming years however will not be the same as in the past. It is becoming clear that the main growth areas for information technology, and hence for IBM, will be centred on distributed information and automation in office and factory. A key area will be the convergence, by means of SNA, DCA, and DIA, of the various different IBM product architectures. IBM will thus be setting the standards once again, and may eventually provide, at long last, a homogeneous standard right across the range.

When a company reaches the worldwide size and dominance of IBM in such a strategic industry as information technology, the threat of government intervention cannot be ignored.

*Dorn:*
*As IBM grows, the chances for long-term legal action rise. There is an ever broadening stream of notes, papers and articles suggesting IBM is too big and needs to be restrained. Most of this is still a semi-underground movement and little widespread, cogent reasoning has appeared in reputable media supporting a 'break up IBM' movement. Two major negatives to such an action are:*

*1  The politics of the present Washington administration.*

*2  The unhappy experience of US corporations and individuals with the judicially mandated break-up of AT&T....*

*In the final analysis, government restraining actions have always proved inept. IBM either circumvents the rules, changes the rules to suit itself or just fights off the hostile government. In general this occurs because few governments have the technical depth to deal with IBM. They do not understand the game being played....*

## IBM versus AT&T

In the computer market today IBM's dominance is effectively unchallenged. It is difficult to imagine another company making an effective counter-attack. The lesson of the minicomputer, in which IBM allowed firms such as DEC to make the market and effectively set the standards, has surely been well learnt — the combination of IBM's advanced research and development in all the major areas of information technology and an unequalled sense of the market must make it more difficult than ever for a competitor to find IBM unprepared for any eventuality. Certainly most of the traditional computer manufacturers have been caught in a defensive position, forced to react to IBM product announcements rather than lead the field.

However, the information technology market of the future will be much more than just the market for computers. Networks, communications, voice and visual images, will all need to come together. As IBM moves into these new areas — and it must do so to maintain market dominance — it will be competing on unfamiliar ground. A key opponent in several of these areas will be AT&T.

*van Kinsbergen:*
*The communications battle with AT&T will probably not really surface until the 1990s. In order for IBM to compete in this marketplace, it needs to increase its critical mass significantly. Investments made so far do not accomplish this. Potential targets for IBM to acquire or work with include GTE, Western Union, Boeing Computer Services, Geisco, and ADP.*

*IBM has taken a $400 million position in MCI in return for turning the assets of SBS over to MCI. MCI needs this help as its finances are fragile, which leaves it in a difficult position to compete against AT&T. IBM hopes that MCI, given access to IBM's Fortune 500 customers, may be able to use SBS's satellites in a way that IBM was unable to do alone. IBM's investments in SBS and MCI show that it believes it must supply data communications support and not just the computers that run user applications.*

*The acquisition of MCI has angered AT&T. This may be just the action required to push AT&T forward. Potentially, AT&T could acquire a computer firm in order to become more of a full service corporation to compete with IBM. The candidates mentioned most often are Digital Equipment Corporation and the Apple Corporation.*

*The battle lines are now drawn. IBM's acquisition of MCI gives it access to MCI's 350 000 commercial customers as well as a 20 000-mile nationwide network. This is a crucial ingredient in IBM's pursuit of its integrated architecture. In short, AT&T is no longer the obvious choice for corporate communication customers.*

*Lamond:*
*Another factor preventing IBM from dominating the newer minicomputer, personal computer and communications markets is competition from AT&T, the only corporation in the information processing industry possessing a size and finance comparable to IBM's own. Before it divested itself of its local Bell Telephone companies in the US, AT&T's annual turnover was three times IBM's (but its profit much smaller). Since divestiture, the new AT&T is about IBM's financial size, but geographically still largely restricted to the US whereas IBM operates worldwide. To date, the long-heralded fight between the two has been fought with 'wet noodles' as 'Datamation' magazine put it. This is partly because AT&T has been distracted until now by the major reorganisation forced on it by the divestiture of its local US telephone operating companies, and the deregulation of the long-distance communications business that it has been allowed to retain. But it is also the result of an understandable caution on the part of two managements who respect each other, and who see their task as maximising profits for their shareholders rather than engaging in publicity campaigns.*

*Each of these companies dominates a core business that the other does not intend to challenge. IBM's is in large mainframe host computers, AT&T's in long-distance communications lines and public telecommunications switching exchanges. Each corporation's activities in the other's core business are designed mainly to maintain an open competitive market rather than gain a major market share.*

Just as IBM is moving into areas such as voice and communications which AT&T has made its own, so AT&T is moving into the computer area. The key product here is of course UNIX System V. After many years as an enthusiasts' operating system with no support from its supplier, UNIX has now become a strategic product, very actively marketed.

Why is AT&T pushing UNIX? The simple answer is that it is now permitted, following the change in its legal position and its divestiture of the local telephone companies in the US, to start selling computer products in a way that was previously denied to it. But this is not the whole story for the value of a UNIX licence to AT&T on a unit price basis is barely enough to make it worth the effort of marketing. The real reason lies in AT&T's avowed intention to become the world's leading supplier of computer hardware. In order to achieve this aim it will clearly have IBM to contend with, but the approach is not unlike that which IBM has applied in other cases: to establish the standard, to make it publicly available so that other suppliers will take it up and make it truly an 'industry standard', and then to compete in this area with the advantage of always being one step ahead of the competition.

## Pointers to the IBM of the future

In a marketing-led company such as IBM, the future strategy can often be discerned from reorganisations of the marketing structure. We have already noted the formation back in 1975 of GSD and GBG, intended to re-inforce the sales of the small and medium systems, which might otherwise have been neglected in the shadow of the then dominant mainframes, but which were seen by top management as a key element in IBM's future development. The removal of this structure in 1981 showed that the products in question had become well established, and was no doubt also a response to the views of users who were confused and irritated by receiving competing proposals from two different IBM salesmen. It also reflected the much reduced likelihood of the company being broken up as a result of the anti-trust litigation.

A later structure (in the US, and mirrored with different terminology in other countries) was the division between National Accounts Division, dealing with the biggest customers, and National Marketing Division, dealing with the smaller customers. The 1985 reorganisation swept this structure away and replaced it with two divisions based on a geographical split. At the same time, IBM has strengthened its National Distribution Division (NDD), which manages the relation with third parties. The growth of NDD recognises the increasing importance of third parties such as systems houses and Value Added Resellers (VARs). In the UK, an Information Systems Distribution Marketing Division has been created, along the same lines as the NDD.

The entry of IBM into the personal computer market was facilitated, as McIntyre describes, by the use of a special organisational approach, the Independent Business Unit (IBU). The reabsorption of the IBU into the mainstream of the company clearly indicates the changed status of the PC.

*McIntyre:*
*Entry Systems is now a traditional IBM product division, with development and product management responsibilities. The management of the dealer channel, which was so vital to the success of the PC, and such an unusual feature of Entry Systems, is now the responsibility of a new division, Information Systems Distribution Marketing (ISDM), which handles all of IBM's third-party marketing channels. These changes recognise two facts of IBM life. Firstly, that the PC family and derivatives are now fundamental elements in IBM's line of products and no longer a new venture in any sense of the words, and secondly, that product sales through third parties have become a major business for IBM and that business sense demands the grouping together of the various channels for management by specialists in that field.*

With the same sales force now able to sell the entire IBM product range too much overlap in market position between the different product lines would be an unwanted complication. IBM can, therefore, be expected to promote convergence between the main product lines. In the medium systems area particularly there are just too many products and some of them will disappear. It is clear, for instance, that IBM is actively pushing the System/36, and there have for some years been rumours that the 8100 would be discontinued.

*Hughes:*
*Many people have predicted the demise of the 8100, but with over 12 000 machines worldwide, IBM has again shown its ability to make things work. The latest machine — the 8150 range — is new in almost everything and, together with the latest versions of software, it is reported to be making existing users very happy. IBM Germany has had a recent order for 4000 machines from the Bundespost. The 8100 position with System/36 is difficult to predict, but it is felt that the two of them will be retained for some time. One area where the System/36 is weak is in its lack of database management facility while the 8100 has the (host dominated) Database and Transaction Management System (DTMS).*

Another possible marketing change is greater adaptation of products to geographical markets. IBM Japan has long had a number of specialised offerings, for instance the JX version of the PC, essentially a superior version of the PC Junior, now launched also in an English-language version in Australia, but there may be also a move to more specialised products for the European markets.

*FinTech (021):*
*In the beginning, IBM tried to create a PC with universal appeal. Now, its design philosophy is changing. In a bid to consolidate its lead in Europe, IBM planners are working on customising the next generation of PCs to produce a range of models with maximum local appeal in each market it serves.*

*Although the company is not ready to predict when the first products for local consumption will be put on sale, the initiative must pose a serious threat to other vendors. It could undermine local advantages which established European manufacturers enjoy in their home markets. US and Japanese manufacturers, with smaller European market shares, could also be hard pressed to compete.*

*But IBM executives believe that the company will need to show greater awareness of local preferences if it is to make the most of its opportunities as a multinational vendor. This is because much of the untapped market potential in Europe is among businesses that have still to adopt information technology.*

Meanwhile, IBM is preparing for greater flexibility to meet national requirements.

*Brett:*
*... IBM is said to be examining the inclusion [in DCA/DIA] of a single ROM with all Western character sets in every output device, be it printer, screen or whatever. This would provide the base for accommodating different nationalities in the office — without a recurrence of the problems that have arisen with non-European keyboards and software....*

## The prospects for open architecture

One of the major questions which IBM-watchers seek to answer is whether IBM will adhere in the future to an 'open architecture' approach, following international standards and other standards which have become established in the market, or whether it will turn its back on the outside world and set its own standards which others will try to follow.

Newman has identified two strategies which IBM adopts in its approach to dominating the market.

*Newman (022):*
*Strategy One, the normally successful IBM approach, is to create an IBM standard by exploiting its market penetration. Other manufacturers have to follow the standard if they are to compete in the IBM market at all, but since IBM controls the standard (or architecture) IBM always has the upper hand. Examples included the System/370 architecture, binary synchronous communications protocols, SNA and more recently DIA/DCA.*

*Strategy Two is a newer approach. This handles instances where IBM missed the inception of a new market and so needs to gain control. The best example is the PC. It is doubtful that anyone saw the potential of the micro before Apple was born; but by coming into the market late, IBM was able to pick out the best features of the current PCs and bring out hardware slightly better than the rest (at that time). But the heart of Strategy Two, in the PC's case, was the decision to buy in an existing standard operating system (PC-DOS) and encourage a proliferation of software through a very un-IBM openness about internals and interfaces.*

*Having captured its 50 per cent or more of the market, the company can set about standardising the PC.... Gradually the PC's open interfaces will close up, and IBM will clearly gain control of the professional PC market's destiny.*

Healey believes that TopView marks the beginning of a move away from open architecture by IBM.

*Healey:*
*The key factor now is that TopView, not PC-DOS, controls applications programs. A next release of 'TopView' (possibly in the first quarter of 1986) will be a native mode 286 operating system with TopView and PC-DOS compatibility but with the true multitasking capability needed for taking the LAN products from the interesting but limited PC Network into true SNA software. At that point IBM will have 'gone it alone'. Only the application providers will be welcome from the outside world. MS-DOS, products like VisiOn, Framework MS-Windows, Desq, are all eliminated....*

*Thus with TopView, IBM is creating an enormous gap between itself and the other personal computer suppliers, including the clones. An IBM PC/AT clone is going to be strangled by software, not hardware, pricing.*

An alternative view is put forward by McIntyre, who believes that it is in the interests of IBM as well as its customers to promote a more open architecture.

*McIntyre:*
*There are several factors which would make a retreat from the 'open' policy counter strategic for IBM, including the following:*

*1  Limitation of future PC sales opportunities to only those applications supported by IBM proprietary application software, and vice versa....*

*2  Making obsolete the past investments by IBM itself and the industry....*

*3  The requirement for application software for personal computers in every environment in the strategic timeframe will take the combined efforts of IBM and the rest of the industry to fulfil.*

*4  As hardware becomes more and more 'generic' the information industry will depend increasingly on the software. Working with the industry and developing an IBM-quality software publishing capability which can harness the best developments in the software world must be of major importance. To walk away from the third-party software industry at this stage would appear to be self-defeating.*

## New applications

The future of the computer industry will be determined in part by advances in technology and decisions by IBM and others whether to implement them; another source of change is the need to cope with new types of application. We have noted the increased importance of new 'unstructured' applications, and a number of these are related to the whole area of 'decision support' (deciding who to promote to use our previous example) and the associated subjects of Intelligent Knowledge-Based Systems (IKBS), expert systems, and Artificial Intelligence (AI).

## Artificial Intelligence

The area of AI has been studied by academic institutions for a good many years but little so far has appeared on the market of real interest to the end user. One area in which some progress has been made is that of expert systems. The term expert system properly describes a particular way of storing and using information which differs both from the traditional DP concept of fields and records and also from the word processing approach of free-format documents. An expert system consists primarily of a 'knowledge base' and an 'inference engine'. The inference engine supplies the logic needed to manipulate the knowledge base in order to find answers to the problem being considered. The knowledge base comprises a number (typically a few hundred) of rules which can be used to draw conclusions based on given facts. These rules are supplied to the system by a person who is an expert in the chosen subject. Typical applications include medical diagnosis and geological prospecting but the technique is applicable to a wide range of subjects, including business problems.

> *Hemsley et al:*
> *Expert systems achieved their high profile in the early 1980s due largely to their success in the medical and oil/mineral exploration fields. Transfer of the potential to the business field and management in particular is occurring, although not at the fast rate that had been projected by suppliers. Examples of promising applications in business and management are:*
> * *Finance, eg credit assessment*
> * *Maintenance/diagnostic, eg car engines*
> * *Design, eg aircraft wings....*
>
> *Complex expert systems require significantly greater processing power and memory than even the IBM AT can offer. However basic expert system shells, small expert systems and special expert system programming languages such as PROLOG and LISP are becoming available on the IBM PC.*

IBM's own offerings in this area were re-inforced during 1985 with the announcement of several products aimed at the VM user, with PROLOG now proclaimed as the language of choice for developing expert systems applications. PROLOG thus takes its place alongside LISP as an IBM-supported vehicle.

Meanwhile, in the micro area, the running is being made by third-party suppliers, with the release of products such as Deja Vu (a significant step forward) promising to bring expert systems nearer to the end user. These products could become an accepted element in the variety of applications that go to make up 'personal computing'. Another application of AI techniques could be to provide 'natural language' processing.

> *Hemsley et al:*
> *... it is in the area of natural language processing of text that the biggest impact will be seen in the next few years. This will occur in special application fields rather than in general conversational English which, despite the excessive claims of some advertisers, is still many years away....*
>
> *The type of practical situation in which natural language processing is already applicable is fortunately now easy to identify and achieve where a natural language system is used as a front-end to a database in a specific situation where the total vocabulary required to express all reasonable requests for access and application is small. Fortunately, many existing conventional databases are of this kind. Therefore there are considerable market opportunities for new natural language products to exploit advances in natural language processing....*
>
> *The potential effectiveness of such focused applications of natural language processing is high. Further extensions are anticipated within the next few years as work currently at the research and development stage is incorporated in new products on the market.*

## New architectures

## Reduced Instruction Set Computer (RISC)

While reducing its types of product in the more traditional areas of computing, IBM is still investigating new architectures. An example is the RISC. The RISC concept was developed by IBM in the late 1970s as a reaction against the growing complexity of computer processor design. Over the years, processors — microprocessors as well as mainframes and minis — have been provided with ever fuller instruction sets. Research by IBM and others has shown that most of the time the more recondite instructions are not actually used; the time and effort needed to test and debug the chips and squeeze ever more functions into the limited physical area of the silicon are a substantial, and arguably unnecessary, overhead on chip design. Meanwhile, at the minicomputer level, the growing use of microcode has led to a two-level implementation of machine instructions which is seen at its most striking in the System/38.

The IBM 801 minicomputer was essentially a research venture, not a product. Its aim was to develop a minicomputer, compiler and control program which would achieve 'significantly better cost/performance for high-level language programs than that attainable by existing systems'. By having a very small instruction set, giving only the most frequently used instructions, it would be possible to avoid microcode and have the entire instruction set hardwired. Software, rather than microcode, would then be used to build up more complex instructions where necessary.

The 801 never became a product, and meanwhile other manufacturers developed the RISC concept. But in mid-1985, IBM announced the Quicksilver engineering workstation. Ultimately descended from the 801, it has been reduced to a single-chip processor, rated at two million instr/sec — although this is not a valid measure since the instructions are by definition not really comparable with pre-RISC machines. Interestingly, its operating system, AIX, is a version of UNIX, supplied by Interactive Systems, originators of VM/IX and PC/IX. Quicksilver is aimed at the engineering and CAD markets, and could set a new standard for very high-power graphics workstations, but it is not at all clear how it will fit in, if at all, with the rest of the IBM product line. One rumour is that it could eventually be offered in office as well as scientific applications and provide a successor to the System/36. The product was launched in January 1986 as the 6150 and 6151, under the generic title of PC/RT (for RISC Technology).

## Parallel processing

A key restriction in virtually all computer systems up to now has been the need to organise processing to proceed in a serial fashion. This is appropriate for many functions, particularly those to which computing has been most successfully applied in the past. However, there are inherent physical limits (dictated by the speed of light and the size of electronic components) to the speed of any computing machine, and for certain applications these limits are already becoming significant. Parallel processing, by allowing several things to be done at once, is a potential key to vast increases in the speed available.

Some degree of parallel processing has of course been common in computers for some time: witness the multiple processors of the System/36, or 'pipelining' (fetching one instruction while the previous one is being executed) as provided on the Intel 80286 and hence the PC/AT. But these are parallel processing only in a very limited sense. True parallel processing involves a large number of general-purpose processors, each of them able to carry out the types of task, and organised in such a way as to divide the total task between them. This is, after all, the way in which the human brain (using a matrix of far slower and less powerful processors than today's computers, but in enormous numbers) is able to carry out functions such as pattern recognition which are far beyond the scope of current computers.

Parallel processing will thus probably be the key to unlocking some of the more intractable problems of AI, as well as tackling problems such as weather forecasting which essentially consist of vast numbers of calculations to be done in parallel. The state of the art in parallel processing took a major step forward in 1985 with the launch of the long-awaited Transputer from the British company Inmos. Essentially a simple but very powerful processor, able to be connected in parallel in large numbers and with its own programming language, OCCAM, the Transputer still awaits the application software which will convert it into the basis of a computer system.

IBM's own work in this area, includes the Research Parallel Processor Project (RP3) being worked on at the Thomas J Watson research laboratory. RP3 is purely experimental and is being developed in conjunction with outside academic institutions. However, it indicates that IBM has not neglected this area. It uses a highly parallel architecture of 64 processors, with the possibility to link eight such machines together giving 512 processors altogether. It also has the ability to simulate other parallel computer architectures.

Parallel processing is not yet the solution to every problem; technical difficulties remain, such as what to do with problems which are difficult to split up for parallel processing: small serial parts of a problem can have a severely limiting effect on the speed of the system as a whole. The questions of simultaneous access to data which arise with multitasking in a serial environment also occur in a different way with parallel processing. However, we can see more and more machines with this type of architecture in the future.

## Fault tolerance

Until now the area of fault-tolerant machines has been left to other manufacturers, but IBM is showing an interest.

*Hughes:*
*In 1985, IBM announced an OEM agreement with Stratus to market its fault-tolerant product as System/88. The System/88 incorporates processors and other components in identical pairs, so that if any component fails, its twin part can instantly and automatically take over the function. With System/88, a failing component causes the computer to diagnose the problem and automatically dials up the System/88 support centre.... If appropriate, a replacement part is despatched to the customer who can replace the failed part himself.*

*To what extent IBM will 'grow' this product is debatable. Certainly, there is an increasing demand for fault tolerance, but as other systems hardware becomes extremely reliable, it is difficult to predict the extent of the System/88's growth. It is likely that all IBM's products will one day gain fault-tolerance status anyway.*

## New information technology

The history of IBM, and of information technology generally, has so far been chiefly concerned with data in the form of text, but office automation in the real world encompasses information in other modes, such as voice and visual images. Already DCA is able to mix voice, data and image, although actual software and hardware devices to support this are not yet available. IBM is rumoured to be developing a compound electronic workstation to handle documents containing a mixture of text, data and images, with voice annotation.

## Voice processing

IBM has been working on speech recognition since the 1960s (eg the 'Shoebox' project). Even so, its experience with voice processing is vastly less than that of its main rival, AT&T. The older IBM PABXs (1750, 3750) are now well out of date and have not been replaced. IBM's current strength in this area is mainly from its ownership of Rolm, but this is not the same as having the capability actually as part of IBM.

There are, in fact, several aspects of voice processing, all of which IBM will need to address if it is to keep up to date in this area:
● Voice store and forward
● Voice annotation of text
● Voice recognition
● Speech synthesis
● Telephone management.

Voice store and forward is a form of electronic mail enabling the sender and recipient to be 'decoupled' in time, just as the telephone has decoupled them in space, while still preserving the naturalness of the voice medium. IBM's ADS voice messaging system, based on a Series/1, is a step in this direction, but a very expensive product. As in many other areas, incompatibilities of the technology are holding it up: ADS was designed for the American touch-tone exchanges, and in Europe is only available as an add-on to IBM PABXs. Its future seems dim: it has been withdrawn in the US, and has also been the subject of legal wrangles with Elk Industries of Miami, which claims that ADS infringes its patents.

*Brett:*
*For voice it is apparent from the relationship with Rolm, that IBM perceives its own Private Automation Branch Exchange (PABX) voice systems to be in decline. The 1750/3750 analogue exchanges are outdated. The ADS voice messaging system, based on the seemingly eternal Series/1, is a first and expensive step towards reducing the 70 per cent failure rate on telephone calls. More can be expected, although the ability to connect to non-IBM PABXs in Europe remains in question — as much because of IBM marketing policy as technical difficulty. The fact that Rolm has its own voice messaging system only further complicates the issue.*

Voice annotation of text is beginning to be supplied in a number of office systems. Typical uses would be for a manager to dictate corrections to a draft prepared by a typist, or for someone receiving an electronic mail item in text form to add a comment by voice before sending it on to a colleague. IBM is said to be considering adding voice annotation to its PROFS system.

Such simple applications as voice annotation and voice store and forward are no longer really at the leading edge of technology: some problems remain, but they are not fundamental, being concerned for instance with the user interface and the large amounts of storage and communications bandwidth involved. A much more challenging aspect of voice technology, and one which will become increasingly important in the remaining years of this century, is the conversion of information from voice to text or vice versa.

Speech recognition could ultimately revolutionise the office and make information technology far more accessible to non-specialist users. A type of speech recognition was demonstrated as long ago as 1939, but many problems still remain. Today we can identify two types of speech recognition:

1 Limited speech recognition: having a small vocabulary and used, for instance, to give commands to a computer. This is now established technology and available on home micros.

2 Full speech recognition: eg for dictating text into a word processor. This is still at the leading edge of technology.

Clearly full speech recognition could, in due course, have an enormous effect on the office, essentially eliminating the job of the typist. Authorities disagree fundamentally, however, as to when it will be an economic proposition. IBM is conducting a major research project into full speech recognition, but there is not even a rumour that this research will lead to a product announcement in the near future. IBM's experimental system shows impressive results, but is not yet a viable proposition for general office use.

> *Hunter (023):*
> *The IBM system required a lot of hardware, including a 4341 mainframe working with three floating point array processors.*
>
> *IBM's two major breakthroughs are a 5000 word vocabulary and the ability to operate in real time. The company's system needs a short delay to process the speech, converting the sound waves into digital signals which are then compared with stored templates or sound patterns of each word.*
>
> *Previous systems were more limited in vocabulary ... but even 5000 is not enough for word processing, as on average about five per cent of spoken words (equivalent of one word for every two lines of A4 text) would still be missing from the vocabulary. A 20 000 word vocabulary is generally considered necessary for word processing, as then only one per cent or less of the spoken words are lost.*

IBM is planning to increase its vocabulary to 20 000 words during 1986.

There are other difficulties with the state of the art in voice recognition. For instance, most systems so far have required each user to train the system by dictating every word in the vocabulary. This is reasonable for the small-scale use that has been made of speech input so far but would be impossible with a 5000-word vocabulary. The IBM system enables the user to train the system by dictating a short standard text.

IBM is thus well advanced in the area of speech recognition, although it is probably well behind AT&T. A product currently at the field trials stage by AT&T allows the use of normal connected speech removing the need to pause between words. One of the application areas which AT&T is working on is a system which the public would converse with for dealing with telephone directory enquiries.

Speech generation from text is less difficult in principle than speech recognition, but the quality of the speech generated is still not entirely satisfactory.

A final area of voice processing is that of 'telephone management' — an aspect of office automation which has become fashionable recently and is exemplified for instance in the ICL 'One Per Desk' executive workstation. Given the large amount of time that many office workers spend making telephone calls, a facility to combine the card index of telephone numbers with an automatic dialler would be extremely useful.

## Voice processing for the PC

IBM's interest in voice processing is shown by a striking set of PC products announced in October 1985. Between them, these products cover nearly all of the aspects of voice processing that we have discussed.

The Voice Communications Option comprises an adaptor card with connections for microphone, external speaker and up to two telephone lines. The associated software comprises the following:

1   The telephone management program: this allows the user to create telephone directories, use the directory to dial a call with one keystroke and enter reminders in a calendar. With additional programs the system can act as a modem and also convert text into synthetic speech.

2   The augmented phone service: intended for those with speech or hearing difficulties. The user types text into the PC and the text can then be converted into speech at the other end of the telephone.

3   The telephone access to office system: provides access to documents contained in office applications such as Personal Services/36 and /38. The documents can be converted into speech so that a user can listen to his electronic mail rather than have it read to him.

4   The voice-activated keyboard utility: allows the user to control programs by voice commands rather than by keyboard input.

5   The voice/phone assistant: allows the PC to act as an answering machine. Voice messages can be received and stored and a list of incoming messages can be viewed on the PC screen and selected for playback in any order.

With these new facilities the PC is even more firmly established as the multifunction workstation of the automated office.

## Image processing

The manipulation of visual images is another area where new development can be expected. Again we have several different types of application — store-and-forward facilities, incorporation into textual documents and conversion between image and text.

The Scanmaster is IBM's main offering in the image area. It allows pictures to be scanned, transmitted, reproduced and incorporated within DCA/DIA. Under DISOSS, a Scanmaster document can be filed in a host document library and users can access it by means of various types of terminal. They cannot normally see the image itself since IBM does not supply a suitable display screen. What they can do is to view, and in some cases update, the document profile (the DIA 'envelope' surrounding the actual DCA document). They can add search terms, search on existing documents, send them on to other people, and so on. The actual image content of the document can only be viewed by having it printed out on a Scanmaster.

> Brett:
> Scanmaster, with the recent announcement of 3270 viewing of image documents via IVF/GDDM under MVS, is unique. It is a blend of facsimile, photocopier, scanner (onto DASD devices) and near letter-quality printer. At £8000 its price/performance is remarkable — if you have a host DISOSS environment.

The Scanmaster is capable of being used either as an office copier or as a facsimile device, but IBM says it is neither of these things. As a further complication, it is capable of limited optical mark reading: 'cover sheets' are provided, using boxes in predetermined positions. The cover sheet can be marked up by hand and fed through the scanning device. It will then tell the system the destination of the document on the following sheet.

The next stage in image processing is optical character reading, to convert a printed or typed paper document to machine-processable text. A number of devices exist to do this, some indeed combining this function with facsimile transmission, but they are generally restricted in the typefaces they can deal with. Further developments in this area, which IBM seems to have left alone so far, can be expected.

## New storage technologies

Both text and voice are very demanding of data storage and will help to push the storage requirements of future systems far beyond what is now economically feasible with magnetic storage media. To some extent this may be overcome by means of software. For instance, in speech generation, AT&T is claiming substantial advances with the use of multipulse linear predictive coding, which uses the inherent redundancies in speech to reduce the storage requirement for a second of speech from 64 000 bits to 9600. However, it is clear that the demand for ever higher capacity storage media will continue.

Optical disk is widely seen as the storage medium of the future. The precise details vary, but the principle is simple: the data is written using a high-powered laser which causes a local change in the optical properties of the medium. Using a lower-powered laser, the information can be retrieved. The advantage of optical storage is that the data can be packed much more tightly onto the disk than with traditional magnetic technology; moreover the data, once recorded, is much less prone to damage or accidental erasure.

In technological terms, the concept is entirely feasible; the problems so far have been economic: namely the production of a sufficiently cheap and compact recording device.

In some areas, optical disk has already made a breakthrough in the form of video disks and audio 'Compact Disk' (CD). Video disks have had limited success: people typically want to be able to record television programmes off the air rather than merely access prerecorded material. But CD has found a secure niche in the hi-fi market, providing a very high quality sound at reasonable cost. Both these applications are 'read-only', in that the information is recorded once when the disk is manufactured, the user can access the recorded information but not update it. Similarly in the data processing area there are read-only applications: 'CD-ROM' has been adopted as a medium of distributing large volume information such as that which is available on on-line databases. DEC has entered this market with a read-only CD system for its MicroVAX.

The real breakthrough for optical disk will depend on a system which allows the user to write as well as read. Such systems are beginning to appear. The initial versions are 'read-once', in other words allowing the user to add new information but not change what is already there. Such a system could have obvious benefits for security and audit trails. The next generation of optical disk storage will allow erasing and rewriting of information.

IBM's involvement with optical disk dates from its participation in the DiscoVision venture in the late 1970s which was aimed initially at the videodisk entertainment market at a time when extravagantly optimistic forecasts were being made for this market. It seems not to have been a profitable enterprise for IBM which sold its share in the DiscoVision business in 1982 at a reputed cost of $100 million. The IBM statement at that time gave no real clues as to its future intentions with the technology.

In 1985, Verbatim (now part of Kodak) announced a prototype 3½-inch read/write optical disk for the IBM PC, capable of storing up to 40 Mbytes, thus giving the capacity of today's Winchester disks, with the exchangeability of floppies. The access time on the other hand is longer — as with most optical systems — typically twice the time required for a Winchester. The Verbatim device, unlike many of those appearing, is erasable, so that old data can be overwritten with new data.

The day of the optical disk is thus clearly coming, but IBM seems, as yet, to have done little in this area. A third-party optical disk add-on could be the next development in expansion options for the PC. If it catches on, we can expect IBM to adopt optical storage, and put its stamp on the developing standards.

## Flat-panel displays

One of the limitations of today's computers and workstations is the large 'footprint' they require on the user's desk — a problem largely caused by the inherently bulky nature of the cathode ray tube technology which is still the norm for VDUs as well as television sets. A flat display screen is an obviously desirable innovation, but this is another area where the technological breakthrough seems permanently just round the corner.

Of the various technologies currently available, plasma displays, and to a lesser extent electroluminescent displays, suffer from high cost and high power requirement. Liquid Crystal Displays (LCDs) are familiar in digital watches, and have appeared on a number of lap-held personal computers, but their main drawback lies in problems with visibility.

Most flat-panel displays are monochrome only (the actual colour varies according to the technology), but Toshiba has announced that it expects to have a 10-inch colour LCD for VDU purposes by 1987, and a television version by 1989.

IBM has a plasma display screen for use with the PC but it is definitely not a lap-held device, being large and expensive, and suitable perhaps for display to groups of people, or where clarity and the absence of the geometrical distortion inherent in a traditional curved VDU screen are more important than cost. Meanwhile there are repeated rumours of an IBM lap-held machine, but the company's official position is that it is waiting for a sufficiently legible portable flat display to become available.

Ultimately there is no doubt that the bulky VDU or personal computer display of today will disappear and be replaced by a flat panel lying on the desk, hanging on the wall, or perhaps propped up at an angle. However the date when this will be achieved is still difficult to predict.

## Conclusions

Information technology today is on the threshold of change in many areas. We have looked briefly at some of the qualitative changes that may take place, but perhaps even more important will be the quantitative changes facilitated by lower cost and more user-friendly systems, in the number of computer workstations. IBM's own predictions show the growth expected in this respect.

*Fintech (021):*
*IBM projections of workstation penetration during the next five years* [show] *that the ratio of employees to workstations in various sectors develop as follows:*

|  | 1985 | 1990 |
|---|---|---|
| *Asset management (including inventory control and plant utilisation)* | *40:1* | *10:1* |
| *Administrative and clerical* | *5:1* | *2:1* |
| *Business outlets (including travel, finance and insurance)* | *20:1* | *4:1* |
| *Business professional staff* | *4:1* | *1:1* |
| *Data processing staff* | *2:1* | *1:1* |
| *Engineering and science* | *7:1* | *1.5:1* |
| *Text handling (including secretaries)* | *4:1* | *1:1* |

*IBM expects that overall usage ratio in these two sectors will reach about one workstation for every two employees by 1990. The prospect offers glittering prizes for vendors able to gear their designs to demand.*

On the basis of these figures, there is clearly an enormous future for information technology. Given IBM's stated business goals, to grow as fast as the industry, to maintain technological and product leadership, and to be the most efficient and low cost producer (given also the enormous technological and marketing strengths of the company which should ensure that it is as well placed as any company to achieve these goals) it is clear that IBM will continue to account for a very large share of this market.

*001*
*Woods J*
'The impact of IBM in Europe'
Frost & Sullivan Ltd
(June 1985)

*002*
*Drucker P F*
'The age of discontinuity: guidelines to our
changing society'
Heinemann
(1969)

*003*
*Sobel R*
'IBM, colossus in transition'
Truman Talley (1981)

*004*
*Nixon Sir E*
'A letter to the stakeholders'
In 'Annual Review 1984'
IBM UK Holdings Ltd
(1985)

*005*
*Scott M D*
'The law according to IBM'
In 'IBM: the blue horizon'
State of the Art Conf
Pergamon Infotech Ltd
(Mar 1985)

*006*
*Dale R*
'User relationships'
In 'IBM: the blue horizon'
State of the Art Conf
Pergamon Infotech Ltd
(Mar 1985)

*007*
*Hughes A*
'Software environments'
In 'IBM: the blue horizon'
State of the Art Conf
Pergamon Infotech Ltd
(Mar 1985)

*008*
*Wilkins G*
'System/36 and the PC —
a commercial and
strategic analysis'
In 'IBM Systems '85:
PCs and the System/36'
Xephon Annual Review
Xephon Technology Transfer Ltd
(Sep 1985)

*009*
*Wells P*
'The 80286 microprocessor'
Byte
McGraw-Hill Inc
(Nov 1984)

*010*
*Banks M*
'286: why it fits the AT'
PC magazine
VNU Business Publications
(Oct 1984)

*011*
*Hatch T F, Geyer J B and
Prange P E*
'Choosing the best operating system'
Computer Design vol 23 no 11
Penwell Publishing Co
(1 Oct 1984)

012
*Bellinger A P*
'The Pick operating system: the computer
industry's best kept secret'
In 'The software development process'
State of the Art Rep
vol 13 no 2
Pergamon Infotech Ltd
(1985)

013
*The Economist*
'IBM in the Akers era'
The Economist vol 296 no 7392
The Economist Newspaper Ltd
(4 May 1985)

014
*Deitel H M*
'An introduction to operating systems'
Addison-Wesley
(1984)

015
*Ritchie D M and Thompson K*
'The UNIX timesharing system'
The Bell System Technical J
American Telephone and Telegraph Co
(July/Aug 1978)

016
*Digitus Ltd*
'The UNIX report: market prospects for the
UNIX system in the UK 1985-1988'
Digitus Ltd
(1985)

017
*Gradwell D J L*
'Application development tools for IBM systems'
In 'IBM: the blue horizon'

State of the Art Conf
Pergamon Infotech Ltd
(Mar 1985)

018
'A marriage of convenience'
PC Management
(Apr 1985)

019
*IBM*
'IBM token ring network PC marketing guidance'
IBM (1985)

020
*Novell Inc*
'Local area network software report'
Novell Inc
(1985)

021
*FinTech*
'IBM works on PC designs for Europe'
FinTech: personal computer markets
Issue 43
Financial Times Business Information
(29 Oct 1985)

022
*Newman M*
The IBM System User
EMAP Business and Computer
Publications Ltd
(Feb 1985)

023
*Hunter P*
'Voice recognition: speak and you shall be
answered'
The IBM system user
(Nov 1985)

# Bibliography

# An annotated bibliography of IBM small and medium systems

**R C Burgess**

Digitus Ltd
London
UK

## Introduction

The range of books and articles available on IBM and its systems varies greatly with the type of system being discussed. The IBM PC is a 'glamour' product which has captured the imagination of end users and provoked a wide variety of ancillary products, both hardware and software. Consequently, it has been well covered in books, particularly for the end users, and magazines, largely supported by advertisements from third-party suppliers. By contrast, the medium range machines, the System/36 and System/38, despite their widespread use in commercial applications, have little immediate end-user appeal and have never generated a mass market in the same way. As a result, good references on these systems are few and far between.

Looking at operating systems we see a similar picture, for similar reasons. The 'fashionable' systems — MS-DOS in the end user area, UNIX and its variants in academic circles — have provoked a substantial literature, while the solid workhorse, Pick, much used but little shouted about, has only a meagre coverage.

Another area of interest is networks and communications. Here there is indeed a large volume of literature in the periodicals, but too much is written either strictly for the experts, thus making it impenetrable to the rest of us, or by authors attempting to describe the latest products, with a limited grasp of what the issues are really about.

This bibliography aims to give as balanced a coverage (as the literature will allow) of references which are helpful in clarifying the issues, or have been significant in developing the continuing debate about IBM and its products.

# Abstracts

## General developments in the computer market

*100*
'The world on the line:
telecommunications, a survey'
The Economist (special survey)
The Economist Newspaper Ltd
(23 Nov 1985)

A review of the telecommunications business in various countries — some already deregulated, like the US and the UK, some like Japan in the process of deregulation, others with telecommunications still very much a state monopoly. Includes a well-presented comparison of the two 'circling giants', AT&T and IBM, and their different problems.

*101*
'The changing computing environment'
EDP Analyser vol 22 no 9 (whole issue)
Canning Publication Inc
(Sep 1984)

A review of the reports in 'EDP Analyser' over the previous few years and an examination of the trends that were apparent. The conclusion is reached that none of the trends were in fact surprising.

*102*
*Kanter J (editor)*
'A historical perspective: mainframes to micros'
In 'Management information systems'
pp 164-201

Prentice-Hall Inc
(1984)

A concise and readable history of the development of computing (both hardware and software).

*103*
*McClellan S T*
'The coming computer industry shakeout:
winners, losers and survivors'
John Wiley & Sons Ltd
(1984)

Personal predictions by a top Wall Street computer analyst of what will happen in the computer industry in the rest of the 1980s. The chapter on IBM, entitled 'The elephant romps again', predicts that IBM will have difficulties in the years ahead, but still turn over $100 billion by 1990.

*104*
*Serlin O*
'Departmental computing: a choice of strategies'
Datamation vol 31 no 9
Technical Publishing Co
(1 May 1985)

Examines the question of multi-user systems compared to networks of PCs for the office automation market. The decision between these alternatives should not be seen as purely a technical one: it should be related to the applications and the nature of the corporate computer environment.

*105*
Informatics Daily Bulletin
VNU Business Publications BV

An indispensable aid for anyone wishing to keep

312

up to date with the latest developments in computing and information technology.

## IBM and its market position

*106*
*Burton K*
'Anatomy of a colossus'
PC: the independent guide to
IBM Personal Computers
Ziff-Davies Publishing Co
(Jan-Mar 1983)

A series of three articles tracing the history of IBM from its foundation. In the first era (up to 1945) IBM was formulating its corporate beliefs and testing them in the marketplace. The second era, from 1946 onwards, was characterised by sweeping technological change. The three articles explore these two generations and IBM's plans for the future.

*107*
*Dale R M*
'User relationships'
In 'IBM: the blue horizon'
State of the Art Conf
Pergamon Infotech Ltd
(Mar 1985)

IBM is a name that arouses a wide range of emotional reactions. Among customers, there are very few who have discarded IBM completely. An IBM customer has an ongoing relationship with the company through the salesman, and this relationship can be made use of to the customer's advantage, for instance in bypassing some of the IBM bureaucracy to speed up delivery of a machine. It is also helpful to promote regular liaison meetings and to take part in user groups.

*108*
Special IBM issue
Datamation vol 31 no 3
Technical Publishing Co
(1 Jan 1985)

Several feature articles on IBM, including: *J W Verity* and *W Schatz*, 'Fast break in Armonk' (IBM in the new more liberal US political climate), *B Jeffrey* 'Shopping for market share' (IBM in the telecomms market) and *I S Nesbit* 'A generous portion' (the PC software market).

*109*
'IBM in the Akers era'
The Economist vol 296 no 7392
The Economist Newspaper Ltd
(4 May 1985)

Since the anti-trust suit was dropped in 1982 IBM has competed very aggressively and is dominating the computer market. Its success dates from the decision in the mid-1960s to go for a unified standard for mainframes, and the mainframe has been the soul of IBM ever since. Even the growth of plug-compatible mainframes has swelled IBM's coffers in the form of software licence fees. However, the trend away from the mainframe may still pose a threat to IBM's continued dominance, especially as the company moves into new business areas where its competitors have as much or more experience. IBM's marketing and management skills may yet make it the dominant force in the wider information processing area, but nothing is certain.

*110*
*Fertig R*
'IBM's strategy moves'
Computer Weekly
Business Press Intl Ltd
(14 Nov 1985)

Reviews IBM's strategy for its small business computers in the light of new developments for the System/36 and System/38 which are seen as a hub for IBM's office systems plans, with an enormous installed base and software range for the System/36 in particular. The next step could be a System/38-like relational database for the System/36.

*111*
*Foy N*
'The IBM world'
Eyre Methuen
(1974)

A rather old, but still relevant, account of the development of IBM, with some predictions about its future, some of which make interesting reading.

*112*
'Dipping a big blue finger
in every pie'
IBM Computer Today
Electrical-Electronic Press
(25 Sep 1985)

Discusses the very wide range of outside interests among IBM's board of directors, linking the company to major centres of power in politics, the media, finance and industry.

*113*
*Jeffrey B*
'Three faces of IBM'
Datamation vol 31 no 14

Technical Publishing Co
(15 July 1985)

Describes in some detail the new marketing organisation, with its three-fold division: National Accounts Division (NAD) looking after the 2000-plus largest customers; National Marketing Division (NMD) looking after small to medium customers; and National Distribution Division (NDD) looking after 6000 distributors, 81 US Product Centres, and IBM Direct (mail order).

114
*Scott M D*
'The law according to IBM'
In 'IBM: the blue horizon'
State of the Art Conf
Pergamon Infotech Ltd
(Mar 1985)

The original aims of the US anti-trust laws were to preserve competition, seen as a socially desirable goal. In recent years however there have been moves to restrict the law to cases where competition can be shown to be beneficial. A prime example of this is the dismissal of the case against IBM. The key points of the legislation are described, and also the history of cases against IBM. In disputes with other companies, IBM's size enables it to 'bury' its opponents in expensive litigation. On the other hand IBM is also very responsive to legitimate complaints, for reasons of public image and the need to preserve its relationship with customers. Aggrieved parties are therefore best advised to try to resolve disputes without going to court. In negotiating contracts, there is never any scope for changing standard clauses, but some details can be negotiated, provided the customer has the option to go elsewhere.

115
*Sobel R*
'IBM, colossus in transition'
Truman Talley Books
(1981)

Traces the history of IBM from its origins as Computing-Tabulating-Recording, through the Watson years and the punched card tabulator era to the early computers and the emergence of the System/360, and the subsequent moves into small business computers. An excellent introduction to the ethos of the company as it developed in its earlier years — an ethos which has changed only little since then.

116
Outlook on IBM
Phillips Publishing Co

A monthly briefing covering the latest IBM developments, with specific coverage of telecommunications, local area networks, robotics and personal computers. Includes notes on suppliers, management moves and analysis of current and future IBM joint ventures.

117
*Weiner H*
'Gazing into the big blue yonder'
IBM Computer Today
Electrical-Electronic Press
(8 Jan 1986)

Predictions for the future of IBM over the next 10 years. During this period, IBM will go through two or three more generations of large mainframes, running a new operating system that will succeed MVS/XA and VM/XA. Real memory will grow still further, but will be made to look like disk storage to avoid the problems of another change in addressing. The mid-range market will diminish in importance, despite important improvements in hardware and software. In the small business machines all processors will be built in LSI, while RISC architectures will become important. A single family of relational database systems will succeed System/36 and System/38. The PC will remain an open architecture product and incorporate Macintosh-style user friendliness in response to the competition. Other IBM ventures will be into optical disk. There may be further acquisitions, of software as well as hardware suppliers.

118
*Uttal B*
'Is IBM playing too tough?'
Fortune Intl
Time Inc
(10 Dec 1984)

IBM's war with its competitors is producing a fast rising casualty list, as other computer companies reel under the shock of IBM's deep price cuts, aggressive marketing and unprecedented flood of new products. IBM's traditional practices — selling a product for four or five years and keeping prices stable until the end of the cycle — gave competitors the opportunity of undercutting. In the late 1970s, however, IBM discovered that cutting its prices provoked more new businesses than expected, and it has responded with lower prices and massive investment to reduce costs. This, and the ability to produce new products, have hit competitors hard, first in mainframes, then in peripherals, latterly in PCs. Competitors are now complaining about IBM tactics, and even threaten legal action in some cases.

**119**

*Watson Jr T J*
'A business and its beliefs: the idea
that has helped build IBM'
Dawsons of Pall Mall
(1963)

The classic statement by the then head of IBM of
the company's basic principles, which have changed very little since. Indeed, as the author says,
'If an organisation is to meet the challenges of a
changing world, it must be prepared to change
everything about itself except its beliefs'.

**120**

*Woods J*
'The impact of IBM in Europe'
Seminar notes
Frost & Sullivan Ltd
(June 1985)

Discusses the strengths and weaknesses of IBM in
the European marketplace, with detailed analysis
of the various machines and figures for their sales.
Also includes predictions of what the future will
be of the various product lines.

**121**

'The report on IBM'
Capitol Publications Inc

An independent weekly publication giving the
latest news on IBM developments, with occasional special supplements.

## Communications

**122**

*Dew C W*
'Managing the micro/mainframe environment'
In 'IBM: the blue horizon'
State of the Art Conf
Pergamon Infotech Ltd
(Mar 1985)

The use of micros linked with mainframes is
described with reference to IMI Computing Ltd.
Potential problems include the possibility of dis-
crepancies arising as local users fill their hard disk
with data downloaded from the mainframe. 3278
emulation is a common means of connection, but
not good for fast file transfer; RJE connection
overcomes this problem but requires a second TP
connection. At IMI a special Host Interface
Manager (HIM) has been devised, to help users
with the complexities and problems of interfacing
with the mainframe software. DCA and DIA are
used for text transfer. Users are supported by
staff at the information centre.

**123**

*Ettinger J*
'Communication networks:
private networks within
the public domain'
Pergamon Infotech Ltd
(1985)

An examination of how public networks are likely
to evolve in the near future and suggestions for
possible approaches to network management.
Starting with the evolution of computer networks,
and the structures of the publicly provided services in the UK and US, the book also covers the
X.25 packet switching procedures, the concept
and future development of Integrated Services
Digital Network (ISDN), and the practicalities of
planning communications connected to the public
networks.

**124**

*Hosier J*
'Little and large —
a story of untapped potential:
PC to mainframe links'
PC Management
EMAP Business and Computer
Publications Ltd
(Nov 1985)

A survey of IBM sites in the US and Europe
shows that over 90 per cent of them have PCs
communicating to mainframes, but only 1/5 of the
use of the PCs involves the mainframe. 3278
coaxial connection is the most common. SDLC
the most common protocol (BSC for VM users).
Irma the *de facto* standard. There is no transparent access to PCs. None suffered violations
of mainframe security. Only a minority use the
mainframe to support back-up and restore.

**125**

*Jennings F*
'Practical data communications:
modems, networks, and protocols'
Blackwell Scientific Publications Ltd
(1986)

A comprehensive guide to the many and varied
ways of connecting a terminal to a computer,
covering interfaces, modems, networks and data
link protocols. It covers all the different types of
data communications equipment currently in use
in the UK.

**126**

*Leibert A*
'Ways to make ends meet'
PC Management
EMAP Business and Computer

Publications Ltd
(Apr 1985)

Micro/mainframe links are entering the second phase of their development. The first was not a resounding success. In the IBM world, PCs are most commonly connected via a 3274. The security problems of connecting a micro are discussed.

### 127

'The micro to mainframe
communications directory'
Architecture Technology Corp
(1984)

A directory of products (hardware and software) concerned with the communications between mainframes (particularly IBM) and personal computers.

### 128

*Tuma F*
'IBM and the information centre'
In 'IBM: the blue horizon'
State of the Art Conf
Pergamon Infotech Ltd
(Mar 1985)

The Information Centre, launched by IBM in the late 1970s, was intended to stimulate latent demand by end users for more DP support, and hence more sales for IBM. An implementation of an information centre at IMI plc is described. The various IBM mainframe products for end-user computing are described.

### 129

*Rich B*
'Communications and the PC'
In 'Microcomputing'
Pergamon Infotech State of the Art Rep
Series 13 no 5 pp 75-87
Pergamon Infotech Ltd (1985)

Examines the various types of communications which are now being expected of the PC and the technology available to support them, with a discussion of some future trends.

### 130

'Data transfer between microcomputers
and mainframes'
Guidelines for computing management no 87
National Computing Centre (1984)

A guide for both the novice and the more experienced user to this currently topical area. Includes a glossary of communications terms, a list of recommended reading, and a summary of available software.

### 131

'Personal computer data communications'
Intl Resource Development Inc
(1984)

Communications is widely hailed as the next growth area for personal computing, but this report points out that the products at present available have a great many limitations. This situation will change in the future, as VLSI technology becomes applied in this area. The report predicts that modems, multiplexors, protocol converters, and network terminal interfaces, will all be implemented on chips by 1994.

## Database

### 132

*Date C*
'IBM and the case for relational databases'
In 'IBM: the blue horizon'
State of the Art Conf
Pergamon Infotech Ltd
(Mar 1985)

Relational systems are the way of the future. A definition is given of the relational model and the functions select, project and join. The case for the relational model is presented in terms of simplicity, extendability, performance and acceptance. Date suggests that relational database is not necessarily less efficient and he discusses the problems of converting from non-relational systems.

### 133

*Martin J*
'Computer database organisation'
Prentice-Hall Inc
(1975)

Still perhaps the most comprehensive introduction to database theory and practice, with descriptions of not only the currently favoured relational approach, but also the older but still widely-used hierarchical models. Part II on physical organisation covers a number of practical points such as hashing, index organisation, and inverted file structures. The whole book is lavishly illustrated with examples and diagrams.

## Medium systems

### 134

*Sanford R*
'System/34 for the microcomputer'

PC Tech J vol 3 no 5
Ziff-Davies Publishing Co
(May 1985)

Describes a software product for the IBM PC which enables it to emulate the System/34. Also discusses some of the differences between the PC and System/34 environments.

*135*
*Carlyle E C*
'Out of gas'
Datamation vol 31 no 24
Technical Publishing Co
(15 Dec 1985)

The honeymoon is over for the System/36. Users are complaining about its shortcomings, including: 16-bit processor; inefficient database management system; no growth path; poor word processing with DisplayWrite/36. Some users claim that the System/36 was never designed for office automation or as a departmental machine, and does not perform well in this role. There is continued speculation of a new machine, codenamed 'Fort Knox', to cover all the mid-range machines, and emulate System/36, System/38 and the 4300. Two years ago IBM and Wang had between them 60 per cent of the office automation market; now DEC and Data General have achieved major shares.

*136*
*Wilkins G*
'System/36 and the PC —
a commercial and strategic analysis'
In 'IBM Systems '85:
PCs and the System/36'
Xephon Annual Review
Xephon Technology Transfer Ltd
(Sep 1985)

The introduction of the 5364 Desktop/36 probably increased the market for the System/36 tenfold. A three-user system can now be acquired for less than £20 000, compared to a previous entry level price of £50 000 and upwards. For small multi-user systems, a Desktop/36 can now be cheaper and give more facilities compared to a network of PCs. There are clues to IBM's thinking for the future in its terminology of 'information centre' (370 architecture), 'departmental solution' (System/3X), and 'general-purpose workstation' (PC). The software produced for the PC will continue to be *personal* because of the limitations of PC-DOS and the need to achieve a very large market. IBM's strategy for selling the Desktop/36 is most confusing at present, but IBM can be expected to act quickly to rationalise it.

*137*
*Hill D*
'Preparing for promotion'
The IBM System User
EMAP Business and Computer
Publications Ltd
(Mar 1985)

Reviews the 1984 additions to the System/38 range which give substantially increased power. The System/38 is now directly comparable in processing power to the 43XX mainframes and much easier to use. With the addition of new communications and graphics facilities, and better system management, CPF has now become a very comprehensive operating system and the dividing line between System/38 and the mainframes is becoming increasingly blurred.

*138*
*Newman M*
'The frying pan's other alternative'
The IBM System User
EMAP Business and Computer
Publications Ltd
(Oct 1985)

For the small IBM mainframe user considering a hardware upgrade, the change to a System/38 is an increasingly attractive alternative. This article considers the objections likely to be raised and some answers to them.

## Networks

*139*
*Brooks T*
'New technologies and their implications for local area networks'
Computer Communications
vol 8 no 2
Butterworth Scientific Ltd
(Apr 1985)

Standing aside from the current debate about standards and competing products, this article looks to the slightly longer term future and the possible impact on networking of new technological developments such as artificial intelligence, optical disk, video telephone, and personal identification devices. External carrier services such as VANs and cable television are also considered.

*140*
'IBM's ring of confidence'
PC Management
EMAP Business and Computer
Publications Ltd
(Jan 1986)

An early review of IBM's token-passing ring. To the surprise of many observers, IBM has announced just what it said it would: a token ring LAN which will use the IBM cabling system as the physical medium. Alternatively, the network could use existing twisted-pair wiring, but it is unlikely that anyone will do this. For software there is a choice between the SNA interface (LU6.2) or the Netbios interface as with the PC Network. There is no application software included and the author expects that existing suppliers such as Torus will adapt the products they produced for the PC Network hardware. Current customers should ignore the token ring, unless they are about to re-cable their building anyway.

*141*
'Introduction to local area networks'
FOCUS: standards for IT
(technical guide 101/5)
Department of Trade and Industry
(Dec 1984)

Gives an overview of the state of the art in LANs and recommendations to allow British industry to work towards Open Systems Interconnection. The basic principles of telecommunications are introduced, together with specific problems of local networking, and a rather more detailed look at two types of LAN implementation, CSMA/CD and the token ring.

*142*
'Intercept recommendations
for LANs according to the
token-passing ring access method'
FOCUS: standards for IT
(technical guide 101/4)
Department of Trade and Industry
(Dec 1984)

Discusses the IEEE standard 802.5 for token ring LANs, with guidance on methods of implementing a network on this basis.

## Futures

*143*
*Solomon A and Goldberg J*
'A future favourite is unveiled'
PC vol 3 no 1
VNU Business Publications BV
(Jan 1986)

With Intel's 32-bit microprocessor, the 80386, recently announced, the prospect of a much more powerful version of the IBM PC becomes realistic. Such a product will not appear until at least 1987. In the meantime, the authors have constructed a theoretical machine around the new chip. The 'PC32' will be fully IBM PC-compatible, but will work about 10 times as fast. There will be 1 Mbyte of RAM, expandable to 4 Mbytes, with DOS held in 512 Kbytes of ROM. There will be a much higher resolution display, with a flat screen as an option. The operating system will be 'DOS 5.0', not UNIX, but very similar to UNIX under the bonnet, and with virtual memory.

*144*
*Holder K*
'Gurus or geese?'
Computer Weekly
Business Press Intl Ltd
(9 Jan 1986)

An amusing summary of the various predictions by IBM watchers and 'gurus' of what IBM would do. There have been some remarkable conflicting stories, notably the PC2, which a well known company claims to have actually seen and tested, although IBM denies its very existence. There were also predictions of the demise of the 4300 and 8100, both of which still seem to be going strong. One thing is certain, however, there are always a few surprises, as IBM announces new products which no one has predicted.

*145*
*Watson A*
'Voicing a marketing hitch'
Infomatics vol 6 no 6
VNU Business Publications BV
(June 1985)

Voice/data integrated workstations have achieved very little success in the market so far, but just about every major manufacturer has such a machine in the pipeline. This article examines the reasons for this and makes predictions for the future growth in this area.

## Office automation

*146*
*Bate J St J and Burgess R C*
'The automated office'
Collins (1985)

An introduction for the general reader to the concepts and goals of office automation and the various technologies that are increasingly becoming available to satisfy them, with notes on the effects that automation will have on office workers.

*147*
*O'Keefe L*
'IBM's OA puzzle'

Datamation vol 31 no 3
Technical Publishing Co
(1 Feb 1985)

IBM has an impressive array of office products, with the PC now clearly taking its place as the workstation and the System/36 as the strategic departmental machine. However IBM office automation solutions are long-term strategic ones — there is no simple answer here and now for automating the office the IBM way, but different approaches will apply in different organisations. The next move could be 'user-integrated' systems, using existing software products to produce customised applications software without programming.

*148*
'Office automation:
practising what big blue
preaches'
The IBM System User
EMAP Business and Computer
Publications Ltd
(Oct 1985)

PROFS is central to IBM's internal OA system. Under NOSS all incoming mail is 'frozen' and typed into the electronic mail system. PROFS is also used by Micro Focus with linked mainframes in Newbury and the US.

*149*
*Giglio L*
'PROFS, DISOSS, what's different?'
Information Week no 025
C M P Publications Inc
(29 July 1985)

IBM's Professional Office System (PROFS) is popular because it is inexpensive and easy to install. Another aspect of its popularity is that, unlike DISOSS (Distributed Office Support System) it is available under the VM operating system. IBM hopes that shipments of Personal Services (PS) will end the confusion between PROFS and DISOSS. A glossary is supplied to explain some of the more confusing IBM terminology.

*150*
'A marriage of convenience'
PC Management
EMAP Business and Computer
Publications Ltd
(Apr 1985)

The PC has much to recommend it as the standard OA workstation: cost-effectiveness, installed credibility and familiarity, high availability, good

software, low running costs. Problems include non-standard user interfaces, inadequate local communications, limited DIA/DCA support, lack of data interchangeability between OA, DP and personal computing, slow processing of large disk files, out of date error-checking and recovery, less integration of function, inefficient text-handling. The AT gives the sort of power needed for OA and is also suitable as a work group computing machine for very small work groups.

*151*
*Kutnick D*
'Office automation'
In 'State of the Art Review —
the information initiative'
Pergamon Infotech Ltd
(Nov 1985)

Word processing is no longer the main driving force in office automation. Specific personal computing applications, as opposed to integrated solutions, have taken its place. Office automation may today be better described as office anarchy, with PCs leading the revolution. The anarchy is beginning to disappear as PCs become professional workstations, giving access to corporate information resources. Today PCs are widely linked using ASCII and 3270, but much closer links will be required in the future. IBM's strategic office automation directions are reviewed. IBM controls the high ground (mainframes) and the low ground (workstations). The battleground will be in the middle ground of the departmental computer.

*152*
*Jelley S*
'Journey to the centre of the blue office'
The IBM System User
EMAP Business and Computer
Publications Ltd
(Dec 1985)

An overview of the history of DISOSS, IBM's major mainframe office automation system, with comments from users and experts. The introduction of a competing system, PROFS, confused the position, but DISOSS is seen as the strategic product, and the PS series gives an interface into DISOSS for System/36 and PC users. DISOSS is only just coming into its own and will involve a great deal of work to implement it.

## Operating systems

*153*
*Deitel H M*
'An introduction to operating systems'

Addison-Wesley Publishing Co
(1984)

The authoritative text on operating system theory and practice, with useful chapters on UNIX, MVS and VM, as well as CP/M and the DEC VAX systems.

*154*
*Hatch T F, Geyer J B*
*and Prange P E*
'Choosing the best operating system'
Computer Design vol 23 no 11
Penwell Publishing Co
(1 Oct 1984)

No one operating system can suit everyone. OS/360 was the first commercially acceptable general-purpose operating system and provided a complete shell surrounding the hardware. Any operating system must provide at least hardware resource management, runtime services, and command language processing. Many operating systems offer a wide range of additional functions, but this can lead to a loss of performance. UNIX exemplifies the 'bare bones' approach, keeping the operating system simple and flexible. Its weakness is the lack of data management facilities. By contrast, Honeywell's GCOS 6, a descendant of the project that gave rise to UNIX, exemplifies the other extreme, with built-in features such as indexed sequential file access, concurrency controls, and journalling on transactions.

*155*
*Greenberg K*
'The DOS drivers'
PC World vol 3 no 7
CW Communications
(July 1985)

An interview with leading figures in Microsoft, including its Chairman and Chief Executive Officer, Bill Gates. Discusses the history and future of the MS-DOS operating system, with particular reference to the needs for networking and the likelihood of multitasking in future versions. Microsoft's own MS Networks product is predicted to co-exist with networking offerings from IBM and other suppliers. Microsoft expects that some customers will use its redirector software in workstations, but will not necessarily use the server software. For serious information sharing, a dedicated server is required, but in smaller networks one PC may act both as a server and as a workstation. A multitasking version of DOS will be required to support this effectively. Microsoft sees DOS outselling XENIX by ten to one, but it is intending to provide greater compatibility between them.

*156*
*Philips M*
'MS-DOS: leader of the pack'
PC Business World
CW Communications Ltd
(7 Jan 1986)

Discusses MS-DOS and its alternatives — including some lesser-known ones such as BOS and the UCSD p-System. The big battle for PC operating systems is of course between Microsoft and Digital Research. They started off equal — CP/M-86 and MS-DOS Version 1 were both straight copies of 8-bit CP/M underneath — but the support of IBM meant that CP/M-86 had lost the first round. Digital Research now has the advantage of a multitasking version (Concurrent DOS), but the problems of compatibility with MS-DOS continue, only resolved with the 286 version for the PC/AT. A multitasking version of MS-DOS will almost certainly appear. Multi-user systems such as Pick and UNIX will appeal to only a minority of PC users, and the author predicts that MS-DOS is likely to be the standard for a long time to come.

*157*
*Awalt D*
'Concurrent PC-DOS'
PC Tech J vol 3 no 3
Ziff-Davies Publishing Co
(Mar 1985)

A review of this alternative PC operating system from Digital Research. It is found to have a well thought-out user interface suitable for those requiring limited multi-user capability or concurrent processing, but only if performance is not a major concern. Weaknesses include very slow performance, lack of support for pathnames, and poor security with IBM DOS format diskettes.

*158*
*Bate J St J and Wyatt M*
'The Pick operating system'
Collins
(1986)

A comprehensive overview of the Pick operating system, its facilities and its uses, with special reference to the use of tools such as the ACCESS enquiry language.

*159*
*Rochkind M J*
'Pick, Coherent, and Theos'
Byte vol 10 no 11
(special IBM issue)
McGraw-Hill Inc
(1985)

A review of three alternative operating systems for the IBM PC: Pick and two UNIX-like systems. The comments on Pick, although based only on a short evaluation, are interesting as a rare view of it not by a Pick enthusiast.

## Personal computers

*160*
*Bird E*
'Controlling the micro'
In 'Microcomputing'
Pergamon Infotech
State of the Art Rep
Series 13 no 5 pp 3-11
Pergamon Infotech Ltd
(1985)

The question of how to control the flood of microcomputers into organisations has provoked much comment. This paper advocates a 'soft control' approach, whereby end users can be supported and guided to follow corporate information aims.

*161*
*Healey M*
'Alternative systems'
In 'Microcomputing'
Pergamon Infotech
State of the Art Rep
Series 13 no 5 pp 27-35
Pergamon Infotech Ltd
(1985)

Examines the strategy of IBM in the personal computer field and compares the IBM offerings with those from alternative suppliers.

*162*
*McIntyre J M D*
'The development of IBM's marketing strategies for the PC'
In 'The impact of IBM in Europe'
Frost & Sullivan Ltd
(June 1985)

The launch of the IBM PC was a new approach for the company, in terms of organisational freedom, an emphasis on the development of systems for the individual, and the unusual experience for IBM of joining a market, not leading it. The marketing aims of the PC are described, as well as the open architecture that arose out of them. The effect of the PC on the market has been that reasonable technical standards have emerged. At the same time, fierce price-cutting has made it difficult for dealers to invest in support and service. Developments since the PC was first launched have meant that the product has evolved considerably, and personal computing in the future will develop far beyond what it is today.

*163*
*Wells P*
'The 80286 microprocessor'
Byte
McGraw-Hill Inc
(Nov 1984)

An examination of the (then) head of the Intel 8086 family, by a member of Intel's microprocessor operation. Discusses the special features of the 80286, in particular memory management and protection.

*164*
*Dravnieks D E*
'The IBM Personal Computer handbook'
And/Or Press Inc
(1983)

A guide for users and potential users of the IBM PC, with sections on the history of the machine, what to buy (and how to buy it), and a directory of products and suppliers.

*165*
*Eggebrecht L*
'Interfacing to the IBM Personal Computer'
Prentice-Hall Inc
(1983)

An authoritative guide to the technical use of the IBM PC, written by one who was involved as a team leader in the original design of the machine.

*166*
*Ogden S*
'Multi-user miscellany'
PC User
EMAP Business and Computer Publications Ltd
(Jan 1986)

Compares the various ways of achieving multi-user capability with the IBM PC: stand-alone PCs, XENIX on an AT, the IBM PC Network, the System/36-PC, and the Series/1-PC. Not surprisingly the conclusion is that they all have their advantages and disadvantages, and the best solution will depend on the organisation's particular circumstances.

*167*
*Bonnet J*
'Personal computing'
In 'Data management (a special supplement)'
Management Today

Haymarket Publishing Group Ltd
(Dec 1985)

The personal computer has gained a level of stability in the market such as it took the mainframe at least three times as long to achieve. The reason for stability is that the dominant company has succeeded in establishing an industry standard. The newer and faster machines will continue to present the same face to the user; the main improvements currently appearing are in software and in peripherals such as printers. This in-depth review covers: the rise and fall of the PC; the purchase decision; following the leaders; the user-friendly system; icons, windows, and other aids; the PC paper makers; how to choose a printer; printing the full price; add-ons and back-ups; IBM and the PC dwarfs.

### 168
'Inside the IBM PC'
Byte vol 10 no 11
(special IBM issue)
McGraw-Hill Inc
(1985)

A full issue of the leading US 'small systems journal' devoted to the IBM PC, with articles on the hardware, operating systems, application software, and many other topics.

### 169
*Norton P*
'Inside the IBM PC: access to advanced features and programming'
Robert J Brady Co
(1983)

This book has been hailed as a classic in the field of IBM PC technical literature. It is aimed at the technical user, but nonetheless clearly presented, and includes a glossary of PC technical terms.

## SNA

### 170
*Gurugé A*
'SNA — theory and practice'
Pergamon Infotech Ltd
(1984)

A much-needed guide to Systems Network Architecture, one of IBM's most complex and confusing products. It covers the needs that SNA was devised to address, its specification and the way the implementation has been different in practice, the concepts of LUs, sessions and other SNA concepts, and the way in which existing IBM protocols and products such as 3270 relate to the overall architecture.

### 171
*Krumrey A*
'SNA strategies:
IBM's Systems Network Architecture reaches its full potential with the PC'
PC Tech J vol 3 no 7
Ziff-Davies Publishing Co
(July 1985)

A useful introduction to SNA and its concepts. The seven layers of SNA are compared to the seven layers of the ISO Reference Model for Open Systems Interconnection (OSI), and the concepts of DIA, DCA, LUs and PUs are explained. Written before the announcement of the token-passing ring, the article concludes that in the local area network field watching and waiting could be the best course for the moment.

### 172
*Passmore L D*
'Coming: a new SNA'
Datamation vol 31 no 22
Technical Publishing Co
(15 Nov 1985)

SNA needs to continue to evolve. Its structure reflects the various incompatible IBM products at the time it was devised, but it has not coped well with dial-up connections, X.25 packet switching, or local area networks. A new, more flexible form of SNA is to be expected. Some details are given of this 'new' SNA, with peer-to-peer connections and the possibility for the use of fibre optic cabling.

### 173
*Verity J W*
'The shifting shape of SNA'
Datamation vol 31 no 22
Technical Publishing Co
(15 Nov 1985)

At each stage of computer history, one standard interface was by far the most important: in the 1950s the 80-column card, in the 1960s connection between the System/360 and its peripherals, in the 1970s the System/370 instruction set. Today it is SNA. SNA is complex and difficult to understand. The documentation does not help very much: LU6.2 is poorly described, despite 800 pages of small print. Moreover IBM itself does not follow the manual. SNA is likely to remain stable in broad outline, but it is vital for IBM to keep it moving along. Keeping up with SNA will therefore continue to be a problem for third-party suppliers.

# Software development

*174*
*Creane J*
'The limited joys of translated software'
PC Tech J vol 3 no 1
Ziff-Davies Publishing Co
(Jan 1985)

This article traces the beginnings of application software for the PC, almost all of which was translated from software originally written for the CP/M environment, and some of the packages still show traces of this origin. Five different methods of translating software are discussed and their various limitations explored. The reputation of a CP/M application, no matter how justified, is often an inadequate basis for buying an IBM version. Now of course, application software is being written to take full advantage of the PC, but the translation question still crops up, as PC software is translated to the Apple Macintosh. Some software which was converted from the 8080 or Z80 to the 8088 is now being run on the PC/AT with its 80286.

*175*
*Gradwell D J L*
'Application development tools
for IBM systems'
In 'IBM: the blue horizon'
State of the Art Conf
Pergamon Infotech Ltd
(Mar 1985)

Fourth Generation development tools are becoming more important, for several reasons: the increasing burden of maintenance; the limitations of package software; the increased user demand fuelled by cheaper hardware. Applications differ in the degree of structure. Products are more suited to one type of application than another, but are converging on the middle ground. The facilities needed in an ADT include the ability to define screen and report layouts, logic and data. The information required to do this needs to be stored in a data dictionary (no longer a very appropriate term), surrounded by various utilities. The products available for IBM mainframes are considered, appropriate methodologies are discussed and the impact on the organisation. By mid 1985 a range of mainframe ADTs will be available on the IBM PC.

*176*
*Stiegler M and Hansen R*
'Programming languages: featuring the IBM PC and compatibles'
Pocket Books Inc
(1984)

A critical evaluation of the different programming languages available on the PC and its compatibles. Discusses the strengths and weaknesses of BASIC, FORTRAN, APL, FORTH, RATBAS, C, Pascal, Modula-2, Ada, LISP, and Assembler. Gives examples of each language, illustrated with charts and tables.

*177*
*Mirecki T*
'COBOL performs'
PC Tech J vol 3 nos 6 7 8
Ziff-Davies Publishing Co
(June-Aug 1985)

A review of eight COBOL compilers for the IBM PC, including products from Micro Focus, Microsoft, mbp, Ryan-McFarland, Realia, Digital Research, and IBM itself.

*178*
*Barnes R*
'Considering PL/1'
PC Tech J vol 3 no 8
Ziff-Davies Publishing Co
(Aug 1985)

A review of the PL/1 language itself, and specifically of the PL/1 compiler produced by Digital Research Inc (DRI) for the IBM PC. Originally promoted as the one language to replace both COBOL and FORTRAN, PL/1 also shows a strong ALGOL influence. It failed to replace other languages perhaps because, by the time it appeared, COBOL was well established and PL/1 was not so much better as to justify retraining costs. Also, the language is so large that few users could understand all its facilities. ANSI therefore designed Subset G (for general use) omitting some of the more esoteric features. The DRI compiler supports a modified version of Subset G; it has the same features as mainframe PL/1, but in some ways it is a new language. In speed of execution it compares well with other languages on the PC.

*179*
*Tozer E E*
'Planning for use of
Fourth Generation languages'
In 'Microcomputing'
Pergamon Infotech State of the Art Rep
Series 13 no 5 pp 99-113
Pergamon Infotech Ltd
(1985)

This paper discusses the need for faster system development and the ways in which this may be achieved by the use of Fourth Generation languages. In the past systems have taken far too long to develop and the use of new technology, including so-called 'Fourth Generation languages' has been disappointing as a means of improving the situation. Organisational changes are also necessary. The type of application is also very relevant. Implementation methods are examined, and the author offers a set of steps to be followed.

180
*Dee D*
'Developing PC applications'
Datamation vol 31 no 4
Technical Publishing Co
(15 Feb 1985)

The traditional method of systems development — structured, efficient, dominated by technical experts — is contrasted in this article with interactive PC development, which is seen as spontaneous, unstructured and dominated by application experts. Users want quick results and the 'try this and see if it works' approach enables them to try again easily if the result is unsatisfactory, which would be much more expensive in the traditional approach.

## UNIX

181
'The UNIX report: market prospects for the UNIX system in the UK 1985-1988'
Digitus Ltd
(1985)

The UNIX operating system has at last begun to take off in the UK. Two thirds of all the licences in use by the end of 1984 were bought in that year alone, indicating that the long predicted rapid growth has at last happened. By the end of 1988 the number of UNIX systems in use will be more than ten times the 1984 figure. Much of this growth will happen at the small multi-user end of the market, with the IBM PC/AT running XENIX a very important part of the picture. Detailed market predictions are given, together with a summary of the main features of UNIX and an assessment of their importance in market terms. The role of IBM, AT&T and other suppliers is also examined.

182
*Marvit P*
'PC/IX: IBM's "credible" UNIX'
In 'The UNIX system encyclopedia'
Yates Ventures
(1984)

An interesting but somewhat dated review of this product, now itself put in the shade by IBM PC XENIX. PC/IX (a version of UNIX for the IBM PC/XT, by Interactive Systems) is being sold by IBM from April 1984. PC/IX is essentially identical to Interactive Systems' existing offering, IS/3. IBM appears to have chosen this as being better established than XENIX 3.0 and closer to 'standard' UNIX. PC/IX is a single-user implementation. It includes the basic System III elements, with a few enhancements to support specific features of the PC (such as the function keys), but lacks the 'Berkeley enhancements' such as the C shell and the vi editor.

183
*Yates J C*
'Software licensing: the UNIX operating system'
In 'The UNIX system encyclopedia'
Yates Ventures
(1984)

Licensing the UNIX operating system from AT&T is not only complex, it can be totally baffling. This article explains some complexities and contractual differences between System III and System V.

184
*Hansen A*
'PC/IX: IBM's version of UNIX for the PC'
PC Tech J vol 3 no 7
Ziff-Davies Publishing Co
(July 1985)

A generally favourable review of this version of UNIX, which the author describes as a 'simple but solid implementation', with power, speed and a wide range of programming tools. Performance is good on the PC/XT; it is 'a joy to use' on the AT, with tasks running three to four times faster than on the XT. PC/IX is of course a single-user implementation, based on UNIX System III, and runs in real-address mode only on the AT: the author expresses a wish for IBM to provide a multi-user protected-mode version based on System V. Clearly this was written before the arrival of IBM XENIX, which is indeed a multi-user protected-mode version, with System V compatibility expected soon.

185
*Hansen A*
'XENIX for the XT'
PC Tech J vol 3 no 6
Ziff-Davies Publishing Co
(June 1985)

A review of the Santa Cruz Operation (SCO) version of UNIX for the IBM PC/XT. The author says that users who have worked with UNIX will find this version comfortable and familiar, but a bit slow. The performance declines noticeably as additional processes are added. XENIX is ideal for single-user, multitasking but the author concludes 'I cannot recommend its use in multi-user mode on the XT'.

*186*
*Hansen A*
'Reflections of UNIX'
PC Tech J vol 3 no 5
Ziff-Davies Publishing Co
(May 1985)

A comparative review of six operating systems for the PC/XT: three versions of UNIX (PC/IX, VENIX/86 and XENIX) and three UNIX 'look-alikes' (Coherent, QNX and uNETix). The availability of application software is also discussed.

*187*
*Brown P et al*
'Introduction to PC/IX and PC XENIX'
Addison-Wesley Publishing Co
(1985)

An introductory guide to the two major UNIX implementations for the IBM PC/XT. Aimed mainly at beginners, the book uses many examples to explain UNIX concepts and demonstrate the power and facilities of the two systems.

*188*
*Walker A N*
'The UNIX environment'
John Wiley & Sons Ltd
(1984)

An account of the author's personal experience with UNIX. Rather than just a multi-user operating system, UNIX is seen as a philosophy and an environment, overcoming many of the drawbacks of previous operating systems. Well written for the person with some computer knowledge. The book concentrates on Version 7, but looks back at Version 6 and is thus somewhat out of date.

*189*
'The UNIX time-sharing system'
The Bell System Technical J
vol 57 no 6 part 2
American Telephone and Telegraph Co
(July-Aug 1978)

A collection of classic papers on UNIX and its development. Indispensable for anyone interested in the subject.

*190*
'The UNIX time-sharing system'
The Bell System Technical J

vol 63 no 8 part 2
American Telephone and Telegraph Co

A further collection of basic papers on UNIX from its originators.

## User interface and windowing

*191*
*Eason K D*
'The man/machine interface
for the intermittent user'
In 'State of the Art Review —
the information initiative'
Pergamon Infotech Ltd
(Nov 1985)

The target for computing is no longer dominated by the specialist user. The target is now the occasional or intermittent user who has little interest in computing. Man/machine interfaces which can be satisfactorily employed by the dedicated user are major obstacles to the intermittent user. This paper examines the various forms of under-utilisation which occur when the end user is an intermittent user, and suggests ways in which the design of the user interface can help to promote more effective use of computer systems.

*192*
*Hebditch D*
'Presenting information'
In 'Microcomputing'
Pergamon Infotech State of the Art Rep
Series 13 no 5 pp 37-50
Pergamon Infotech Ltd
(1985)

A useful overview of the various techniques for graphical presentation of data, with recommendations for the use of graphics in the office.

*193*
*Wheelwright G*
'Can GEM be set to shine?'
PC vol 3 no 1
VNU Business Publications BV
(Jan 1986)

A review of Digital Research's GEM windowing product for the IBM PC and some of the application packages produced for it. The article concludes that GEM is a well-designed and enjoyable product, but really needs the speed of the AT with hard disk. The article is accompanied by boxes discussing the competitive products, Microsoft Windows, TopView, and Taxi. For more on a related subject (packages giving concurrency) see the article by D Awalt in the same issue.

## Reference sources

In the list of bibliographic references above, journal titles are abbreviated as little as possible. The full address from which the publication is available is given below. Book publishers and other sources are also included in the list.

Addison-Wesley Publishing Co
53 Bedford Square
London
WC1B 3DZ
UK

American Telephone and Telegraph Co
Bell Laboratories
J F Kennedy Parkway
Short Hills
NJ 07078
US

And/Or Press Inc
PO Box 2246
Berkeley
CA 94702
US

Architecture Technology Corp
PO Box 24344
Minneapolis
MN
US

Blackwell Scientific Publications Ltd
Osney Mead
Oxford
OX2 OEL
UK

Robert J Brady Co
Bowie
MD
US

Business Press International Ltd
Quadrant House
The Quadrant
Sutton
Surrey
SM2 5AS
UK

Butterworth Scientific Ltd
PO Box 63
Westbury House
Bury Street
Guildford
Surrey
GU2 5BH
UK

Canning Publication Inc
925 Anza Avenue
Vista
CA
US

Capitol Publications Inc
Suite 1600
1300 N 17th Street
Arlington
VA 2209
US

C M P Publications Inc
111 E Shore Road
Manhasset
NY 11030
US

Collins
8 Grafton Street
London
W1X 3LA
UK

CW Communications
555 De Haro Street
San Francisco
CA 94107
US

CW Communications Ltd
99 Gray's Inn Road
London
WC1X 8UT
UK

Dawsons of Pall Mall
Cannon House
Folkestone
Kent
UK

Department of Trade and Industry
1 Victoria Street
London
SW1H OET
UK

Digitus Ltd
10-14 Bedford Street
London
WC2E 9HE
UK

The Economist Newspaper Ltd
25 St James' Street
London
SW1A 1HG
UK

Electrical-Electronic Press
Quadrant House
The Quadrant
Sutton
Surrey
SM2 5AS
UK

EMAP Business and
Computer Publications Ltd
67 Clerkenwell Road
London
EC1R 5BH
UK

Eyre Methuen
11 New Fetter Lane
London
EC4P 4EE
UK

Financial Times
Business Information
Tower House
Southampton Street
London
WC2E 7HA
UK

Frost & Sullivan Ltd
104 Marylebone Lane
London
W1M 5FU
UK

Haymarket Publishing Group Ltd
30 Lancaster Gate
London W2
UK

William Heinemann Ltd
10 Upper Grosvenor Street
London
W1X 9PA
UK

IBM United Kingdom Ltd
PO Box 32
Alencon Link
Basingstoke
Hampshire
RG21
UK

International Resource
Development Inc
30 High Street
Norwalk
CT 06851
US

McGraw-Hill Inc
1221 Avenue of the Americas
New York
NY 10020
US

National Computing Centre
Oxford Road Manchester
M1 7ED
UK

Novell Inc
1170 Industrial Park Drive
Orem
Utah 84057
US

Penwell Publishing Co
119 Russell Street
Littleton
MA 01460
US

Pergamon Infotech Ltd
Berkshire House
Queen Street
Maidenhead
Berkshire
SL6 1NF
UK

Phillips Publishing Co
7315 Wisconsin Avenue
Bethesda
MD 20814
US

Pocket Books Inc
1230 Avenue of the Americas
New York
NY 10020
US

Prentice-Hall Inc
Englewood Cliffs
NJ 07632
US

Prentice-Hall Inc
66 Wood End Lane
Hemel Hempstead
Hertfordshire
HP2 4RG
UK

Technical Publishing Co
875 Third Avenue
New York
NY 10022
US

Time Inc
10880 Wilshire Boulevard
Los Angeles
CA 90024-4193
US

Truman Talley Books
The New York Times Book Co Inc
Three Park Avenue
New York
NY 10016
US

VNU Business Publications BV
53-55 Frith Street
London
W1A 2HG
UK

John Wiley & Sons Ltd
Baffins Lane
Chichester
Sussex

PO19 1UD
UK

Xephon Technology
Transfer Ltd
27-35 London Road
Newbury
Berkshire
RG13 1JL
UK

Yates Ventures
4962 El Camino Real
Suite 111
Los Altos
CA 94022
US

Ziff-Davies Publishing Co
One Park Avenue
New York
NY 10016
US

Index